THE COMPOSITION OF JOHN'S GOSPEL

BRILL'S READERS IN BIBLICAL STUDIES

VOLUME 2

THE COMPOSITION OF JOHN'S GOSPEL

Selected Studies from Novum Testamentum

COMPILED BY

DAVID E. ORTON

BRILL
LEIDEN · BOSTON · KÖLN
1999

This book is printed on acid-free paper.

Cover design: BEELDVORM, Leidschendam

On the cover: The evangelist John. MS. Patmos 80,
fol. 192 vo., 13th century. After A.D. Kominis, *Patmos. Die Schätze des
Klosters*, Athens: Ekdotike Athenon S.A., 1988, p. 317.

ISSN 1389-1170
ISBN 90 04 11158 1

PRINTED IN THE NETHERLANDS

CONTENTS

PREFACE

This is the second in a series of publications designed to make previously published journal material available in a more convenient and accessible form. The material presented in this series, then, though it certainly contains some previously neglected but valuable studies alongside established "classic" essays, does not claim to be more than a convenient selection. However, convenience can easily translate into usefulness and indeed use, and many university and seminary teachers will find the selections suitable not only for their personal use, but also for their classes.

The present selection has been made from the best and most useful articles on the origins, purpose and literary composition of the Fourth Gospel to have appeared to date in the journal, *Novum Testamentum*. As far as possible, an attempt has been made to offer a balanced representation of the discussion over a period of four decades, but it so happens that the decade of the 1970's was a particularly productive period in this field. The constraint of maximum international usefulness has meant that only English-language articles could be included. Those interested in a complete listing of articles published in this field in *Novum Testamentum* up to 1994 may be referred to the relevant entries in *An Index to Novum Testamentum Volumes 1-35* (ed. W.E. Mills & J.H. Mills; Brill, 1994).

As the compiler of this collection, I must bear responsibility for the choice. I am not, of course, responsible for the original publication of the articles, which resulted from the due process of peer review and editorship by the incumbent editorial boards of *Novum Testamentum*. It has not been possible to correct errors in the original articles for this collection. To some extent the individual articles are snapshots of scholarship at different stages of Johannine research, and when using them, readers should of course bear the date of the articles in mind. The essays, which are listed in chronological order of original publication, speak for themselves, and are offered without editorial comment, in conformity with the ethos of the journal.

DEO
Leiden, 1998

PLACES OF ORIGINAL PUBLICATION

The articles of this book first appeared in *Novum Testamentum*.

Howard M. Teeple, 'Qumran and the Origin of the Fourth Gospel,' *NT* vol. IV (1960-1961), pp. 6-25.

C.F.D. Moule, 'The Individualism of the Fourth Gospel,' *NT* vol. V (1962), pp. 171-190.

Herman Ridderbos, 'The Structure and Scope of the Prologue to the Gospel of John,' *NT* vol. VIII (1966), pp. 180-201.

A. Wind, 'Destination and Purpose of the Gospel of John,' *NT* vol. XIV (1972), pp. 26-69.

Peder Borgen, 'Logos was the True Light,' *NT* vol. XIV (1972), pp. 115-130.

Joseph A. Grassi, 'The Wedding at Cana (John II 1-11): A Pentecostal Meditation?,' *NT* vol. XIV (1972), pp. 131-136.

Robert Kysar, 'The Source Analysis of the Fourth Gospel—A Growing Consensus?' *NT* vol. XV (1973), pp. 134-152.

James D. Purvis, 'The Fourth Gospel and the Samaritans,' *NT* vol. XVII (1975), pp. 161-198.

Paul S. Minear, 'The Beloved Disciple in the Gospel of John,' *NT* vol. XIX (1977), pp. 105-123.

John J. O'Rourke, 'Asides in the Gospel of John,' *NT* vol. XXI (1979), pp. 210-219.

John Ashton, 'The Identity and Function of the Ιουδαιοι in the Fourth Gospel,' *NT* vol. XXVII (1985), pp. 40-75.

Bruce Grigsby, 'Washing in the Pool of Siloam—A Thematic Anticipation of the Johannine Cross,' *NT* vol. XXVII (1985), pp. 227-235.

QUMRAN AND THE ORIGIN OF THE FOURTH GOSPEL

BY

HOWARD M. TEEPLE
Buckhannon, W. Va. U.S.A.

I

One theory concerning the parallels between the Dead Sea scrolls and the Fourth Gospel is that they indicate that many or all of the traditions in that Gospel are authentic. W. F. Albright concluded that "the books of the Essenes from the first century B. C. provide the closest approach to the Gospels (particularly St. John) and the Pauline Epistles, so far as conceptual background and terminology are concerned, that has yet been discovered" and that they show that "both narratives and *logia* of John's Gospel certainly or presumably date back to oral tradition in Palestine, before A.D. 70; they were probably transmitted orally in the Diaspora for at least a decade—possibly two decades—before being put into writing. . . . That the needs of the early Church influenced the selection of items for inclusion in the Gospel we may readily admit, but there is no reason to suppose that the needs of that Church were responsible for any inventions or innovations of theological significance. . . . we may rest assured that it [the Gospel of John] contains the memories of the Apostle John . . .' [1])

Frank M. Cross, Jr., after examining the parallels of the Fourth Gospel with Qumran literature, apparently favors a similar con-

---

[1]) W. F. Albright, "Recent Discoveries in Palestine and the Gospel of St. John," in W. D. Davies and D. Daube, eds., *The Background of the New Testament and its Eschatology*, Cambridge, England 1956, pp. 169-71. Professor Albright previously had claimed that John's substratum was orally transmitted Aramaic tradition (*The Archaeology of Palestine*, pp. 240, 248) and that there are some "illustrations of the accuracy of local colouring in John, which clearly indicates that these traditions were put into substantially their extant form before A. D. 66-70" (*ibid.*, p. 244). As the scrolls from Qumran became known, Albright employed them to support his conviction that the tradition in John is early and authentic.

clusion: "We must look for a Sitz im Leben for the development of Johannine tradition where Jewish Christianity was dominant, and where Essene influences persisted. Some have suggested that John may be regarded no longer as the latest and most evolved of the Gospels, but the most primitive, and that the formative locus of its tradition was Jerusalem before its destruction. This is not to suggest that the present form of the book has not had an elaborate literary history; the point is that John preserves authentic historical material which first took form in an Aramaic or Hebrew milieu where Essene currents still ran strong." [1])

Kurt SCHUBERT, too, views the Qumran scrolls as decisive support for a conservative conclusion concerning the origin of the Fourth Gospel. "Thus one of the most important results of Qumran research has been to prove the Jewish origin of the Gospel of John conclusively." [2]) "The similarities in style between the Gospel of John and the Qumran texts are so striking that a close connection cannot be denied." [3])

Criticism of such views has been steadily mounting. In 1957 Frederick C. GRANT made this comment: "The theory that, in view of certain parallels found in the Dead Sea Scrolls, the [Fourth] gospel must have been written in Palestine, preferably southern Palestine, and at a fairly early date, perhaps shortly before or after the Fall of Jerusalem, and by an apostle, presumably John the son of Zebedee, is surely an example of the wish fathering the thought. Included in the vast array of parallels found in Hellenistic religious literature, especially Greek, Egyptian and Near Eastern. . ., the few which are found in the Dead Sea Scrolls are really minor and only 'more of the same.' They simply testify to the widespread religious syncretism which existed in that period and influenced the most diverse types of religious life and thought, even Jewish, even Essene—or 'sectarian Jewish'—especially in their religious imagery. [4])

Millar BURROWS criticizes Professor ALBRIGHT's position and comments: "How much in the Gospel of John comes from Jesus and

---

[1]) Frank Moore CROSS, Jr., *The Ancient Library of Qumran and Modern Biblical Studies*, London 1958, pp. 161-2.

[2]) Kurt SCHUBERT, *The Dead Sea Community: the Background to the Dead Sea Scrolls*, New York 1959, p. 152.

[3]) *Ibid.*, p. 153.

[4]) Frederick C. GRANT, *The Gospels: Their Origin and Growth*, New York 1957, p. 175.

how much from the evangelist himself is a difficult question which cannot be answered by parallels with the Dead Sea scrolls. It is somewhat confusing also to be told that the Synoptics and John differ especially at the points of closest resemblance with Essene teaching, and at the same time that the parallels with the scrolls in the Synoptic Gospels are in the areas of closest agreement with John." [1])

Recently Cyril BLACKMAN has observed: ". . . what appears to have been taken over by Christians from the Qumran stock of ideas may simply derive from contemporary Judaism or from the original common source in the Old Testament, just as parallels with Qumran ideas in Mandaean sources may not imply direct borrowing but only an ultimate derivation from the Old Testament or from Iranian dualism." [2])

If the scrolls really indicate that the traditions in the Fourth Gospel are early in origin, it must be demonstrated that these traditions contain features derived from the Palestinian Essene background rather than from other environments. What methods should be employed to solve this problem? At the outset the Johannine Epistles should be separated from the Gospel of John, for the old view that all were written by the same author is not supported by the evidence. The inclusion or exclusion of these Epistles, however, does not change the conclusions of this study.

Features in the scrolls but not in the Fourth Gospel

One approach to the problem is to note the differences between the scrolls and John. Some differences are to be expected, but differences in *basic* features constitute evidence against a close relationship between the two. One group of differences consists of characteristic terms and ideas which are in the scrolls but absent from John. These include the following: a) 'Belial" (בליעל) as the name for the personification of evil (1QS 1 : 18, 24; etc.; 1QM 1 : 1 ff.; etc.); b) belief that the sect has a "new covenant" (הברית החדשה, CD 6 : 19; etc.); c) expectation of an eschatological war (1QM); d) emphasis upon ethics; e) light and darkness are contrasting *spirits* (1QS 3 : 25); f) *both* the good and evil spirits are from God (1QS 3 : 18; contrary to 1 John iv 1); g) hatred of all

---

[1]) Millar BURROWS, *More Light on the Dead Sea Scrolls*, New York 1958, p. 129. See also pp. 123-30.

[2]) Cyrill BLACKMAN, "The Critical Quest," *The Christian Century*, vol. 76, p. 1176, Chicago 1959.

outsiders, gentiles included; [1] h) degrees of rank among the members; [2] i) necessity of repentance (1QS 10 : 20; CD 2 : 5; 8 : 16; neither μετανοέω nor μετάνοια occur in John); j) revelation as a vital possession of the sect (1QS 9 : 13); k) the spirit of truth is opposed to the spirit of evil (IQS 3 : 19; 4 : 2 ff); l) interpretation of Torah as the primary source of doctrine; [3] m) the term "saints" (אנשי הקודש, "the men of holiness," 1QS 8 : 23; 9 : 8; cf. CD 20 : 8, קדושי עליון, "saints of the Most High." The Greek equivalents, ἄγιοι and ἡγιασμένοι, are not in the Fourth Gospel); n) the terms "the elect" or "those whom God has chosen" as applied to the religious group (בחירי ישראל, "elect of Israel," CD 4 : 3-4; 1QS 8 : 6; cf. 1QS 4 : 22; 11 : 7, 16; in John the disciples are never the ἐκλογαί or ἐκλεκτοί). Some differences would result from adaptation to the Christian ideas, but would the author have omitted all of these if the background were Essene?

In connection with these features which are absent from the Gospel of John, some further remarks may be made. Not only is the term "Belial" absent, but the characteristic term in that Gospel is the Greek word διάβολος, "devil," and not the Jewish terms "Belial" and σατανᾶς, "Satan." Σατανᾶς occurs only once in John (xiii 27) and this is probably derived from Luke xxiii 3. John never describes the devil in the language employed in the scrolls.

The chief ethical note in John is the commandment to love one another, and this is included not because the author has a general concern for ethics, but because he recognizes the need for unity in a church torn by dissension. In the scrolls, however, the deep concern for ethics constantly appears. The question of ethical dualism will be discussed later.

As for revelation, at Qumran it came through interpretation of the Torah and was the main source of the sect's rules and doctrines, whereas in John Torah is spurned as the Jews' law and is valued only as testimony of Christ. The noun ἀποκάλυψις, "revelation," does not occur in the Fourth Gospel. The verb ἀποκαλύπτω occurs only once (Jn. xii 38); it appears not because it is a term in the

---

[1] 1QS 1 : 4, 10; however, cf. CD 12 : 6-9. Although John is hostile to the *world*, the author never hates outsiders in general, but only Jews.

[2] 1QS 3 : 20-3; 4 : 21-4; etc. On the other hand, there is "no indication of a fixed order or rank among the disciples" (Burrows, *op. cit.*, p. 126).

[3] For Qumran's interpretation of Torah see the present writer's monograph, *The Mosaic Eschatological Prophet*, Philadelphia 1957, ch. 2.

author's vocabulary, but because it happens to be in a quotation from Isaiah liii 1.

If the Fourth Gospel had been influenced by Qumran, would it have omitted the idea of a new covenant, or at least a covenant, a basic doctrine in the scrolls and in early Christianity as well? Would the author, contrary to Jesus and to Judaism in general, have been so relatively uninterested in ethics? Would he have omitted completely both the word and the doctrine of repentance, which were characteristic of Palestinian Christianity as well as Qumran?

Features in the Fourth Gospel but not in the scrolls

A second group of differences between John and the scrolls consists of characteristic features present in the Gospel and absent from the scrolls. These include: a) the necessity of abiding in the Son of God and in his love (xv 1-8); b) the Messiah as an incarnate god (i 14); c) "Son of Man" as a messianic title (i 51; etc.); d) the doctrine that salvation depends upon eating the flesh and drinking the blood of a god (vi 53-4); e) semi-Gnostic ideas such as knowing the Father (xiii 3), rebirth (iii 3), physical dualism (iii 6), and concern for "whence" and "whither" (iii 8; viii 14; etc.).

The title "Son of Man" occurs thirteen times in the Fourth Gospel. Unless it has been discovered very recently, this messianic title has not been found at Qumran. On the other hand, belief in a Messiah who is a descendant of David was prevalent both at Qumran [1]) and in early Christianity, but it is absent from John, except on Jewish lips (vii 42). If the Fourth Gospel were influenced by Qumran, would its Christology be so radically different?

The sixth chapter of the Gospel of John makes eating the flesh and drinking the blood of the Son of Man a requirement for salvation. The idea of eating the flesh and drinking the blood of either God or Messiah never occurs in ancient Jewish literature; in fact, such an idea was utterly repugnant to all Judaism, even Hellenistic Judaism. If the Fourth Gospel's background were Palestinian, would it have included such a doctrine?

Helmer RINGREN has pointed out that the sect at Qumran was not Gnostic. [2]) Concerning the Fourth Gospel, Robert M. GRANT has stated: "Even though the Gospel of John is not fully Gnostic,

---

[1]) I.e., the Son of David. Florilegium; Commentary on Genesis 49.

[2]) "Gnosis i Qumrantexterna," *Svensk Exegetisk Årsbok*, vol. 24, pp. 41-53, Uppsala 1959.

it remains a fact that in it we find a portrait of Jesus which is
essentially mythological." [1]) He observes also that John's language
is "semi-Gnostic." [2]) Although the Fourth Gospel is not *fully* Gnostic,
it certainly is much closer to Gnosticism than is the Qumran literature. Thus the semi-Gnosticism in John is an element which is absent
from the scrolls. The Dead Sea scrolls are dualistic, but not semi-
Gnostic.

Alleged parallels

A second approach to the problem of the possible relationship of
the Fourth Gospel to the scrolls is to search for and to examine the
parallels between them. Some *alleged* parallels, however, are too
remote or too general to deserve to be called parallels.

Eschatology is not a significant parallel, for it was very prominent
at Qumran, but in the Fourth Gospel it is minimized. John's
eschatology lacks the characteristics of that of primitive Christianity. Considering that eschatology was so prevalent in both Judaism
and primitive Christianity, is it reasonable to assume that a Gospel
which minimizes and reinterprets eschatology has a Palestinian
background or presents authentic tradition?

The baptism with the Holy Spirit in John is not a parallel to the
role of the spirit in the scrolls, for in the latter the spirit does not
cause one to be born from above, but rather causes his sins to be
atoned and precedes the "washing" in water which purifies the
flesh (1QS 3 : 6-9). [3])

It has been alleged also that the role of the Logos or Word in
John is parallel to the role of God's knowledge in the scrolls: God
created all things through each. [4]) These are not really parallel because, unlike the Logos, God's knowledge in the scrolls is not a
personified agent of God.

Jean DANIELOU suggests that Jacob's well in John may possibly
be a symbol of the Jewish Law, as is the well in the Damascus
Document. [5]) This is extremely doubtful, for the well in John is

---

[1]) R. M. GRANT, *Gnosticism and Early Christianity*, New York 1959, p. 173.
[2]) *Ibid.*, pp. 172-3.
[3]) The common practice in the English language of capitalizing "Spirit"
in the Fourth Gospel and not capitalizing it in the Dead Sea scrolls causes
the difference to seem larger than it really is, however.
[4]) F. M. CROSS, Jr., alleges that 1QS 11 : 11 and 3 : 15-17 are parallels to
the Prologue of John (*op. cit*, p. 161, n. 34).
[5]) Jean DANIELOU, "Eglise primitive et communauté de Qumran,"
Etudes (May, 1957), pp. 216-35, Paris.

Jacob's, not Moses'. The well in the Damascus Document, on the other hand, is connected with Moses in Numbers xxi 18, the passage cited, and then associated with the sect's Interpreter of the Law (CD 5 : 21-6 : 8).

Opposition to the Temple is not a parallel, as Oscar CULLMANN has claimed, [1]) for the cause of the opposition in John has a completely different basis (namely, opposition to Judaism as a whole), and the kind of worship substituted for the Temple is very different. John's interest in the Jewish feasts is not a parallel to Qumran's interest in the calendar, for, as BROWN and BURROWS have observed, [2]) Qumran's deep concern for the proper times for celebrating the feasts is lacking in John. Gnosticism is not a parallel, for as noted above, the Gnostic tendency in John is not matched at Qumran.

"Modified dualism" is alleged by Father BROWN to be common to John and Qumran, that is, both believed in two opposing principles which were created by God. [3]) This is not a true parallel, however, for in John the dualism is not between two spirits as at Qumran, and furthermore Christ, one of the opposing principles, is not created, but is begotten as in Gnosticism.

Various scholars have claimed that John's dualism is "ethical" like that of Judaism, rather than physical like that of Gnosticism. It is true that the Fourth Gospel has a dualism of light versus darkness, and darkness is associated with evil, while light is connected with "doing truth" (iii 19-21). This is an ethical dualism, but not the same type as that at Qumran. In the scrolls the way of the spirit of light consists of humility, slowness to anger, goodness, and zeal for righteous laws (1QS 4), whereas in John iii the main interest in ethics is simply to use them as a means to denounce those who do not believe in the Son. The role of the term "walk" in this matter is discussed below. In this Gospel ethical dualism is rather incidental, whereas with the Essenes and Pharisees it was a major theme.

---

[1]) Oscar CULLMANN, "The Significance of the Qumran Texts for Research into the Beginnings of Christianity", *Journal of Biblical Literature*, vol. 74, pp. 222-3, Philadelphia 1955. Also by the same author, "L'Opposition contre le Temple de Jerusalem, Motif Commun de la Theologie Johannique et du Monde Ambiant," *New Testament Studies*, vol. 5, pp. 157-73, Cambridge, England 1959.

[2]) Raymond E. BROWN, "The Qumran Scrolls and the Johannine Gospel and Epistles," in Krister Stendahl, ed., *The Scrolls and the New Testament*, New York 1957, pp. 201-2. Millar BURROWS, *op. cit.*, p. 126.

[3]) In STENDAHL, *op. cit.*, pp. 184-6.

Furthermore, there *is* a physical dualism in John which sets spirit and flesh in opposition. ". . . unless one is born of water and the Spirit, he cannot enter the kingdom of God. That which is born of the flesh is flesh, and that which is born of the Spirit is spirit" (iii 5-6). Dualism of this type is not present in the scrolls of Qumran.

The frequent occurrence of the term κόσμος, "world," in the Fourth Gospel is related to the physical dualism of the Hellenistic world. In John the world is naturally sinful and needs to be saved (i 29; iii 17) by light because the world is darkness (xii 46), hence Jesus' kingdom is "not of this world" (xviii 36). Consequently it is stated explicitly that "God is Spirit" (iv 24). Although the author combined ethical and physical dualism, the ethical is made subordinate to the physical.

That predestination is a parallel is very doubtful. Although John xv 16 implies some determinism, other passages in John speak of choice of light or darkness. BROWN has called our attention to the fact that while some passages in the scrolls suggest determinism, other passages require freedom of the will. [1]

Parallels in language but not in thought

There are some linguistic parallels which are not parallel in thought; the same terms are employed, but they convey different ideas. Admittedly, some adaptation to Christianity would naturally take place; but when these expressions occur in John they vary from the Essene usage, not in the direction of primitive Christian thought, but in the direction of Hellenistic Christian thought!

Although "light" and "darkness" are opposed to each other in both the scrolls and the Fourth Gospel (1QS 3; Jn. i 5), they are identified with very different things. In the Manual of Discipline light and darkness are the spirits of truth and error, respectively, but in John they are Christ and the world, respectively.

In Judaism the verb "walk" (הָלַךְ) was often employed metaphorically to describe an ethical way of living (Ps. ci 6; 1QS 1 : 8; CD 2 : 15-16; etc.). The characteristic Jewish expressions, "walk perfectly," "walk humbly", "walk in God's ways," etc., are not in the Fourth Gospel. In the Manual of Discipline the sons of righteousness "walk in the ways of light" and the sons of perversion "walk in the ways of darkness" (iii 20-1). This has been cited as a parallel to John's "walk in the day" (xi 9) and "walk in

---

[1] *Ibid.*, pp. 189-92.

the darkness" (viii 12; xii 35; cf. 1 Jn. i 7, "walk in the light"). Unlike typical Jewish usage, this usage in John is not directly connected with ethics, but rather is associated with belief and knowing whither one is going (xii 35-6). Linguistically, there are closer parallels in the Old Testament to John's usage than there are in the scrolls. In the Qumran writings walking is "in the ways of light" or "in the ways of darkness," while in John one walks directly in light or darkness. This grammatical form without the word "way" is paralleled in the Old Testament (the form with the term "way" occurs there too). Close linguistic parallels in the Old Testament are "walk in the light" (Isa. ii 5; Ps. lvi 13 (Heb. lvi 14)) and "walk in the darkness" (Eccl. ii 14; Ps. lxxxii 5 (LXX 81 : 5); Isa. l 10).

Frank M. Cross, Jr., maintains that Essene reference to the sect as a Unity (often translated as "Community") is a parallel: "The Johannine phrases, 'that they may be one,' 'become perfectly one' (Jn. xvii 11, 21, 23) use typical Essene diction." [1] The parallelism is the closest in the phrases "to be one" (להיות ליחד, 1QS 5 : 2; ἵνα ὦσιν ἕν, Jn. xvii 11, 21) and "gather (or "assemble") into one" (בהאספם ליחד, 1QS 5 : 7; συναγάγῃ εἰς ἕν, Jn. xi 52). The idea that Christians are "one" is not limited in the New Testament to Johannine literature, however; it is found, for example, in 1 Cor. xii 12 and Eph. iv 3-5. The sense in which the members of each group are "one" is very different. At Qumran the sect is a unity in Torah and wealth, whereas in the Fourth Gospel the group is one in a mystical sense—"one" even as the Father and Son are one. The unity of religious groups was a common idea in the ancient world. Millar Burrows disagrees with Professor Cross' view and comments that the words "be one" or "become one" "are associated with Christ and God in a way that is not all Essene." [2]

"Do the truth" (לעשות אמת; ποιεῖν τὴν ἀλήθειαν) is another linguistic parallel which in both religious groups referred to doing what the group taught. The nature of this truth differs, however. At Qumran doing the truth is associated with ethics, righteousness and justice (1QS 1 : 5; 5 : 3; 8 : 2), whereas in John it is associated with belief in the Son of God (iii 21).

The phrase, "the works of God" (מעשי אל; τὰ ἔργα τοῦ θεοῦ), was employed by the scribes at Qumran as well as by the author of John.

---

[1]) Cross, op. cit., p. 156.
[2]) Burrows, op. cit., p. 127.

At Qumran it was the duty of the Supervisor of the camp to instruct the Many in the works of God (CD 13: 7-8) and members have a mighty wisdom which is faithful in all the works of God (1QS 4 : 3-4). In John it is the work of God to believe in the Christ whom God has sent (vi 29) and a man was born blind that the works of God might be manifest (ix 3). At Qumran God's works apparently are his mighty deeds in history, especially in connection with the history of the sect. In John God's works consist of the Christ's miracles and Christian belief in the Christ.

Whether or not "knowledge" is a linguistic parallel is an open question, since the scrolls prefer the noun and John has only the verb. Nevertheless, in both there is present the idea that the members of each group possess knowledge, the ultimate source of which is God. There are major differences, however, in the nature of the knowledge and in the means by which the knowledge is given to the group. At Qumran the knowledge of God (1QS 4 : 22) does not refer to knowing God so much as it does to knowing the knowledge which comes from God (1QS 11 : 17-18). This knowledge consists of knowledge of righteous laws (1QS 3 : 1), of mysteries (1QS 4 : 6), of good (1QS 4 : 26), and of the Community's councils (1QS 8 : 18). The way in which this knowledge is revealed is through the Torah and the interpretation of the Torah.

In the Fourth Gospel what one should know consists of knowing God, the Father (xvii 3; vii 28; viii 55; xiv 7; xvi 3; xvii 25), knowing Jesus Christ (xvii 3; x 14; xiv 7, 9; xvi 3) and who he is (vi 69; viii 28), knowing that the Father is in the Son and that the Son is in the Father (x 38; xiv 20), knowing that the Son is sent from the Father (xvii 8, 23, 25), knowing that Jesus' teaching is from God and that Jesus does not teach on his own authority (vii 17; viii 28; xvii 7-8), knowing the truth (viii 32), knowing the Spirit of Truth (xiv 17), knowing that Christians are in the Son and he in them (xiv 20), knowing that the Son loves the Father (xiv 31), knowing that the Son has loved the disciples (xvii 3). Jesus, too, knows the Father (vii 29; viii 55; x 15 (and the Father knows him); xvii 25). Jesus has made known to the disciples all that he has heard from the Father (xv 15) and the Father's name (xvii 26). This knowledge differs from that at Qumran not only in content, but also in the means by which it is disclosed, namely, by the Son and by the Spirit which he will send. These semi-Gnostic concepts of knowledge are utterly alien to the religion of Qumran.

Parallels in language and perhaps in thought

Some of the linguistic parallels between the scrolls and the Gospel of John are not identical in thought content, but have some similarity and *perhaps* should be classified as parallel in thought. "Eternal life" (חיי נצח, 1QS 4 : 7; CD 3 : 20; ζωὴ αἰώνιος, Jn. iii 15; etc.) refers to immortality. The extent of the parallelism in thought is open to question, for there is considerable ambiguity as to the precise concept of immortality in both the scrolls and the Fourth Gospel. Certainly the means of qualifying for eternal life is very different.

"Light of life" is another verbal parallel which may have some similar connotations. At Qumran it is "through the spirit of God's true counsel" that all of man's "iniquities will be atoned so that he may look upon the light of life" באור החיים, (1QS 3 : 7). John viii 12 represents Jesus as saying, "he who follows me will not walk in darkness, but will have the light of life" (τὸ φῶς τῆς ζωῆς). The light of life is not precisely defined in either source, but in both it is associated with immortality.

The phrase "sons of light" is a term for the sect in both John and the scrolls. It is found in the Manual of Discipline (i 9, בני אור) and repeatedly in the War scroll. Christians are "sons of light" (υἱοὶ φωτός) in John xii 36. Paul applies the same phrase to Christians in 1 Thess. v 5. The basis of becoming a member of the group and a son of light, however, is different in the scrolls and in John. In the scrolls membership in the sect is based upon observance of the Torah and upon the Community's statutes which are derived from interpretation of the Torah. In John it rests upon faith in the Son, the Light (xii 36, 46).

"Spirit of truth" (רוח אמת; τὸ πνεῦμα τῆς ἀληθείας) is a parallel in that in both sources it is a spirit which is divinely given in the new age. Furthermore, there is a parallelism in function in that in both sources the Spirit teaches things. In the Manual the spirit of truth counsels religious virtues for the sons of truth (iv 2-6); in John the Spirit of truth will teach all things to the disciples (xiv 26).

An additional similarity in function is that the Spirit of Truth provides help. The Greek term παράκλητος occurs in the Fourth Gospel four times (xiv 16, 26; xv 26; xvi 7) and has been variously translated as "Comforter" (AV), "Counselor" (RSV), and "Helper" (Moffatt; Goodspeed). The literal and probably best translation is

"Helper." This Helper is called "the Spirit of Truth" (τὸ πνεῦμα τῆς ἀληθείας) in John xiv 17 and xv 26. The Manual of Discipline states that "the God of Israel and the angel of his truth helped (ומלאך אמתו עזר) all the sons of light" (iii 24-5). The angel of truth apparently is synonymous with the "spirit of truth" (רוח אמת) in iv 21. [1]) In both the scrolls and John the spirit or angel of truth helps the members of the religious group.

There are, however, some important differences. In the Manual of Discipline God himself will cause the spirit to come, whereas in John the Son will send it from the Father. According to the Manual of Discipline God will cleanse man by sprinkling the spirit of truth upon him (iv 21; cf. iv 19-20). This is not a true parallel to God's sanctifying the disciples in or by truth (John xvii 17), for the Hebrew verb in the Manual of Discipline is not קָדַשׁ, to "sanctify" or "make holy," but טָהֵר, to "cleanse," "purify." Also, this function is quite different from that in John xv 26 where the Spirit of Truth will bear witness concerning the Son. The content of the teaching which the Spirit gives is a further difference. Furthermore, in John the Spirit of Truth is not synonymous with light (Christ), whereas in the Manual of Discipline it is (iii 18-19, 25).

In one respect the concept of the Spirit of Truth is a closer parallel to Qumran in I John iv 6 than in the Fourth Gospel, for in I John it is in opposition to the "spirit of error" (cf. 1QS 3 : 18-19).

"Witness of truth" is another linguistic parallel. The members of the community at Qumran are "witnesses of truth" (עדי אמת, 1QS 8 : 6). In John both Jesus and John the Baptist "witness to the truth" (μαρτυρήσω τῇ ἀληθείᾳ, xviii 37; etc.; μεμαρτύρηκεν τῇ ἀληθείᾳ, v 33; etc.). Thus there is agreement that the truth should have witnesses, but as noted above, the concept of the truth differs. Besides, at Qumran, but not in John, the members are witnesses of truth.

Parallels in general ideas

There are some *general* ideas in both the scrolls and John which are parallels in thought. a) Darkness is bad and is connected with evil (1QS 3 : 21-2; Jn. i 5; iii 19). b) Light and darkness are opposed to each other (1QS 3; Jn. i 5). c) Light is equated with truth (1QS 3 : 18-19, 25; Jn. i 4-5, 9; viii 12). d) It is the duty of each member

---

[1]) Cf. Burrows, *ibid.*, p. 283.

of the group to love all the other members of the group (1QS 1 : 9;
Jn. xiii 34-5; xv 12). e) Truth is opposed to evil (1QS 4 : 24; Jn.
iii 20-1).

Admittedly, the last three sections (Parallels in language but
not in thought; Parallels in language and perhaps in thought;
Parallels in general ideas) overlap and are not separated from each
other by clear lines. Possibly they should all be grouped together as
partial parallels.

II

With three exceptions, all of the parallels listed above occur also
in the Old Testament and/or the Apocrypha and Pseudepigrapha.
The metaphorical use of the terms "light" and "darkness" abound
in the Old Testament. "Walking in the light" is contrasted with
"walking in the darkness" in Isaiah (ii 5; l 10; lix 9) and in Psalms
(lvi 14 (Heb.); lxxxii 5). The "fool walks in darkness" is in Eccle-
siastes ii 14. The terms "light" and "darkness" are used symbolically in Psalms of Solomon (iii 15), in 1 Enoch (lviii 5) and 2 Baruch
(xvii; xviii; xlvi 2; lix 2). Light is typically associated with
righteousness and observance of the Law and darkness is connected
with the opposite. Thus Qumran's concepts of metaphorical light
and darkness are very similar to those characteristic of other
ancient Jewish literature, whereas John's concepts are not.

The use of the term "walk" to refer to a way of life, etc., is quite
common in the Jewish background. In addition to the examples
cited in the paragraph above, there is reference to walking in
uprightness (Isa. lvii 2), walking in the ways of the Lord (Hos. xiv 9;
Mic. iv 2), walking in an evil way (Isa. lxv 2) and walking in the
Lord's truth (Ps. xxvi 3; lxxxvi 11). The Wisdom of Solomon charges
that kings did not "walk according to the purpose of God" (vi 4).
1 Enoch blesses "those who walk in the way of righteousness"
(lxxxii 4). In 2 Baruch the righteous walk in God's law, but the
wicked walk in vanity and in their own works (xiv 5; xxxviii 4;
xlviii 38). Here, too, Qumran's usage is similar to that which is
typical of Judaism, whereas John's usage is not.

The application of the term "one" or "unity" to a religious group
is another feature which is not limited to the scrolls and the Fourth
Gospel. Psalms cxxxiii 1 notes how good it is when brothers dwell
in unity (יַחַד). Speaking of Jews in general, 2 Baruch observes,
"we are all one celebrated people" (xlviii 24). These are very different

from the Johannine mystical usage, but the concept in Psalm cxxxiii is very similar to that in the scrolls.

The phrase, "do the truth," is another expression found in Judaism outside of the scrolls. Tobit iv 6 states that if "you do the truth" (ποιοῦντός σου τὴν ἀλήθειαν) your ways will prosper through your deeds. The Testament of Benjamin admonishes its readers to "do the truth," each one to his neighbor (x 3). In comparison, note that in the Psalms God does not do the truth, but all of his deeds are "done in truth" (xxxiii 4; cxi 8). As at Qumran, "doing the truth" is associated with ethics, not with belief in the Messiah.

As for the expression, "the works of God," it occurs frequently in ancient Jewish literature. It refers to God's creation of the world (Ecc. xi 5) and to his deeds in history for Israel (Jos. xxiv 31). We find the phrase in Job (xxxvii 14) and Daniel (ix 14), and it abounds in the Psalms (xlvi 8; etc.). Sirach xxxix: 16 states: "All things are the works of the Lord, for they are very good." 1 Enoch v 2 notes that God's "works go on from year to year." Once again we have an expression which Qumran used in typical Jewish fashion, while the Fourth Gospel's usage is not typical of Judaism.

The idea that "knowledge" comes from God, a concept in both the scrolls and John, is found, for example, in Proverbs ii 6 and Wisdom vii 17. The idea that man should know God is very prevalent, occurring, for example, in Isaiah xix 21, Jeremiah xxxi 34, Psalm xxxvi 10, and repeatedly in the Wisdom of Solomon (ii 13; etc.). The Fourth Gospel's emphasis upon knowing God thus has its parallels in Judaism, but its stress upon knowing the Messiah is not a Jewish characteristic.

In the category of parallels in language and perhaps in thought, there are two which are present in Judaism outside of the scrolls. First, there is the phrase "eternal life." According to Daniel xii 2 and Psalms of Solomon iii 16, the righteous dead will awake to life eternal. "Eternal life" refers to immortality repeatedly in 1 Enoch, e.g., xl 9 and lviii 3.

The second expression in this category is "the light of light." This occurs in Psalm lvi 13 (Heb., lvi 14) with the usual connotation of immortality: "For thou hast delivered my soul from death . . . that I may walk before God in the light of life."

As for the parallels in general ideas listed above, all were prevalent in Judaism outside of Qumran. Darkness is bad and connected with evil in Isaiah (xlii 6-7), Proverbs (iv 19) and the Book of Wisdom (chap. xvii). Sinners die in darkness in 1 Enoch (cii 7).

In addition to the examples previously cited, there are many passages in ancient Jewish writings in which symbolic light and darkness are opposed to each other. Examples in the Old Testament include: "when I sit in darkness, the Lord will be a light to me" (Mic. vii 8) and "to the upright light arises in the darkness" (Ps. cxii 4). In the Parables section of the Book of Enoch we read: "And darkness to the sinners in the name of the Lord, who made a separation between the light and the darkness, and divided the spirits of men" (xli 8). Outside of the Parables section is this statement: "And he [the righteous man] shall walk in eternal light, and sin shall perish in darkness forever" (1 Enoch xcii 4-5). A similar opposition between light and darkness is described in the Testament of Naphtali: "there is a division between light and darkness . . . neither while you are in darkness can you do the works of light" (ii 7, 10).

Light and truth are closely associated with each other in Psalm xliii 3, "send out thy light and thy truth." In the Testament of Asher we read that "all truth is under the light" (v 3).

An approximate parallel to the idea that members of a religious group should love one another occurs in Leviticus xix 17-18, which commands, "love your neighbor (fellow Israelite) as yourself."

Finally, the general idea that truth is opposed to evil is implied in Old Testament passages which associate truth with God. An ideal in the Psalms is to walk or be lead in God's truth (xxv 5; xxvi 3) and the Lord is a God of truth (xxxi 5).

In these parallels the usage at Qumran invariably is much closer to that in other Jewish literature than is the usage in the Fourth Gospel. If it becomes established—which at present seems improbable—that 1 Enoch and the Testaments of the Twelve Patriarchs originated at Qumran, then the examples from those two composite books should be subtracted. The removal of those examples, however, would not change substantially the general pattern of the evidence.

Since all of the above parallels were so current in Judaism, is it reasonable to maintain that they necessarily indicate Palestinian origin of Johannine traditions? The author of the Fourth Gospel could have derived these expressions and ideas from Judaism elsewhere just as readily as from Palestine.

There are three parallels between John and the scrolls which are not found in the Old Testament. These parallels consist of the expressions "sons of light" and "Spirit of truth," and the concern for witness to or of religious truth. Of these three, the phrase "sons of light" occurs elsewhere in the New Testament. In John —unlike the scrolls—the Spirit of truth is sent from the Father by the Son, will dwell in Christians and will speak things to them. In John Jesus and the Baptist are the witnesses, while at Qumran the members of the sect are the witnesses; also, these sources do not agree on the nature of the truth.

Do these three parallels indicate a Palestinian connection for the traditions of the Fourth Gospel? Hardly, when in the case of two the similarity is so remote, and in the case of the third it occurs in Paul's writing (1 Thess. v 5). The present writer has not searched thoroughly through all of the ancient Jewish literature, and perhaps all three of these parallels exist there. Even if they do not exist today, it must be remembered that much ancient literature has been lost.

A third approach to the problem of the possible relationship of the Fourth Gospel to the Qumran literature is to look in the New Testament outside of the Gospels and the Johannine writings for parallels to the scrolls. If we find them in books written outside of Palestine, we may well question such parallels as reliable evidence for the Palestinian origin of the parallel Johannine traditions.

The parallels to the Dead Sea scrolls are just as numerous in the rest of the New Testament as they are in the Johannine literature. Paul regards the "angel of light" as a good angel (2 Cor. xi 14), and Qumran contrasts the "angel of truth" with the "angel of darkness" (1QS 3 : 20-5). Paul, too, can call the devil "Belial" and associate him with darkness (2 Cor. vi 14-15). The members of the group are brethren (Rom. i 13; 1 Cor. i 10; etc.). Colossians i 13 views darkness as bad, for God "has delivered us from the power of darkness." Darkness is bad also in the passage in 2 Corinthians vi.

The belief that God has chosen or elected the righteous, an idea so prominent at Qumran, occurs in Ephesians i 4 which asserts that God chose Christians in Christ before the foundation of the world. The phrase, "eternal life," is found in Romans ii 7 and 1 Timothy i 16. God is the Father of the righteous people in the Old Testament (Isa. lxiii 16; lxiv 8, "O Lord, thou art our Father"), at Qumran (1QH 11, "thou art a Father to all the sons of thy truth"), and repeatedly in the New Testament (1 Cor. i 3; etc.). Paul and the author of Hebrews, as well as the Essenes, believe that man should know God (1 Thess. iv 5; 2 Thess. i 8; Heb. viii 11).

The opposition of light to darkness is almost as characteristic of Paul's letters as it is of the Johannine Gospel and Epistles: "What fellowship has light with darkness?" (2 Cor. vi 14); "Let us therefore lay aside the works of darkness, and put on the armor of light" (Rom. xiii 12); "For you are all sons of the light and sons of the day. We are not of night, nor of darkness" (1 Thess. v 5). A similar view is in the non-Pauline books, Ephesians and 1 Peter: "For you once were darkness, but now you are light in the Lord. Walk then as children of the light . . ." (Eph. v 8); "But you are a chosen race . . . [God] called you out of darkness into his marvelous light" (1 Pet. ii 9).

The expression "sons of light" was employed by Paul (1 Thess. v 5) as well as by the Essenes and the author of the Gospel of John. The idea that all of the members of the group are "brothers" and should love one another is very characteristic of the New Testament in general and of Qumran. Paul exhorts Christians to love one another as brothers (Rom. xii 10; xiii 8), as does the author of 1 Peter (i 22). The ideal of human perfection, with God's help, which was stressed at Qumran (1QS 1 : 8; etc.), appears also in the Epistle of James (i 4; iii 2), in Paul's letters (1 Cor. xiii 11; Phil. iii 15), and elsewhere in the New Testament (Heb. xiii 20-1; etc.).

Truth is opposed to evil in various New Testament books besides the Johannine writings, for example, Romans i 25 and ii 8, and Ephesians v 9. Virtue lists, so prevalent in ancient Jewish literature, occur both in the Manual of Discipline (4 : 2) and Paul's letter to the Galatians (v 22-3). The expression "walk by the Spirit" is in both the scrolls and Paul's letters, but not in the Fourth Gospel. In the Manual of Discipline the sons of truth walk by the spirit of truth (1QS 4 : 6), and Paul exhorts to "walk by the Spirit" instead of gratifying the desires of the flesh (Gal. v 16, 25). This is not a full parallel, for Paul does not call the Spirit the "Spirit of Truth."

The Jewish expression, "the works of God," is in Acts ii 11 in the Pentecost story, when the inspired Christians tell "the mighty works of God." Presumably this refers to God's miracles in history, especially through Jesus. Paul uses the phrase in the singular to refer to Christian fellowship or perhaps to Christ's death (Rom. xiv 20).

In addition, there are three *partial* parallels. One is the idea of walking in the light. At Qumran the sons of righteousness "walk in the ways of light" (1QS 4 : 20). In Romans Christians are instructed to put on the armor of light and walk as in the day (xiii 12-13). These are not identical linguistically, but both refer to an ethical manner of living. More remote in parallelism is the association of truth with the means of purification in both the Manual of Discipline and 1 Peter. In the former God will cleanse man by sprinkling the spirit of truth upon him (1QS 4 : 21). In 1 Peter i 22 Christians have cleansed their souls by their obedience to the truth.

The term "way" as a metaphor for a pattern of living was prevalent in Judaism, especially among the Essenes. It is repeated many times in the Dead Sea scrolls (1QS 3 and 4; 5 : 7; 10 : 21; etc.) where it refers to living according to the teachings of the sect. The author of 2 Peter uses the expressions "way of truth" and "way of righteousness" to refer to Christian faith and doctrine in contrast to heresies (ii 2, 21), which is not a close parallel in thought. Even in Acts "the way of God" (xviii 25-6) probably refers more to beliefs concerning Jesus himself than the ethics he taught.

Of the above group of parallels between the scrolls and the rest of the New Testament, all but two are in the Old Testament. Those two are the phrase "sons of light" and the idea that truth is associated with the means to purification.

Without resorting to statistics, it can be truly said that there are about as many parallels between the scrolls and the New Testament outside of the Gospels and the Johannine Epistles as there are between the scrolls and the Fourth Gospel. But what of the Johannine Epistles? In the Johannine Epistles these parallels to Qumran occur: the members of the group are brethren (1 Jn. iii 13-14; 3 Jn. 3) and should love one another (1 Jn. ii 9-10); two opposing spirits, the "spirit of truth" and the "spirit of error" (but their functions are different: in 1 John they inspire true and false prophecy, respectively (1 Jn. iv 1-6), while at Qumran they determine behavior in general); "doing the truth" (1 Jn. i 6); "walk in the light" or "walk in the darkness" (1 Jn. i 6-7); "walk in the truth" (2 Jn. 4; 3 Jn. 4).

Even if we add these parallels from the Johannine Epistles to those from the Fourth Gospel, there are still about as many parallels to the scrolls to be found in the rest of the New Testament as in the Johannine writings.

In summary, certain questions should be asked. Since there is so much dissimilarity between the Dead Sea scrolls and the Fourth Gospel in that each literature has so many important features which are not in the other, and since so many alleged parallels are too remote to be real parallels, how can it be maintained that the traditions in each necessarily come from the same environment? Since so few of the parallels are very close or are parallel in both language and thought, is it very probable that there is much relationship between their origins? When John's parallels differ from Qumran thought, they usually differ in a direction *away from* primitive Christianity and *toward* the Hellenistic background and the later church; is this compatible with the claim for the authenticity of Johannine tradition? Since the vast majority of the parallels between Qumran and John occur in the Old Testament and Apocrypha which were used by virtually all Christians, and/or in the Jewish Pseudepigrapha of which part originated in Alexandria, why should anyone jump to the conclusion that these parallels necessarily point to Palestinian origins? Why should anyone think that John is very Jewish when its use of Jewish terms is, unlike Qumran, so far from Jewish usage? Again, since as many parallels with Qumran occur in the rest of the New Testament as in the Johannine writings, and since the parallels in these other Christian writings are usually non-Palestinian in origin, what evidence is there that the Johannine parallels point in a different direction, namely, to Palestine? As for those few scholars who have claimed that the Qumran parallels indicate that the Fourth Gospel's traditions are Palestinian and early, have they not neglected to see the total historical situation?

Do the Jewish parallels with the Fourth Gospel necessarily indicate that its author was a Jewish Christian, as many scholars seem to think? Hardly.

The Gospel of John is full of evidence that the author was a Gentile Christian. His attitude toward "the Jews," the Jewish patriarchs, and "your law" is that characteristic of Gentile Christians, not Jewish Christians. [1] The Fourth Gospel contains parallels to Gentile thought which have never been found in Jewish or Jewish-Christian writings. These parallels include eating the flesh and drinking the blood of a deity (vi 52-8), turning water to wine

---

[1] See Howard M. TEEPLE, "Early Jewish-Christian Writing," *The Journal of Bible and Religion*, vol. 25, pp. 301-5, Brattleboro, Vermont 1957.

as in the Dionysos cult (ii 1-11), and the close parallel in John iii 4, 6-8, to spiritual rebirth in the Hermetic cult.

These Gentile attitudes and ideas are very strong evidence that the author was a Gentile. If he was a Gentile, however, could his Gospel have so many Jewish traits? This could easily happen.

The most probable situation is that the author was a "God-fearer" before his conversion to Christianity; that is, he was a Gentile who attended the Jewish synagogue services prior to his joining Christianity. In light of the fact that this type of convert was numerous in the early church, it is amazing that so many scholars assume that some Jewish features imply Jewish Christian authorship. If the author formerly attended the synagogues, he would naturally become familiar with rabbinic language, thought and exegesis.

A second possibility is that the author was a Gentile who acquired his knowledge of Judaism after he became a Christian. He may have been converted by a Jewish Christian church and have been a member of that community for a while. Or, more probably, he may have been a member of a mixed church; that is, he may have belonged to a church in which some members had been Jews and some had been Gentiles before conversion. The Christian communities in Antioch and Alexandria must have been churches of this type. The author of the Epistle of Barnabas may be in this category.

A third possibility is that prior to conversion the author lived in a pagan community which had absorbed some Jewish ideas and diction. Professor C. H. Dodd has suggested that paganism in Alexandria may have been influenced by Judaism. [1]) All of the syncretism between Judaism and paganism may not have moved in one direction; paganism may have learned from Judaism as well as vice versa.

These three possibilities are not mutually exclusive. The author could have had some knowledge of Judaism before conversion, either in paganism or as a God-fearer, then joined a mixed church with both Jewish and Gentile members.

Finally, it should be remembered that of the parallels between John and Qumran discussed in this study, all but three could have been suggested to the author of John by the Septuagint, the Bible of all Gentile Christians, including those who had no special contact with Judaism or Jewish Christianity.

---

[1]) C. H. Dodd, *The Bible and the Greeks*, London 1935 and 1954.

THE INDIVIDUALISM OF THE FOURTH GOSPEL

BY

C. F. D. MOULE
Cambridge, England

I

Individualism was more at home in the 'Liberal Protestant' world than it is in the present climate of theology. For the 'Liberal Protestant' frame of thought it was easy to recognise the kingship of God in each individual who accepted the will of God, but harder to grasp the idea of Christianity as incorporation by baptism into membership of the Body of Christ—a corporate existence, entered upon and maintained sacramentally and institutionally. It is one of the results of the revival of 'biblical theology' that, of the two, the latter emphasis—the corporate and the sacramental—has come to be widely recognised as closer to the roots of authentic Christianity.

But this recovery of a theology of the Church has tended to swing the pendulum too far, sometimes actually to distort the picture and to engender an unwarranted suspicion of anything that sounds 'individualistic'. The famous Lucan saying (Lk. xvii 21) about the kingdom of God being ἐντὸς ὑμῶν is today generally so interpreted as to rescue it from the unacceptable inward and individual sense; or, if there were an acceptable alternative today, it might be to blame 'Luke the Hellene' for introducing an alien individualism into the doctrine of the kingdom. It is almost a slur on a biblical writer—or else on his expositor—if an individualistic note is detected.

That may be a caricature of the situation. But if it contains even a modicum of truth, then perhaps it is not untimely to enter a plea for a reappraisal of the Johannine outlook in this particular respect. To that end I offer this essay, uncertain whether it will meet with approval from the distinguished scholar in whose honour it is presented; certain only that I am deeply indebted to him, both for warm personal friendship when I stayed at Erlangen in 1952, and for all that I have learnt from the publications he has generously presented to me, including a copy of his important *Theologie des*

Neuen Testaments. Since the essay was first drafted, my attention has been drawn to an early paper by another very good Erlangen friend, Dr. G. STÄHLIN (now of Mainz), which in part anticipates my theme, and to which I am indebted for further insights. [1]) Something of my viewpoint is also shared with Dr E. SCHWEIZER in the works cited below.

My thesis is that the Fourth Gospel is one of the most strongly individualistic of all the New Testament writings, and that the 'realized eschatology' which is so familiar a feature of this Gospel is the result rather of this individualism than of anything more profound or radical in its thought. This may sound a foolish thesis. St John's Gospel is generally thought of as one of the chief documents of Christian unity and organic life. One's thoughts immediately fly to the temple of Christ's body, to the Shepherd and the one flock, to the vine and the branches, to the *ut omnes unum sint.* [2]) Of course! But is that the whole story?

II

Picking up the point about 'realized eschatology' first, I begin trom xiv 21-23, which, I submit, is a far more explicitly individualistic type of eschatology than even the Lucan ἐντὸς ὑμῶν interpreted in the 'inward' sense. The immediate antecedents of this passage are a reference to a return of Christ after his departure (v. 18 οὐκ ἀφήσω ὑμᾶς ὀρφανούς, ἔρχομαι πρὸς ὑμᾶς), and the interpretation of His return not as a public manifestation to the whole world but as a manifestation to the disciples only (v. 19 ὁ κόσμος με οὐκέτι θεωρεῖ, ὑμεῖς δὲ θεωρεῖτέ με). For them, admittedly, it will be an understanding of something that seems emphatically 'corporate'—the 'mutual coinherence' of Christ and the Father and of Christ and the disciples (v. 20 γνώσεσθε ὑμεῖς ὅτι ἐγὼ ἐν τῷ πατρί μου καὶ ὑμεῖς ἐν ἐμοὶ κἀγὼ ἐν ὑμῖν). And yet, this seems to be immediately interpreted (in keeping with v. 19) in such individualistic terms that

---

[1]) G. STÄHLIN, ,,Zum Problem der johanneischen Eschatologie'', *ZNTW* 33 (1934), 225.

[2]) 'Nun gibt es freilich im Neuen Testament kaum eine Schrift, die die Einheit der Kirche so stark betont wie gerade das vierte Evangelium (x 16; xvii 20 f.)' — E. SCHWEIZER, ,,Der Kirchenbegriff im Evangelium und den Briefen des Johannes', in *Studia Evangelica* (*Texte und Untersuchungen* 73. Band = V. Reihe, Band 18, 1959), 372 ('The Concept of the Church in the Gospel and Epistles of St John', in *New Testament Studies* ed. A. J. B. HIGGINS, 1959, 236).

one of the disciples, Judas (not the Iscariot) is scandalised. Jesus says that he will love and manifest himself (ἐμφανίσω . . . ἐμαυτόν) to anyone who loves and obeys him. Judas exclaims, 'But what has happened, that you should manifest yourself to us and not to the world?' In reply, Jesus simply reiterates (v. 23) that the Father and he will come (ἐλευσόμεθα) and stay with anyone who loves and obeys. That could be interpreted—whether rightly or not remains to be seen— as a 'realized eschatology' indeed, but one which finds its realisation only on the level of the individual. The Fourth Evangelist habitually makes his point by a dialogue containing a misunderstanding and its correction; and here, by means of Judas' misunderstanding, the point seems to be deliberately sharpened that, insofar as there is any 'coming' to be realized in the near future, it is essentially not a world-wide manifestation but a secret, private coming to each individual as he realizes the fact of the resurrection, loves God in Christ, and accepts him.

It is perhaps not inopportune at this point to make the observation that indeed any eschatology that is to be immediately 'realized' must, of necessity, be only partial or 'inaugurated' or 'sich realisierende'; and is therefore inherently bound to show an individualistic tendency: the more fully realized, the narrower the scope. Is it not, then, proper to ask whether the widely recognised emphasis of the Fourth Gospel on the realisation of the coming as already about to take place is not largely achieved by a corresponding individualism? [1]) Similarly the rabbis, as we know, sometimes spoke of individuals 'accepting the yoke of the kingdom'— that is, accepting God's will and conforming to his sovereignty. [2]) But any realisation of the kingdom of God in a fuller, more nearly total, more corporate sense was, for rabbinic thought, an expectation only for the future. Whether there is here a clue to the Evangelist's milieu, who can say? In the Jerusalem of our Lord's time, there were probably rabbinical views such as this, side by side with Zealot revolutionary ideals, apocalyptic hopes, and many others. [3]) But equally at Ephesus, near the end of the first century, there was no doubt a motley variety of religious views—indivi-

---

[1]) As G. STÄHLIN puts it (loc. cit.), John, as contrasted with Paul, lacks 'Telosstrebigkeit': his thinking is, in that sense, more static; but this does not mean that he is without a futurist expectation.

[2]) References in S.-B. i. 608 ff., on Mt. xi 29.

[3]) See E. STAUFFER, e.g. Jerusalem und Rom (1957), passim.

dualistic gnostic types of thought, millennarianist ideals, and a host of others. It would be too much, therefore, to hope to find in this eschatological saying a clue to the Gospel's provenance.

But to return: are there any other passages in the Fourth Gospel that redress the balance in the direction of a less individualistic eschatology? The references to judgment or acquittal as having already taken place (iii 18, v 24), and to the passing from death to life as a fait accompli (v 24), are in terms of individuals, except when it is the judgment of the world or of its ruler, which is accomplished by Christ's death (xii 31, xvi 11). Conversely, the only quite clearly 'collective' and 'corporate' allusion (other than these allusions to Christ himself and his conquest of cosmic powers) is in terms not of 'realized eschatology' but of the 'orthodox' future event, not yet realised (v 28 f.). This confirms the view that the only 'realized eschatology' in the Fourth Gospel is on the individual level; and such a type of 'realized eschatology' so far from *replacing* a futurist eschatology, need be only its correlative. Indeed, in vi 40, 44, 54 it is possible to see the two together, side by side: ... ἵνα πᾶς ὁ θεωρῶν τὸν υἱὸν καὶ πιστεύων εἰς αὐτὸν ἔχῃ ζωὴν αἰώνιον, καὶ ἀναστήσω αὐτὸν ἐγὼ ἐν τῇ ἐσχάτῃ ἡμέρᾳ, etc.; cf. xi 24.

III

This leads to an observation on the relation between Luke and John. It is often said that the eschatology of the Fourth Gospel is in sharp contrast with that of Luke-Acts. It is a familiar fact that in other respects there are striking traces of a common tradition between Luke and John (e.g. the traditions of the Bethany family); but it is usually held that, in their theological approach and outlook, the two writers are vastly different, and, in particular, that their attitude to history and to eschatology sets them at a distance from one another. If Luke-Acts strings out the events, narrative-wise, in a sequence of 'moments'—the ministry, the death, the resurrection, the ascension, the coming of the Spirit, and (in the future) the coming again of Christ—the Fourth Evangelist, it is said, chooses instead to present the great verities in their mutual relationship as a single, indivisible unity: the entire ministry is the self-giving; the exaltation on the cross is the exaltation in glory; the Spirit is Christ's own *alter ego*; and there is no concern about a future παρουσία, for the coming of the Spirit is 'the coming', absolutely.

Now, obviously there is a measure of truth in this. Luke is essentially a narrator, and, whatever his theological intention, he achieves it through the use of at least a seeming chronology. John, by contrast, thinks 'theologically' and is ready to fuse different members of his structure together by the use of multivalent words like ὑψοῦν in such a way that there might seem to be less place in his treatment of his theme for time-sequences or successiveness.

And yet, to leave such a statement unqualified is to simplify deceptively, and means ignoring the fact that, seldom though this is observed, Luke and John have something in common even in the territory of such themes as ascension and the doctrine of the Spirit and of eschatology.

John alone, it must be remembered, shares with (Mk.) xvi and Lk.-Acts an explicit reference to ascension in addition to the resurrection. Jo. xx 17, whatever its obscurities, clearly represents the already risen Christ as declaring that he is also 'ascending' or about to 'ascend': that is, it distinguishes ascension from resurrection, and underlines ascension as though it added something of theological significance to the resurrection. It is another matter to determine the meaning of the *noli me tangere*, especially when contrasted with the express injunction to Thomas to feel the Lord. But it is very difficult, in my opinion, to believe (with C. H. DODD and others, *in loc.*) that the Evangelist intends us to understand that, between the meetings with Mary and Thomas, the 'ascension' has somehow been consummated and that it is this that explains the contrast between the 'touch me not' to Mary and the 'reach hither thy finger . . .' to Thomas. It is surely much simpler to explain the words to Mary to mean that she need not cling to the Rabbi, for he really is still 'with' her and not yet withdrawn from sight. By contrast, then, what Thomas needs is to be met upon his own ground and, since he has resolved to demand tactual evidence, to be offered it—if only to convince him, in the very act, that it may be dispensed with. On this showing, the contrast lies entirely in the needs and circumstances of the two disciples, and not in any differrence in the state of the Lord as between the two encounters. In that case, this Evangelist, like Luke, is recounting certain 'resurrection-appearances' as taking place between the resurrection and the ascension. This interpretation of the words spoken to Mary Magdalene fits, incidentally, with the Matthean picture of the women approaching Jesus and grasping his feet (ἐκράτησαν αὐτοῦ τοὺς πόδας, Mt. xxviii 9) and being told μὴ φοβεῖσθε—meaning, perhaps, again, that they need have no misgivings, for it is really the Lord whom they see: he has not yet ascended, he is no phantom.

But returning to the allusion to resurrection, we must recognise, of course, that the word ἀναβαίνειν (apart from its uses with reference to going up to Jerusalem) is used earlier in the Gospel also, and in a striking way. Is this compatible with so 'Lucan' an interpretation as I have just offered? In iii 13 the words are: καὶ οὐδεὶς ἀναβέβηκεν εἰς τὸν οὐρανὸν εἰ μὴ ὁ ἐκ τοῦ οὐρανοῦ καταβάς, ὁ υἱὸς τοῦ ἀνθρώπου ὁ ὢν ἐν τῷ οὐρανῷ (if, with A Θ 1 etc. 13 etc. 579 and others, we read this last difficult clause). It is simplest to accept this (which would otherwise be a hopelessly dark and oracular saying) as a post-resurrection formulation of the Church's faith. [1]) For the post-resurrection Church, Christ is both the one who came down from heaven and also the only one who has returned thither. If the last clause is indeed original and if this is a post-resurrection point of view, then it is not irrelevant to our enquiry that Christ is spoken of as *now in heaven*: that is precisely in line with the *Lucan* eschatology, and by no means conforms with what is usually (but I suspect not quite correctly) thought of as the eschatology of the Fourth Gospel. On the Lucan view, Christ, seated at the right hand of God in heaven, is represented on earth by the Spirit; and that, I suspect, is in fact the Fourth Evangelist's 'pattern' of thought also. The other comparable use of ἀναβαίνειν is in vi 62 ἐὰν οὖν θεωρῆτε τὸν υἱὸν τοῦ ἀνθρώπου ἀναβαίνοντα ὅπου ἦν τὸ πρότερον; But here there is no reason, as far as I can see, to look further than the most obvious sense—that the Son of Man, now ἐπὶ τῆς γῆς (to use the Synoptic phrase) will soon be exalted and vindicated (cf. Mk. xiv 62): it is simply an anticipation of that for which the ascension stands, and thus fits into the same comparatively simple 'pattern' of resurrection and ascension which we have seen implied in the post-resurrection narratives both of Luke and John. Certain peculiarities in the use of the term 'the Son of Man' will be discussed later. For the moment, the result of the enquiry is, I suggest, to confirm the thesis that John shares, substantially, Luke's 'pattern' of ideas.

---

[1]) E. M. SIDEBOTTOM, *The Christ of the Fourth Gospel* (1961), 120, proposes to translate 'No one has ascended . . . but one has descended'; but, while I agree that εἰ μή need not mean 'except', I cannot see how ὁ καταβάς can thus be turned into an indicative clause.

With much les confidence, and only as a tentative suggestion, it may now be asked whether the σύ μοι ἀκολούθει of Jo. xxi 22b may not be brought within the same scheme. Of course if we regard Jo. xxi as an extraneous addition, any affinities it may show to the standard 'pattern' which we are calling Lucan will be irrelevant to the authentic Johannine viewpoint. But there is little or nothing *in style* (to the best oi my knowledge) to distinguish it trom the rest of the Gospel; [1]) and if it is pronounced unauthentic it will be mainly for three reasons: first, because of the obvious climax in xx 30 f. (but that only means that xxi is an addition, not necessarily that it is by another hand); secondly, because oi the possibility that, since xxi 24 f. is manifestly by another hand, the whole chapter may be by another hand (but that is only a possibility); thirdly, because of the alleged incongruity of its eschatology. But if the eschatology of the preceding chapters is, after all, compatible with the standard Lucan type, which reckons with post-resurrection appearances followed by a final withdrawal from sight (ascension), then even the 'follow thou me' might refer less to a spiritual, 'unearthly' leadership than to the leading of the disciples up to Jerusalem by the risen Lord for Pentecost which (as I am beginning to suspect) the Acts narrative implies. If such an idea is ruled out, it will be only on the grounds of the unacceptability of such crass, physical literalism, not on the ground of language. Now Luke certainly did entertain such literalistic ideas: the post-resurrection accounts demonstrate this clearly—so much so that I am inclined (in parenthesis) even to accept the συναλιζόμενος of Ac. i 4 as = συναυλιζόμενος—Jesus bivouacking with the disciples.[2]) But what is interesting for the present purpose is that John also exhibits a physical literalism about the post-resurrection appearances, for is it not he alone who expressly mentions the stigmata (xx 25-27)? Luke's allusion to the hands and the feet (Lk. xxiv 39) reaches the same result, but only by implication.

Further, before we leave the subject of the resurrection appearances, it is worth while to observe that St John is quite careful about the timing of them. The first (xx 14) is in the continuous context of the early morning visit to the tomb (xx 1); the next is οὔσης ὀψίας τῇ ἡμέρᾳ ἐκένῃ τῇ μιᾷ σαββάτων (xx 19); the next, μεθ'

---

[1]) See CASSIEN, Évêque de Catane, 'Saint Pierre et l'Eglise dans le N.T.', *Istina* 3 (1955), 291 f. and literature there cited.

[2]) See C. F. D. MOULE 'The Ascension', *E.T.* lxviii 7 (April 1957), 205 ff.

ἡμέρας ὀκτώ (xx 26), i.e. the following Sunday. Only the appearance in Galilee in xxi is more vaguely dated as μετὰ ταῦτα. There is not much here, I submit, to encourage the notion that John is concerned only to fuse together into a sequence-less unity all the timeless 'moments' of his theological interpretation. Not a whit less than Luke, he gives us a narrative sequence. [1])

IV

Next, the 'going and coming' terminology of this Gospel must be examined. The relevant phrases are set out in the accompanying conspectus. So far as they refer to Jesus, they seem, for the most part, to fall into three main categories—allusions to the coming or coming forth or coming down from heaven, allusions to the going or the departure from sight or the ascending to heaven, and allusions to the coming or coming again or return to visibility. It is that third, of course, that is generally treated as taking the place of the παρουσία at the end of time. Now I suggest that the simplest possible way to interpret these phrases is to apply the first category to the incarnation, the second to the death, and the third to the resurrection, the return from death.

It is manifestly impossible to remain content with so simple an identification, because the second category certainly includes phrases which seem to refer to going in terms of going back to the Father, ascending to heaven, and so forth; while the third appears to include a mystical return such as is not to be identified *tout court* with reappearance after death: there is xiv 2 πάλιν ἔρχομαι καὶ παραλήμψομαι ὑμᾶς πρὸς ἐμαυτόν, and there is the already-discussed xiv 21 ff. which seems to describe an inward and spiritual coming to individuals. Moreover, further complexity is imparted to this third category by the introduction of the sayings about the coming of the Paraclete side by side with references to the coming of Christ.

It is this overplus to the simple going and coming categories, together with such phrases as 'the hour cometh *and now is* . . .', which lends plausibility to the idea that the Fourth Gospel is describing the death and resurrection as themselves the ultimate coming of Jesus—and that, in terms of the Spirit. The extreme form of such an interpretation would be that, for this Evangelist,

---

[1]) My colleague M. F. WILES has pointed out, however, that, if the point about Thomas is to be made at all, there must be a time interval: and what more theologically apt than that between Sunday and Sunday?

there is no παρουσία at the end, nor even a strictly time-involved sequence of resurrection appearances, but rather a single coming—the incarnation—which is seen to be final and decisive because of the triumph through death. The triumph through death, releasing the Spirit, marks the beginning of the era of realised eschatology; and this 'coming' is the only coming that matters. For DODD (*in loc.*) the 'ascension' is complete or consummated by the time of the appearing to Thomas and in the ascension is completed also the true *coming.*

But since we have already seen with what care the Evangelist describes and dates the resurrection appearances, is such a notion really in keeping with his own frame of thought? There are, so far as I can see, no references to the Spirit's coming which show decisively that the Evangelist intended to substitute the Paraclete for the παρουσία. xiv 16 is the most that might be quoted to support such a thesis—ἄλλον παράκλητον δώσει ὑμῖν ἵνα ᾖ μεθ' ὑμῶν εἰς τὸν αἰῶνα. But εἰς τὸν αἰῶνα need only mean 'for good and all' in a purely relative sense (cf. Ex. xxi 6, Philem. 15, etc.) and in contrast to the transitory, earthly ministry of Jesus which was about to be terminated. There is scarcely here sufficient evidence to show that the coming of the Spirit is conceived in any other way than as Luke—or, for that matter, Paul—conceives it, as the abiding presence of God with his Church on earth and as the firstfruits or pledge of a consummation yet to come. What is more, the only other guides we possess in the New Testament point decisively away from the assumption that the presence of the Spirit is to be equated with the final consummation. Not only does St Paul notoriously call the Spirit only the first fruits and *pledge* of something yet to come (Rom. viii 23, etc.); 1 John itself, recognising the presence of the Spirit (iii 24), adds, iii 2, . . . ἐὰν φανερωθῇ . . . Why, then, should it be assumed (unless there is cogent evidence) that the Fourth Gospel takes a different view? As for the 'now is' sayings (iv 23, v 25), these only represent the combination of realised with future which is a recognized phenomenon also in the Synoptics. [1] It is certainly true, however, that the coming or return of Jesus is described in terms which cannot be altogether confined to the mere post-resurrection appearances, just as also the 'going away' evidently contains in some instances a more pregnant idea than that merely of

---

[1] Cf. STÄHLIN *loc. cit.* 257 f.

temporary departure in death. 'To go to the Father', 'to go to prepare a place for you', clearly mean a consummation corresponding more closely to the ascension than to the death alone. As G. B. CAIRD well says, 'on the Cross Jesus goes to the Father not as an individual resuming a place which He relinquished when He came down from heaven, but as the representative of those who are to share with Him this place He has constantly occupied' ('The will of God: II. In the Fourth Gospel', *E.T.* lxxii 4 (Jan. 1961), 115 ff.).

Yet such phrases by no means have the monopoly in the category of 'going'; and in the 'coming' or 'returning' category they are represented only by xiv 2, 21 ff. It looks, then, as though St John were working with what I have called the ordinary 'Lucan' pattern, but sometimes adding phrases which transcend it in such a way as to suggest that the going in death and the return in the resurrection are actually fraught with greater, indeed with ultimate, significance [1]—that the going in death is also a return to the Father, in the sense that it represents the completion of Christ's earthly ministry, and that the return from death means the taking of the disciples up into the heavenly life of the new age (cf. xvii 24). As BENGEL says, on xiv 18, 'Adventus primi *continuationes* sunt ceteri potius, quam iterationes'. But neither of theses pregnant uses precludes the holding of a 'normal' expectation of a future consummation in addition. It is not a realised eschatology in exchange for a futurist, but merely an expression of that element of the realised which inheres in any Christian eschatology (cf., as noted above, vi 40, 44, 54).

V

And in fact one only has to read 1 John to see how the eschatology of the Fourth Gospel works out in post-resurrection terms. It is often said that the eschatology of the Johannine Epistles is more 'temporal' than that of the Gospel—that is, that it fits more directly into the 'orthodox', Lucan time-scheme ('die Mitte der Zeit'), looking back to the ministry of Jesus and forward to his reappearing. But two questions need to be asked before one concludes that this eschatology is therefore essentially different: (i) Is not the more 'temporal' factor due simply to the more corporate setting of the

---

[1] '. . . alles Entscheidende schon geschehen ist', E. SCHWEIZER, *Gemeinde und Gemeindeordnung im Neuen Testament* (1959), 105.

thought? (ii) Is there anything in the eschatology of 1 John which is actually incompatible with the Gospel's teaching? [1]) One may freely admit that there is no explicit parallel in the Gospel to the references in 1 John ii 28, iii 2 (cf. ii 18, iv 17) to the coming (again) of Christ. But if it be once allowed that the Gospel recognises an *ascension* (in the 'Lucan' manner), it is not going beyond the evidence to say that this also implies a *return*. Otherwise, why did not the Fourth Evangelist remain content with a more timeless, a more 'mystical', a more theological ascension? [2]) The epistle's conception of a return of Christ, and its recognition of the presence of the Spirit meanwhile (iv 13) are not essentially out of harmony with the presuppositions of the Gospel. For the rest, it shares with the Gospel the conception of Christ as sent by the Father (iv 9, 14), as coming or appearing from heaven (iii 8), as bringing victory over the world (ii 13, iv 4); and it has as much—and as little—as the Fourth Gospel about 'realized eschatology'. If in the Gospel's prologue the true light was just coming into the world (for so, perhaps, it is best to interpret Jo. i 9), in the epistle that true light is already shining (ii 8); the recipients of the epistle have, like the believer of the Fourth Gospel, already passed from death to life (iii 14); they are already sons of God (iii 1); already the expectations about the Spirit's instruction are being fulfilled (ii 20 ff.). Perhaps most significant of all, the very same kind of realised eschatology is recognised as we examined in Jo. xiv 21 ff.: in 1 Jo. iv 12 f. 'No one has ever seen God', but God does abide within the Christian community if its members love one another, and the token of this is the presence of the Spirit. That is only one degree less 'individual' than the Gospel passage: the 'presence' is confined to the community of believers; it is invisible; it is achieved in terms of the Spirit. All this goes to confirm that this degree of 'realised' eschatology is perfectly compatible with a vivid expectation of a *future* consummation; and that there is no need to find a frame of reference for the Fourth Gospel other than that of the epistle—or of St Luke. It may well be that the Johannine epistles were a corrective, in some respects, to the Gospel, or to a misreading of the

---

[1]) Cf. F. M. Braun, *Jean le Théologien* (1959), 36.
[2]) If there is ἀρχή, is it mistaken to assume τέλος ? cf. G. Stählin, *loc. cit.* 255 f. This is where perhaps J. A. T. Robinson, in *Jesus and His Coming* (1957), over-estimates the alleged 'distortion' of a Johannine theological unity by the other writers (see e.g., p. 165).

Gospel, and that part of the correction was in the direction of a greater stress on the corporate, leading to a correspondingly greater explicitness about the future consummation. [1]) But, if so, this only confirms the thesis here advanced.

VI

If, as I believe, the significance of the choice of the word παρά-κλητος is that the Spirit is viewed as the Vindicator or Champion of the cause of God, as the Advocate, pleading God's cause against disobedience everywhere, first in the Church and next (through the Church's obedient acceptance of God's judgment) in the world, then this, again, is exactly in line with the picture presented by the Acts. [2])

My conclusion thus far, [3]) then, is that the Fourth Evangelist's eschatology is much more 'normal' than is often assumed [4]); and that, where it is of an emphatically realised type, there the individualistic tendency of this Gospel is also at its most prominent; and that the peculiar *depth* of the Fourth Gospel lies largely in its penetrating analysis of the meaning of individual relations with God in Christ.

VII

All this being said, we may now go back for a while, behind the eschatological question, to note how often, throughout the Fourth Gospel, it is the individual who is in question. As E. SCHWEIZER has reminded us, [5]) the Fourth Gospel is practically without the words ἐκκλησία, ἀπόστολος (only xiii 16), ἅγιος (only πάτερ ἅγιε, xvii 11); and only once is there any mention of the

---

[1]) Cf. E. SCHWEIZER, *T. und U.*, ut sup., 376 (*N. T. Essays*, ut sup., 239).

[2]) As BENGEL says on Jo. xvi 8: Hujus loci impletio habetur in Actis Apostolorum. Vide ibi exemplum elenchi, de *peccato infidelitatis*, c. 3, 13 s. de *justitia*, c. 13, 39. cum antecedenti: de *judicio*, c. 26.18. I would not have chosen these passages; but if we substitute (i) v 4, 9; (ii) iv 13-16 (iii) xix 13-20, we get the same results.

[3]) With which cf. the thesis of G. STÄHLIN, *loc. cit.*

[4]) There is, I think, no necessity to read Jo. xix 37 as an instance of realised eschatology. The 'looking' of Zech. xiii 10 is not here (I would believe) intended to have been already fulfilled by the Roman soldier and his companions: only the piercing is fulfilled, in order that, on the *future* occasion of Christ's return, it may be upon him whom they pierced that his enemies must gaze.

[5]) *T. und U.*, ut sup., 370 f. (*N.T. Essays*, ut sup., 235); and *Gemeinde und Gemeindeordnung* (1959), 110 f.

Twelve (vi 67). That might be taken as a mere chance of vocabulary, were there not other, more unmistakable, indications pointing in the same diretion. In the Synoptists, the term 'the Son of Man' is used in a way which is at least compatible with the 'human' figure in Daniel—the figure which stands for the group of loyal Jews who chose martyrdom rather than surrendering their faith. But in the Fourth Gospel generally, the nearest approach [1]) to this is only in the 'Jacob's ladder' saying (i 51), where the corporate reference is perhaps obliquely hinted by the substitution of the Son of Man for Jacob (= Israel). Otherwise, the Son of Man is a pre-existent figure—and presumably therefore an individual: he is nearer, at least in this respect, to what we find in I Enoch XXXVII-LXXI (although I am far from convinced that those chapters were extant in the time of Christ). [2]) Here, then, instead of the true Israel, who, in the last analysis, is true Man, including and comprehending man, we meet something more like an individual Saviour. [3]) Again, the Fourth Gospel is full of encounters between Jesus alone with an individual or with very small groups: two disciples (i 38), Peter (i 42), Philip (i 43), Nathanael (i 47), Nicodemus (iii), the Samaritan woman (iv), the infirm man (v), the brothers of Jesus (vii 6), the blind man (ix), the Bethany family (xi, xii), the Greeks (xii).

Springing from these encounters are numerous sayings about the relation between Jesus and individuals: life belongs to anyone who believes; such a one has passed from death to life; anyone who drinks the living water will find thirst satisfied, whoever eats the living bread will not go hungry; the true worshipper is the one

---

[1]) On this passage see E. SCHWEIZER, „Die Kirche als Leib Christi in den paulinischen Homologoumena", *Th. Literaturz.* 1961, No. 3, Sp. 169. I doubt whether C. H. DODD's ingenious linking of Jo. xv 1 ff. with the Son of Man via Ps. lxxx (*The Interpretation of the Fourth Gospel*, 1953) is really convincing.

[2]) Yet, note in Enoch XLII that Wisdom found no place to dwell among men, so returned to take her seat among the angels. This is strikingly parallel to 'his own received him not' (i 11), and 'having come forth . . . he returned (xiii 3); and the taking of his own to the dwelling-places (xiv 2 f.) follows very naturally. See C. H. DODD *op. cit.* 275 for other parallels from the Wisdom Literature.

[3]) I do not, of course wish to deny that Jesus was 'the true self of the human race' (C. H. DODD, *op. cit.*, 249), but I do question whether such a conclusion is justly extracted from the use of the term 'Son of Man' in the Fourth Gospel; and I am inclined to think that, even if the conclusion, more broadly based, is a true one, it scarcely represents the *prevailing emphasis* of this Gospel. It better describes St Paul's outlook.

whose worship is not localised in a temple but is inward and spiritual·
And is it not, perhaps, significant that what appears to be, short of
the death and resurrection itself, the greatest of all the σημεῖα—
the crown of the whole series—is the restoring to life of one individual, Lazarus? It is clear enough that for Paul the resurrection
of Christ is an inclusive event as wide as Mankind: for Paul the
resurrection of Christ is *the* resurrection at the last day, not the
resuscitation of one individual; and it is difficult to imagine that
Paul would have been content to use any merely human individual's
restoration to life as a symbol for this essentially *final* and *all-
inclusive* event. For Paul, Christ is the first-fruits of the whole
human race; Paul's Christology is of the size of an anthropology.
But when the Johannine Christ is shown as anticipating the final
resurrection, it is on an individual scale. Martha says that she knows
that her brother will be raised at the last day. Jesus replies that he
himself *is* the resurrection, he *is* life. But what follows suggests that
this is in the sense not that in him the total resurrection of man is
included, but rather that each individual who puts his trust in him
becomes possessed of an unassailable life. It is a one-by-one salvation that is here envisaged. It could very easily give rise to that
individualistic heresy alluded to in 2 Tim. ii 18—that the resurrection had already taken place. Even when Christ is the Vine [1]),
it is a matter for each branch, individually, to remain or to be
detached. When he is the good Shepherd, it is the individual
sheep who listen and respond or who are deaf to his voice. This is
not, of course, to deny that the fact that disciples are spoken of
as *in Christ*, and Christ is *in God* (xvii 21, etc.) bears witness to that
mysterious inclusiveness—that 'corporate personality'—which is
characteristic of the New Testament estimate of Christ generally:
it is merely to affirm that in this Gospel it is the individual relationship that is the more prominent.

Perhaps E. KÄSEMANN was right, then, in picturing the Elder of
the Johannine Epistles (and I am ready to believe, with him, that
this is also the author of the Gospel) as the anti-ecclesiastical,

---

[1]) And I have no wish to controvert the assumption that behind this
figure lie the characteristically corporate and collective Hebrew ideas associated with the vine as representing Israel. See E. SCHWEIZER, ,,Die Kirche
als Leib Christi in den paulinischen Homologoumena'', *Th. Literaturz.* 86
(1961), Spp. 168 ff.

pietistic believer; [1]) and perhaps the Evangelist (though, in my opinion, no anti-sacramentalist, *pace* Bultmann, but, on the contrary, constantly alluding to the sacraments) is more interested in the great realities that underlie all sacraments—and, indeed, all life—than in their more narrowly sacramental embodiment and their corporate, ecclesiastical regularisation. In other words, perhaps the Fourth Evangelist is consciously and deliberately interpreting the sacraments themselves in terms of other categories, rather than interpreting other categories by means of the sacraments. And even if one allows a very direct allusion to the sacraments in this Gospel, it is noticable that the Pauline idea of incorporation in Christ in his death and resurrection is not made explicit: instead, it is rebirth by water and Spirit (iii), or enlightenment (ix). The nearest we come to a hint of baptismal incorporation is at xiii 8 ἐὰν μὴ νίψω σε, οὐκ ἔχεις μέρος μετ' ἐμοῦ: but that is still a long way from the Pauline idea of the death of Christ as 'the one baptism', [2]) involving the baptism of all by incorporation: here is no Pauline sacramentalism in terms of entry into the Body of Christ crucified and raised.

VIII

If there is any truth in these observations, they will help to explain why it is that the Fourth Gospel is so particularly precious to all pastors and evangelists who set store by personal dealing. This is the Gospel, par excellence, of the approach of the single soul to God: this is the part of Scripture to which one turns first when trying to direct an enquirer to his own, personal appropriation of salvation. Here, then, is an emphasis which is precious in the extreme. Only, it is not a total, inclusive view. It is as one-sided (in depth) as Luke-Acts tends to be (in breadth). The thinker who most organically and most profoundly combines the two planes is Paul. His doctrine of the Spirit not only as Advocate and Champion pleading our cause, but also as Christ's sonship crying in us the 'Abba' of Christ's filial obedience, and yet, still only the 'first fruits'

---

[1]) „Ketzer und Zeuge" in *Exegetische Versuche und Besinnungen* (1960), 168 ff. (first published in *ZThK* 48 (1951), 292 ff.).

[2]) See O. CULLMANN, *Die Tauflehre des Neuen Testaments* (1948), 18 ff. etc.; J. A. T. ROBINSON, 'The One Baptism as a Category of New Testament Soteriology', *S.J.T.* 6.3 (Sept. 1953), 257 ff.; cf. W. NAUCK, *Die Tradition und der Charakter des ersten Johannesbriefes* (1957), 179.

of a consummation in the future, goes further than John or Luke to combine depth and perspective. The function of Luke and John, in the divine dispensation, seems rather to be to stress each one side of the picture, although Luke's picture happens to be in the nature of a two-dimensional map into which it is possible to introduce the great depth of the Fourth Evangelist's insight— possible, because it is the same 'map' that he himself also accepts and uses.

Thus, each writer has his special vocation in the Lord, and each must be balanced by the other. [1]) It is in the New Testament collectively that we find reflected ἡ πολυποίκιλος σοφία τοῦ θεοῦ.

---

[1]) 'Vielleicht gibt es keine anderen Schriften im Neuen Testament, die derart anregend und fruchtbar werden können wie gerade diese (d. h. Joh.). Aber sie (d.h. die Kirche) hat sie neben die anderen Schriften gestellt, neben die Synoptiker und die Paulusbriefe. Nur mit ihnen zusammen und von ihnen her auch modifiziert und interpretiert ist Johannes zu hören.' — E. SCHWEIZER in *T. und U.*, ut sup.; (*N.T. Essays*, ut sup., 243).

Coming, going, and returning in St. John's Gospel (mainly xiii-xvii)

Coming (from pre-existence)	Going (? in death)	Returning
i 9 ἦν τὸ φῶς τὸ ἀληθινόν, . . ., ἐρχόμενον εἰς τὸν κόσμον.		
i 11 εἰς τὰ ἴδια ἦλθεν.		
iii 2 ἀπὸ θεοῦ ἐλήλυθας διδάσκαλος.		
iii 13	οὐδεὶς ἀναβέβηκεν .εἰς τὸν οὐρανὸν εἰ μὴ	
ὁ ἐκ τοῦ οὐρανοῦ καταβάς, ὁ υἱὸς τοῦ ἀνθρώπου.		
iii 19 τὸ φῶς ἐλήλυθεν εἰς τὸν κόσμον.		
iii 31 ὁ ἄνωθεν ἐρχόμενος . . . ὁ ἐκ τοῦ οὐρανοῦ ἐρχόμενος.		
vi 14 ὁ προφήτης ὁ ἐρχόμενος εἰς τὸν κόσμον.		
vi 33 ὁ γὰρ ἄρτος τοῦ θεοῦ ἐστιν ὁ καταβαίνων ἐκ τοῦ οὐρανοῦ.		
vi 38 καταβέβηκα ἀπὸ τοῦ οὐρανοῦ.		
vi 46 ὁ ὢν παρὰ τοῦ θεοῦ.		
vi 50 ὁ ἄρτος ὁ ἐκ τοῦ οὐρανοῦ καταβαίνων		
51 . . . ὁ ἄρτος ὁ ζῶν ὁ ἐκ τοῦ οὐρανοῦ καταβάς.		
vi 58 ὁ ἄρτος ὁ ἐξ οὐρανοῦ καταβάς.		
vi 62	ἐὰν οὖν θεωρῆτε τὸν υἱὸν τοῦ ἀνθρώπου ἀναβαίνοντα ὅπου ἦν τὸ πρότερον;	
vii 28 ἀπ' ἐμαυτοῦ οὐκ ἐλήλυθα.		
vii 33	ἔτι χρόνον μικρὸν μεθ' ὑμῶν εἰμι καὶ ὑπάγω πρὸς τὸν πέμψαντά με . . . ὅπου εἰμὶ ἐγὼ ὑμεῖς οὐ δύνασθε ἐλθεῖν . . . ποῦ οὗτος μέλλει πορεύεσθαι . . .;	
vii 21		[τὸ πνεῦμα] οὗ ἔμελλον λαμβάνειν οἱ πιστεύσαντες εἰς αὐτόν· οὔπω γὰρ ἦν πνεῦμα, ὅτι Ἰησοῦς οὐδέπω ἐδοξάσθη.
viii 14 οἶδα πόθεν ἦλθον ὑμεῖς δὲ οὐκ οἴδατε πόθεν ἔρχομαι	καὶ ποῦ ὑπάγω· ἢ ποῦ ὑπάγω.	
viii 21	ἐγὼ ὑπάγω καὶ ζητήσετέ με . . . ὅπου ἐγὼ ὑπάγω ὑμεῖς οὐ δύνασθε ἐλθεῖν.	

Coming (from pre-existence)	Going (? in death)	Returning
22	ὅπου ἐγὼ ὑπάγω ὑμεῖς οὐ δύνασθε ἐλθεῖν.	
viii 42 ἐγὼ γὰρ ἐκ τοῦ θεοῦ ἐξῆλθον καὶ ἥκω· οὐδὲ γὰρ ἀπ' ἐμαυτοῦ ἐλήλυθα, ἀλλ' ἐκεῖνός με ἀπέστειλεν.		
ix 39 εἰς κρίμα ἐγὼ εἰς τὸν κόσμον τοῦτον ἦλθον.		
xii 47 οὐ γὰρ ἦλθον ἵνα κρίνω τὸν κόσμον, ἀλλ' ἵνα σώσω τὸν κοσμον.		
xiii 1	εἰδὼς ὁ Ἰησοῦς ὅτι ἦλθεν αὐτοῦ ἡ ὥρα ἵνα μεταβῇ ἐκ τοῦ κόσμου τούτου πρὸς τὸν πατέρα . . .	
xiii 3 εἰδὼς ὅτι . . . ἀπὸ θεοῦ ἐξῆλθεν	καὶ πρὸς τὸν θεὸν ὑπάγει . . .	
xiii 33	ἔτι μικρὸν μεθ' ὑμῶν εἰμι . . . ὅπου ἐγὼ ὑπάγω ὑμεῖς οὐ δύνασθε ἐλθεῖν . . .	
xiii 36	κύριε, ποῦ ὑπάγεις; . . . ὅπου ὑπάγω οὐ δύνασαί μοι νῦν ἀκολουθῆσαι,	
37	ἀκολουθήσεις δὲ ὕστερον. διὰ τί οὐ δύναμαί σοι ἀκολουθῆσαι ἄρτι; τὴν ψυχήν μου ὑπὲρ σου θήσω.	
xiv 2	πορεύομαι ἑτοιμάσαι τόπον ὑμῖν.	
3	καὶ ἐὰν πορευθῶ καὶ ἑτοιμάσω τόπον ὑμῖν,	πάλιν ἔρχομαι καὶ παραλήμψομαι ὑμᾶς πρὸς ἐμαυτόν, ἵνα ὅπου εἰμὶ ἐγὼ καὶ ὑμεῖς ἦτε.
4	καὶ ὅπου ἐγὼ ὑπάγω οἴδατε τὴν ὁδόν.	
5	οὐκ οἴδαμεν ποῦ ὑπάγεις . .	
6	ἐγώ εἰμι ἡ ὁδὸς . . . οὐδεὶς ἔρχεται πρὸς τὸν πατέρα εἰ μὴ δι' ἐμοῦ.	
xiv 12	ὅτι ἐγὼ πρὸς τὸν πατέρα πορεύομαι.	
xiv 16		ἄλλον παράκλητον δώσει ὑμῖν, ἵνα ᾖ μεθ' ὑμῶν εἰς τὸν αἰῶνα, τὸ πνεῦμα τῆς ἀληθείας, ὃ ὁ κόσμος οὐ δύναται λαβεῖν, ὅτι οὐ θεωρεῖ αὐτὸ οὐδὲ γινώσκει· ὑμεῖς γινώσκετε αὐτό, ὅτι παρ' ὑμῖν μένει καὶ ἐν ὑμῖν ἔσται.
xiv 18		οὐκ ἀφήσω ὑμᾶς ὀρφανούς, ἔρχομαι πρὸς ὑμᾶς.

Coming (from pre-existence)	Going (? in death)	Returning
19	ἔτι μικρὸν καὶ ὁ κόσμος με οὐκέτι θεωρεῖ	ὑμεῖς δὲ θεωρεῖτέ με, ὅτι ἐγὼ ζῶ καὶ ὑμεῖς ζήσετε. ἐν
20		ἐκείνῃ τῇ ἡμέρᾳ γνώσεσθε ὑμεῖς ὅτι ἐγὼ ἐν
21		τῷ πατρί μου . . . .
xiv 23		ἐμφανίσω αὐτῷ ἐμαυτόν. πρὸς αὐτὸν ἐλευσόμεθα καὶ μονὴν παρ' αὐτῷ ποιησό-
xiv 26		μεθα. ὁ δὲ παράκλητος, τὸ πνεῦμα τὸ ἅγιον ὃ πέμψει ὁ πατὴρ ἐν τῷ ὀνόματί μου . . .
xiv 28	ὑπάγω ἐχάρητε ἂν ὅτι πορεύομαι πρὸς τὸν πατέρα . . .	καὶ ἔρχομαι πρὸς ὑμᾶς . . .
xv 22 εἰ μὴ ἦλθον καὶ ἐλάλησα αὐτοῖς . . .		
xv 26		ὅταν ἔλθῃ ὁ παράκλητος ὃν ἐγὼ πέμψω ὑμῖν παρὰ τοῦ πατρός, τὸ πνεῦμα τῆς ἀλη- θείας ὃ παρὰ τοῦ πατρὸς ἐκπορεύεται . . .
xvi 5	νῦν δὲ ὑπάγω πρὸς τὸν πέμ- ψαντά με, καὶ οὐδεὶς ἐξ ὑμῶν ἐρωτᾷ με· ποῦ ὑπά- γεις;	
xvi 7	συμφέρει ὑμῖν ἵνα ἀπέλθω. ἐὰν γὰρ μὴ ἀπέλθω,	ὁ παράκλητος οὐ μὴ ἔλθῃ πρὸς ὑμᾶς.
8	ἐὰν δὲ πορευθῶ,	πέμψω αὐτὸν πρὸς ὑμᾶς. καὶ ἐλθὼν ἐκεῖνος . . .
xvi 10	πρὸς τὸν πατέρα ὑπάγω καὶ οὐκέτι θεωρεῖτέ με.	
xvi 13		ὅταν δὲ ἔλθῃ ἐκεῖνος, τὸ πνεῦμα τῆς ἀληθείας . . .
xvi 16	μικρὸν καὶ οὐκέτι θεωρεῖτέ με,	καὶ πάλιν μικρὸν καὶ ὄψεσθέ με.
17	μικρὸν καὶ οὐ θεωρεῖτέ με, ὅτι ὑπάγω πρὸς τὸν πατέρα;	καὶ πάλιν μικρὸν καὶ ὄψεσθέ με; καὶ
xvi 19	μικρὸν καὶ οὐ θεωρεῖτέ με,	καὶ πάλιν μικρὸν καὶ ὄψεσθέ με;
20	ὑμεῖς λυπηθήσεσθε,	ἀλλ' ἡ λύπη ὑμῶν εἰς χαρὰν γενήσεται.
xvi 23	νῦν μὲν λύπην ἔχετε·	πάλιν δὲ ὄψομαι ὑμᾶς, καὶ χαρήσεται ὑμῶν ἡ καρδία,

Coming (from pre-existence)	Going (? in death)	Returning
		καὶ τὴν χαρὰν ὑμῶν οὐδεὶς αἴρει ἀφ' ὑμῶν. καὶ ἐν ἐκείνῃ τῇ ἡμέρᾳ ἐμὲ οὐκ ἐρωτήσετε οὐδέν.
xvi 25	ταῦτα ἐν παροιμίαις λελάληκα ὑμῖν·	
		ἔρχεται ὥρα ὅτε οὐκέτι ἐν παροιμίαις λαλήσω ὑμῖν, ἀλλὰ παρρησίᾳ περὶ τοῦ πατρὸς ἀπαγγελῶ ὑμῖν.
26		ἐν ἐκείνῃ τῇ ἡμέρᾳ ἐν τῷ ὀνόματί μου αἰτήσεσθε ...
27 ἐγὼ παρὰ τοῦ θεοῦ ἐξῆλθον.		
28 ἐξῆλθον ἐκ τοῦ πατρὸς καὶ ἐλήλυθα εἰς τὸν κόσμον·	πάλιν ἀφίημι τὸν κόσμον καὶ πορεύομαι πρὸς τὸν πατέρα.	
xvi 30 ἀπὸ θεοῦ ἐξῆλθες.		
xvii 8 παρὰ σοῦ ἐξῆλθον ...		
xvii 11	καὶ οὐκέτι εἰμὶ ἐν τῷ κόσμῳ ... κἀγὼ πρὸς σὲ ἔρχομαι.	
xvii 13	νῦν δὲ πρὸς σὲ ἔρχομαι, καὶ ταῦτα λαλῶ ἐν τῷ κοσμῷ ..	
xvii 24	θέλω ἵνα ὅπου εἰμὶ ἐγὼ	κἀκεῖνοι ὦσιν μετ' ἐμοῦ [?]
xviii 37 εἰς τοῦτο ἐλήλυθα εἰς τὸν κόσμον ...		
xx 19		ἦλθεν ὁ Ἰησοῦς καὶ ἔστη εἰς τὸ μέσον ...
xx 24		ὅτε ἦλθεν ὁ Ἰησοῦς.
xx 26		ἔρχεται ὁ Ἰησοῦς ... καὶ ἔστη εἰς τὸ μέσον ...
xxi 22		ἐὰν αὐτὸν θέλω μένειν ἕως ἔρχομαι ...
23		ἐὰν αὐτὸν θέλω μένειν ἕως ἔρχομαι ...

THE STRUCTURE AND SCOPE
OF THE PROLOGUE TO THE GOSPEL OF JOHN

BY

HERMAN RIDDERBOS

Kampen

I

Anyone who attempts to form a judgment as to the place and significance of the Gospel of John in the canon of the New Testament, and at the same time take notice of those points which have been raised in the history of scientific investigation up to the present day, finds himself confronted with a confusing plenitude of problems. Scholars who have immersed themselves in these matters speak, each in his turn, of the "riddle" of the Fourth Gospel [1]). If one inquires in what this riddle consists, then it appears that in more than one respect the Gospel is difficult to place, historically and geographically (when and where was it written, and whom must one suggest as the author?), and especially theologically. What did the author intend by the Gospel? What was his spiritual background? What is the world from which he derives his peculiar terminology and content of ideas and which, for example, causes him to transmit the words of Jesus in so different a form from that of the other evangelists? And finally, is not what is described as his "Christology" another, much further removed from the historical Jesus-image, than that of the synoptics?

These and similar questions have governed the discussion for many decades. If one looks more closely, then the historical and theological questions appear to be intimately related and not a little dependent upon each other for their solution. The historical objections against the old tradition that the Gospel originates with the Apostle John would not weigh so heavily were not many of the

---

[1]) So already A. v. HARNACK, *Lehrbuch der Dogmengeschichte* I[5], Tübingen, 1931, p. 308. R. SCHNACKENBURG, "Logos-Hymnus und johanneischer Prolog", *Bibl. Zeitschrift*, Vol. I, 1957, pp. 66-109, cf. p. 69. E. KÄSEMANN, "Zur Johannes—Interpretation in England", *Exegetische Versuche und Besinnungen* II, Göttingen, 1964, speaks of "die rätselhafteste Schrift des Neuen Testaments", p. 148.

opinion that the content of the Gospel has undergone a very marked modification through the influence of a world quite different from that in which one can suppose an eye-witness and disciple of Jesus to have moved. It is true that the time is past when a radical criticism could assert that the Gospel originated in the latter half of the second century, contains no trustworthy tradition, and, indeed, that it does not intend to give an historical account but rather to present in historical dress a certain idea of Christ [1]). The discovery of fragments written on papyrus and dating from the first decades of the second century in Egypt has demonstrated that the Gospel could not have been written later than the period in which it is placed by tradition. This does not remove the fact, however, that many consider the Fourth Gospel to have been thoroughly influenced and conditioned by thoughts stemming from a world different from that which one may presume of John the son of Zebedee. Specifically is this the case with two prominent interpretations in our time: i.e., those of C. H. Dodd [2]) and R. Bultmann [3]). Both seek the spiritual background of the fourth evangelist in the Hellenistic-Greek world view, though each in his own way and without much mutual agreement. While Dodd makes use of the philosophical ideas of Philo and the Hermetic writings of the second century in the interpretation of the Gospel, Bultmann here again seeks the background against which we must understand the Gospel in the thoughts and ideas of the later Gnostic writings.

Nevertheless, these investigations have anything but solved the riddle; in their essential diversity of point of view and in their different predilections for what in the old religious and philosophical systems might be the background of the Fourth Gospel, they represent rather, in great style, the precariousness of any attempt to seek the key to the solution in a world that is absolutely different from the core of the Gospel. It may be for this reason that, however great the prestige of the investigators and whatever the extraordinary learning and talent they, each in his own way, have shown, one cannot in general say that they have found many followers. They are rather more praised for their efforts, than belie-

---

[1]) For these conceptions (as of F. C. Baur) see Feine—Behm—Kümmel, *Einleitung in das Neue Testament*[12], Heidelberg, 1963, p. 133.

[2]) *The Interpretation of the Fourth Gospel*, Cambridge, 1958.

[3]) *Das Evangelium des Johannes* (in Meyer's *Kritisch-exegetischer Kommentar über das Neue Testament*) [11], Göttingen, 1950.

ved in their results. Indeed, one must observe that, also in the judgment of many whom one cannot reproach with immoderate zeal for the conservation of ecclesiastical tradition, a certain turn in the tide of opinion is taking place. Here again the historical and theological aspects of the problem as formulated hang closely together, though it be now conversely. There are further new indications which point emphatically to Palestine for the historical background of the Fourth Gospel and, indeed, to the time before the fall of Jerusalem. The accuracy of various topographical references in the Gospel has been established by such experts in the archaeology of Palestine as W. F. ALBRIGHT [1]) and JOACHIM JEREMIAS [2]). It is no less important that in the Qumran writings a rich source of material for comparison has been opened, which has proved at least that for the explanation of various Johannine ideas and motifs it is not necessary to look so far afield as has often been supposed [3]). How positions are in process of changing may be clearly seen in an article by the well-known writer, Bishop J. A. T. ROBINSON: "The New Look on the Fourth Gospel" [4]). In it he argues that the suppositions which have long ruled the interpretation of the Fourth Gospel are increasingly being brought into question. These suppositions are, among others, that the background of the evangelist must have been another than that of the events which he related; that he cannot be regarded seriously as a witness to the historical Jesus, but only to the Christ of the faith of the later ecclesia; that he thus also could not have been the Apostle John or an immediate eye-witness. Still more important than this critique of that which formerly appeared to some to be unassailable are the positive contributions which have been made

---

[1]) See, e.g., his essay "Recent Discoveries in Palestine and the Gospel of St. John", in *The Background of the New Testament and its Eschatology* (ed. by W. D. DAVIES and D. DAUBE in honour of Ch. H. DODD), Cambridge, 1956, pp. 153-171. See also his *From the Stone Age to Christianity*, Baltimore, 1940, pp. 304 ff. Cf. further the judgement of G. E. WRIGHT, *De Bijbel ontdekt in aarde en steen* (translation of *Biblical Archaeology*), Baarn, 1958, p. 276.

[2]) See his *Die Wiederentdeckung von Bethesda*, 1949.

[3]) See, e.g., K. G. KUHN, "Johannesevangelium und die Qumrantexte", in *Neotestamentica et Patristica, Suppl. to Novum Testamentum* Vol. VI, 1962, pp. 111-122; G. QUISPEL, "l'Évangile de Jean et la Gnose", in *Recherches Bibliques* Vol. III, *l'Évangile de Jean*, Louvain, 1958, pp. 197 ff. See also the balanced evaluations of P. BENOIT, "Qumran et le Nouveau Testament", in *New Testament Studies* Vol. VII, 1961, pp. 276-296.

[4]) *Twelve New Testament Studies*, London, 1962, pp. 94 ff.

by others to understand the Gospel of John from the Palestinian situation before the year 70, and of which the essay of the Utrecht Professor VAN UNNIK, concerning the aim of the Gospel of John, constitutes a fine example [1]).

II

Meanwhile, these general considerations do not yet bring us to the matter itself. I should like to do so by asking attention for a subject that in the whole discussion of the Gospel of John has continually played a great part: i.e., *the structure and scope of the Prologue to the Gospel.* To be sure, it is especially in the Prologue that we come in contact with what is often seen as the most conclusive evidence that the concepts and ideas of the fourth evangelist must have been oriented by a different world from that of the other evangelists, and certainly from that of Jesus himself. In particular is this said to be the case with the Logos mentioned at the very beginning of the Prologue, his pre-existence with God as a personal being, his relationship to the world of all that is created, his entrance into the world as the Only-Begotten of the Father.

I am aware that, in the space allotted to me on this occasion, not all the problems which are connected with the Prologue to John's Gospel, or brought into connection with it, can be adequately treated, or, indeed, even so much as mentioned. I wish, therefore, to limit myself to a few chief considerations which I have attempted to draw together under the title: "Structure and Scope of the Prologue". At the same time, I shall refrain from giving an inventory of all the suggestions which have been made concerning this subject. Well-known, for example, is the dilemma suggested by VON HARNACK: Is the Prologue intended to provide a paedagogical introduction to the whole of the Gospel for the Hellenistic reader, or a short summary of the Gospel itself [2]) ? But others, e.g., HAENCHEN [3]) and KÄSEMANN [4]), have rejected this dilemma as false, and

---

[1]) W. C. VAN UNNIK, "The Purpose of St. John's Gospel", *Studia Evangelica*, ed. by KURT ALAND a.o., Berlin, 1959, pp. 382 ff. In his footsteps also J. A. T. ROBINSON, "The Destination and Purpose of St. John's Gospel", *o.c.*, pp. 107-125.

[2]) A. v. HARNACK, "Über das Verhältnis des Prologs des vierten Evangeliums zum ganzen Werk", *Zeitschrift für Theol. und Kirche* Vol. II, 1892, pp. 189 ff.

[3]) E. HAENCHEN, "Probleme des johanneischen ,,Prologs" ", in *Gott und Mensch, Gesammelte Aufsätze*, Tübingen, 1965, pp. 114-143.

[4]) E. KÄSEMANN, "Aufbau und Anliegen des johanneischen Prologs", in *Exegetische Versuche und Besinnungen* II, Göttingen, 1964, pp. 155-180.

each has come to another formulation of the intent of the Prologue. HAENCHEN, indeed, has argued that one cannot really speak of a Prologue, but that in these verses the writer makes a direct beginning with the Gospel itself [1]), in so far, that is, as he relates the revelation of the Logos in the various phases of his existence before the incarnation. Rather than to go into all these conceptions, I should like to set out *medias in res*, recognizing that, in the nature of the case, some answers must inevitably be given to the questions which have been posed.

The first issue which here arises is whether the Prologue as we now have it is on the whole to be understood as a unity. This matter is closely connected with a second: i.e., whether the Prologue is an original unity or an adaptation of an earlier composition or song, as many take it to be, which then may be described as the original Logos song or Logos hymn. There are, in turn, various opinions as to the source of this song. According to BULTMANN [2]), it is of pre-Christian origin, deriving from the former disciples of John the Baptist. Following his reasoning, they applied the Logos name and Logos idea to their hero: namely, John the Baptist. The *Logos figure* himself must again be traced still further back and is said to have been borrowed from what BULTMANN calls the Gnostic Redeemer myth. In the form in which the followers of the Baptist applied it to their revered master, the Logos figure was taken over by the evangelist, and adapted and transferred to Jesus Christ with the intention, among others, of claiming for Christ the honour ascribed by the song to the Baptist. This hypothesis has found little or no support, in so far as it brings the previous Logos song into relationship with John the Baptist. However, the suggestion that the Prologue stems from an already existing Christ song has found acceptance, especially in Germany[3]), but also elsewhere [4]). This song, so the argument runs, was entirely and throughout governed by the Logos motif and dedicated to Christ. In the hands of the evangelist, however, it was provided with all manner of additions and interpretations, and thus for the most part lost its original

---

[1]) HAENCHEN, *o.c.*, p. 117.

[2]) BULTMANN, *o.c.*, pp. 4 ff.

[3]) So e.g. HAENCHEN, KÄSEMANN, but also SCHNACKENBURG (cf. p. 180, note 1); A. WIKENHAUSER, *Das Evangelium nach Johannes*, Regensburg, 1961, pp. 39 ff.

[4]) Cf. e.g. M. F. LACAN, "Le Prologue de Saint Jean", *Lumière et Vie* Vol. VII, 1957, pp. 91-110.

rhythmical form. Proceeding from this hypothesis, various scholars
with a fine stripping knife have sought to bring out once more the
original song, though it must be said that, in all the operations
which have been undertaken, no two have led to the same result, [1]
and in the relevant literature we meet with a whole series of hypotheses as to how the original song must have appeared.

At this point the sober question may be asked whether the whole
matter of the existence of an earlier Logos song has any significant
importance for the exegesis of the Prologue as it lies before us. It
is with this, after all, that we are concerned. It may be pointed out
that such English commentators as DODD, BARRETT [2]), and Hos-
KYNS [3]), not so committed to the *Quellenscheiderei* as their *formgeschichtliche* colleagues in Germany, cheerfully engage in their
exegesis, quite unconcerned with all the joints and seams which,
according to the supporters of the hymn theory, are everywhere
to be observed in the Prologue. Nevertheless, the matter is not
without importance even for exegesis. I mention three considerations
which take us to the heart of the matter with which we are concerned
in this investigation.

The *first* is of a somewhat more formal nature. Only by viewing
the Prologue as an adaptation of an earlier song can it become
clear, so we are told, how it is that the rhythm of the first verses
is repeatedly interrupted further along and passes into a more
prosaic style. This applies particularly to the passage about John
the Baptist in vv. 6-8, which exhibits a much more prosaic form.
Further on, in verse 9, the pattern of the hymn is resumed. But
gradually the exactness of the form, so striking in the opening
verses, is relaxed. Especially does verse 15, where the Baptist is
mentioned again, strike a discordant note, though it is true that the
whole of the conclusion appears to trouble itself increasingly less
about the rhythm. Some think, indeed, that the song extends no
further than verse 14 in the Prologue [4]).

These are, one may say, observations in the area of style criticism
which in themselves are not of decisive significance for the exegesis.

---

[1]) This—so much must one concede to SCHNACKENBURG, *o.c.*, p. 72—does
not yet prove that the whole hypothesis is unsound. Certainly it, on this account, loses probability.
[2]) C. K. BARRETT, *The Gospel according to St. John*, London, 1956.
[3]) E. C. HOSKYNS, *The Fourth Gospel*, ed. by F. N. Davey, London, 1947.
[4]) So KÄSEMANN, *o.c.*, p. 168.

It is important, however, that the *second* point which I should like to make is closely related to them. We are told that in the structure of thought, too, this interrupting element reveals itself. And this faulty thought structure only becomes clear when one realizes that in the Prologue we have to do with an original in which the Logos motif had a more central place and a stricter thematic development than in our Prologue, which appears frequently to digress away from the Logos in order later to return to him. Moreover, the opinion is not infrequently expressed that the earlier hymn must have spoken of the Logos in a manner different from what now is the case in the Prologue [1]). Thus, we are told, the original, before coming to the incarnation of the Logos, gave detailed attention to the entry of the Logos into the world as the Logos *a-sarkos*, before his incarnation. This is then said to be recoverable in a somewhat defective form in vv. 4 ff. and 9 f., and could also appear out of the emphatic pronouncement in v. 14: "and the Word became flesh", words which indeed give the impression that nothing has yet been said about the incarnate Logos until v. 14. With the adaptation of the Logos song, however, this progression of thought from the pre-existent Logos, the Logos *a-sarkos* in the world of the gentiles and of Israel, the Logos *en-sarkos* in Christ, was more or less wiped out and everything concentrated upon the advent of Jesus Christ in the world. It is clear that all this is of cardinal significance for the exegesis. Some, as, e.g., HAENCHEN, go so far as to prefer to exclude from consideration certain verses of the Prologue which, so the argument goes, have corrupted the earlier thought pattern of the hymn, because we are under no obligation to permit the intrusion of the conception of a later interpreter or modifier [2]). Others opposed to this, e.g., BULTMANN, certainly distinguish between the original sense of the Logos hymn and that of the Prologue, but attempt even so to interpret the Prologue as a new whole. A third group, e.g., that of SCHNACKENBURG, who are also of the opinion that exegesis has surely to deal with the text as we have it before us, nevertheless repeatedly cast a look at the hymn in the form in which they consider themselves able to reconstruct it, and permit it at some points to condition their exegesis of the Prolo-

---

[1]) So also BULTMANN.

[2]) HAENCHEN, *o.c.*, pp. 141 ff., who ascribes vv. 12, 13, 15, not to the evangelist, but to a later *"Ergänzer"*, p. 332. He distinguishes no less than three layers or *"Ebenen"* in the Prologue, p. 143.

gue [1]). It is evident that in this way important opposing points of
view appear on the scene in the exegesis of the Prologue. There is,
as it were, an attempt to press the pleats of the cloth in one direction,
while the original material was creased in an opposite, or at least
another, direction. This all can certainly bring what is characteristic
of the Prologue to the fore, but at the same time it compels an
exegesis which bears more the character of a re-interpretation than
of an unprejudiced explanation of that which we have before us.

Finally, yet a *third* point, perhaps the most important of all. If
one accepts that the name and figure of the Logos derive from an
earlier song, pre-Christian or indeed Christian, then this name did
not arise nor is it to be explained from the context of the Fourth
Gospel, but was introduced from a Christian or, as most certainly
assume, an ultimately pre-Christian source. To a certain extent the
same applies to the position—that of Dodd and others—according
to which there is no necessity to accept an earlier and already
existing Logos song, but which, nevertheless, supposes that the
evangelist in the Prologue has identified Jesus Christ in his pre-
existence with a pre- or non-Christian Logos figure. No one can
escape the fact that all this places the exegesis under the burden
of a not unimportant a priori or, one may say, a heavy mortgage.
For it means, surely, that the Prologue—and with it the whole
Gospel—receives its opening and tone from a motif which does not
spring from the Gospel itself. This does not necessarily signify
that this motif must work as a *corpus alienum* in the Fourth Gospel;
on the contrary, even they who are of the conviction that we have
to do here essentially with a pre-Christian motif, whether one calls
it Hellenistic-Jewish or Hellenistic-Greek, take pains to demonstrate that this motif is entirely integrated, Christianized, re-
fashioned in a Christian sense, or however one may wish to describe
it. But nevertheless, this does not remove the exegetical a priori,
that the evangelist sought to attach his Gospel in some way or other
to an already existing thought milieu. This means, at the same
time, that the purpose of the Gospel at once is sought in a very
definite direction. The evangelist, also in the event that he was a
Jew, attempted to present the Christ of his Gospel in such a way as

---

[1]) So SCHNACKENBURG calls v. 5, so very important for the progression of
thought of the Prologue, "eine abschweifende Bemerkung" of the evangelist,
and he attempts in this way to bring to bear on the exegesis of the Prologue,
too, the "original" progression of thought of the hymn, *o.c.*, pp. 103, 104.

to find acceptance in a world of thought more or less conversant with the Logos figure, or capable of being addressed by it. And the conclusion drawn from this then is that that world can be no other than the world of Hellenistic or pre-Christian Gnostic religious thought. For where else than there, so the opinion goes, can one find in the pre-Christian world such a Logos figure to which a divine existence was ascribed? Perhaps one may here make reference to the personified wisdom of the later Jewish Wisdom literature. But it is clear, in the first place, that this is nowhere called the Logos, and, second, that it is at most a personification of a divine attribute, but never represented as a divine person. Hence, it is said, one in any case must search in the pre-Christian, non-Jewish world [1]). Thus, the Hellenistic objective and interpretation of the Prologue, and of the whole of the Fourth Gospel, is really an inescapable postulate. Truly—we may be permitted to say—that is no small exegetical a priori.

All this makes of quite extraordinary interest the question as to whether the structure and scope of the Prologue are capable of being understood in another way than as an adaptation of an intrusive Logos motif, whether that is considered to be the incorporation of an already existing Logos hymn or only the utilization of definite Hellenistic terms and ideas.

III

As I have already observed, the matter has a style critical aspect. I do not wish to dwell on that, but even so, we cannot entirely pass it by, because the hypothesis of the Logos song rests partly upon considerations of style and rhythm. At this point, however, we are no longer on uncharted ground. A great deal of very exact work has been done in the last decades, by which, generally speaking, the stylistic unity of the Fourth Gospel is clearly established. Specifically, the minute research of RUCKSTUHL [2]) is well-known, research in which he has compiled a list of not less than fifty carefully selected peculiarities of the Johannine style and demonstrated that these are scattered over the whole Gospel with such frequency

---

[1]) Cf. BULTMANN, o.c., pp. 8 ff.
[2]) E. RUCKSTUHL, Die literarische Einheit des Johannesevangeliums, Freiburg, 1951; for that matter following E. SCHWEIZER, Ego Eimi, Göttingen, 1939. Also the work of B. NOACK, Zur johanneischen Tradition, Kopenhagen, 1954, deserves to be mentioned in this respect.

and evenness that in general the literary unity of the Fourth
Gospel can no longer be brought into question. Following these
criteria, he has also investigated the Prologue, and powerfully
maintained its original unity against BULTMANN's hypothesis of
the Logos hymn. Still others, e.g., SCHNACKENBURG, while recognizing RUCKSTUHL's style criteria [1]), have nevertheless sought to
defend the hypothesis of an earlier Logos hymn; however, they
are compelled at the same time, if they wish to remain outside the
style criteria of RUCKSTUHL, to apply the ax ever more deeply: i.e.,
continually to ascribe more and more to the evangelist and increasingly less to the hymn [2]). The question then automatically
arises whether this whole style critical analysis of the Prologue is
not in the process of collapsing under its own weight. One may
in any case assert that the involved discussions about rhythm,
metrical feet, *"Zweizeiler"* and *"Dreizeiler"*, cannot lead us to any
conclusive decision concerning the real character and scope of the
Prologue [3]), but rather urge us to concentrate our attention on the
question as to whether or not the *content* of the Prologue as we have
it before us can be understood as a self-contained unity. This
brings us at last to the investigation of the structure of thought of
the Prologue itself.

A first and very important question is this: What is one to think
of the often defended conception that the Prologue—be it not so
evident as it must have been in the presupposed Logos song—even
in its present form intends to furnish a description of the Logos in
his various modes of existence and revelations: first as the pre-
existent Logos, then as the light of the nations and of Israel before
his incarnation, finally as the Logos incarnate in Christ [4])? If one
feels constrained to give an affirmative answer, then we have to
do in the Prologue with an elaborate Logos theology. If one answers
in the negative, then, as we shall see, the character of the Prologue

---

[1]) SCHNACKENBURG, *o.c.*, pp. 78 ff.

[2]) Even v. 14 can no longer be considered as an original unity, SCHNACKEN-
BURG, *o.c.*, pp. 79 ff.

[3]) HAENCHEN, too, warns in this respect against all too artificial criteria.

[4]) This conception is also proposed by authors who do not start from an
original Logos hymn. Very extensively, e.g., by M. E. BOISMARD, O.P.,
Le Prologue de Saint Jean, Paris, 1953. He comes, however, into great difficulties with the vv. 6-8, pp. 38 ff. He considers it probable that these vv.
originally stood between vv. 18 and 19, and were later inserted into the
Prologue, "au moment de l'édition définitive de l'Évangile, par les disciples
de Jean". But this, too, is a *tour de force*.

and the significance of the Logos motif become entirely different.

Now, the acceptableness of the conception referred to is in very large measure brought into question by the fact that John the Baptist is already brought upon the scene in v. 6 as witness to the light, of which there was also mention in v. 5. That is to say, thus, that already in v. 6 the light and the Logos are discussed as these have appeared in Christ. And this has a very evident reference to the exposition of the preceding "light". It is a natural conclusion that thus already in v. 5 the light is discussed which *in Christ* shines in the darkness and that, consequently, no place remains in the Prologue for a revelation of the Logos before the incarnation. At this juncture certain proponents of the hymn hypothesis have answered that it is exactly those verses which speak of John the Baptist which have interfered with the train of thought of the original Logos hymn and given it a turn which the original did not have. Hence, vv. 4 and 5 should—according to this point of view— still be understood of the Logos *a-sarkos*. But KÄSEMANN [1]) has correctly observed—himself a supporter of the hymn hypothesis— that the words of v. 5, "and the light shines in the darkness and the darkness apprehended it not", must in any case be understood of the light which has appeared in Christ. This is indicated not only by the present tense, "the light shines", but also by the renewed use of the same form of expression in v. 9. There the same thing is said, though in other words: i.e., that that light is shining which lights every man. And in spite of all attempts to understand the "shining" of vv. 9 f. once more as an illuminating work of the Logos before the incarnation, there can be reference here in vv. 9 f. in the context of the Prologue only to the appearance of the light *in Christ*. For in v. 12 it is said of those who have accepted this true light that they have received from Him power, liberty, to become children of God. And that, as is indicated by the whole of the New Testament, is the gift of Christ and of the eschatological redemptive time that has commenced with Him. Surely, some promotors of the Logos song theory ascribe these words of v. 12 to the adaptation of the hymn and not to the original hymn itself; but the grounds for this assumption are—even from the viewpoint of style criticism— too weak to bear the burden. And as for the material point of view, no one can, on reasonable grounds, maintain that the words,

---

[1]) *O.c.*, pp. 159 ff.

"to them he gave power to become the sons of God", do not fit in the context. We may thus conclude that wherever in the Prologue the revelation of the Logos is spoken of as the light which shines in the darkness, v. 5, which lights every man, which was in the world and which came to his own, the revelation of the Logos in Jesus Christ is regularly and exclusively intended. This is an exceedingly important point of departure for the ascertainment of the character and structure of the Prologue. Though we must guard against false antitheses, yet one is surely able to say this: that the real subject of the Prologue is not the revelation of the Logos, who also at last received *form* in the person of Jesus Christ. Rather the reverse: the Logos, who was in the Beginning, who was with God and was Himself God, is discussed under the point of view of that which has taken place in Jesus Christ and has been seen and heard in Him. In a word: Jesus Christ is, in essence, the subject of the Prologue, the Logos the predicate. And not the reverse.

This general point of view must now, however, be applied to the progression of thought of the Prologue itself. The present occasion does not permit the giving of an elaborate analysis of all the separate transitions in thought which are here to be observed. I shall rather, on the basis of such an analysis, attempt to indicate the principal idea. That principal idea unfolds itself (we may be permitted to say) in three concentric circles, all three of which relate to the revelation of the historical Christ: i.e., in the vv. 1-5, 6-13, and 14-18. This unfolding takes place, on the one hand, in the reiteration and recurrence of the same motifs, and, on the other, in the continuing diffusion and broadening of the pattern of thought according to the nature of Johannine speech. In addition it is essential to note that the evangelist speaks and argues from the kerygmatic situation and point of view. The atmosphere of the Prologue is not that of pious meditation, of mystical contemplation, or of theological speculation; it is altogether that of the *evangelist* who stands in the midst of the struggle between those forces to which he will refer again and again: the light and the darkness, the truth and the lie; and who before he comes to the narrative itself, the record of what has taken place and been accomplished, of what has been heard and seen, wishes to indicate first the purport, the scope, of that which he will relate, as well as the grounds upon which he summons men to the faith that Jesus is the Christ, the Son of God (xx 31).

This observation—that the evangelist is speaking and arguing out of the kerygmatic point of view—makes it extremely improbable that the first circle of thought rounds off with v. 4 [1]), which speaks of the Word that was in the Beginning with God and Himself God: "in the Word was life, and the life was the light of men". It is far more in accord with the drift of the whole Prologue that all these *imperfecta*, which arrange themselves together in sublime monotony and describe the pre-existence and "being" of the Word preceding all existence and experience, have their essential point and meaning—and observe there the kerygmatic situation—in the pronouncement emanating from them as a flash of lightning and illuminating the actual situation: "And the light shines in the darkness; and the darkness apprehended it not". Only there, with that statement which at once penetrates the actuality of the proclamation, does the first thought circle end. The light, the light of the Word of life, which was with God and was God, that light shines in the darkness as present, continuing reality. And the darkness has not apprehended it.

With that statement the first thought circle is concluded, and it is exactly here that the second is now joined to it, vv. 6-13. It begins specifically with a reference to John the Baptist, the man sent from God as witness of the light, an obvious new commencement which, however, takes up precisely where the first cycle left off. John is here specifically introduced upon the scene, *first*, because his witness still more strongly accentuates the contrast of the shining of the light in the darkness and the failure of the darkness to apprehend it. The darkness should have apprehended it, and could have apprehended it, for there was no uncertainty, there was a man sent from God to bear witness of the light. And *second*, John is mentioned because by him *e contrario* the majesty of the light must appear more markedly still [2]). For however much he had been sent of God and however powerful his witness was, he was not the light.

It is exactly these verses concerning John which have often been made to serve as proof that the Prologue is not an original unity; they are said to disturb both the rhythm and the progression of

---

[1]) As is defended by KÄSEMANN, in agreement with BULTMANN. He fears that otherwise that parallelism between v. 5 and v. 9 f. is imperilled, which, however, with our conception is not the case.

[2]) How far here "polemic" is conducted against the adherents of John the Baptist can remain an open question. The pronouncement that he was not the light, also independent of this presupposition, makes good sense.

thought of the Logos song. In the matter of rhythm, it must be
said that there is something to this, if one regards the structure of
the first five verses as determinative for the whole. But one *cannot*
say that the stately new beginning, composed in the manner of the
Old Testament [1]), "there was a man sent from God whose name was
John", strikes a different key from that which precedes. Again with
regard to the rhythm, as soon as one borrows the criteria for the
original unity of the Prologue from it, he entangles himself, as well
for what follows, in insoluble difficulties. In our opinion, however,
the harmonious place occupied by the mention of the Baptist in
the structure of thought is decisive. The critical situation which,
according to v. 5, has been created by the appearance of the light
is in a very particular way characterized by the figure of the Baptist.
He was the unmistakable witness who asked for belief. At the same
time, his greatness demonstrates the exclusiveness of Him who
alone was the true light. Therefore, the repetition of the categories
from the first thought circle follows now forthwith upon mention
of him, in order to indicate in this way the full critical significance
and the all-encompassing import of the decision with regard to the
light shining in the darkness. He, of whom John bore witness, was
the true light, who through his coming into the world lights every
man. He was in the world, and the world had been made by Him.
He came to the world as to His own. But the world—and here
the *votum* of v. 5 recurs, and the concentric character of the order
of thought becomes apparent—did not know Him, and His own
did not receive Him, Him who was thus. But therefore, because He
was who He was, the reverse side must now also be manifested in
its all-embracing significance. Because He was who He was, therefore He had authority over the sonship of God, for those who
received Him and believed in His name. And therefore also, the
life that He was able to give them is not of human power or impulse,
but was born of God. For in Him was life, because He was the Word
in the Beginning, with God and Himself God.

So the circle closes once more. And one may wonder whether all
has not now been said of that which must qualify the content and
scope of the Gospel. Nevertheless, the heart of the matter only
appears to be reached in the monumental commencement of the
third cycle, carrying everything to its climax: "And the Word

---

[1]) For this see, e.g., BOISMARD, *o.c.*. p. 40.

became flesh, and dwelt among us". It is for this reason, therefore, that the attempt has been made in every possible way to understand all that precedes as the revelation of the Logos before the incarnation, in order thus to keep the way free for the climax.

For those for whom this way is impassable, the question forces consideration of the specific point of view of this third and last thought cycle. BULTMANN, who also wishes to understand the Prologue as a—be it then secondary—unity, is of the opinion that the great turning point comes here, the solution to the riddle which lies locked up in what has preceded. For how does it come about that, though the Light shines and the Light is the Light of the Logos, in the Beginning with God and Himself God, yet the world has not known Him? The answer is: because the Word became flesh, that is—thus BULTMANN—man, no other than man, and not more than man. The revelation has come as hiddenness. It is, he argues, from this principle that the Gospel of John should be viewed and the Prologue understood as indication of all that follows [1]).

However profound this explanation may be, and however much the words, "and the Word became flesh", have been similarly understood in the history of theology and even come to live a life of their own apart from the context, yet in connection with the Prologue they appear under another, and perhaps one may say, contrary perspective. For the statement, "and the Word became flesh", is followed by "and dwelt among us, and we beheld His glory, glory as of the only begotten of the Father". The incarnation of the Word does not constitute an indication of the hiddenness, but rather of the manifestness of the revelation; it serves, therefore, not as an explanation of the riddle of unbelief, but rather to point out the foundation and certainty of faith.

But with this then the new and peculiar viewpoint of the third thought cycle has also been given. All that has so far been said of the Word and the Light has already been said of the Christ and not of the Logos *a-sarkos*. But the word *sarx* has not yet been mentioned. What has not yet been said is this: that the Word which was with God and was God *so* came into the world and *so* was in the

---

[1]) ... "das ist die Paradoxie, die das ganze Evg. durchzieht, daß die δόξα nicht neben der σάρξ oder durch sie, als durch ein Transparent, *hindurch* zu sehen ist, sondern nirgends anders als in der σάρξ .... Die Offenbarung ist also in einer eigentümlichen Verhülltheit da", *o.c.*, p. 41.

world as the Word that became *flesh* and that dwelt among us. Here, we may say, one comes upon the last preparations for the transfer from the Prologue to the narrative. For it is here, in the Word which became flesh and which dwelt among us, that the way is opened for the evangelist to testify and to tell of the *beholding* of the glory of the Only-Begotten of the Father.

It has been correctly pointed out again and again that a change of persons takes place here. No longer are "those who received Him" spoken of in the third person, but rather now in the first person: "We beheld Him". This "we" should not be misunderstood. It is the same "we" as that of I John i 1, where the purport of it becomes still clearer: "That which we have seen with our eyes, which we have beheld, and our hands have handled, of the Logos of life". It is not simply the "we" of the believers, or the "we" of the ecclesia. For not all who believe, or will believe, have also seen. Later on it will be said: "Blessed are they who have not seen, and yet have believed", xx 29. Therefore, this "seeing" or "beholding" has a very specific significance, and the mention of it corresponds with what the evangelist at the close of his book indicates to have been the purpose for all his writing: "Many other signs therefore did Jesus *in the presence of the disciples*, which are not written in this book; but these are written, that you may believe that Jesus is the Christ, the Son of God", xx 30, 31. And it is with the mention of this incarnation and of this "we" that the evangelist seeks the transition to his narrative, his narrative as evangelist of the *history* of Jesus. Therefore also, the third cycle can speak so much more exuberantly than the first and second of the glory of the Light. Therefore—I can now only indicate the principal line—anew the appeal to the Baptist as fellow-witness of this divine, pre-existential glory of Him who came. Therefore the experience of all who were permitted to behold Him and receive from His fulness grace for grace. And therefore, too, the comparison with Moses. Moses also stands in the line which runs from the beginning to the present, in the service, too, of the divine Word; for through his mediation the law was given to Israel. But grace and truth are by Jesus Christ, and not only given, but also *become*. All the "it" of God in history becomes "He" in Him. Therefore finally, yet once again, the reference to the *beholding*: "No man has seen God at any time". This does not intend a limitation which one, in spite of all, must take into consideration, but rather indicates the exclusiveness and absoluteness of the knowledge of God through Him who is in the bosom of the Father. He has brought the knowledge of God: namely, through His incarnation and that which we have seen of Him.

In summary, it may be established above all that the Prologue of the Fourth Gospel forms in itself a closed, impressive unity of thought. One is able to speak of an ellipse with two foci. These two foci are marked by the Logos concept, initially with the opening as the Word which was in the beginning with God, after that once again in v. 14 as the Word which became flesh and dwelt among us. Out of these two foci the whole content of the Kerygma is qualified as light-bringing, life-creating, separation-making, fulness of grace and truth. But both foci also define each other reciprocally, for they are one. For just as one must return to the beginning of God's creation in order to understand and find adequate expression for who He was, who dwelt among us and whose glory we beheld, so only can He, who was from the Beginning, thus be spoken of, just because He became flesh and dwelt among us. So the beginning (the alpha) casts the light upon the ending (the omega); but in the same way the beginning can only be understood from the ending. In this manner the Prologue qualifies the content of what now further will be narrated of the glory of Him who was with God. And that all, as it is written at the close, "that ye may believe that Jesus is the Anointed, the Son of God", xx 31.

IV

All this gives us some grasp by which to mark off the sense of the Prologue and in some respects even the character of the Gospel itself along certain sides.

1. In the first place, we must return to the opinion of those (e.g., HARNACK, DODD, BULTMANN, SCHNACKENBURG) for whom the Logos idea is a kind of paedagogical introduction to the Gospel for Hellenistic readers, who by virtue of their pagan religious background were to some extent acquainted with the Logos concept. Yet, irrespective of the enormous objections which present themselves when one wishes to place the Johannine Logos idea in the Hellenistic background—objections upon which I cannot now dwell at length, but which are generally recognized—the Prologue itself points in another direction. For the question may be asked: Is there a more Israelitish opening to the Gospel conceivable than the words: in the Beginning? Is not in this way all that follows

brought into the context of all God's works, as everyone who had
been reared in *Israel's* holy Scriptures had learned to understand
them? And is it not true that not only the initial words, but also
the concept of the Logos itself, and all that is said about the power
of the Logos to bring light and to make separation between light
and darkness, refer to the frequently repeated "And God said",
and to the effecting of that speaking in Genesis i? BULTMANN, one
of the great promotors of this *religionsgeschichtliche* method of
interpretation, admits that the evangelist could hardly have begun
with the words, "in the Beginning", without thinking of Genesis i 1;
but he adds that the absolute use of "the Word" is an indication
of the distance which separates the Prologue from the Old Testament. For while in Genesis i, and throughout the Old Testament,
the Word of God is an event going out from God, in John i the
Word is the eternal being who from the very beginning is with
God. Thus, he argues, the Logos of John i is not to be explained
from the Old Testament, but its origin must be sought elsewhere [1]).
One can fully agree with this, provided that this reasoning is not
made to serve as a postulate for the Hellenistic or Gnostic interpretation, and as a thereto oriented stipulation for the character of
the Prologue. For there is another way and another origin, indicated
in the structure of the Prologue itself. I refer to the two foci in the
Prologue which reciprocally define each other. In the unmistakable
mutual dependence between the Word that was in the Beginning
and the Word that became flesh lies, it seems to me, the real
explanation of the Prologue. On the one side: if the evangelist
wishes to express the glory of Him whose witness he is, then he
falls back upon the beginning of all God's ways, then he cannot
think otherwise than in the categories of a new creation, a new
Genesis. But the reverse is no less true. When the Word has become
flesh, the speaking of God which creates and brings light in the
Beginning and in the history of salvation can no longer be considered and understood apart from the glory which has been revealed
in Christ. That which was the Word from the Beginning, the life,
the light of men, that was He. The First Epistle of John speaks in
the same way about the Word, the Logos of life, which was from
the Beginning: "The life was manifested, and we have seen, and
bear witness, and declare unto you that eternal life, which was with

---

[1]) BULTMANN, *o.c.*, pp. 6 ff.

the Father, and was manifested unto us", I John i 1 ff. In Him is the speaking of God, is the life that was with God, made flesh and blood, so that henceforth this Word, this life, this light, this truth, must be spoken of in the personal categories of "He was" and "I am". That which brings the evangelist from the "it" to the "He", from the event to the person [1]), is not a body of ideas from another religious world, but the beholding of the glory of God in Christ. Reflection about this and designation of it was certainly a matter of time and development. One may also point out that both the Old Testament and Judaism, if they wish to give expression to the divine glory, whether of the Messiah or of the Wisdom or of the law, always reach back again to the glory of God in the Beginning. Lines had been drawn within which the reflection about the glory of Christ as well could move. But the real secret of this designation of Christ as the Word lies, for all that, not in the profound *reflection* about the person, but in the person Himself. In a word: By calling Christ the Logos, the evangelist does not reach into another world for a name of honour, nor does he identify Him with a figure or idea well-known elsewhere, but he gives expression to the manner in which he beheld the glory of God in Christ. Therefore, it is not strange—as it otherwise would surely be—that the name of the Logos is not mentioned again. Jesus Christ is the great subject of the Gospel and of the Prologue, and the Logos is the predicate [2]), and not the reverse.

2. In the second place: In what has gone before, is there any indication of the general character, the objective, the *Sitz im Leben*, of the Fourth Gospel? At the conclusion the evangelist himself says that he has written these things in order that his readers may believe that Jesus is the Anointed, the Son of God. That thought originated in Judaism: that Jesus is the Anointed One [3]). The same may be said of the Prologue, in so far that in it, too, the fundamental

---

[1]) Cf. the penetrating discussion of the problem in G. SEVENSTER, *De Christologie van het Nieuwe Testament*[2], Amsterdam, 1948, pp. 224-232. Concerning the person of the Logos he writes, p. 226: "Het gaat in de eerste verzen van het hoofdstuk over den achtergrond van zijn (Jezus Christus') verschijning op aarde. Daardoor wordt het reeds volkomen begrijpelijk, dat de schrijver ook deze figuur van den Logos als een zelfstandige persoon laat optreden".

[2]) Cf. J. WILLEMSE O.P., *Het vierde evangelie. Een onderzoek naar zijn structuur*. Hilversum/Antwerpen, 1965, p. 224.

[3]) Cf. VAN UNNIK, *o.c.* (see p. 183, note 1).

structures are derived from the revelation of God given to Israel:
In the Beginning, the Word of God which creates and brings salvation, Christ as the Coming One, the comparison with Moses, all are
key thoughts of Israel. However, one cannot say, on the other
hand', that the Prologue is set in the Israelitish or Jewish expectation of the Messiah. The Messiah is the Son of God in a broader,
more universal sense than had been the case with the Son of God
in Israel. And the question in the Prologue as to who the Messiah
is goes beyond Israel, beyond Moses, and even beyond Abraham.
It goes back to the Beginning. And there it links up with the universality of salvation. For the light shines in the world, and lights
every man by its coming into the world. The question as to who
must be supposed to have been the readers of the Fourth Gospel,
in the nature of the case, cannot only be answered upon the basis
of the Prologue. But the Israelitish and the universal are here
clearly connected. Perhaps one may say that this gives support
to the suggestion that the Gospel was intended for the Jews outside Palestine, in their peculiarity as Jews and in their committment
to the world in which they lived.

3. In the third place: On the basis of the Prologue, can anything
further be said about the Christology of the Fourth Gospel? Must
one see in the opening proof that the Fourth Gospel views Jesus
exclusively out of the faith of the ecclesia as it later progressed,
proof, too, that that which we find here informs us more as to the
development of Christology than as to the course of Jesus' earthly
life?

Here again the answer can only be fragmentary. But there is,
nevertheless, a clear indication in what we have called the two foci
as to the nature of that which is termed the "Christology" of the
evangelist. One must say of it, at the same time, that a more exalted,
more divine, and a more historic, more human Christology is not
to be conceived. And further, that these two are one: What he has
to say of the Word which was with God in the Beginning and was
Himself God, what he has to say of the Word which became flesh and
dwelt among us. His Kerygma is his eye-witness, and his faith
is his beholding. One should perhaps say that this cuts in a decisive
manner across the modern statement of the problem concerning
the historical Jesus and the kerygmatic Christ. But the character
and purpose of the Gospel are indicated in this way, and not other-

wise. The Gospel, therefore, is not in the first place a witness of the faith, but of that which has been seen and heard and handled with the hands. And, therefore, whoever asserts that the background of the faith of the evangelist is another than that of the event which he narrates, attacks not only the narrative, but also the Kerygma of the evangelist at its very heart. On the other hand, the Prologue particularly, in its simplicity and impressive formulation, is an expression of that which has been so long and so intensely considered that it could be formulated with this great and grand simplicity. Is there a more fitting explanation of these two aspects possible than that which tradition gives us concerning the authorship of the Apostle John at the end of his life?

4. Finally, a word about the eschatological (and *heilsgeschichtliche*) point of view. With the synoptic writers, Jesus stands in the center of the great dramatic motif of the coming of the kingdom and derives from that His significance as the Son of man, Messianic king of Israel, Redeemer of the world. In Paul also the *heilsgeschichtliche* point of view remains dominant, as he describes the significance of Jesus Christ in ever broader spheres as the seed of Abraham, the second Adam, the First-Born of all creation. Does not the fourth evangelist begin where Paul seems to end, and does not this bring with it an *Enteschatologisierung* of the original gospel, whether this be interpreted then in an idealistic or an existentialistic way? Here again we must confine ourselves to the Prologue. One cannot say that the *heilsgeschichtliche* point of view here becomes blurred or, indeed, is absent. For with the "in the Beginning" of the opening, the whole of the gospel is qualified as the second Genesis, the beginning of the new creation of God. In addition, here already in the Prologue are Moses and the Baptist, through whom the form of Him who came is related to the *history* of God's saving acts. One may certainly say that, in the manner in which the Prologue introduces and announces the gospel narrative, the person of Christ stands out in a still more absolute way than in the preaching of the kingdom in the synoptics and of the fulness of time in Paul. Here, too, there is no antithesis, for the Christ of the synoptics is also the *auto-basileia*; and Paul's eschatology is also essentially nothing other than Christology. But in the Fourth Gospel all descriptions which intend to express the redemptive significance of Christ appear to simplify and concentrate themselves in the final and utter

identification of person and matter. The Word became *flesh*. In the relationship to Him lies the relationship to God, to the world, to history, to the future. He comprehends them all. For the *Word* became flesh. It is in harmony with this very core of the Prologue that the answer to all questions in the Gospel can be reduced to the most personal formula that is possible: *Ego eimi*, I am.

DESTINATION AND PURPOSE OF THE GOSPEL OF JOHN

BY

A. WIND

Leiden

After the discovery of the Dead Sea Scrolls in Qumran, a growing number of N. Test. scholars pointed to a Palestinian background of the Gospel of John because of the affinity of terminology and thoughts with Qumran-documents [1]).

The ideas about the address and purpose of the fourth Gospel also changed, though there is not yet a common opinion. Formerly as an exception f.i. K. BORNHÄUSER defended the thesis that this Gospel was addressed to Jews [2]), but in more recent times more and more authors got this conviction, e.g. VAN UNNIK, ROBINSON and recently H. MULDER [3]). The original conclusion of the latter about origin and purpose of this mysterious Gospel [4]) brought me to a comparison of his article with those of VAN UNNIK and ROBINSON. VAN UNNIK concluded: "The purpose of the Fourth Gospel was to bring the visitors of a synagogue in the Diaspora (Jews and God-fearers) to belief in Jesus as the Messiah of Israel" [5]).

ROBINSON defended an almost similar thesis: "... in its present form it is an appeal to those outside the Church, to win to the faith

---

[1]) ROBINSON f.i. spoke about a "new look": J. A. T. ROBINSON, "The new Look on the Fourth Gospel", Twelve N.T.Stud. (Stud. in Bibl. Theol. 34) 1962, p. 94-106 (repr. from Stud. Evang. vol. I, T. U. 73, 1959, p. 338-350); cf. also St. NEILL, The Interpretation of the N.T. 1861-1961, 1966, p. 308 ff.

[2]) K. BORNHÄUSER, Das Joh.ev. eine Missionsschrift f. Israel, 1928.

[3]) W. C. v. UNNIK, "The Purpose of St. John's Gospel", Stud. Evang. I. o.c.p. 382-411; J. A. T. ROBINSON, "The Destination and Purpose of St John's Gospel", Twelve N.T.St. o.c. p. 107-125 (repr. from N.T. St. VI, 1960); H. MULDER, "Ontstaan en Doel v. h. vierde Ev." Geref. Theol. Tijdschrift 69, 1969, p. 233-258.

[4]) Cf. E. KÄSEMANN, "Z. Joh. Interpr. in England", Exeg. Versuche u. Besinnungen II, 1964, p. 148: "rätselhaft"; cf. MULDER o.c. p. 233; v. UNNIK pointed to the words of v. HARNACK 50 years ago (Lehrb. d. Dogm. gesch. I 5 A. 1931, p. 308), that the origin of John was the greatest riddle of the ancient Church, o.c. p. 303.

[5]) VAN UNNIK, o.c. p. 410.

that Greek-speaking Diaspora-Judaism to which the author now finds himself belonging" [1]).

MULDER however rejected a primarily missionary purpose, he thought that the Gospel was more an apologetic work, written by the apostle John on behalf of the Churches in Asia Minor, in order to urge them to keep their faith amidst the turmoil after the definite exodus of the Jewish Christians out of the synagogue [2]). Though Gentile-Christians also were involved in these disturbances it is clear that the destination of the Gospel was in the first place: Jewish Christians [3]).

In the history of N. Test. studies many different answers have been given on the question of the destination and purpose of John's Gospel. MULDER did not defend his solution against other opinions, VAN UNNIK and ROBINSON gave only a brief survey of other conclusions [4]). This is understandable because of the variety of opinions, but I think it is worthwhile to attempt to make such a survey.

It is however impossible to deal with all the nuances or combinations of viewpoints; I'll not strive after any completeness. To mention all the arguments of the quoted authors is also impossible. I did not keep a chronological order of quoted works, my only purpose is to give an impression of the diversity of viewpoints regarding purpose and address of the fourth Gospel.

In order to get a sharp picture I'd like to mention the answers given on three important questions:

1. To which kind of readers was the Gospel addressed: to Jewish or non-Jewish groups, or to mixed circles? Apart from the question whether these readers were Christians or not.

2. What was the destination of the Gospel: non-Christians (a missionary purpose, for Jews or non-Jews) or Christians, the Church? In case of the Church, his purpose must have been related to the

---

[1]) ROBINSON, "Destination", *o.c.* p. 125.

[2]) MULDER, *o.c.* p. 258. He refered to C. K. BARRETT, "Zweck d. viert. Ev.", *Z. syst. Th.* 22, 1953, p. 257-273 and to F. NEUGEBAUER, who stressed the non-miss. character of John, *Die Entsteh. d. Joh.ev.*, 1968, p. 14f.

[3]) Cf. MULDER, *o.c.* p. 253, 256f.

[4]) Cf. VAN UNNIK, *o.c.* p. 386f. ROBINSON expressed himself very briefly: "to win the faithless, to establish the faithful or to counter the gainsayers", "Destination" *o.c.* p. 108. If one assumes an apologetic purpose, the question is, whether the opposition was Jewish, Baptist-movement, Gnostic or even Christian. None of these viewpoints got more adherents than another, because as Robinson stated, there is no clear evidence for one special solution.

situation of the Churches, with different possibilities: only edification of the faith or polemical and apologetical against menacing dangers as heresies, attacks from outside, or a theological reïnterpretation written from a special point of view, being that of the evangelist or of the circles addressed in his work. In case of a theological reïnterpretation usually the relation of the Fourth Gospel to the Synoptics plays an important rôle, therefore I like to mention the adherents of this point of view together with the answers given on a third question:

3. Was the purpose of this Gospel partly or fully conditioned by its relation to the Synoptic Gospels? There are again different possibilities: to supplement the Synoptics, to correct them or to replace totally the Synoptic tradition, or: there was no relation at all. Special attention could be given to the idea that the fourth Gospel has been written against a totally different background compared with the Synoptics, e.g. the Christian faith in its concrete contemporary situation with the intention of a theological reinterpretation [1]).

4. Finally some authors could be mentioned who have a remarkable view f.i. those who recognized a dramatic character in the fourth Gospel, based upon style and structure of this Gospel.

I am hopeful that on this way at least some paths could be shown in the forest of viewpoints regarding this matter.

ad 1. *Which kind of readers: Jews or non-Jews?*

a. The Gospel was addressed to Jewish readers (apart from the question whether they were Christians or not). This was the conviction of o.a. K. BORNHÄUSER, W. C. V. UNNIK, R. M. GRANT, P. WINTER, T. C. SMITH, J. A. T. ROBINSON, and H. MULDER [2]).

b. The readers were not Jews, but Hellenistic Gentiles or Gentile-

---

[1]) The variety of answers is connected with the viewpoints of the authors on writer, date and background of the fourth Gospel, problems too complicated to deal with in this article.

[2]) VAN UNNIK expressed his agreement with BORNHÄUSER, but on totally different arguments, *o.c.* p. 410; R. M. GRANT, "The Origin of the Fourth Gospel", *J.B.L.* 69, 1950, p. 305-322: the Gospel was addressed to Jewish Christians at the end of the first cent., many of whom had been fallen back into Judaïsm, p. 320; GRANT refered to B. S. EASTON; P. WINTER, "Z. Verständnis d. Joh.ev.", *Vox Theol.* 25, 1955, p. 149-157 (about the famous book of C. H. DODD), esp. p. 155f; T. C. SMITH, *Jesus in the Gospel of John*, 1959, had an almost similar view as VAN UNNIK, about the conclusions of ROBINSON and MULDER, see above.

Christians. Other scholars rejected the whole dilemma as a false one because the Gospel is too universal and addressed to everyone or to the whole Church. I mention here W. OEHLER, A. OEPKE, C. H. DODD, F. W. GROSHEIDE, W. NEIL, ST. SMALLEY and many others in ancient and recent times [1]). The majority of them also defended an apologetical-polemical tendency in this Gospel and/or stressed the differences between this Gospel and the Synoptics. C. K. BARRETT even doubted whether the Gospel had a concrete address [2])!

ad 2. *Did the fourth Gospel have a missionary purpose or not?*

a. Many scholars defended a missionary purpose (apart from the question whether it was addressed to Jews or not), e.g. BORN-HÄUSER, OEHLER, OEPKE, SMITH, VAN UNNIK, ROBINSON, DODD, NEIL and SMALLEY, already mentioned above. So too E. STAUFFER, F-M. BRAUN, C. F. D. MOULE, ST. NEILL a.o.[3]).

b. Others rejected the interpretation of John xx 31 in a mission-ary sense or stated that no decision could be made on the basis of

---

[1]) Cf. W. OEHLER, *Das Joh. ev. eine Missionsschrift f. d. Welt*, 1936; *id.*, "Z. missionscharakter d. Joh. ev.", *B.F.C.T.* 42, 4, 1941; A. OEPKE, "Das miss. Christuszeugnis d. Joh. ev.", *E.M.Z.* 2, 1941, p. 4-26; C. H.DODD, *The interpretation of the Fourth Gospel*, 1953, p. 8, 9: "a non-Christian public to which he wishes to appeal ... in the varied cosmopolitan society of a great Hellenistic city"; F. W. GROSHEIDE, *Het hl. Evang. vlgs. Joh.*, I 1950, p. 53: to the Church after the definite separation between Christians and Jews; W. NEIL, *Harpers Bible Comm.* p. 401f: "to show Jesus, not as He was for Jews in Palestine, but as He is for all times and everyone; NEIL thinks that the evangelist made a deliberate use of the language of the Hellenistic world for a miss. purpose; see also G. H. DAVIES, A. RICHARDSON and C. I. WALLIS, *Twent. Cent. Bible Comm.* 1955, p. 440f: "for serious-minded in the gentile world"; ST. SMALLEY, "New Light on the F. Gospel", *Tyndale Bull.* 17, 1966, p. 36-62, esp. p. 39: "the scope of this writer is finally as wide as it possibly could be"; Smally speaks about "inside or outside the Church, Jew or Greek"; cf. also SMALLEY, "Liturgy and Sacrament in the Fourth Gospel", *Ev. Quart*, 1957, p. 161f.

[2]) C. K. BARRETT, *The Gospel acc. to St John*, 1955, p. 115: "he wrote primarily to satisfy himself. His Gospel must be written; it was no concern of his whether it was also read".

[3]) STAUFFER called the Gospel "ein Programmschrift an Täufergemeinden", *Th.L.Z.* 1956, p. 146; F-M. BRAUN in *Rev. Thom.* 55, 1955, p. 294; C. F. D. MOULE, *The Intention of the* "Evangelists," *N.T. Essays in mem. T. W. Manson* 1959, p. 165-179, esp. p. 175: the fourth evangelist wrote "with more than half an eye on outsiders", p. 168; cf. also MOULE, *The Birth of the N.T.* 1962, p. 93f; ST. NEILL, *o.c.* p. 276: "the Fourth Gospel is expressely missionary in its purpose".

an exegesis of this verse [1]). Many other arguments brought them to
the conclusion that the Gospel was addressed to Christian readers.
In that case we have to ask for the concrete situation of the Church
being the reason why the evangelist wrote this Gospel. A variety
of answers has been given. I think we could discern at least four
directions:

1. a positive purpose: to strengthen the faith;
2. an apologetic goal or polemics;
3. a theological reïnterpretation of the Christian tradition;
4. in connection with liturgical motives.

ad 1. Many authors stressed the positive intention of the evangelist, but often combined it with a polemical secondary motive,
related to the threatened position of the Church in those days. I
mention a.o. W. R. Inge (no polemical intention), F. W. Grosheide,
Feine-Behm-Kümmel, C. K. Barrett, A. J. B. Higgins, R.
Schnackenburg, M. Dods, W. de Boor [2]). The idea of a missionary
purpose was rejected by K. G. Kuhn because of the view and attitude of the Church itself in those days, but F. Hahn rightly corrected
these arguments, in my opinion [3]).

---

[1]) Some scholars defended not only the present tense in this text but
declared also that it expressed a "remaining" in the faith, e.g. Grosheide,
o.c. II p. 547; W. de Boor, "Das Ev. d. Joh." (*Wuppert. Stud. Bibel*) II,
1970, p. 249. That no conclusion is possible here was the conviction of
Kümmel, *Einl. i.d. N.T. begr. v. P. Feine/J. Behm neu bearb. v. W. G. Kümmel*,
15 A. 1967, p. 157; cf also R. Schnackenburg in a reaction upon the article
of Van Unnik and Robinson: "Die Messiasfrage im Johannesevangelium",
in *Neutestl. Aufsätze, Festschr. J. Schmid, z. 70 Geburtst.*, hrsg J. Blinzler,
O. Kuss and F. Mussner, 1963, p. 240-264, espec. on p. 257/258.

[2]) W. R. Inge, *Hastings Dict. of Christ a. the Gospels*, vol. I 1907, p. 885 ff:
"to edify and teach the faithful"; Inge thought about an attempt to reconcile
the gnostic "pneumatics" and the simple faithful within the Church; Feine-
Behm-Kümmel: "Das Joh. ist also jedenfalls geschrieben um den Glauben
der Christen zu festigen und zu sichern", o.c. p. 158; C. K. Barrett, *Zweck*,
o.c. p. 272: a "Kirchenbuch"; A. J. B. Higgins *The Historicity of the Fourth
Gospel*, 1960, p. 13 f, 21; R. Schnackenburg in *Lex. f. Theol. u. Kirche* vol.
V 1960, p. 1102; M. Dods, *Gospel of St. John, The Expos. Greek Test* 1927,
p. 657 f: doubted a polemic against Cerinthus but stated that it seemed to
be necessary for the Church to stress the faith that Jesus was the Messiah,
the Son of God; W. de Boor, "Ev. d. Joh." o.c. I 1968, p. 29.

[3]) K. G. Kuhn, "Problem d. Mission", *E.M.Z.* 11, 1954, p. 167: the Church
to which this Gospel has been written had no missionary attitude any more,
but isolated itself antithetically from the world; F. Hahn, "Mission in the
N.T." (*Stud. in Bibl. Theol.* 47) 1965, p. 153 admitted that the Gospel had
no direct missionary intention, but the clearly missionary perspective was

ad 2. The majority of the authors combined a positive purpose
of the Gospel with an apologetic and especially polemical motive
against heresy or attacks from outside the Church. This polemical
intention of the evangelist was thought to be directed against:

a) heresies, e.g. docetism or generally: Gnosticism, or:
b) against disciples of John the Baptist, or:
c) against the Jews (Judaism).

ad a). Already Irenaeus [1] mentioned the polemical intention of
this Gospel against docetism, connected with Cerinthus. This
view point has still its defenders, f.i. R. H. STRACHAN, F. W. GROS-
HEIDE, M. MEINERTZ, W. F. HOWARD, W. WILKENS, W. GRUND-
MANN, A. WIKENHAUSER, W. DE BOOR a.o.[2], but was also opposed
f.i. by R. M. GRANT and FEINE-BEHM-KÜMMEL [3]. Some scholars
assumed an anti-gnostic tendency in the fourth Gospel [4]. Other
authors went into another direction, looking for an ecclesiastical
polemic against a false interpretation of the sacraments [5].

---

an element of the whole conception of the Church in this Gospel; so too
R. SCHNACKENBURG: the Mission was for John: Aufgabe der Kirche. "Die
Messiasfrage", o.c. p. 264.

[1] IRENAEUS, Adv. Haer. III, 14, 1. He mentioned also a polemic against the
Nicolaitans.

[2] R. H. STRACHAN, The Fourth Gospel, 3ed. 1941, p. 44f; cf. the critique
of D. GUTHRIE, N.T. Introd. Gospels and Acts, 1965, p. 251; F.W. GROSHEIDE,
o.c. II, p. 549; M. MEINERTZ, "Einl. i. d. N.T." 5A. 1960 (R. Cath.); W. F.
HOWARD, The Interpr. Bible vol. VIII 1952, Introd. p. 437-463; W. WILKENS,
Die Entsteh.gesch. d. viert. Ev. 1958: in his theories about the growth of the
Gospel out of a "Grundevangelium", he thought that this growth was
conditioned by anti-docetic features; cf. the review of his book by J. M.
ROBINSON, "Recent Research in the F. Gospel", J.B.L. 78, 1959, p. 242ff;
W. GRÜNDMANN, Zeugnis u. Gestalt d. Joh. Arb. z. Th. 7, 1960; A. WIKEN-
HAUSER, Einl. i. d. N.T., 4A, 1961, hrsg. A. Vögtle; W. DE BOOR, o.c. vol. I,
p. 29.

[3] R. M. GRANT, o.c. p. 311ff; FEINE-BEHM-KÜMMEL, o.c. p. 158 refering
to W. MICHAELIS, Einl. i. d. N.T., 2A, 1954, p. 121 and O. MICHEL, C.B.L.
1959, p. 658ff.

[4] Cf. FEINE-BEHM-KÜMMEL, refering to S. SCHULZ, "Komposition u.
Herkunft d. Joh. Reden", B.W.A.N.T. 5, F. 1, 1960; cf. also W. MICHAELIS
o.c. p. 121; D. GUTHRIE, o.c. p. 251; more generally E. C. HOSKYNS/F. N.
DAVEY, The Fourth Gospel, 2ed. 1948, p. 48f.

[5] See f.i. W. F. HOWARD, Christianity acc. to St. John 1943, p. 143-150;
D. GUTHRIE, o.c. p. 255f; also J. JEREMIAS, Die Abendmahlsworte Jesu 2A,
1949; about allusions to the sacraments in John, cf. O. CULLMANN, Early
Chr. Worship (Engl. Transl.) 1933, p. 37ff; C. K. BARRETT, "Gospel", o.c.
p. 69-71; W. BAUER, "Das Joh. ev." (Handbuch Lietzmann) 2A. 1925,
p. 95ff (3A. 1933); HOSKYNS-DAVEY, o.c. p. 363f; E. LOHSE, "Wort u.
Sakrament i. Joh. ev.", N.T. St. 7, 1961, p. 110-125 attributed these allusions

ad b). Very often we meet the idea that the Fourth Gospel had the intention to be a polemical writing against disciples of John the Baptist (cf. Acts XIX 1 ff). So already in the 19th century K. G. BRETSCHNEIDER and W. BALDENSPERGER [1]).

In this century a.o. W. BAUER, R. SCHNACKENBURG, R. H. STRACHAN, R. BULTMANN, W. MICHAELIS, W. F. HOWARD, O. MICHEL, T. HENSHAW, FEINE-BEHM-KÜMMEL [2]). The hypothesis has been opposed a.o. by SMITH and ROBINSON [3]).

ad c. The polemical character of the Gospel of John against the Jews always got much attention. Therefore many scholars were convinced that the Gospel somehow was to be connected with a conflict between Judaïsm and the Christian Church: already from the eighteenth century onwards, a.o. C. WEIZSÄCKER, W. WREDE, JÜLICHER-FASCHER, LORD CHARNWOOD, G. H. C. MACGREGOR, V. TAYLOR, Fr. BÜCHSEL, R. M. GRANT, C. F. D. MOULE [4]). Cf. also the authors mentioned by FEINE-BEHM-KÜMMEL, for whom the anti-Judaïstic tendency was thought to be an important secondary purpose [5]).

---

to an editor; cf. the discussion between J. JEREMIAS, *Z.N.W.* 44, 1952/3 p. 256f and G. BORNKAMM, "Die euch. Rede i. Joh.ev.", *Z.N.W.* 47, 1956, p. 16ff; M. MICHAELIS, *Die Sakramente i. Joh.ev.* 1946.

[1]) K. G. BRETSCHNEIDER, *Probabilia de Evang. et Epistularum Joannis apostoli ind. et orig.* 1820; W. BALDENSPERGER, *Der Prolog d. viert. Ev.* 1898.

[2]) W. BAUER, "Komm." *o.c.* p. 14ff (refers to Mandaeism); R. SCHNACKEN-BURG, "Das viert. Ev. u. d. Joh. jünger". *Hist. Jhrb.* 77, 1938, p. 21ff; R. H. STRACHAN, *o.c.* p. 109; R. BULTMANN, "Das Ev. d. Joh."(*Kr. Ex. Komm. Meyer*) 11 A. 1950, p. 3ff: the Prologue as revision of a gnostic hymn from circles of disciples of the Baptist); W. MICHAELIS, *o.c.* p. 121; W. F. HOWARD, *The F. Gospel in rec. Criticism and Interpr.*, 2ed. 1955, ed. C. K. BARRETT, p. 57ff; O. MICHEL, *C.B.L. o.c.*; T. HENSHAW, *N.T. Liter. in the Light of mod. Scholarship*, 2ed. 1957; FEINE-BEHM-KÜMMEL, *o.c.* p. 158: at least a "Neben-motiv"; so also GUTHRIE, *o.c.* p. 254f.

[3]) T. C. SMITH, *o.c.* p. 50f; J. A. T. ROBINSON, "Elijah, John and Jesus, an Essay in Detection", *Twelve N.T. St. o.c.* p. 28-52 (repr. fr. *N.T. St.* 4, 1958, p. 263ff), esp. p. 49ff.

[4]) WEIZSÄCKER, cf. FEINE-BEHM-KÜMMEL, p. 158; W. WREDE, "Char. u. Tendenz d. Joh.", *Vortr. u. Stud.* 1907, 2A 1933; A. JÜLICHER-E. FASCHER, *Einl. i. d. N.T.*, 7A 1931; LORD CHARNWOOD, *Accord. to St. John* 1925; G. H. C. MACGREGOR, "The Fourth Gospel, the Backgr. of Chr. Experience", *J.B.L.* 49, 1930, p. 150-159; V. TAYLOR, *The Gospels*, 5ed. 1945, p. 98; cf. GUTHRIE, *o.c.* p. 250, note 3; F. BÜCHSEL, *N.T.D.*, "Ev. d. Joh." 5A. 1949, p. 12f; R. M. GRANT, *J.B.L. o.c.* p. 318ff; C. F. D. MOULE, *Birth, o.c.* p. 94ff.

[5]) E.g. WIKENHAUSER, MEINERTZ, FEINE-BEHM, HENSHAW, D. W. RIDDLE-H. H. HUTSON, *N.T. Life and Liter.* 1946. A remarkable view in P. WINTER, *o.c.* p. 155f: against missionary activity of Jews, cf. the critique of VAN UNNIK, *o.c.* p. 410 note 2. See about anti-Jewish tendencies also E. GRÄSSER, "Die Anti-jüd. Polemik i. Joh.ev.", *N.T. St.* 11, 1964/65, p. 74-93.

ad 2. b. 3. *Theological reïnterpretation*

Many adherents of the religio-historical school went into this direction. It is clear that for them the differences between the fourth Gospel and the Synoptics played an important rôle, therefore I prefered to mention this group of scholars within the category of answers given on the third question. (See below)

ad 2. b. 4. *Liturgical motives*

In the first place has to be mentioned now the theory of A. GUILDING [1]: the Gospel was addressed to Jewish Christians recently expelled from the Synagogue (cf. the similarity with MULDER's theory), therefore John reproduced the preaching of Jesus originally connected with the Jewish calendar of festivals as a proof of the fulfillment of Judaism in Jesus, in the original liturgical setting.

A triennial Jewish lectionary lies behind this Gospel. The material has been ordered as a commentary on O.T. passages within this setting of the Jewish calendar. The hypothesis was criticized by many [2]. RANEY pointed to hymns in prose-form in this Gospel, destinated for liturgical use [3].

3. The answer on our third question: has the purpose of the Fourth Gospel been conditioned *by its difference with the Synoptic Gospels*?

We could discern different answers:

a. Adherents of the *"Supplementary"*-theory: the Gospel of John presupposes the Synoptic tradition and aims to supplement it.

b. The *Correction-theory*: the fourth Gospel aims to correct the Synoptic Gospels because it claims to have a more accurate knowledge of the facts.

---

[1] A. GUILDING, *The Fourth Gospel and Jewish Worship*, 1960.

[2] Cf. a.o. GUTHRIE, *o.c.* p. 257, 286f; FEINE-BEHM-KÜMMEL *o.c.* p. 159; J. R. PORTER, "The Pentateuch and the Triennial Lection. Cycle, an exam. of a recent Theory" in: *Promise and Fulfillment, Essays pres. to S. H. Hooke*, ed. F. F. Bruce, 1963, p. 163-174; L. MORRIS, *The N.T. and the Jewish Lectionaries* 1964.

[3] W. H. RANEY, *The Relation of the Fourth Gospel to the Chr. Cultus* 1933; cf. the critique of GUTHRIE, *o.c.* p. 257, note 3, who also mentions other attempts to find a liturgical frame behind the structure of John's Gospel, p. 286f, refering to E. LOHMEYER, "Über Aufbau u. Gliederung d. viert. Ev.", *Z.N.W.* 27, 1928, p. 11-36, to A ROBERT/A. FEUILLET, *Introd. à la Bible* II 1959, p. 623 and D. MOLLAT in the Jerusalem Bible.

c. This Gospel has the purpose to *replace* fully the Synoptic Gospels. Many scholars supposed that it was meant to be a theological reinterpretation of the life and teaching of Jesus Christ, written from the point of view of the contemporary Christian faith.

ad 3 a. *John's Gospel is supplementing the Synoptics*

This viewpoint is a very old one and has still many defenders. The difference between John and the Synoptics already drew the attention of the early Church. Therefore Clement of Alexandria and Origenes proposed as a solution: John is a "pneumatic" Gospel [1]). In more recent times this hypothesis of a supplementary purpose of John has been defended a.o. by GOGUEL, SIGGE, GROSHEIDE, SCHÄFER, BOISMARD, CASSIAN and NEIL [2]).

ad 3 b. *Correction of the Synoptics*

This idea has been defended a.o. by E. STAUFFER [3]).

----

[1]) CLEM. OF ALEX., *Hypotyposes*, quoted by EUSEBIUS, H. E. VI, 14, 7. There is some difference of interpretation of the contradistinction: "τα σωματικα" and "πνευματικον — εὐαγγελιον". W. SANDAY f.i. interpreted the latter as the Gospel that sought to bring out the divine side of its subject, supplementing the Synoptics: W. SANDAY, *The Criticism of the F. Gospel*, 1905, p. 71; R. M. GRANT, *J.B.L. o.c.* p.306 however interpreted "pneumatic" as gnostic, refering to CLEMENT's distinction between two kinds of gnosis, f.i. inhis *Stromata*, V, 7, 4-5. ORIGENES too gave a similar interpretation in his commentary on John i 4; cf. GUTHRIE *o.c.* p. 248f; FEINE-BEHM-KÜMMEL, p. 159; see for a survey of the various standpoints regarding the relation between John and the Synoptics, a.o. H. WINDISCH, "Joh. u. d. Synoptiker", *U.N.T.* 12, 1926 and P. GARDNER SMITH, *St. John and the Synoptic Gospels* 1938.

[2]) M. GOGUEL, *Introd. au N.T.* vol. II 1922, p. 158ff; T. SIGGE, "Das Joh.ev. u. d. Synopt." *NTA* 16, 2/3, 1935, p. 213f; F. W. GROSHEIDE, *comm. o.c.* I, p. 36 refering to a similar conclusion in the works of GODET, ZAHN, BERNARD (*I.C.C.* vol. I, p. XCVI); K. TH. SCHÄFER, *Grundriss d. Einl. i. d. N.T.* 2A. 1952; M.E. BOISMARD, in *Rech. Bibl.* III, "L'Év. de Jean, Ét. et Probl." 1958; Bishop CASSIAN, "The Interrelation of the Gospels Matthew-Luke-John (Luke after Matth. and before John)", *Stud. Evang.* I *o.c.* p. 129-147 (esp. p. 147); W. NEIL, *o.c.* p. 401. Cf. also A. M. HUNTER' "Recent Trends in Joh. Studies," *Exp. T.* 71, 1960 p. 164-167, 219-222 (esp. p. 219ff).

[3]) E. STAUFFER "Histor. Elemente i. viert. Ev." in: *Bekenntnis z. Kirche, Festschrift E. Sommerlath*, 1960, p. 33ff. It is a remarkable fact that the historical reliability of the Johannine tradition has been accepted by more and more scholars in recent times. See f.i. the articles of A. M. HUNTER, also J. A. T. ROBINSON, *New Look, o.c.* p. 100f and D. GUTHRIE, *o.c.* p. 298-300.

ad 3c. *Replacing the Synoptic Gospels*

H. WINDISCH proposed the idea that the Fourth Gospel aimed
to replace the Synoptic Gospels. Also W. BAUER, RIDDLE-HUTSON,
R. M. GRANT a.o. went into this direction, but they met a lot of
opposition too [1]). The majority of the scholars assumes a knowledge
of the Synoptics by John or at least acquaintance with the Synoptic
tradition behind these Gospels. It takes too much time to deal here
with the whole problem of the relation between John and the
Synoptics in a more detailed way. This relation has been made still
more complicated by some authors who assumed sources in the
Fourth Gospel (e.g. BULTMANN). Suggestions have been made that
the tradition written down in the Fourth Gospel must have been
much older than the time of its definite publication or that even the
first publication was earlier than generally has been thought.

These suggestions deserve in my opinion more serious attention
than they got [2]).

Those scholars who thought the Fourth Gospel to be a theological
reinterpretation [3]) are again very much divided among themselves:
some thought that the purpose was a stressing of Christology
(particularly because of the background of Gnosticism) as in John
xx 31, others: of eschatology (the postponement of the Parousia,
the realized eschatology in John), or a reinterpretation of the
doctrine of the sacraments (already mentioned above).

---

[1]) H. H. WINDISCH, *Joh. u. d. Synopt. o.c.* p. 87f; W. BAUER, "Joh.ev. u,
Joh. briefe, Th. Rdsch." *N.F.* 1 1929, p. 135-160, esp. p. 139; R. M. GRANT.
"The Fourth Gospel and the Church" *Harv. Th. R.* 35, 1942, p. 95.

[2]) Cf. f. i. V. BURCH, *The Structure and Message of St. John's Gospel* 1928,
who defended a publication even before A.D. 70; cf. also C. H. DODD, *Histor.
Tradition in the Fourth Gospel*, 1963; H. H. EDWARDS, *The Disciple who
wrote these Things*, 1953, related the publication of this Gospel with the
flight of the Christians from Jerusalem to Pella, p. 129f.

[3]) The theory of a theol. reïnterpretation has been stressed a.o. by
W. WREDE, "Charakter", *o.c.* p. 178ff; A. JÜLICHER/E. FASCHER, *Einl. i.d.
N.T.* 1931, 148; W. HEITMÜLLER *Schrift. d. N.T. übers f. d. Gegenwart
erklärt*, 3A. 1920, p. p. 46; cf. also VAN UNNIK, *o.c.* p. 387. FEINE-BEHM-
KÜMMEL concludes: if it is true that this Gospel is neither a supplement nor
a correction or substitute, the only possibility is, "dass es unter stillschweigen-
der Voraussetzung der Bekanntschaft mit schon vorhandenen Evangelien,
seinerseits die jenige Darstellung Jesu geben will, die in vollendeter Weise
erscheinen lässt, dass Jesus der Gesalbte, der Sohn Gottes ist, 20:31, und
so versucht adaequat aus zu drucken was bereits in der früheren Tradition
enthalten, war", *o.c.* p. 160 (refering to a similar point of view in BARRETT's
article, "Zweck", *o.c.* p. 267, R. H. LIGHTFOOT, *Comm. St. John's Gospel*
1906, and R. BULTMANN).

The majority of the authors to be mentioned here are agreeing with the theory that the Gospel of John has been written from the viewpoint, the faith of the Christian community after Eastern or from the convictions of a particular grouping within the Church of those days [1]). The authors differ from each other in their view of the background of this Gospel (Jewish, Hellenistic, Philo, Gnostic, Jewish Gnosticism, Qumran etc.) but they all agree with the idea of a theological reinterpretation of the Christian tradition, which could be found in the Synoptics.

Regarding the interest of the author of the Fourth Gospel into the historical facts of Jesus' life, there is again a variety of opinions. It would bring us too far to discuss more fully all these points of view, I'm only mentioning some of the most important ones [2]). Already E. F. Scott thought Gnosticism to be the background and the principle of understanding of John's Gospel [3]). In the same direction went F. C. Grant, C. K. Barrett, R. Bultmann, E. Käsemann and others [4]).

---

[1]) E.g. M. Dibelius in *R.G.G.*, vol. III 2 A., p. 350: "Joh. bringt . . . zur Darstellung nicht was Jesus war sondern was die Christen an Jesus haben"; cf. also E. Gaugler, "Das Christuszeugnis d. H. Schrift u. d. Kirche", *Beih. Ev.Th.* 1936, p. 41 ff; H. Strathmann, "Ev. d. Joh." *NTD.* vol. 4, 6 A. 1951, p. 22 f; J. C. Fenton saw in the life of Christ in John's Gospel "a projection backwards of the Christian life": "Towards an Underst. of John", *Stud. Evang.* IV, *TU* 102, 1968, p. 28 ff; Cullmann expressed as his view regarding the purpose of John: to prove that the historical Jesus is the Christ of the Church and that the "Church's interests at the time (sacraments, mission) were already found with the Lord", O. Cullmann, in *The Early Church*, ed. A. J. B. Higgins 1956, p. 186.

[2]) Cf. Van Unnik, *o.c.* p. 386: "a book of the Christian community which has to express itself in the terms of its new surroundings", quoting the idea of Feine-Behm, *Einl.* 9 A. 1950 p. 116 ff and W. Michaelis, (*Einl. i. d. N.T.* 2 A. 1954, p. 117 f.)

[3]) E. F. Scott, *The Fourth Gospel its Purpose and Theol.* 2 ed. 1908, p. 86-103: a double reaction on Gnosticism, a positive one of sympathy with Gnostic doctrine (stressing the "ideal value" of Jesus' life, dualism and gnosis) and a negative one: avoiding the use of certain gnostic terms. He dated the Gospel between the first opposition against Gnosticism (Epistle to the Colossians) and the later rejection in the 2d cent. Cf. the critique of D. Guthrie, *o.c.* p. 251.

[4]) F. C. Grant, *The Gospels, their Origin and Growth*, 1957, p. 163 ff: the background of the evangelist was a group of adherents of an early Christian gnostic mysticism; the purpose of the F. Gospel was a re-writing of Jesus' life in the language of this contemporary gnostic mysticism; C. K. Barrett, *Peake's Comm.* 1962, p. 844: the Gospel has a theol. intention: to answer on two burning issues at the end of the 1st cent., the eschatological (postponed Parousia) and the developing Gnosticism. Esp. R. Bultmann spoke about

The discovery of Qumran had a great influence on these discussions, as we stated already. Various elements in John which
formerly were thought to be Hellenistic (Gnostic) dated in the
second century, now proved to be familiar on Palestinian soil in
the terminology and ideas of the community of Qumran in the first
century. After the first enthousiastic reactions on the discovery
of the Scrolls the discussion went on between those who defended
a close affinity between John and Qumran, as f.i. ALBRIGHT,
ROBINSON a.o.[1]) and those who opposed this viewpoint [2]).

BARRETT defended the thesis that John's Gospel aimed to be a

---

a gnostic background in several publications, i.c. the gnostic myth of the
redeemed Redeemer originating in Iran, recognizable f.i. in the Mandaean
writings; cf. his art.: "Die Bedeutung d. neuentschloss. mand. u. manich.
Quellen f. d. Verständnis d. Joh.ev." Z.N.W. 24, 1925, p. 100-146; also in
R.G.G. ("Joh.ev.") III, 3A. 1959, p. 840ff: the fourth Gospel is a "Neu-
gestaltung geschichtlicher Jesustradition" against a Gnostic background,
p. 845; BULTMANN pointed to the affinity with the Odes of Solomon the
letters of Ignatius and gave also a reconstruction of the gnostic myth; cf. the
critique a.o. of ST. NEILL, o.c. p. 167f, 222ff, cf D. GUTHRIE, o.c. p. 251f;
cf. also R. BULTMANN, Theol.d. N.T. 2A. 1954, p. 349ff. About BULTMANN,
see R. GYLLENBERG, "Die Anfänge d. joh. Tradition," NTl. Stud. f. R. Bultmann Beih. Z.N.W. 21, 1954, p. 144ff; E. KÄSEMANN, "Z. Joh. Interpr.",
o.c. II p. 151ff.

[1]) W. F. ALBRIGHT, Recent Discoveries on Palest. and the Gospel of John,
in The Background of the NT. and its Eschat., i. hon. C. H. DODD, 1956,
p. 153ff; J. A. T. ROBINSON, "New Look" o.c.; cf. also R. BROWN, "The
Qumran Scrolls and the Gospel and Epistles of John" in (ed. K. Stendahl),
The Scrolls and the N.T. 1957, p. 183ff.

[2]) So f.i. H. M. TEEPLE, "Qumran and the Origin of the F. Gospel", Nov. T.
4, 1960, p. 6-25. TEEPLE concluded that John has more a Hellenistic than a
Jewish (The Essenes of Qumran) background. Much has been written about
this relation John-Qumran, e.g. G. BAUMBACH, Qumran u. d. Joh. 1958;
H. BRAUN, Qumran u. d. N.T. 1966, vol. I p. 96-138, vol. II p. 118-144 (see
the literature mentioned by him). F. C. GRANT too had the opinion that there
are more parallels with the Hellenistic religious liter. in John than with
Qumran. Moderately critical, was f. i. M. BURROWS, More Light on the Dead
Sea Scrolls, 1958, p. 129. In recent times more and more scholars are inclined
to look for a Palestinian background of the fourth Gospel: the O. Test. but
often combined with a "pre-Gnosticism" from Iranian origin (ethical and
eschatological dualism in contradistinction from cosmic dualism in the later
Hellenistic Gnosticism). Cf. a.o. the survey about the relation John- O. Test.
in SMALLEY, o.c. p. 58ff; O. BÖCHER, Der Joh. Dualismus i. Zusammenh. d.
nach-bibl. Judentum, 1965, p. 11ff, in the line a.o. of B. REICKE, "Traces of
Gnosticism in the Dead Sea Scrolls?", N.T.St. 1, 1954/55, p. 137-140; idem
article R.G.G.: "Iran" II (Iran. Religion, Judentum, Urchristentum) vol. III,
3A. 1959, p. 881-884; K. G. KUHN, "Die Sektenschrift u. d. iran. Religion",
Z.Th.K. 49, 1952, p. 296-316 and "Die i. Palest. gefund. hebr. Texte u. d.
N.T.", Z.Th.K. 47, 1950, p. 192-211.

theological reïnterpretation of the eschatological tradition too [1]).

4. Very briefly I'd like to mention some authors who recognized, in the style and structure of the Gospel of John the features of a drama, apart from the question whether this form was aimed at and edited by the original writer or not. Usually they do not stress the discussions about the addressed readers, but it is clear that in case it was a kind of drama, we have to think more in terms of a Greek than of a Jewish public. I mention as some examples a.o. C. R. Bowen, R. H. Strachan, B. W. Robinson and C. M. Connick [2]).

I hope that this survey in spite of its incompleteness, proves the diversity of the answers given on the question of the purpose and address of the Fourth Gospel.

It is not difficult now, to classify the answers given by the three authors we are dealing with here: Van Unnik, Robinson and Mulder. All three agreed that Jewish readers were addressed, but they differed in their answer on our second question: whether the purpose was a missionary one: the address being non-Christians, or a positive-apologetic aim: to address the Christian Churches.

If we compare the arguments of our three authors, we find that each one had a different startingpoint.

Van Unnik starts with the exegesis of John xx 31, the self-testimony of the evangelist about the purpose of his book: the faith that Jesus is the Christ, the Anointed One, that is the promised Messiah and the Son of God [3]). This belief was the decisive point of discussion between the missionary Church and the Synagogue.

Robinson and Mulder both started with a comparison between

---

[1]) C. K. Barrett, "Gospel acc. to St. John", *o.c.* p. 115 ff: a new interpretation of the primitive eschatological hope: realized eschatology; cf. also Käsemann's review of Barrett's work, *o.c.* II p. 141 ff. Cf. about the eschatology of the Gospel of John, L. v. Hartingsveld, *Die Eschatologie d. Joh. ev.* 1962.

[2]) C. R. Bowen, "The Fourth Gospel as Dramatic Material", *J.B.L.* 49, 1930, p. 292-305; also his "Comments on the Fourth Gospel", *Angl. Theol. Rev.* jan. 1930; Bowen assumes that the present form of the Gospel is not edited by the author himself; R. H. Strachan *The Fourth Evangelist, Dramatist or Historian*, 1925; B. W. Robinson: *The Gospel of John* 1925, also called the form "a dramatic dialogue" or rather "a popular conversational homily", p. 150; C. M. Connick,, "The Dramatic Character of the Fourth Gospel", *J.B.L.* 67, 1948, p. 159-169.

[3]) Van Unnik, *o.c.* p. 384, 387 ff.

the Fourth Gospel and the Synoptics regarding their attitude towards the Gentiles, who in fact do not come into the picture of John, as they did in the Synoptic Gospels.

ROBINSON explains this difference by the fact that the Fourth Gospel was not directed at all towards non-Jews (see the difference with Paul who was interested in the relation between Jews and Gentiles, circumcized and uncircumcized), but towards "the Greek", that is for John: Greek-speaking Diaspora-Jews in their relation to the Synagogue [1]).

MULDER however explains this difference between John and the Synoptics by the argument that the Synoptic Gospels were written before the Jewish war and before the destruction of Jerusalem 70 A.D., while the Gospel of John was published after that time and fully conditioned by the post-war situation and its consequences regarding the relation between Jewish Christians and the Synagogue [2]).

In spite of the fact that the arguments of the three authors are sometimes running parallel, this different startingpoint makes a summarizing survey of the whole complex of arguments more difficult. But I think that we could summarize the most important arguments into four categories:

1. The difference between John and the Synoptics regarding "the Jews" and "the Gentiles".

2. The self-testimony of the Fourth Gospel in John xx 31.

3. The background (Heimat) of the Johannine tradition: Palestine before or after the war.

4. The address of the Greek speaking Jews or Jewish Christians in the Diaspora.

ad 1. *Jews and Gentiles in the Fourth Gospel*

Both ROBINSON and MULDER stress the own character of the Fourth Gospel regarding these topics [3]).

This Gospel with its polemic against "the Jews" who rejected Jesus, seems to be the most anti-Jewish book of the New Test., but both authors agree with Lightfoot that the Gospel of John "is

---

[1]) ROBINSON, "Destination", *o.c.* p. 111 ff, 116 ff.
[2]) MULDER, *o.c.* p. 233 f, 239 ff.
[3]) Cf. ROBINSON, *o.c.* p. 109 ff.; MULDER, p. 234 ff.

the most Hebraic book in the N.Test, except perhaps the Apocal-lypse" [1]).

MULDER therefore compares it specially with the Gospel of Matthew. He comes to a similar conclusion as ROBINSON, that in the Synoptic Gospels "we are conscious always of the Gentiles pressing in on the wings" [2]). But in John we find the term "the Jews" at least 70 times, nowhere however "the Gentiles" are mentioned expressis verbis [3]). At the other hand John's Gospel has been called the most universalistic Gospel [4]): again and again we meet the word "κοσμος".

How to combine this universalism with the lack of any trace of Gentile mission?

ROBINSON and MULDER again differ in their answer, which is decisive for their different solutions.

ROBINSON states that the typical Pauline problem (the relation Jewish Christians-Gentile Christians, cf. Galatians) does not come into the picture of the Fourth Gospel [5]).

---

[1]) J. B. LIGHTFOOT, *Bibl. Essays* 1893, p. 135; cf. ROBINSON *o.c.* p. 109, MULDER *o.c.* p. 234; ROBINSON remarks that the Jews are not condemned "from without" but always "from within". He admits that Jesus speaks about "your" law (viii 17; x 34) and "their" law (xv 25) but at the other hand the fact that Jesus was a Jew Himself, gets a special stress (cf. i 11; iv 9, cf. iv 22; xviii 35, He is the King of the Jews xix 19). The expressions "your" and "their" therefore have to be interpreted by their context: the discussion with the unbelieving Jews in the Gospel.

[2]) ROBINSON, *o.c.* p. 110.

[3]) Cf. the remarkable result of a comparison with the Synoptics in the articles of ROBINSON and MULDER. ROBINSON's arguments are a.o.: Jesus is the Revelation for Israel (i 31); in stead of the Syro-Phoenician woman in the Synoptics, we read about the Samaritan woman who still could say: "our father Jacob" (iv 12, cf. MULDER *o.c.* p. 236f); in stead of the healing of the son of the Roman centurion, we find the son of the royal officer, perhaps a Jew, a Herodian (iv 46-54); the only Roman who plays a rôle, is Pilate (cf. MULDER, p. 237); the Romans will destroy Jeusalem (xi 48) but the Kingdom will not be given to others (cf. Matt. xxi 43; MULDER remarks that the parables about the relation of Israel to the gojim are not found in John); the disciples will be banned from the synagogues (xvi 2) but not brought before governors and kings (Matt. x 18); Jesus always remains in Palestine; MULDER points to the strange fact of the lacking of any suggestion of the mission among the Gentiles after the time of Paul's missionary work, *o.c.* p. 238. ROBINSON states that the "world" in John is the Jewish world, including "the Greeks" (vii 35 xii 20f) *o.c.* p. 111f, 116f.

[4]) See f.i. i 9, 29; iii 16f; xii 32: "all".

[5]) *O.c.* p. 113f. We never find an appeal to the Gentiles. John vii does not mean missionary activity but a public demonstration before the Jews. "Cosmos" as such is the world as the object of God's love or as the hostile

As I said before, the "Greek" in this Gospel are for ROBINSON those, mentioned in 7:35: the Dispersion among the Greeks, the Greek speaking Diaspora Jews [1]).

A comparison between John and Paul shows that the important contrast for John was not: Jews-Gentiles, but: Jewish Christians and non-Christian Jews [2]). John uses the symbol of the vine-tree, Paul that of the olive-tree, both O.Test. symbols for Israel [3]).

John is no Judaizer, the transition to the Christian faith is nothing less than a "rebirth" [4]), but what matters is: to be a true Jew, that is to be a true Christian [5]). John's problem is the question of Nicodemus: how is this possible? (iii 9) [6]). How could someone become a Christian without ceasing to be a Jew, in spite of the fact that he is banned from the synagogue? [7]) On that question the Gospel wants to give an answer.

---

power opposing Jesus, but never the Gentile world over against the Jews. They who hear the voice of Jesus are Jews, represented by some individuals as Nathanael, Nicodemus, the blind man a.o.

[1]) See below, ad 4.

[2]) ROBINSON, o.c. p. 113. The contrast between light and darkness in John is not that between Jews and Gentiles. The problem of Paul in Romans ix-xi and Eph. ii (the barrier) is unknown to John.

[3]) ROBINSON, o.c. p. 113; MULDER, p. 238. In both symbols the act of lopping off the branches, is important, but "for John there is no grafting in of alien branches". But I must remark here that the function of the symbol in John's Gospel totally differs from that in Paul's letter to the Romans. I'm doubting whether it is allowed to compare therefore these two O.T. symbols in such a way with so important consequences.

[4]) By the word "rebirth" John makes it clear that the entire existing system of Judaism is challenged and transcended in Jesus Christ: the law (i 17), the ritual (ii 6), the temple (ii 19), its localized worship (iv 29), its Sabbath-regulations (v 9-18): ROBINSON, o.c. p. 113. And yet there is "nothing in Jesus alien to Judaïsm, truely understood. He is the true shekinah (i 14), the true temple (ii 21). Salvation is from the Jews" (iv 20ff).

[5]) ROBINSON, l.c. What matters for John is the relation between Judaïsm and the true Israel, the true vine, Christ. Therefore the O. Test. plays such an important rôle in his Gospel: Moses (i 46; v 39-47), Abraham (viii 39, 56), Isaiah (xii 41): they were witnesses of Christ and condemn their unbelieving descendants. Jesus is the "Holy One of God" (vi 69), the Prophet (vi 14; vii 40, cf. Deut. xviii 15).

[6]) Exactly Nicodemus is typical: member of the Jewish Council and teacher of Israel.

[7]) MULDER comes to a similar conclusion as ROBINSON: the problem is the banning of Jewish Christians from the synagogue, but his arguments are different. ROBINSON also deals with the other problems Paul had in Galatians. For John the questions of the Torah and the circumcision were not "the fence between Judaïsm and the Gentile world, barriers of exclusivism to be broken down", but "what must be transcended by Judaïsm within its own life because they belong to the level of flesh and not spirit,

MULDER however thinks that John knew the fact that the Gentiles received salvation in Christ and that he often alludes to this fact. A remarkable difference of interpretation I found therefore between MULDER at the one hand and VAN UNNIK and ROBINSON at the other hand, regarding John x 16 [1]).

But is seems to be only an abstract theory for John, stated MULDER. The only important thing is the relation between Israel and Jesus Christ. The reason is that the background of this Gospel has to be sought in Palestine after the Jewish war, in the more and more hostile relations between Jewish Christians and the Synagogue.

The striking frequency of the term "the Jews" brought ROBINSON to his theory that it was John's purpose to point to the "hopelessly divided Judaïsm" divided against itself, when faced with the claims of Jesus. This theory is related to his remarkable interpretation of the geographical and topographical data in this Gospel.

For MULDER however, this frequent use of "the Jews" was an argument for his view of the rôle of the Pharisees after the war. We'll come back upon this difference later.

ad 2. *The Testimony of the Gospel itself: John xx* 31

In my opinion VAN UNNIK was right in taking his startingpoint in this own testimony of the Gospel. He proved that the word "Christ" in his verse is no proper name, but a title in the full etymological sense: the Anointed One, the Messiah promised in the O. Test.[2]). After a comparison with some texts from Acts (xvii 2, 3;

---

whether a single Gentile wanted to enter the Church or not", ROBINSON, *o.c.* p. 116.

[1]) VAN UNNIK thinks that "the other sheep ... not belonging to this fold", probably were Jews in the Diaspora, *o.c.* p. 407. ROBINSON points to the O.T. background in Ezek. xxxiv 37, Jer. xxiii 31, dealing with the gathering of the dispersed Jews and he too concludes that not the Gentiles but Jews in the Dispersion are meant here, o.c. p. 121. But MULDER quotes this verse as a proof of the universalistic character of his Gospel and as allusion to the fact that also the Gentiles are saved by Christ, *o.c.* p. 237. My first comment here is, that if this latter exegesis is true, it would be impossible to speak of "an allusion" only. We find a clear proof then that the Gentiles are in the picture of John's Gospel.

[2]) VAN UNNIK, *o.c.* p. 390f. John is the only author in the N.T. who uses the word "Messiah" without translation (i 42), moreover in the same context he speaks about Jesus as the King of the Jews (i 49). Therefore VAN UNNIK rejects the opinion of BAUER that John "heaps on Jesus all the traditional

xviii 5, 28), VAN UNNIK concluded: "that Jesus is the Christ, this Johannine phrase is a formula which has its roots in the Christian mission among the Jews" [1]. A comparison with Christian writers in the second century (Hegesippus),[2] especially Justin's Dialogue with the Jew Trypho, proves that this theme: "Jesus the Christ" was the decisive point in the discussions between the Church and the Synagogue, but in a missionary, not an apologetic setting [3]. Different from Justin, quoting O.T. citations, in John it is by his works (signs) that Jesus proved to be the legitimate Anointed One, sent by God [4]).

Therefore VAN UNNIK and ROBINSON both interpret the addition in xx 31: "the Son of God" as the ground of the certainty that Jesus is the Messiah, his divine legitimation, however much this Sonship of God was the great stumblingblock for the Jews [5]).

It is clear that this stress on the proof that Jesus, the man from Galilee by his work done in Palestine, was the promised Messiah, points into the direction of Jewish readers [6].

The Palestinian background of the Johannine tradition brings me to my third theme of discussion:

---

names current in the Chr. Church of his days, without a thinking in Jewish categories" (p. 392). Based upon different arguments, VAN UNNIK cocnludes: although the nationalistic Messianism is not shared by John, he stands on the ground of Jewish Messianic belief. Cf. about these things also ROBINSON, "Destination", o.c. p. 114: except in i 17 and xvii 3, "Christ" is always a title in John, no proper name, vide the article.

[1]) VAN UNNIK, o.c. p. 397.
[2]) Cf. EUSEBIUS, H.E. II, 23, 8-10.
[3]) VAN UNNIK, o.c. p. 397.
[4]) VAN UNNIK points to the difference between John and Justin's approach of this theme, o.c. p. 398-403; SCHNACKENBURG rightly said, that the Person of Jesus, his signs and the faith of those who met Him, are the central elements in John, not the O.T. quotations, Die Messiasfrage, o.c. p. 242-243.
[5]) VAN UNNIK, o.c. p. 404; ROBINSON: the term "Son of God" "stands as an epexegetic of the Christ", with a Jewish background, o.c. p. 114. He points to the metaphors used by Christ about Himself: manna, light, shepherd a.o. all associated with the O.T. and later Judaism as symbols of the true Israel of God. Cf. also the frequent use of "ἀληθινος", the true Israel over against Israel after the flesh, o.c. p. 114.
[6]) VAN UNNIK, o.c. p. 406: the Gospel therefore was addressed to the synagogue, Jews or God-fearers. Other arguments of VAN UNNIK are: Jesus is always called "Rabbi or Teacher of Israel (John iii); the prophecy that the disciples will be banned from the synagogue will be the sign of the hate of the cosmos; cf. also the expression: afraid of the Jews (ix 22) and the fact that the temple and the synagogue as places of Jesus' public teaching, represent "the world", xviii 20.

ad 3. *The Background of the Gospel of John: Palestine before or after the War?*

All three authors agree that this background is a Palestinian one, but on this point the ways of ROBINSON and MULDER diverge.

ROBINSON found as the "Heimat" of the tradition behind the Fourth Gospel: South Judaea, the place of Jewish opposition without contacts with the Gentile world [1]).

MULDER however finds the "Sitz im Leben" in the isolated Jewish Christian communities after the destruction of Jerusalem in a time in which the contacts between Palestine and the Diaspora were very few and the stormy development in the Christian Churches of the Diaspora were unknown in Palestine [2]).

A striking fact is that both authors point to the Qumran-community as an example of an isolated community [3]).

In relation to this background in South Judaea, ROBINSON points to the already mentioned motive of the divided Judaism, faced with the claims of Jesus, the Christ [4]).

The geographical indications in the Fourth Gospel are also seen by ROBINSON in this light: especially the division between Galilea and Judaea. ROBINSON gives an own theological interpretation: Jesus, the man from Galilea comes to South Judaea, Jerusalem, to his true "Heimat" [5]).

MULDER however directed his attention to the post-war situation,

---

[1]) ROBINSON, "Destination", *o.c.* p. 116: "The Gentile world except as represented by the Romans, is miles away".

[2]) MULDER, *o.c.* p. 239f. This isolation was promoted also because the rabbis tried as much as possible to continue the past, a fact that must have influenced the Jewish Christians, with the consequence that they did not seek much contact with their fellow Christians in the Dispersion.

[3]) Cf. ROBINSON, *o.c.* p. 116: the children of darkness in Qumran are not the Gentiles (Kittim) but the faithless Israel; MULDER, *o.c.* p. 240f.

[4]) ROBINSON, *o.c.* p. 117. There are tensions f.i. between the common people and the Jerusalem authorities, sometimes designated as "the Jews"; there is a division within the authorities, between members of the Sanhedrin and Pharisees, and "moreover the various groupings — the Pharisees, the common people, the Jews who believed in him and the Jews who did not — are split among themselves", *o.c.* p. 117. But the still more far-reaching division "is that between metropolitan Judaism and the Diaspora", p. 118.

[5]) ROBINSON, *o.c.* p. 118f. "The Jews" are with a few exeptions always Jews from Judaea, the Jewish country is the Judaean country, Jesus' true "home-land" in spite of the fact that He originated from Nazareth. Probably vii 42 "presupposes that John knows the tradition of his birth at Betlehem". He entered his own realm, that is Judaea, but there people disowns him as a Galilaean and even as a Samaritan (viii 48).

especially the strengthened position of the Pharisees, the new organisation of Jewish life in Jamnia.

Exactly the Pharisees are characterized by their irreconcilable attitude in this Gospel. This situation fits with that after the war. After the supple attitude of Jokanan ben Zakai came the "stern line" of Gamaliël II, culminating in the addition of the "Birkat-ha-minim", the curse against the Christians, to the "Schemone-es're" (The Eighteen Prayers), forcing them to leave definitely the Synagogue [1]. MULDER gave much attention too, to the topographical pecularities of the Fourth Gospel, but he did not interpret them in a theological sense, but from an archaeological point: they are topographical indications of places, which were still recognizable as ruins after the war [2].

All things point to a post-war situation, thinks MULDER, just as they all point to a pre-war South-Judaean situation as place of origin of the Johannine tradition, in ROBINSON's article!

ad. 4. *The address: the Greek Dispora*

All three authors agree about the thesis that the Jews to whom the Fourth Gospel was addressed, lived in the Greek Diaspora [3].

---

[1] MULDER, *o.c.* p. 241-245. Therefore the Herodians and Sadducees are no more mentioned in John and the Pharisees are irreconcilable (John vii). This explains also the attention of the Gospel for the crypto-faithful, p. 242. The hesitation of Samuel the Little who had formulated the new prayer against the "minim", was interpreted by MULDER as a reminiscence of the possible sympathy of many Jewish leaders for Jewish Christians, MULDER, *o.c.* p. 245, esp. note 64. The banning of Jewish Christians from the synagogue caused a lot of disturbance and confusion. So MULDER came to his solution of the purpose of this Gospel.

[2] MULDER states that John always locates the events very accurately, but the geographical map of the Jewish land in his Gospel looks different from that in the Synoptics, *o.c.* p. 245, 246. This difference is caused by the war which destroyed the country. MULDER mentions some examples e.g. the name "Tiberias" (vi 1; xxi 1, MULDER p. 246f), Bethany (p. 247), Bethesda and Siloam (p. 247, 248), Solomon's cloister, the treasury of the temple (p. 249) and Gabbatha (p. 249/250) and concludes: the indications of John have to be understood against the background of the sombre scenery of a burned city, where normal life was almost impossible, p. 250.

[3] Cf. ROBINSON, *o.c.* p. 116: "quite patently his Gospel is in Greek and for a Greek-speaking public". ROBINSON points to the striking difference between John and Paul: for Paul and Luke (Acts), the distinction between Jews and Greeks means: Jews and Gentiles, circumcized and uncircumcized; for John however: Jews in Palestine- Greek-speaking Jews in the Dispora. This is seen from a Palestinian standpoint and that is exactly the standpoint

Not only linguistic data, but also the evidence of some texts in the Gospel point clearly into this direction. The rôle of the "Greeks" and the "Dispersion among the Greeks", the explanation of Jewish customs, all these things bring Van Unnik and Robinson to the conclusion: this Gospel is a missionary writing for Greek-speaking Diaspora-Jews [1]).

Mulder however thinks that the motive for the writing of this Gospel was the confusion among Christians in the Diaspora, especially in Asia Minor, because of the Birkat-ha-minim.

---

of the writer of this Gospel, *o.c.* p. 117. Also Van Unnik points to the typical Greek expressions in the language of John's Gospel, *o.c.* p. 407.

[1]) Cf. vii 35: The Dispersion among the Greeks as distinct from Babylon, Egypt or Rome. Van Unnik thinks that possibly we meet a piece of irony here: what seemed unbelievable for the Jews, happened by the mission, *o.c.* p. 408. Important is also xi 52, the prophecy of Caiphas. Robinson interprets the words "the whole nation" by metropolitan Judaïsm and "the scattered children of God" are the Diaspora-Jews, *o.c.* p. 120. Van Unnik points to the fact that the words "scattered children etc." purposely are added by the evangelist because of his special interest into them. Both Van Unnik and Robinson, refer also to xii 20f, the Greek who liked to see Jesus. We saw that Robinson thought that they were Greek speaking Diaspora-Jews, *o.c.* p. 111. Their coming means for Jesus the hour of his glorification (p. 120). Cf. also Robinson's interpretation of x 16 mentioned above. In xvii 20f Jesus' prayer for the unity of the faithful, Robinson thinks that the unity of the Jewish people was meant, not the unity of divided Christianity, *o.c.* p. 121. The careful collecting of the pieces of bread into twelve baskets, vi 12f, was also seen by Robinson as a sign of the fullness of Israel and the pastoral and missionary care of John that all who are destinated for life would be saved, *o.c.* p. 121. Robinson admits that John's nationalism is not exclusivistic, but vindicates that all have the right to become children of God (as in Romans) and that he never reduces salvation to the Jews only (cf. xvii 21), but because John writes for a special public (Jews) he formulates his Gospel in their own language and speaks as a Palestinian Jew (cf. Paul in I Thess. ii 14f), Robinson, *o.c.* p. 121/122. About the explanation of Jewish customs (purification, ii 6, burial-customs xix 40) cf. Van Unnik, *o.c.* p. 407. Robinson refutes the objection that John speaks so objectively about "the Jews" as if he was not a Jew himself. He explains facts from the life of Aramaic speaking Judaism for Jews who were no longer acqainted with these terms and customs. Very important is the expression "a feast of the Jews" usually for Jesus the occasion to go to Judaea: Jesus the man from Galilea has to go to the "land of the Jews", Judaea, see above. Therefore every detail is important, Robinson, *o.c.* p. 123. Cf. also Mulder, *o.c.* p. 251. Van Unnik wants to prove that his solution fits nicely with the picture of the relation Synagogue-Church in Acts, *o.c.* p. 407f. The polemical tendency against the disciples of the Baptist points to Ephesus, thinks Van Unnik, as the place of origin of this Gospel (cf. Acts xix 3ff). In Asia Minor the disputes took place between John and the Synagogue, in accordance with the old tradition of Irenaeus (Adv. Haer. II, 22, 5 and III, 1, 1-4), Van Unnik, *o.c.* p. 409, 410.

The apostle John took note of this confusion after his return from exile on the island of Patmos. He wrote the Gospel in order to comfort, to encourage the Christians, i.c. the Jewish Christians in the Dispersion and to insist on persistency of faith [1]). He draws the lines of Jesus' preaching, in Jesus' days already disputed and rejected by the Pharisees who were loyal to the Torah, and the experience of those who came to believe Jesus, on till his own time and the situation of his readers in Asia Minor, confronted with the definite separation from the synagogue and Judaism [2]).

We conclude that VAN UNNIK and ROBINSON [3]) assume a missionary purpose behind the Gospel but MULDER thinks that the readers

---

[1]) MULDER, *o.c.* p. 251/252 ff. Mulder admits that we don't know much about the reactions of the Diaspora-Jews on the addition of the Schemonees're and probably these reactions differed from place to place. He thinks that there must have been confusion also among the Gentile Christians, because they were accustomed to a friendly relation between Jewish Christians and Jews. No one was more capable to give information than the apostle John, who had been in Palestine during the war (only afterwards he went to Ephesus) and therefore was well acquainted with the development on the political and religious field. He was able to answer the question (cf. Peter on the first day of Pentecost): what are we to do? John answered: the true Jew is he who confesses his faith into Jesus as the Christ, the Son of God, though the risks a definite break with his fellow-Jews. The examples in the Gospel (Nathanael/Thomas, Nicodemus, the man born as a blind, all Jews who were converted in spite of the opposition of their fellow-countrymen) were mentioned by John, in MULDER's opinion, as examples for all, who had to confess their faith also in difficult circumstances, as f.i. on that moment in the Diaspora, *o.c.* p. 255f. On this way John wants to comfort and encourage them in their spiritual crisis. In Revelation too we find traces of this hostility of the Jews against the Churches (Rev. ii 9; iii 9). MULDER agrees with Epiphanius (Adv. Haer. 2, 51, 12) —that John wrote his Gospel after his return from Patmos, in spite of the fact that this information has not been found in the writings of the earlier Fathers.

[2]) John wants to prove that the same elements which confused the minds in Asia Minor already played a rôle in the days Jesus preached his message of salvation to the Jews in Judaea, MULDER, *o.c.* p. 257. The elements stressed in this Gospel would then be the threat of excommunication from the synagogue, the discussions with fanatic Jews (cf. Jesus and the Pharisees in the Gospel) and even the threat of persecution.

[3]) ROBINSON compares John with Philo, who also addressed himself to Greeks (Hellenistic readers), but with a totally different aim and on a totally different way, "Destination", *o.c.* p. 123 f: "Philo was commending Judaism to Greek-speaking paganism, John was commending Christianity to Greek-speaking Judaïsm and between those two aims there is a world of difference", p. 124. John was not interested in the world of the speculative Hellenistic philosophy as Philo was, but he stood in the "pre-gnostic" stream of Jewish wisdom-mysticism, new light on which is constantly coming before us", *o.c.* p. 124.

were already Christians who had to be encouraged in order to keep their faith, that Jesus is the Christ, the Son of God. John did not find the other Gospels suitable enough for this purpose.

It is clear that the interpretation of John xx 31, "that you may believe" (R.S.V.) in the article of MULDER differs from that of VAN UNNIK and ROBINSON [1]).

This striking difference gives me reason for a critical approach. I'll restrict myself to the following issues:

1. The self-testimony of the Gospel.
2. The "Sitz im Leben".
3. The background of John's Gospel.
4. The address and purpose of the Fourth Gospel.

ad. 1. *The Self-testimony of the Gospel*

We find in John xx 31 a wellknown textcritical difficulty [2]), but I think this is not so important for our goal, because I agree with many scholars who concluded that the tense of the verbs in this verse are not decisive for the solution whether the Gospel was addressed to Christians or to non-Christians [3]).

The comparison with the first Epistle of John however, made f.i. by Robinson, convinced me that a missionary intention is most likely in this text. John also stresses in his Gospel the "holding'

---

[1]) MULDER does not stress this interpretation, but he clearly presupposes that the words mean a "remaining in the faith". ROBINSON on the contrary stressed the difference between John's Gospel and the first Epistle of John. In the latter it is clear that faith is already presupposed, cf. I John ii 21, 24, esp. v 13: "ὑμῖν ... τοῖς πιστεύουσιν". In the Gospel however the things are written "that you may believe", the faith being the goal just as the possession of eternal life through this faith, ROBINSON, *o.c.* p. 124. He rejects therefore the opinion of E. C. COLWELL, "John defends the Gospel" and states that this is true for the Epistle, but not for the Gospel. The material in this Gospel originated from "teaching within a Christian community in Judaea" living amidst the oppression and rejection by the Jews in that area, but the Gospel itself in its present form is a missionary appeal to Greek-speaking Diaspora-Jews, to win them for the faith that Jesus is the Christ. The author himself belongs now to these Jews in the Diaspora, ROBINSON, *o.c.* p. 124/125.

[2]) Some MSS (B, ℵ *, 157) have " πιστευητε", the others: "πιστευσητε". If the coniunct. Aor. was right, it could be an Aor. ingress., but this too is not necessary; cf. SCHNACKENBURG "Messiasfrage", *o.c.* p. 257; the editors of the Greek N.T. are divided, the versions too: R.V.S.: "that you may believe", but *New Engl. Bible* (Oxford/Cambr. U.P. 1961): "that you may hold the faith".

[3]) See above, note 1, p. 30. FEINE-BEHM-KÜMMEL, SCHNACKENBURG, also C. K. BARRETT, "Zweck", *o.c.* p. 258.

or „keeping" of the faith (esp. in the farewell-speeches) but then he sometimes uses the verb "μενειν" (viii 31; xv 4-10) [1]).

Other arguments against a missionary purpose as used f.i. by R. SCHNACKENBURG (the addition of the words "Son of God") [2]) and by H. MULDER (comparison with Peter's answer in Acts ii 37) did not change my opinion [3]). I would like to suggest now already that perhaps the pecularity of this Gospel, mixing facts and words of Jesus with own commentary and interpretation, points to the early use of the tradition in the first missionary preaching of the Church of which we find examples in Acts. I'll come back upon these things.

---

[1]) FEINE-BEHM-KÜMMEL points to these texts in order to prove that John did not have primarily a missionary aim, o.c. p. 158. But it is a fact that the context always deals with people who already believed (viii 31: Jews; xv 3: you are clean). Therefore these texts are not decisive for the exegesis of xx 31. For ἵνα with the coniunct., pointing to a not yet realized aim, cf. xiii 19.

[2]) R. SCHNACKENBURG, "Die Messiasfrage", o.c. p. 257. If the words "Son of God" only aimed to deepen the understanding of the messianic expectation of Jews, I could agree with SCHNACKENBURG that also Gentile-Christians could have been addressed, esp. in the light of Luke's writings, to which he refered. But the expression "Son of God" in John has the special element of legitimation: sent by God, fulfillment of God's promise. On this point exactly the unbelieving Jews opposed Jesus. I am agreeing with SCHNACKENBURG that John was in line with the tradition of the early Church in stressing the fulfillment of the O.T. promises in Jesus Christ. This explains the Christological interest of the Fourth Gospel, so much stressed by SCHNACKENBURG (p. 241ff, 245, 262). I agree that this does not exclude non-Jewish readers, but I'm doubting whether this would make a missionary purpose also difficult to accept. I admit that the farewell-speeches, whose missionary intention were doubted also by VAN UNNIK, are an integral part of the Gospel (SCHNACKENBURG, p. 262/263). Maybe we have not to make this dilemma for John: missionary or not! SCHNACKENBURG's thesis: "Das Joh-Ev. ist ein Buch für die Kirche und erschliesst nur in der Kirche seinen wahren Sinn und Gehalt" (p. 263), is at least as one-sided as the viewpoint of VAN UNNIK and ROBINSON, rejected by him.

[3]) MULDER compared the purpose of John with Peter's answer on the question in Acts ii 37: What are we to do?, o.c. p. 254. But it is clear that Peter spoke to non-Christians and asked for conversion, ii 38ff: a missionary situation. MULDER himself therefore also spoke about conversion and it seems that he does not exclude this motive in spite of his statement that the purpose of John was not primarily: missionary activity, in order to win Gentiles or Jews for the faith, o.c. p. 256. As examples of discussions and facts from Jesus' life, important for the Jewish Christians to whom John addressed himself, MULDER mentions (p. 255): Nathanael — but he had difficulties in accepting the fact that Jesus came from Nazareth—, Thomas, — but his doubt had nothing to do with the opposition of Jews, loyal to the Torah. I don't see how we could find in these descriptions "struggles of of Jewish Christians with Pharisaic scribes".

2. The "Sitz im Leben"

In spite of the great value of this term originating from the school of Formcriticism, not only on the field of source- and tradition-criticism, but also on that of redaction-criticism, there is in my opinion always the danger for those who use this term, that a stressing of the concrete life-situation of the Christian Church or of the evangelist in the days he wrote the Gospel, being the true "Sitz im Leben" of his book, closes the eyes of the scholars for the fact that the Gospels want to tell facts and words from Jesus' life and times.

I think we could recognize this danger in the redaction-critical works of those who used a theological motive to interpret the Gospels, e.g. LOHMEYER, MARXSEN and CONZELMANN [1]).

Especially those theologians who think that the Fourth Gospel is a theological reinterpretation written from the standpoint of the contemporary Church, sometimes consequently speak about a "projection backwards", as f.i. FENTON, and KÄSEMANN [2]).

The three authors I deal with here, do not speak about such a projection backwards, nevertheless sometimes I got the impression that John mentions contemporary situations, discussions and problems rather than facts from Jesus' times.

VAN UNNIK speaks about the "Sitz im Leben" of John, being his solution of the purpose of this Gospel: to bring the visitors of a synagogue in the Diaspora to belief in Jesus as the Messiah of Israel [3]). He states that the place of the disputes between John and the synagogue was somewhere in Asia Minor [4]). These disputes between Christians and Jews in John's days were in the mind of the author, when he wrote his Gospel, therefore a comparison with Justin's Dialogue with the Jew Trypho in the second century could be useful for VAN UNNIK.

Therefore I think SCHNACKENBURG rightly asked: "Wieweit spiegelt das Evangelium das Zusammentreffen des (joh.) Christentums mit dem Judentum seiner Umgebung wider?" And: "Sind

---

[1]) E. LOHMEYER, *Galiläa und Jerusalem*, 1936; W. MARXSEN, *Der Evangelist Markus*, 2A. 1959; H. CONZELMANN, "Die Mitte der Zeit" (*Stud. z. Theol. d. Lukas, Bh.Th.* 17), 4A. 1962.

[2]) J. C. FENTON, *Towards an Underst. of John*, cf. note 1, p. 36; KÄSEMANN: "eine Rückprojektion des Christus präsens in der Vergangenheit", *o.c.* p. II, p. 140.

[3]) VAN UNNIK, *o.c.* p. 410.

[4]) *Idem*, p. 409.

das Dinge die schon zu einem früheren Zeitpunkt der Traditions-
geschichte des Joh-Ev. als Problem aufgetaucht sind, oder erst im
christlich-jüdischen Streitgespräch um die ersten Jahrhundert-
wende, durch die Umgebung des Verfassers, ihre eigentliche
Schärfe erhielt ?" [1])

My objection against VAN UNNIK's hypothesis is not that the
Fourth Gospel has its own background, written with an eye on
the contemporary situation, but that he gives sometimes the
impression that the disputes between Jesus and "the Jews" were
in concreto the disputes between John and the Synagogue about
Jesus [2]).

ROBINSON speaks about the "Heimat" of the Johannine tradition,
South-Palestine, Judaea, the Christian missionary activity there [3]).

---

[1]) R. SCHNACKENBURG, "Messiasfrage", o.c. p. 260, 261. SCHNACKENBURG
admits the disputes between Christians and Jews in the 2d cent., o.c. p. 250.
He also agrees with the idea, that "ein zeitgeschichtliches Interesse mit
konkreten Anlässen" is to be found in John and refers to ideas of D. DAUBE,
The N.T. and Rabbinic Judaism, 1956, p. 308 ff, o.c. p. 260. But he doubts
whether the disputes about Jesus' Messiahship (as f.i. between Justin and
Trypho) urged the fourth evangelist too, because in John Jesus stresses
always that the Jews do not know his origin, because of their unbelief. It
is much more the christological interest of the evangelist himself, that marks
his Gospel, o.c. p. 251, 252.

[2]) Though John gives a free reproduction mixed with own interpretation,
I still believe that the disputes and discourses of Jesus have their basis in
a historical reality. The same objection I have against SCHNACKENBURG too,
who stated f.i. that possibly the withess of the Baptist about Jesus' pre-
existence was inserted by the evangelist in i 15, not only because of a polemical motive, but also because of his Christological interest, o.c. p. 245.
SCHNACKENBURG continues then: "Die göttliche Weisheit über deren'Funktion
man in hellenistischen Judentum spekulierte, der Logos über den man im
gebildeten Heidentum sprach, ist in Jesus von Nazareth gekommen, ist
in dieser geschichtlichen Person da gewesen, so hart und anstössig das auch
klingen mag: Das wollte das Christentum in die damalige Welt hineinrufen
und so seinen Christus in der Tiefe seines Wesens bekennen", o.c. p. 245/246.
I would like to add: therefore it was very important that the Christ, preached
by the Church in John's days, was the historical Jesus of Nazareth described
in the Gospels.

[3]) The address of the present form of the Gospel is however: Greek-
speaking Jews in the Diaspora and the purpose was to bring them to the
acceptance of Jesus as the Messiah, though " the people of Jerusalem and
their rulers did not recognize him" (Acts xiii 27), ROBINSON, "Destination",
o.c. p. 116, 119. Cf. SCHNACKENBURG's summary of ROBINSON's hypothesis:
"dass die joh. Sicht und Gestaltung aus einer Zeit stammt wo Joh. das Ev.
unter Juden verkündigt, schon um die Mitte des ersten Jahrhunderts". The
"Sitz im Leben" was: "christliche Mission unter den Juden von Judäa; in
seiner jetzigen Gestalt aber sei das Joh-Ev für die Mission unter den Diasporajuden gedacht", SCHNACKENBURG, o.c. p. 261.

He points to the disdain of Galilea in Judaean circles, but I think he exaggerates in stating "a recurrent and bitter altercation between Judaea and Galilea" [1]).

Usually "the Jews" in the Fourth Gospel are Judaeans, as ROBINSON stated, but he admitted himself that there are some exceptions. The solution for this phenomenon is simple, that the Fourth Gospel gives special attention to Jesus' ministry in Jerusalem and Judaea and therefore of course speaks more about the Judaeans than the Synoptics [2]).

Important for us now is the impression given by Robinson, that he thinks: the fact of the concentration of Jesus' ministry in Jerusalem and Judaea, in John, proves that the Johannine tradition came into existence in that area. I am doubting this kind of conclusion. Behind the tradition in this Gospel we find Jesus' own real ministry. That does not mean that I reject the idea that Judaea was a centre of Christian mission and that the tradition had a function and developed especially in the preaching in that area.

MULDER too distinguished between the background of the tradition in John's Gospel: Palestine after the war, where John still lived for some time and the address of the Gospel: Christians in Asia Minor after the addition of the Eighteen Prayers with the Birkat-ha-minim. He points to the dominant and fanatical rôle of the Pharisees and explains the lack of any trace of mission among the Gentiles by the isolation of Jews and Jewish Christians in Palestine after the war [3]). Because of the topographical indications in John, MULDER concludes: John placed the story in his Gospel against the background of the situation after the war. Jesus' preaching goes on in his Gospel till a society who had got a new shape through a series of catastrophal events [4]). However, why did

---

[1]) Cf. Joh. i 46; iv 44 f; vii 41, 52. In i 46 we hear a certain view of Nathanael about Galilea, but his doubt was in my opinion caused not so much by his contempt for Nazareth as well by his knowledge of the O.T. prophecy. In iv 44 f Galilea is called Jesus' homeland, we find an allusion to the Synoptic tradition of his rejection in Nazareth. That the Galileans give Him welcome because they had seen his works in Jerusalem, does not say anything about the contrast Galilea-Judaea. In vii 41, 52 Galilea is contrasted with Bethlehem, again based upon the O.T. prophecy.

[2]) Cf. ROBINSON's arguments, o.c. p. 118, which did not convince me. I agree with him that i 11 points to Israel, but there is no reason to restrict this to Judaea only.

[3]) MULDER, o.c. p. 239, speaks of a proper soil for the origin of the Fourth Gospel.

[4]) MULDER, o.c. p. 250.

John not address his Gospel to his Palestinian fellow-countrymen, but to the Diaspora-Jews? "What made John in Ephesus write with so many details about the bitterness and hostility, which had risen in the Jewish country between the Jews and Jewish Christians?" (own translation, A.W.) [1]. This goes too far for me. I agree that the preaching of Jesus' words and deeds in the Gospels functions against the background of the contemporary situation and it is clear that MULDER uses expressions which are the contrary of "projection backwards", but I'd like to ask: did the evangelist write about a situation so many years after Jesus' death, i.c. the hostility between Jews and Jewish Christians, or about Jesus' ministry on this earth?

The same difficulty I have with MULDER's argumentation about the position of the Pharisees in the Fourth Gospel [2]. Suppose it is true that in Asia Minor in John's days, we could meet an almost similar situation as in Jesus' times, when they rejected his Person and message and even though it is then probable that John selected his material against this background, I'm doubting whether in the hesitation of Samuel the Little reciting the Birkat-ha-minim, could be found an allusion to the crypto-believers among the Jewish leaders and that the Gospel paid so much attention to them, because there were still many of them in John's days [3].

3. *The Background of John's Gospel:* how to explain some peculiar characteristics of this Gospel?

a. *The Gospel of John and "the Gentiles"*

We saw already that both ROBINSON and MULDER stressed the fact that "the Gentiles" are not mentioned expressis verbis in this Gospel. But there is too a remarkable universalism in the Fourth Gospel, shown f.i. by the frequent use of the word "κοσμος" [4].

---

[1] *Idem*, p. 251.

[2] SCHNACKENBURG expressed himself more cautiously, also refering to the Birkat-ha-minim (cf. the literature mentioned by him on p. 249, note 28): "auch wenn der Bann und die übrigen Massnahmen (11 : 57, Anzeigepflicht) zur Zeit Jesu *möglich* waren, so lässt sich nicht übersehen, dass der Evangelist-schon durch die sprachliche Gleichformulierung — von der damaligen Bannandrohung eine Linie zum späteren Ausschluss aus der Gemeinde Israel ziehen wollte. Die joh. Darstellung bewegt sich also auf verschiedenen Ebenen und verfolgt sicher mehr als ein Ziel", "Messiasfrage", *o.c.* p. 249.   [3] MULDER, *o.c.* p. 245.

[4] Cf. ROBINSON: "There are no more universalistic sayings in the N.T., than in the Fourth Gospel", "Destination", *o.c.* p. 112.

ROBINSON thinks that he could speak here only of a "cosmic perspective" and he interprets the word "κοσμος" by: "not the world outside Judaism, but the world which God loves and the world which fails to respond, be it Jew or Gentile". Essentially however it is only the Jewish world, which comes into the picture [1]).

MULDER accepts the acquaintance of John with the salvation of Gentiles and even points to allusions in the Gospel [2]). But I'm doubting whether the universalism of the Fourth Gospel has got enough weight on this way. I spoke already about the argument of ROBINSON and MULDER, that Paul used the symbol of the olive-tree and John that of the vine-tree. The purpose for which the metaphor was used is too different in the both texts (Romans xi and John 15), to draw any conclusion of the kind ROBINSON and MULDER proposed.

The texts in John's Gospel in which the Gentiles seem to come into the picture, have also been explained by ROBINSON, VAN UNNIK and MULDER on a way they could fit well with their solution, But did they give the right interpretation?

We spoke already about John x 16 [3]). ROBINSON refered to the O.T. background in Ez. xxxiv, xxxvii 21-28; Jer. xxiii 1-8 and xxxi 1-10. If we dealt with a text as Matt. xxvi 31, I would agree with him, but I'm doubting whether these O.T. texts are a background in John x. I prefer to point to Psalm xxiii, where we don't find the motive of the gathering of the dispersed sheep. I cannot find enough evidence to restrict John x 16, "the other sheep . . . not belonging to this fold" to Diaspora-Jews only [4]).

---

[1]) Cf. the critique of SCHNACKENBURG, concluding: "Wie denn auch sei, eine Missionsschrift für Juden müsste doch anders aussehen. Hinzu kommen die oft festgestellten auch von uns oben gestreiften *universalistischen* Züge im Joh-Ev. die ein unverkennbares interesse auch an den Nichtjuden bekunden. So wird man die einseitige Zweckbestimmung, das Ev. sei als Missionsschrift für Diasporajuden gedacht, schwerlich annehmen können", "Messiasfrage", *o.c.* p. 260.

[2]) MULDER, *o.c.* p. 237.

[3]) See above, note 1. p. 42.

[4]) Cf. also the critique of SCHNACKENBURG, "Messiasfrage", *o.c.* p. 258/259. The contrast between "this "and "the other" seems to me to be deeper than that between Palestinian and Diaspora-Jews. Moreover, the context, Jesus' sacrifice, makes a universalistic meaning: salvation for the whole world, very likely in John. I think, generally spoken, that "κοσμος" in John has a broader meaning than the Jewish world. ROBINSON mentioned already the double aspect of the word: object of God's love and hostility against God and Christ, "the evil world"; cf. also O. BÖCHER, *o.c.* p. 27/28 and A. WIND,

Van Unnik and Robinson paid much attention to xi 52, making
a difference between "ἔθνος" (nation): Palestinian Jews, and
"scattered children of God": Diaspora-Jews. I agree with the
critique of Schnackenburg who thinks that "ἔθνος" being not a
geographical but an ethnic term, means the whole Jewish people
and "children of God", being a theological term (cf. 1:12), refers to
the whole Church, believing Jews and Gentiles [1]).

Robinson thought that "the Greeks" in the Fourth Gospel were:
Greek-speaking Diaspora-Jews [2]). Again I could agree with
Schnackenburg, that in vii 35 the interpretation of "οἱ Ἕλληνες"
as Greek-speaking Diaspora-Jews, "nirgends belegt ist" [3]). Indeed,
we don't read in xii 20f that the Greeks who came to Jesus, were
merely God-fearers or former Gentiles, but Robinson too could not
prove that they were Jews! This distinction is clear f.i. in Acts vi 1:
Greek speaking Jews, but there we find the term "Ἑλληνισταί"
and not "Ἕλληνες" as in John xii [4]). The probable solution is, that
"the Greeks" in xii 20f were God-fearing non-Jews, Greeks who
lived in a close contact with the synagogue.

So we can understand why Philip hesitated to pass the request
of the Greeks immediately on to Jesus, xii 22. Against this background we also understand the word "all", xii 32. Nevertheless,
there is a remarkable difference between the Synoptic Gospels and

---

Leven en Dood in h. Ev. v. Joh. en in de Serat Dewarutji, 1956, p. 69f. There
is yet a third aspect: "κοσμος" as created world, dwellingplace of mankind,
scenery of the history of salvation, being again in John a very universalistic
word; cf. i 9, 10. It is my conviction that the cosmos in i 10 has not to be
identified with "his own realm" in i 11, pointing to Israel: *Leven en Dood*,
o.c. p. 71f, 74. This too makes it clear that John from the beginning paid
attention to the relation between Christ and the non-Jewish world.

[1]) Schnackenburg, o.c. p. 258: "Der Evangelist enthüllt hier sehr deutlich
seine universalistische Tendenz, obwohl er selbst von Judentum herkommt".
We find again here that the universal salvation is by the vicarious death
of Christ.

[2]) Robinson, o.c. p. 111f, 117.

[3]) Schnackenburg, o.c. p. 259. "to teach the Greeks" probably means
Jewish mission among the Greeks, to make them proselytes.

[4]) I admit that we are not allowed to conclude too much here, because
Luke has another terminology. I mention only this difference because
Robinson made the same comparison: "The "Ἕλληνες" are for him the
Greek-speaking Jews living outside Palestine in distinction from the
"Ἑλληνισταί" in Acts vi 1; ix 29, who are Greek-speaking Jews resident in
Palestine", p. 117. I agree with Schnackenburg who thought that these
Greeks were "(Halb)-Proselyte griechischer Sprache und Herkunft", o.c.
p. 259.

John regarding "the Gentiles", for which we have to find an explanation.

The question is, whether the hypotheses of ROBINSON and MULDER, that the Gospel, which had come into existence in South-Judaea, without contact with the Gentiles, later was addressed to Jews, so that it was not necessary to mention the Gentiles, or: that the Gospel came into existence in the post-war situation of an isolated Palestine and was addressed to Christians living in a conflict with the synagogue, the question is whether these two hypotheses are the only possible explanation of the omission of "the Gentiles" in John, or not.

I'm doubting whether the development of the mission among the Gentiles, the problems of Paul, the application of the Torah upon Gentile Christians (Galatians) were absolutely unknown to Jewish Christians in South-Palestine. We get a different impression from Acts: cf. the Apostolic Council, the events around Paul's emprisonment etc. Is it true that Jewish Christians after the war in Palestine didn't know anything about the development outside the country [1] ? How was exactly the situation of the Jewish Christians after the war in Jerusalem and its environment? We don't know very much about it. If this war played such an important rôle as the background of the Fourth Gospel, we immediately come across the problem: why don't we find any direct indication of this war in this Gospel? This problem becomes even more difficult if John himself was in Palestine during the war, as MULDER states. Many authors think that the Synoptic Gospels give more indications about the war than John [2]. A new problem is: how many Christians fled to Pella when Jerusalem was besieged—if this flight at least was a historical fact. What did it mean for the relation between Jews and Jewish Christians? [3]. Again some questions came into my mind,

---

[1] MULDER, o.c. p. 238, 240.

[2] They refer a.o. to Matt. xxii 7; Luke xxi 20f. I am aware of the fact that these texts are still in discussion, in relation to the date of the Synoptic Gospels. D. GUTHRIE rightly pointed to the denial of any predictive power of Jesus, in the apocalyptic chapters, by many critical investigators, o.c. p. 43. 70, 106ff. But if one does not date the Synoptic Gospels before or after 70 AD on the ground of these texts, still the difference with John is remarkable.

[3] MAC GIFFERTH states that the definitive break between Jews and Jewish Christians took place when the Jewish Christians fled to Pella and were called traitors by their fellow-Jews, Mc GIFFERTH, A History of Christianity in the Apost. Age, 1914, p. 562ff; cf. also C. B. BAVINCK, "De Ver-

reading in MULDER's article that also in Asia Minor among the Diaspora-Jews, the relations between Jews and Jewish Christians were still so close at the end of the first century, that the Birkat-ha-minim could cause so much confusion within the Christian Churches, not only among the Jewish but also among the Gentile Christians [1]).

We could ask, whether this distinction between Jewish and Gentile Christians still counted, many years after Paul's letter to the Ephesians and his plea to break down the barrier [2]). We don't hear much in the N.Test. (except in the earliest time of the N.T. Church, in Acts) about a friendly relation between Jewish Christians and the Synagogue.

Anyhow, I think that the typical universalism of John's Gospel could be explained also by different solutions, e.g. a very early dating of the tradition written down in this Gospel, even before the mission among the Gentiles was fully developed or by a very late date, many years after Paul, in a time the distinction between mission among Jews and among Gentiles did not count any more. Or possibly a combination of both solutions? I'll come back upon these suggestions.

b. *The Gospel of John and "the Jews", esp. the Pharisees*

MULDER was convinced that the Pharisees played a special rôle in the Fourth Gospel (fanatical opposition) compared with the Synoptics [3]). All the groupings we find in the Synoptic Gospels, as Herodians, Sadducees, disappeared in John, only the Pharisees are mentioned [4]). "The Jews" are not always opponents of Jesus, but

houding v. Kerk en Israel tot aan de Reformatie (relation Church-Israel till the Reformation"), *De Heerbaan* 23, 1970, p. 67f: BAVINCK too has the opinion that the friendly relation between Jews and Jewish Christians couldn't have lasted a long time, because of the problems of rivalry and the missionary activity of the Christians, though from the side of the Rabbins the break with the Christians became definite by the addition of the Birkat-ha-minim. BAVINCK refered to K. H. RENGSTORF in *Kirche u. Synagoge*, and J. JOCZ, *The Jewish People and Jesus Christ*; cf. also *Th.Rdsch.* 35, H. 1, p. 67f.

[1]) Cf. MULDER, *o.c.* p. 252f.
[2]) Cf. GUTHRIE, *N.T. Introduction, The Pauline Epistles*, repr. 1964, p. 108, 122/123. GUTHRIE warns against too easy conclusions regarding the relation between Jewish and Gentile Christians.
[3]) The other evangelists speak about encounters with foreigners, John gives more attention to the discussions with Jews, esp. with the Pharisees, MULDER, *o.c.* p. 236.
[4]) MULDER, *o.c.* p. 241.

the attitude of the Pharisees is irreconcilable [1]). This is for MULDER again an argument to think of a post-war situation, because the Pharisees were the only grouping who got off the war with a whole skin [2]).

I'm however doubting whether this special rôle of the Pharisees in the Fourth Gospel, compared with the Synoptics, could be vindicated. In the Synoptics the Pharisees are also the opponents of Jesus [3]).

[1]) MULDER, *o.c.* p. 241/242. The Pharisees take measures to bann people from the synagogue. SCHNACKENBURG remarks rightly however: "Die ungläubigen und Jesus feindlich gesinnten "Juden" sind nicht etwa nur die führenden Kreise der Synhedristen und der Pharisäer (obwohl es diese mit Vorzug sind)", "Messiasfrage", *o.c.* p. 259.

[2]) MULDER, *o.c.* p. 243. The Pharisees in John are always loyal to the Torah. They built a new apparatus for the study of the law in Jamnia and concentrated on a consolidation and stock-taking of the spiritual heritage of the Jews, MULDER, p. 244.

[3]) A summary of the statistics regarding the terms (plural or singular), used for Jewish leaders (whether opponents of Jesus or not), in all four Gospels. shows the following result:

a. *Pharisees* We meet them in all four Gospels.
Not combined with other groupings, in Mark 6 ×, Matt. 11 ×, Luke 17 × and John 14 ×. John is therefore no exception.
Combined with "chief priests": in Matt. 2 ×, in John 5 × (always as authorities).
Combined with "scribes" (or lawyers): Mark 2 ×, Matt. 10 ×, (esp. Matt. 23), Luke 6 × and in John only in viii 3. In stead of "γραμματεις" Luke uses 3 × "νομικοι", a term used also 4 × without combination in Luke and once in Matt. Remarkable is the expression "scribes of the Pharisees", once in Mark and once in Luke (parallel-text).

b. Scribes (lawyers): "γραμματεις": except in John viii 3 not in the Fourth Gospel. The Synoptics have each 3 × the combination: chief priests and scribes. Without combination we find the word 8 × in Mark 4 × in Matt. and 2 × in Luke.
Combined with "elders", only in Matt. xxvi 57.
The combination chief priests, elders and scribes, we find in the Syn. Gospels only, as an expression for the Jewish Council. Sometimes Matt. has: chief priests and the whole Council and Luke: chief priests and officers (of the temple-police). Sometimes also: chief-priests and elders. (Matt. and Luke)
I think, our conclusion has to be, that there was a variety of terminology in the Gospels for Jewish leaders. The term "chief-priests" we find again in all four Gospels (Mark 4 ×, Matt. 3 ×, Luke 1 ×, John 5 ×). The term "elders" (without combination) we find 4 × in John, but in Luke too.
Perhaps we could say that John prefers the combination "chief priests and Pharisees" while in the Synoptics the combination "chief priests and scribes" prevails. This could be explained by the fact that the Pharisees in the Fourth Gospel always are "lawyers", loyal to the Torah. Perhaps we could then find in the term "chief priests" the johannine expression for the family of the High Priest, the sect of the Sadducees who played an important rôle in the process against Jesus and later against the Church.

We meet the Herodians only once in the Synoptic Gospels, in a special context, while the Sadducees too play a very unimportant rôle, compared with the Pharisees [1]). The activities of the High Priest and his family in the Passion narrative of John do not differ from the data of the Synoptic Gospels.

c. *The Topography of John*

Could the topographical pecularities of the Fourth Gospel give us a clear evidence of a post-war situation, as MULDER suggests ? [2]). He gives interesting and impressive examples as f.i. the name of Tiberias, the cloister of Solomon, recognizable as ruins a.o. But again the question is, whether different explanations are possible or not. Moreover there are many striking names of places, not found in the Synoptic Gospels, who are not explained at all by a

---

Is it true that the Pharisees are more fanatical in their opposition, in John than in the Synoptics ? Apart from their relation to John the Baptist and from the fact that Luke mentions some dinners of Pharisees who invited Jesus, I could find only a few texts in the Synoptics in which the opposition against Jesus was not the important motive, e.g. Matt. xxiii 2; Luke xiii 31; xvii 20. In all other texts the Pharisees are in discussion with Jesus, attempt to test him, play a rôle in the process against Jesus, were warned by Jesus or the disciples were warned against them. Therefore I'm doubting whether their attitude in John is more fanatical and hostile than in the Synoptic Gospels.

[1]) The Sadducees and the Herodians indeed are not found in John. But the Herodians appear only once in Matt. (in connection with the problem of the paying of taxes, together with the Pharisees) and 3 times in Mark (one parallel-text with Matt. xxii, plotting to kill Jesus, iii 6 and in Jesus' warning against their leaven and that of the Pharisees, viii 15). In the paralleltext in Matt. xvi we find Jesus warning against the leaven of the Pharisees and the Sadducees!

The Sadducees too do not play an important rôle in the Synoptics: we meet them in connection with discussions about the resurrection from the dead, Matt. xxii 23, 34 (is Mark xii 18; Luke xx 27) not mentioned by John and in combination with the Pharisees only in Matt. (relation to the Baptist and Matt. xvi). I'll not deny the fact that these groupings are not mentioned by John, but point to the fact that John differs from the Synoptics in so many things because of his special background and purpose. Therefore I'm doubting whether this fact could be used as a proof of a post-war situation. Remarkable is the frequent use of the term "the Jews", usually in a negative, hostile sense. They are represented specially by the opposing Jewish leaders and represent the "evil world". This feature of John cannot be explained fully by the assumption of a post-war situation only. I doubt too whether ROBINSON's stress on the divided Judaism could help us to explain this term. The Synoptics give also an impression of divided Judaism, facing Jesus.

[2]) MULDER, *o.c.* p. 245-250.

post-war situation, e.g. the frequent use of Kana, the names Aenon near to Salem, Bethany beyond the Jordan a.o.[1]).

Solomon's Cloister is also found in Acts iii 11; v 12, as the place where the Christians used to meet and to preach, therefore a place wellknown in the early tradition. Is it allowed to explain the omission of the name Tiberias in the Synoptics by the fact that Jews who were loyal to the Torah wanted to suppress this name? [2]).

Is perhaps the fact that John mentions the distance between Bethany and Jerusalem (xi 18) to be explained by his mentioning of two places with the name of Bethany and not by the Jewish war? [3]).

We find different interpretations of John's topography, which seem to me at least as acceptable as MULDER's solution, e.g. the hypothesis that John's accuracy has its ground in his aim to be historically and geographically reliable as an eyewitness (19:35) [4]).

Or the possibility that the central theme of the incarnation, that the Word became flesh, i 14, means for John: Jesus the Messiah, the Son of God dwelled among us, worked and lived here, therefore the places where He put his footsteps are very important from a salvation-historical point of view [5]).

---

[1]) About Kana cf. ii 1, 11; iv 46; xxi 2; Aenon: iii 23; Bethany i 28.

[2]) MULDER, o.c. p. 246.

[3]) Cf. MULDER, o.c. p. 247.

[4]) The reliability of the Johann. tradition, esp. its topography has been affirmed by the archaeology and is recognized by more and more authors. Cf. o.a. R. D. POTTER, "Topography and Archaeology in the Fourth Gospel", Stud. Ev. I TU 73, o.c. 329-337, who concludes: John "knew the Palestine that they have learned to know" who lived there a long time, p. 335; cf. also A. M. HUNTER, Rec. Trends o.c.: "whoever applied the topography must have known Jerusalem and its neighbourhood before AD 65", p. 222; S. SMALLEY, "New Light", o.c.: the archaeology "upholds the reliability of the joh. tradition in its singular record of Palestinian topography as well as of Jewish institutions existing before AD 70", p. 73; cf. H. N. RIDDERBOS, Opbouw en Strekking, o.c. about the accurate and detailed knowledge of Jewish life in the period before the fall of Jerusalem, p. 224, 225f; GUTHRIE is right, I think, in stating that the great number of places in South-Palestine, found in John, simply depends on John's stressing of Jesus' ministry in Judaea, p. 226, note 4.

[5]) Cf. f.i. D. MOLLAR, "Remarques s.l. Vocabulaire spatial du 4ième Év.", Stud. Ev, I, o.c. p. 321-328, who speaks of an "espace religieuse", the connection between a place, a person and a scenery, and concludes: "La signification religieuse de ces lieux s'accomplit dans la présence et les paroles de Jésus; l'espace Palestinien transfiguré par la gloire du Verbe fait chair, se charge de signification nouvelle", p. 322, cf. also p. 325f.

4. *The address of the Fourth Gospel: Jews in the Greek Diaspora?*

We saw in the survey of the answers given on the question of the purpose of John's Gospel already that this point is still in discussion whether the Gospel was addressed to Jews or to Greeks (Gentiles). The difficulty is a.o. that John explains Jewish customs, uses expressions as "a festival of the Jews" etc. I'm doubting whether the explication of ROBINSON that John wrote to Diaspora-Jews who were no longer acquainted with the Palestinian way of life and that for John every detail was significant out of a theological motive, is satisfying [1]). Is it allowed to assume such a gap between Diaspora-Jews and Palestinian Jews, so that purification- and burial-ritual had to be explained? [2]).

Moreover, why did John use the word "logos" in his Prologue in that very singular hypostatic sense? Could this term be attractive for Jewish readers too? C. H. DODD used many arguments for his conclusion that the address was not Jewish but Greek-Hellenistic readers [3]). Therefore we could understand that some authors hesitate to follow ROBINSON and VAN UNNIK, accepting exclusively Jewish readers as the aimed address of John's Gospel. They do not want to be so one-sided. I mention f.i. SMALLEY and SCHNACKENBURG [4]).

---

[1]) Cf. ROBINSON, "Dest., *o.c.* p. 123:" every detail is seen by him as supremely significant for the sign and its interpretation. He is concerned that nothing shall be missed which reveals Jesus as the true fulfillment of Judaism". SCHNACKENBURG rightly doubted this argument, because it was a common tradition in the early Church to prove that Jesus fulfilled the O.T. promises, "Messiasfrage", *o.c.* p. 257, 259. A totally different solution for the frequent use of the expression "feast of the Jews" was given by L. MOWRY, "The Dead Sea Scrolls and the Background for the Gospel of John", *The Bibl. Archaeologist* 17, 1954, p. 87 f: a polemical intention against the official Jewish calendar.

[2]) Cf. DAVIES' opposition against MONTEFIORI regarding the problem of Paul's background: whether rabbinic-Palestinian, or Hellenistic, Diaspora-Jewish, W. D. DAVIES, *Paul and Rabbinic Judaism*, 1965.

[3]) C. H. DODD, "Interpretation", *o.c.* p. 8 ff; cf. also GUTHRIE, *o.c.* p. 252 f. Regarding "logos", I still keep my opinion, defended in my dissertation, that the remarkable use of this word has to be understood not against a Hellenistic background, but against the development within the O.T. and N.T. kerygma; cf. about this issue also a.o. E. HAENCHEN, "Probleme d. joh. Prologs", *Z.Th.K.* 60, 1963, p. 305-334; he saw the Prologue as the direct start of the Gospel, the revision of a hymn (p. 309), by the redactor who added ch. 21 (p. 328 ff) and compared "logos" with "spät-jüdische Aussagen über die Weisheit" (p. 313), Philo and Paul (p. 314 f). It is impossible to deal with these problems in a deeper way, in this article.

[4]) Cf. also note 1 on p. 29 above; S. SMALLEY, "New Light", *o.c.* p. 39, in agreement with C. F. D. MOULE (*Intention*); he admits that John starts with

There are still many authors who defend the thesis that Greek Hellenistic circles are the address of the Fourth Gospel [1]).

This brings me to the already mentioned discussion, which is still going on about the relation between the Fourth Gospel and Gnosticism or pre-Gnosticism, Jewish or Hellenistic and the relation to Qumran [2]). It would take too much place to deal with these problems in a more detailed way, but it is clear that the affinity f.i. with the Dead Sea Scrolls has been as enthousiastically defended as radically rejected [3]).

---

the Jews, wherever they could be found, but "that he begins and ends with the Jews of the dispersion as Dr. ROBINSON would have us to believe, seems to me most unlikely"; he points to DODD's expression: "the universe of discourse" in which John's thoughts move, to the translation of so many Jewish terms (Rabbi, Rabbouni, even Messiah) and his explication of Jewish customs (that the Passover was a festival of the Jews, vi 4 cf. xviii 38), things which could not be unknown for even the most hellenized Jew, SMALLEY, p. 39. SCHNACKENBURG also warns against the danger of onesidedness, assuming that the Gospel was addressed to the Church and he concludes: "im letzten spricht er nicht einzelne Gruppen an, seien es Juden- oder Heidenchristen, Palästinenser oder Menschen in der Diaspora, Samariter, Griechen oder andere Hellenisten, sondern *alle Glaubenden als solche*, alle "Kinder Gottes" (vgl. i 12), alle zu Christus und Gott Gehörigen", "Messias- frage", *o.c.* p. 262. He does not exclude different secondary motives too, e.g. polemics against the disciples of the Baptist, apologetical motives against attacks of Judaism and even rejection of a gnostic heretical view of Christ or to win gnostics for the Christian Saviour, *o.c.* p. 264.

[1]) See f.i. the survey of GUTHRIE, *o.c.* p. 25055, 252ff, cf. above note 2, p. 37; also E. FASCHER, "Christol. u. Gnosis im viert. Ev.", *Th.L.Z.* 93, p. 721-730, pointing to iv 42, "Saviour of the world", a title from hellenistic eschatology; he saw in the Gospel, a demythologisation of the gnostic myth: the Word became flesh; E. HAENCHEN, "Neuere Lit. z. d. Joh. briefe", *Th. Rdsch. NF.* 26, 1960: the Fourth Gospel is not gnostic though "es in die Welt der Gnostiker hineinspricht", p. 276, 288; E. KÄSEMANN (review of BARRETT's comment.), *o.c.* II p. 145: "Sicher steht Joh. i. Zuge seiner hellen. Umwelt in welcher die präsentische Eschatologie immer stärkeres Gewicht erlangt"; KÄSEMANN thinks that John doesn't show any interest in the conflict around the Torah, p. 151 and he stresses the worldwide "Aufgabe" of the evangelist, p. 179; O. BÖCHER does not make a clear choice but he thinks that "jüdische Apokalyptiker" are more likely the address than "Hellenistische Gnostiker", *o.c.* p. 17, note 43.

[2]) Cf. above note 3, p. 36 — note 2, p. 37.

[3]) Cf. a.o. H. BRAUN, "Qumran u. d. N.T. *o.c.* vol. I p. 96-138, II p. 118- 144; S. SMALLEY, *o.c.* p. 39f; A. M. HUNTER, *o.c.* p. 166f; H. N. RIDDERBOS speaks about Qumran as a rich source of material for comparison, proving that many Johannine terms and motives have their origin on Palestinian soil, *o.c.* p. 38/39; RIDDERBOS refers to K. G. KUHN, "Joh. ev. u. d. Qumran- texte" in Neotest. u. Patristica, *Suppl. Nov. T.* VI 1962, p. 111-122; G. QUISPEL, "L'Évangile de Jean et la Gnose", *Rech. Bibl.* III. L'Év. de Jean, 1958 p. 197ff; P. BENOIT, "Qumran et le N.T.", *N.T. St.* 7, 1961, p. 276ff.

Van Unnik said rightly that the relation between John and Qumran is a decisive issue for the future research about the Fourth Gospel [1]). Therefore I have to ask now: what relation does f.i. Mulder's solution have with these problems regarding Qumran and Gnosticism? I mentioned already the remarkable fact that both Robinson and Mulder only refered to Qumran as an example of an isolated Jewish community in Palestine [2]).

There are many questions about the affinity of the Fourth Gospel with the Testaments of the Twelve Patriarchs, the Odes of Solomon, the Gnostic myth, reconstructed by Bultmann, its relation to Jewish apocalyptics and heterodox Judaism etc. In my opinion these problems have to get attention too, if we speak about the purpose and the address of the Fourth Gospel [3]).

How could the encouragement of Jewish Christians who were banned from the synagogue, be combined with the dualistic Johannine terminology? If these two things are not excluding each other, the relation still has to be explored [4]).

It is clear that in spite of the enchaining and sometimes surprising arguments and solutions given by the three authors I dealt with,

---

[1]) Van Unnik, o.c. p. 383/384. The problem is f.i.: was John a disciple of the Qumran-community? Cf. also the Dutch article of Quispel, "Het Joh. ev. en de Gnosis", Ned.Theol.T. 11, 1956/57, p. 173-203.

[2]) Mulder, o.c. p. 240; Robinson, Destination, o.c. p. 116. In his article: "The Baptism of John and the Qumran-community", Twelve N.T.St. o.c. p. 11-27 and in "The New Look", o.c. p. 99f, Robinson relates the johann. tradition with Qumran by the link of the disciples of the Baptist; cf. also L. Mowry, o.c. p. 78-97; rightly Mulder pointed to the difference between the isolation of Qumran and of Palestine after the war, but in my opinion this difference is so essential that we cannot even compare the two. I'm doubting whether the influence of the Essenes was so great that they impressed the example of isolation upon the Jewish people, as Mulder thinks, o.c. p. 241.

[3]) Cf. about these things also E. Stauffer, Theol. d. N.T. 4A. 1948, 1.318ff; idem, "Probleme d. Priestertradition", Th.L.Z. 81, 1956, p. 135-150; E. Haenchen, "Gab es eine vor-christl. Gnosis?", Z.Th.K. 49, 1952, p. 316-349; B. Reicke, "Traces of Gnosticism", o.c. p. 137-141 (he used the term "pre-Gnosticism") cf. p. 141; O. Böcher, "Dualismus", o.c. p. 11ff, who also dealt with the O.T., the Test. 12 Patr. and Qumran; about the affinity with the Odes of Solomon, cf. a.o. R. M. Grant, "The Odes of Solomon and the Church of Antioch", J.B.L. 63, 1944, p. 363-377; L. Mowry, o.c. p. 86 sought a common background in Damascus.

[4]) Mulder stressed the johannine motive of the conflict between Jesus, the Church and the world, cf. f.i. p. 257. In my opinion this is only one of the motives in this Gospel and perhaps not even the most important one.

the questionmarks around the purpose and address of the Fourth Gospel still did not yet vanish.

I did not discuss deeply all the problems regarding Joh's Gospel and its own character, that was impossible. There is only one more issue which has to be touched now, that is the relation between John and the Synoptic tradition.

MULDER presupposed that John was acquainted with the Synoptic Gospels, but did not find them suitable for his purpose [1]).

After the research of some scholars as f.i. GARDNER SMITH, many are doubting this thesis and point to the independency of the Johannine tradition [2]). Personally I am convinced that John at least knew the tradition behind the Synoptic Gospels and that he used this material on his own way, related to his purpose and his own time and added the information he had collected himself as an eyewitness. Gratefully we could state that more and more authors recognize the fact that we find very old tradition in the Fourth Gospel.

Some Conclusions and Suggestions

It is remarkable that so many concrete answers given on questions regarding the Gospel of John prove to be one-sided. I

---

[1]) MULDER, *o.c.* p. 256. They were from an earlier date and did not touch the shocking problems in recent times.

[2]) P. GARDNER SMITH, *o.c.*; cf. als a.o. A. M. Perry, "Is John an Alexandr. Gospel?", *J.B.L.* 63, 1944, p. 99-106, esp. p. 101; R. E. BROWN, "Introd. commentary on John," *Anchor-Bible* 29, 1966 and the review of this book by T. HOLTZ, *Th.L.Z.* 93, p. 348-350; J. A. T. ROBINSON, "New Look", *o.c.* p. 96; E. HAENCHEN, "Joh. Probleme", *Z.Th.K.* 56, 1959, p. 19-54; O. BÖCHER, *o.c.* p. 17: in John we find "eine Fülle älteres und u. U. recht verschiedenen Traditionsmaterials verarbeitet"; BÖCHER refers to SCHULZ, *o.c.* p. 151 and thinks that John did not know the Synoptics, there is no relation to them, only: "Die Parallelen zu synopt. Berichten bezeugen die Abhängigkeit d. Joh. nicht von d. Synoptikern sondern "von der mündliche überlieferten festgeformten Urkatechese" " (cf. E. RUCKSTUHL, *Die liter. Einheit d. Joh. ev.* 1951, p. 219); J. A. BAILEY, "The Tradition common to the Gospel of Luke and John", *Suppl.Nov. T*, VII, 1963, assumes that John at least knew Luke, p. 113; the discussion is going on; cf. the survey a.o. of A. M. HUNTER, *Recent Trends*, *o.c.* p. 219 f (HUNTER assumes: "All we may safely say now is that St. John was generally familiar with the oral tradition which was worked into shape in the Synoptics, but that he went his own masterful way in writing the Gospel"; Hunter tries to prove that also the chronological-historical frame of John fits with the frame of Mark, p. 220 ff); D. GUTHRIE, *o.c.* p. 260, 262-275; FEINE-BEHM-KÜMMEL, *o.c.* p. 136-139: probably John knew Mark and Luke; S. SMALLEY, *o.c.* p. 36 f, 42 ff: "the Johannine tradition is independent of the other Gospels".

could agree with the exegesis of John xx 31 by VAN UNNIK and was convinced too that the Gospel primarily has a missionary purpose. Nevertheless we saw that SCHNACKENBURG mentioned some strong contra-arguments. The fare-well-speeches, the stress on "holding the faith" and other elements give me the impression that probably this dilemma is a false one: missionary or for the Church. We have to drop it. VAN UNNIK, ROBINSON and MULDER collected many arguments to prove that the address of the Gospel must have been Jewish readers.

Nevertheless, the universalistic character of this Gospel, its expressions (festival of the Jews), its explanation of Jewish customs etc. point to a wider circle of readers. Probably we have to drop again a false dilemma.

There is some difference of opinion, whether the Gospel, which shows a real familiarity with the Jewish country and life, points to a pre- or to a post-war situation.

How could we explain the remarkable terminology, e.g. the antitheses "light-darkness, life-death a.o." and its own mode of thinking? Perhaps against the background of a certain—by the different scholars differently defined—movement within Judaism? But does that mean, that maybe also the address could be circles which were attracted by this way of thinking and mode of expression?

Especially VAN UNNIK drew some lines between John and Acts. It is my opinion that we could find more points of affinity here. So f.i. Acts i 8, the earliest missionary programm of the first Christians, mentioning three geographical areas: Jerusalem, Judaea and Samaria and finally the ends of the earth, the whole world. Not Galilea, but South-Palestine and Samaria are mentioned. Different from Matt. xxviii 19, the Gentiles (nations) are not recorded expressis verbis, but the Jews and the Samaritans are mentioned [1].

Exactly this fact was a striking one in John's Gospel. Would it therefore be such a queer theory that the tradition behind this Gospel indeed belongs to the oldest tradition of the N. Test.[2]) and

---

[1]) CULLMANN's hypothesis that John iv 38, the ministry of "others" in Samaria refers to the Hellenists (Philip a.o.) in Acts vi and viii, and his thesis that the author of the Fourth Gospel belonged to the circle of these Hellenists, has no evidence enough in the N.T., I think; cf. O. CULLMANN, "The significance of the Qumran-Texts for Research into the Beginning of Christianity", in STENDAHL, Scrolls and N.T. o.c. p. 18ff, esp. p. 27.

[2]) Cf. D. GUTHRIE, o.c. p. 261f; S. SCHULZ, "Komposition", o.c. p. 151;

was developed within the earliest Christian preaching by the apostles in Jerusalem and Samaria, even before the Church directed itself consciously to the Gentiles? [1]).

This too points into the direction of a missionary purpose of the Gospel. It striked me that not before the preaching of Peter to the Gentile Cornelius, the geographical pattern of the Synoptics became visible in Acts x 37: "all over the land of the Jews, starting from Galilee after the baptism proclaimed by John". It seems that as long as the Gospel was preached only to Jews (and perhaps to Samaritans too), Jerusalem geographically was the centre, because this first preaching was strongly concentrated upon Jesus' death at the cross and his resurrection [2]).

We find also the conception of the predestination (the so-called Johannine determinism) expressed in the beginning of Acts [3]). At

---

R. SCHNACKENBURG, stated that "der johann. Schriftbeweis sich konzentrierte auf den Einzug Jesu in Jerusalem, den Verrat des Judas, das Leiden und die Auferstehung Jesus ein Zeichen für die Verbundenheit des Evangelisten mit der urchristlichen Tradition (vgl. I Kor. xv 3f)", "Messiasfrage", o.c. p. 242.

[1]) I suggested already that it would be possible to explain the method of John, to add interpretative commentary to Jesus' words and deeds, as the method used in the earliest preaching of the Church. MULDER interpreted this feature in the light of John's purpose, to show that the same elements which disturbed the minds in Asia Minor, already played a rôle in Jesus' days, o.c. p. 257. This is not a rejectable idea in itself, but in my opinion is the other interpretation, the use of the tradition in the kerygma at least as acceptable. SMALLEY dealt extensively with this issue, o.c. p. 55 ff. We cannot discuss here the relation between historical facts, words, tradition and the kerygma of the Church, but cf. SMALLEY, o.c. p. 45 ff, C. H. DODD, The Apost. Preaching a. its Development, 3nd ed. 1967, a.o. I'd like to refer only to the examples of the apostolic preaching given in Acts, which make clear that the facts of Jesus' ministry, his death and resurrection were a part of the earliest kerygma. SMALLEY thinks that we could find in John "all the basic elements belonging to the pattern of apostolic preaching", o.c. p. 45. Remarkable is the fact that in Acts the theme "Jesus is the Christ" was a central theme in the preaching; cf. VAN UNNIK o.c. p. 395f, who pointed to Acts xvii 3; xviii 5, 28; ix 20, 22. In my opinion we find this motive already in the earliest preaching, e.g. Acts ii 36; iii 18, 20. Cf. the detailed comparison in SMALLEY's article p. 47 ff, with the conclusion: "In Mark and John we have a literary version however conscious, of the kerygmatic activity reflected and reported in the speeches of Acts", p. 50.

[2]) Cf. f.i. Acts ii 22, "among you"; also ii 23f, 32; iii 13, 15; v 30f. A remarkable fact is also that in Acts viii we find Peter and John still together, but in Acts x, the story of Cornelius, John did not join Peter. Is it possible that somewhere on this point of time the tradition of the Synoptics (Peter-Mark) separated from that of John.

[3]) Acts iv 28. In John the stress is laid upon the salvation of those whom the Father gave to the Son (vi 37, 39, 44; xvii 6, 9, 11), in Acts iv 28 the

the other hand I wouldn't be surprised if there are some objections against this comparison between the Gospel of John and Acts. In the latter book we get the impression that especially the Sadducees, the High Priest c.s. were the main opponents of the Christian Church in the first period [1]), while the Christian communities enjoyed the favour of the common people and even priests and Pharisees joined the Christian faith [2]). But we have to make a clear distinction, in my opinion, between the "chief priests" (hostile) and the priests and we don't read that many of the Pharisees came to believe in Christ. If we assume that "the Pharisees" in John's Gospel are especially "doctors of the law" we have in Acts vi 12 an indication that in Acts too the first persecution was inaugurated from that side.

The fact that the apostles stayed in Jerusalem after the death of Stephen could be interpreted as a sign that the persecution of those days was directed in the first place against the Hellenistic Jewish Christians. But it is my impression that Saul's activity as told in Acts viii 3; ix 2; Gal. iii 13, was directed against the whole Christian community. In that case we could find a background here for the motive of persecution and bitterness in the Fourth Gospel. Finally, already in Acts we find the remarkable Johannine use of the term "the Jews" expressing the opposition against Christ and the Christians [3]).

Whether there exists a special relation between John and heterodox Judaism (apocalyptics, pre-Gnosticism, Qumran etc. cf. Böcher, Reicke, Kuhn a.o.) and how to define this affinity, is not yet clear. If there was such a relation, we could understand why the opposition was guided by the chief priests (esp. the High Priest and his family responsible for the temple-cultus) and the scribes and Pharisees.

Nevertheless I don't have the opinion, in spite of all what I said, that the Gospel of John in its present form, is the earliest Gospel

---

decree of God is applicated on the course of history, esp. the opposition against Christ and the Church, but we find a remarkable "determinism" in both cases.

[1]) Cf. Acts iv 1, 5, 6, 23; v 17, 21, 23.

[2]) Cf. Acts ii 47; v 13; vi 7; xv 5.

[3]) Cf. f.i. Acts ix 23; xii 3; cf. Guthrie, o.c. p. 232f: "It is probable that the term Jew is used more especially in contradistinction from 'Christians', rather than from 'Gentiles' in the same sense in which it occurs in Revel. iii 9". Paul too used the term in this sense, cf. I Cor. x 32.

of all four, as sometimes has been proposed [1]). Except for the external testimonies in the ancient Church, there are also many internal data which point to a publication of the Fourth Gospel at a time, later than the Synoptics, i.e. in the last decades of the first century. The majority of the scholars support this view. Therefore I am inclined, following the suggestion of others, to think of a distinction between a first record of facts and words of Jesus, functioning within the earliest preaching and, many years afterwards, an addition of material and the edition of the Gospel by the aged apostle John in Ephesus. He added f.i. the Prologue to his Gospel and shaped its present form [2]).

By this hypothesis we can understand why "the Gentiles" are not mentioned expressis verbis: in the earliest preaching they were not yet in the picture of the Church and when John edited his

---

[1]) Cf. above, note 2, p. 35 (V. BURCH a.o.).

[2]) Cf. D. GUTHRIE: "there is something to be said for the view that John made notes of our Lord's discourses shortly after hearing them", o.c. p. 261; GUTHRIE refered to the study of EDWARDS, o.c.; cf. also p. 262, note 1; cf. DODD's distinction between the Johannine tradition before AD 70 and the later publication of his Gospel, Hist.Tradition, o.c. The history of the growth of John's Gospel is still a discussed topic. The assumption of sources behind the Gospel has been doubted by many after the research a.o. of E. RUCKSTUHL, Die liter. Einheit d. Joh.ev., 1951; cf. GUTHRIE, o.c. p. 275-284. This does however not exclude the possibility of a development of the Gospel in two or more stages, if the author is the same apostle-eyewitness. It is impossible to deal broadly with the problems of the authorship here. Cf. for the history of development of the Fourth Gospel also a.o. J. A. T. ROBINSON, "The Relation of the Prologue to the Gospel of John", in The Authorship and Integrity of the N.T., S.P.C.K. Theol. Collections, 4, 1965, p. 61-72, following the view of W. SANDAY, "Criticism", o.c. p. 211 f. ROBINSON proposed the following order of writing of the Johannine literature: the bulk of the Gospel, the Epistles, the Epilogue and Prologue of the Gospel, o.c. p. 67; the Gospel originally started with the witness of John the Baptist and was later revised and supplemented by the Prologue. About the relation between the Prologue and the Gospel and the integrity of the Prologue, there have been many discussions. Some suggested that a hymn (Gnostic or from circles of Baptist-disciples or Christian, cf. BULTMANN, KÄSEMANN, S. SCHULZ, "Die Komposition d. joh. Prologs u. d. Zusammensetzung d. viert. Ev.", Stud. Ev. I, TU 73, o.c. p. 351-362, E. HAENCHEN, "Prob. d. joh. Prologs", o.c. p. 309 ff) was basic to the Prologue; cf. also RIDDERBOS, o.c. p. 40 ff. I could not deal with these problems here, but am agreeing with the viewpoint of RIDDERBOS, that a clear unity of thoughts could be found in the Prologue, a real integrity, o.c. p. 51/52; cf. also SMALLEY o.c. p. 54 f. This too does not exclude however the possibility that the Prologue was added to the Gospel by the same author; cf. about the growth of John's Gospel also R. E. BROWN's "Commentary", o.c. who assumed a growth in five stages; this theory is too complicated to be true, cf. the critique of HOLTZ, Th.L.Z. 93, p. 349 f.

Gospel so many years later, the distinction between mission among the Jews and among the Gentiles had no more actuality, the Church was conscious to have a message for "the world" a universalistic message. It is my opinion that the three articles discussed above, make it very clear that the Gospel was directed "first to the Jews", but I'd like to add: "also to the Greeks". This was since the days of Paul the custom of the early Christian Church [1]). John could use the early-recorded material from the beginning of the Christian preaching, for the time in which he wrote the definite Gospel, because still "the Gentiles and peoples of Israel" (Acts iv 27) were opposing the Anointed One, Jesus Christ and his Church.

Probably the Jews became more fanatical in several places after the addition of the Schemone es're by the Birkat-ha-minim, the Gentiles were attracted more and more by syncretistic Gnosticism, the symptoms of which John perhaps had met already in Palestine, commencing to influence Christians too (docetism). It is therefore not improbable that the purpose of John's Gospel is as broad as its universalistic character seems to suggest: "that you may believe", that is the faith that saves and defeats the world (John iii 16 and 1 John v 5).

---

[1]) Also in Acts and in Paul's ministry we find the rule: first the Jew and also the Greek. DAVIES even concluded: "It is this preoccupation of Paul with the Jews in the Book of Acts that has led many to doubt the historicity of the latter", W. D. DAVIES, o.c. p. 69; cf. H. N. RIDDERBOS: though John xx 31 has been thought from a Jewish standpoint, one cannot say the the Prologue has been composed in the terms of the Israelite Messianic expectation. Jesus Christ is the Son of God in a broader, more universalistic sense than Israel spoke about the Son of God. The question, who is the Messiah, goes back in the Prologue behind Israel, behind Moses, even behind Abraham, to the very beginning. This motive is linked with the universality of salvation, because the light is shining in the world, enlightening every man by his coming into the world. The Israelite and the universalistic aspect are clearly combined. Perhaps one could say that this supports the thesis that the Gospel has been addressed in the first place to Jews outside of Palestine as Jews related to the world in which they lived, RIDDERBOS, o.c. p. 54, 55 (my own translation, A.W.). If "in the first place" does not mean exclusivity, and non-Jews are also kept in our mind, I could agree fully with RIDDERBOS.

LOGOS WAS THE TRUE LIGHT*

Contributions to the Interpretation of the Prologue of John.

BY

Dr. PEDER BORGEN
Bergen, Norway

RESEARCH STANDPOINTS

Analyses of the Prologue of John in recent years have concentrated particularly on the question of poetic and prose stylistic forms, and on the question of unity and unevenness in thought, both within the Prologue itself, and the Prologue in relation to the rest of the gospel. As far as form is concerned, several scholars, such as R. BULTMANN, E. KÄSEMANN, R. SCHNACKENBURG and R. E. BROWN, have suggested that the evangelist has used and supplemented a hymn [1].

BULTMANN's analysis of the Prologue has resulted, amongst other things, in the direct reference to John the Baptist, John i 6 ff. and v. 15, being considered a secondary addition, as it is prose, thus not belonging to the original poetic hymn. According to BULTMANN, the evangelist as a former disciple of the Baptist, added these words about him as a testimony to Jesus, to resolve his problem in leaving the Baptist's sect and becoming a Christian.

Other scholars who interpret John's Prologue as a hymn seem to disagree with several aspects of BULTMANN's interpretation of the thoughts piecemeal. Nevertheless, they are in agreement with

---

* Guest lecture delivered at the University of Uppsala, Sweden, upon invitation extended by Professor Harald Riesenfeld. Cf. P. Borgen, "Logos var det sanne lys," *Svensk exegetisk Årsbok*, XXXV 1970, 79-95.

[1] See R. BULTMANN, *Das Evangelium des Johannes, Kritisch-exegetisches Kommentar über das Neue Testament*, begr. v. H. A. W. MEYER, 11. Aufl., Göttingen 1950, 1-5: E. KÄSEMANN, "Aufbau und Anliegen des Johanneischen Prologs", *Libertas Christiana* (DELEKAT Festschrift), München 1957, 75-99; E. HAENCHEN, "Probleme des Johanneischen Prologs", *Zeitschrift für Theologie und Kirche*, 60, 1963, 305-34; R. SCHNACKENBURG, *Das Johannesevangelium, Herders Theologischer Kommentar zum Neuen Testament*, Band IV, erster Teil, Freiburg 1965, 197-207; R. E. BROWN, *The Gospel according to St. John*, I-XII, Garden City, N. Y., 1966, 1-37. Concerning the earlier stages of this exegetical tradition, see C. K. Barrett, *The Prologue of St. John's Gospel*, London 1971, 6ff.

him in regarding the references to John the Baptist as a secondary addition.

E. HAENCHEN's study of John i 1-18 is of particular interest. He believes that the editor who added ch. 21, also added the saying about John the Baptist, i 6-8, 15. This editor thought that John had to be mentioned first, and then Jesus, and thus undertook the necessary revisions of John's Prologue. HAENCHEN's study, however, shows that an essential criterion for eliminating vv. 6-8, 15 has been discarded. In fact, he indicates that the difference in style between poetry and prose cannot be utilised with regard to the Prologue, and thereby this criterion is also weakened with regard to vv. 6-8, 15 [1]).

With this in mind, it is understandable that W. ELTESTER completely rejects the hypothesis of a reworked hymn. ELTESTER maintains that John i 1-18 is a single entity, and that the gospel narrative begins with v. 1. In fact, each section tells of an epoch in salvation history:

i 1-5 Das ,,Wort" als Schöpfungsmittler und als Offenbarer.
i 6-8 Johannes als Gottgesandter und als Zeuge des Offenbarers.
i 9-11 Der Offenbarer und seine Ablehnung durch Heiden und Juden.
i 12-13 Die alttestamentlichen Gotteskinder.
i 14-17 Die Fleischwerdung des ,,Wortes" und der Lobpreis seiner Gemeinde, mit Johannes als Zeugen seiner Pre-existenz und seiner Gnadengaben im Alten Testament und in Jesus.
i 18 Der eingeborene Sohn als alleiniger Künder Gottes [2]).

For ELTESTER, the statements about John have a central function, but his treatment seems rather schematic and strained. He does not give a satisfactory explanation as to why the statements about John appear as early as vv. 6-8, and not just before the verses on the Incarnation, vv. 14 ff. Another objection to ELTESTER is that it is difficult not to interpret vv. 9 and 11 as referring to the Incarnation, as much as v. 14.

At the same time, there are two points of ELTESTER's which seem to be value. When the distinction between poetry and prose is

---

[1]) E. HAENCHEN, *op. cit.* Cf. C. K. BARRETT, *The Prologue*, 14 ff. for further criticism of the criterion of poetic and prose styles as applied to the Prologue.
[2]) W. ELTESTER, "Der Logos und sein Prophet", *Apophoreta* (HAENCHEN Festschrift), Berlin 1964, 109-34, especially 124.

dismissed, it is natural to consider John i 1-18 as a unity [1]). And even if ELTESTER's salvation history epochs are over-schematically presented, but nonetheless one ought to investigate whether or not the salvation history motif is present in the passage. Various studies (among others A. FRIDRICHSEN's and N. A. DAHL's) show that there are, in fact, elements of salvation history within the gospel [2]). Therefore one can expect to find such elements in the opening of the gospel as well.

Thus there is a need to investigate John i 1-18 anew, with regard to both form and content.

THE EVANGELIST AND JEWISH EXEGESIS OF GENESIS

In the study "Observations on the Targumic Character of the Prologue of John", (published in "New Testament Studies") I have attempted to show that the Prologue's basic structure is not primarily dependent on whether the style is prose or poetry, but that this portion is an exposition of Gen. i 1 ff. [3]). This exposition follows the pattern a), b), c)/ c), b), a), which becomes apparent when one identifies the words and phrases based on Gen. i 1 ff., which are used repeatedly in the passage.

vv. 1-2.	*a)*	*vv. 14-18.*

v. 1 ἐν ἀρχῇ ἦν ὁ λόγος, καὶ ὁ λόγος ἦν πρὸς τὸν θεόν, καὶ θεὸς ἦν ὁ λόγος. v. 2 οὗτος ἦν ἐν ἀρχῇ πρὸς τὸν θεόν.

v. 14 καὶ ὁ λόγος σάρξ ἐγένετο καὶ ἐσκήνωσεν ἐν ἡμῖν, καὶ ἐθεασάμεθα τὴν δόξαν αὐτοῦ, δόξαν ὡς μονογενοῦς παρὰ πατρός, πλήρης χάριτος καὶ ἀληθείας ········ v. 18 θεὸν οὐδεὶς ἑώρακεν πώποτε·μονογενὴς θεὸς ὁ ὢν εἰς τὸν κόλπον τοῦ πατρός, ἐκεῖνος ἐξηγήσατο.

v. 3.	*b)*	*vv. 10-13.*

v. 3. πάντα δι' αὐτοῦ ἐγένετο, καὶ χωρὶς

v. 10. ἐν τῷ κόσμῳ ἦν, καὶ ὁ κόσμος δι' αὐτοῦ ἐγένετο, καὶ ὁ κόσμος αὐτὸν οὐκ

---

[1]) Cf. that the theory of an Aramaic hymn has not had convincing force. See R. E. BROWN, *John*, CXXIX f., 22 f.

[2]) A. FRIDRICHSEN, "Missionstanken i Fjärde Evangeliet", *Svensk eksegetisk årsbok*, II, 1936, 39-53; N. A. DAHL, "The Johannine Church and History", *Current Issues in New Testament Interpretation* (PIPER Festschrift), New York 1962, 124-42; cf. P. BORGEN, *Bread from Heaven, Supplements to Novum Testamentum*, 10, Leiden 1965, 148-54.

[3]) P. BORGEN, "Observations on the Targumic Character of the Prologue of John", *New Testament Studies*, 16, 1970, 288-95.

αὐτοῦ ἐγένετο οὐδὲ ἓν ὃ
γέγονεν.

ἔγνω········ v. 13. οἳ οὐκ ἐξ αἱμάτων
οὐδὲ ἐκ θελήματος σαρκὸς οὐδὲ ἐκ
θελήματος ἀνδρὸς ἀλλ' ἐκ θεοῦ
ἐγεννήθησαν.

vv. 4-5.

c) *vv. 6-9.*

v. 4. ἐν αὐτῷ ζωὴ ἦν,
καὶ ἡ ζωὴ ἦν τὸ φῶς
τῶν ἀνθρώπων· v. 5. καὶ
τὸ φῶς ἐν τῇ σκοτίᾳ
φαίνει, καὶ ἡ σκοτία αὐτὸ
οὐ κατέλαβεν.

v. 6. 'Εγένετο ἄνθρωπος, ἀπεσταλμένος
παρὰ θεοῦ, ὄνομα αὐτῷ 'Ιωάννης· v. 7.
οὗτος ἦλθεν εἰς μαρτυρίαν, ἵνα μαρτυρήσῃ
περὶ τοῦ φωτός, ἵνα πάντες πιστεύσωσιν
δι' αὐτοῦ. v. 8. οὐκ ἦν ἐκεῖνος τὸ φῶς,
ἀλλ' ἵνα μαρτυρήσῃ περὶ τοῦ φωτός.
v. 9. ἦν τὸ φῶς τὸ ἀληθινόν, ὃ φωτίζει
πάντα ἄνθρωπον ἐρχόμενον εἰς τὸν κόσμον.

In the aforementioned study in *NTS* (where the details of form-analysis can also be found) it was suggested that a parallel to this pattern is found in the Jerusalem Targum of Gen. iii 24, and similar patterns are found in other Jewish writings.

It would be possible to relate this pattern in the Prologue of John to a source analysis. On this basis one could advance the hypothesis that a source has been reworked and supplemented by the evangelist. In this study, however, we shall put the question: can John i 1-18 be considered a unit, composed by the evangelist? The question could be formulated in another way: does the exegesis compel us to reckon with a reworked and supplemented source?

If we regard John i 1-18 as a unit, composed by the evangelist, its arrangement can be presented thus:

(a) vv. 1-2 and vv. 14-18 Logos and God before the creation, and the Epiphany with the coming of Jesus.

(b) v. 3 and vv. 10-13: Logos which creates in primordial time, and which claims its possession by the coming of Jesus.

(c) vv. 4-5 and vv. 6-9: Light and nightfall in primordial time, and the coming of Light with Jesus' coming, with the Baptist as a witness.

On the basis of this structure it is clear, therefore, that vv. 1-2 must be interpreted first and foremost together with vv. 14-18; likewise v. 3 with vv. 10-13; and particularly vv. 4-5 together with vv. 6-9. In the most essential points in this study we shall concentrate the discussion of vv. 4-5 and vv. 6-9 on Light. We shall see if these verses can be understood as a unity, or if their exegesis leads us to consider vv. 6-8 as a secondary supplement. These interests coincide particularly on the issue of how far Jewish traditions of interpreting Gen. i, and other Jewish traditions, illuminate the train of thought, and partially the terminology, of John i 4-9.

It can be considered very probable that the evangelist has not only reproduced words from Gen. i such as ἐν ἀρχῇ/בראשית, (ὁ) θεός/ אלהים and τὸ φῶς - ἡ σκοτία/אור – חשך, and substituted the words ברא את השמים ואת הארץ in Gen. i with a creation formula δι' αὐτοῦ ἐγένετο (vv. 3 and 11), but that he has also drawn on learned Jewish exegesis.

The term ὁ λόγος is particularly interesting in this connection. It occurs explicitly in vv. 1 and 14, and is referred to in many other verses in the passage. Vv. 4-9 contain important factors towards an understanding of the background to the phrase. This becomes clear when one considers more closely the suggestion that Gen. i 3 forms the background for the term: ויאמר אלהים יהי אור, LXX καὶ εἶπεν ὁ θεός Γενηθήτω φῶς [1]). HAENCHEN raised this objection to interpreting ὁ λογος so: ,,Aber Judentum hat jenes 'und Gott sprach' von Gen. i eben gerade nicht zu einer von Gott unterschiedenen Person hypostasiert'' [2]).

There are several points immediately contradicting HAENCHEN's rejection of this interpretation. For example, it can be asserted that since Logos seems to be identified with light in John i 9 [3]), Gen. i 3 provides the natural basis, since εἶπε there can be understood as light. This occurs in Jewish exegesis, in Gen. R. III: 3, for example, where דבר is interpreted as light. In a quotation from Proverbs xv 23, "A man hath joy in the answer of His mouth; a word in season, how good it is'', the expression "the answer of His mouth'' במענה–פיו is understood as God's creative word in Gen. i 3. Thus it is explicit that "the reply of His mouth'' is דבר, and דבר is, as in John i 9, identified with light: "and a word דבר in season, how good it is; And God saw light, that it was good'' (Gen. i 4) [4]).

HAENCHEN's objection has some validity all the same, for in Gen. R. III דבר is in fact not personified, and is not a greatness

---

[1]) See E. HAENCHEN, op. cit., 305, note 3.
[2]) ibid.
[3]) See P. BORGEN, New Testament Studies, 16, 1970, 289-90. Concerning ὁ λόγος as subject of ἦν in John i 9, see R. BULTMANN, Johannes, 31, note 6.
[4]) Cf. Midr. Ps. 18 § 26. See C. H. DODD, The Bible and the Greeks, London 1935, 115 ff. with regard to the concept of Logos and the story of creation in Poimandres.

independent of God, but is God's spoken word. At the same time. HAENCHEN's objection here overlooks the fact that Philo in Somn, I 75 interprets Gen. i 3, and moves from the spoken word, to Logos as the model behind the work of creation: τὸ μὲν γὰρ παράδειγμα ὁ πληρέστατος ἦν αὐτοῦ λόγος, φῶς—'εἶπε' γάρ φησιν 'ὁ θεός ·γενέσθω φῶς', "for the model was the Word of His (God's) fullness, namely light, for He says "God said, 'Let there be light'"". Philo can then on other places add the personal aspect of Logos as a hypostasis, precisely with reference to Gen. i. Thus in Conf. 148, of "God's first-born", "Logos"; He is called "The Beginning", "Logos", "the Man after His (God's) image". For additional support from Philo it can be mentioned that in Opif. 31 Logos is also characterised as light, against a background of the creation account, that is, the background of Gen. i 3. In the study "God's Agent in the Fourth Gospel", (in the memorial volume to E. R. GOODENOUGH) I have attempted to show that Philo, in "De Confusione Linguarum" and in other places, reworks common Jewish traditions, amongst other ways, within Jewish mysticism [1]). In the light of all this, it must be concluded that HAENCHEN's objection is untenable. Gen. i 3, therefore, presents the most probable foundation for the term Logos in the Prologue of John.

For further support in thus understanding Logos, one can refer to the fact that John builds upon and expands Jewish exegesis also in other places, for example in John v. Against the background of Jesus healing a lame man on the sabbath, and the Jewish sabbath rule against work, John v 17 expresses God's attitude to the sabbath: ὁ πατήρ μου ἕως ἄρτι ἐργάζεται.

The evangelist here presupposes the exegetical traditions, which, based on Gen. ii 2-3 raised the question of whether or not God could rest on the sabbath. The conclusion was that God is always active, at least with regard to certain definite functions [2]). There are also other places in John where it is plain that learned exegesis is either taken up or presupposed by the evangelist [3]). Therefore we have reached the probable conclusion, that the term ὁ λόγος in John i 1 ff. builds upon an exegesis of Gen. i 3 such as we find in Gen. R. III: 1-3 and in Philo in Somn. I 75.

---

[1]) P. BORGEN, "God's Agent in the Fourth Gospel", *Religions in Antiquity* (E. R. GOODENOUGH Memorial Volume), Leiden 1968, 137-48.

[2]) See C. H. DODD, *The Interpretation of the Fourth Gospel*, Cambridge 1953, 319-23.

[3]) See P. BORGEN, *Bread from Heaven*, especially 59-98.

Thus the question is, can Jewish traditions in connection with Gen. i 3 and other traditions, throw light upon John i 4-9 as an entity? Of interest here are the traditions which depict primordial light and dark in primordial time, and thereafter a later revelation of light again. There are several examples of such a tradition. In Chag. 12a are the following points: (a) Primordial light (Gen. i 3) which gave Adam universal sight and the removal of light because of the sin of the generation in primordial time; (b) light's coming in the next age [1]).

This conception can be given various formulation. The coming of light can be directly connected with the Messiah's coming, or it can be connected with events which have already occured in Israel's history, particularly Abraham and Moses' lawgiving [2]).

Against this background, the theme for i 4-9 can be presented thus: primordial light and nightfall in primordial time, vv. 4-5, and light's entry into history, prepared by the coming of John. It would be practical to begin with vv. 6-9 the coming of light into history, prepared by the coming of John.

VV. 6-9: THE ENTRY OF LIGHT INTO HISTORY, PREPARED BY THE COMING OF JOHN

V 6 Ἐγένετο ἄνθρωπος, ἀπεσταλμένος παρὰ θεοῦ, ὄνομα αὐτῷ Ἰωάννης has a style characteristic of historical narrative in the O.T., for example Judges xiii 2, (ויהי איש אחד מצרעה ממשפחת הדני ושמו מנוח) xix 1, 1 Sam i 1 [3]). BULTMANN underlines the fact that it is the O.T. prose style which is used and therefore he reckons vv. 6-8 as an interpolation in a Logos-hymn, as stated [4]). In addition to the objections already expressed to this conclusion, we are now in a position to see that the Jewish traditions of primordial light can readily be connected with the advent of light in history, and more particularly, in Israel's history.

In accordance with the expression of John's appearance in history

---

[1]) Str.-Bill., II, 348, note 2. Cf. Lev. R. XI:7; Esther R. Proem XI:5; Gen. R. XI:2; Tanchuma Shemine 9; Ruth R. Proem VII:5.

[2]) On the light (Gen. i 4) and the Messiah, see Pesiqta R. 36 (161a); and Abraham, cf. Gen. R. II:3; and Moses, 3 Petirat Mosheh 72; Jalkut Reubeni Ki Tissa 111a, cf. Sifre Num. § § 136-37. See B. MURMELSTEIN, "Adam, ein Beitrag zur Messiaslehre", Wiener Zeitschrift für die Kunde des Morgenlandes, 36, 1929, 56. Cf. Syr. Baruch 17-18.

[3]) See R. BULTMANN, Johannes, 29, note 1 and references.

[4]) ibid., 3 f., 29-31.

in v. 6, a statement follows in v. 7 of his task, to witness to the light. Our hypothesis of a Jewish background is borne out by the fact that John here has expressions characteristic of Rabbinical usage, as ἦλθεν εἰς μαρτυρίαν/בא לעדות [1]).

Then, vv. 8-9 characterizes John in relation to Jesus: v. 8, οὐκ ἦν ἐκεῖνος τὸ φῶς which states that John was not the primordial light of Gen. i 3, whereas v. 9 ἦν τὸ φῶς τὸ ἀληθινόν states that Logos was.

V. 9 needs closer consideration. As for the question of the subject of ἦν, it could be understood in the verb: he, namely Logos; or it could be τὸ φῶς τὸ ἀληθινόν, the true light was . . . . BULTMANN asserts, rightly, that it is ὁ λόγος, mentioned in vv. 1-4. In support of this interpretation he cites vv. 10 and 11 where the verbs ἦν and ἦλθεν also have Logos as the subject, due to the fact that the pronoun αὐτόν in v. 10b is masculine and must refer back to ὁ λόγος [2]).

The term τὸ φῶς connects v. 9 to the preceding, where the same term is used. This fact counts against taking v. 9 together with the following verse, even though the term ὁ κόσμος provides a link with v. 10 [3]).

In v. 9, light is identified as the true Light, τὸ φῶς τὸ ἀληθινόν. There is a sharp contrast between this genuine, actual light, and John as the supposed light, v. 8. Again, an observation which speaks for the idea that vv. 6-9 belong together. If vv. 6-8 are removed as an interpolation, it is in fact not so clear what it is that provides the contrast to the true light, despite the fact that the true light may be understood as a more exact precision of Light in v. 4 [4]). The most difficult grammatical problem remains in vv. 6-9, that is the participle ἐρχόμενον in v. 9. The seemingly obvious is to take the participle in connection with the preceding πάντα ἄνθρωπον. Even though a Rabbinical formula about becoming man seems to lend support to this approach, it is not satisfactory. The

---

[1]) *ibid.*, 29, note 1.
[2]) *ibid.*, 31, note 6.
[3]) See further P. BORGEN, *New Testament Studies*, 16, 1970, 291 and 294.
[4]) R. BULTMANN, *Johannes*, 32, maintains that in the original hymn the true light was contrasted with the earthly light. Against this point of view it can be said that vv. 1-5,9 which belonged to the hymn, does not make this contrast clear. R. SCHNACKENBURG, *Johannesevangelium*, 229, gives a more precise characterization of the light in v. 4 by saying that it is of unique kind. Again it can be stated that the most obvious contrast found in the context is that between the preparatory light of John and the true light of Jesus.

context, and John iii 19 and xii 46, show that it concerns the coming of light, and not the birth of every man [1]).

This problem disappears if ἐρχόμενον is taken as a periphrastic form together with ἦν: "the true light was about to come into the world". Otherwise, ἐρχόμενον can be understood as a loosely connected participle construction to τὸ φῶς "he was the true light which enlightens and which is coming". But even these interpretations are not without difficulties. It is rather unusual that a whole relative clause separates ἦν from the participle in its periphrastic form, and in the case of a loosely connected participle construction, one would have expected the article to have been positioned before the participle [2]).

On the other hand, there is another alternative which is grammatically defensible and which renders good sense. The participle ἐρχόμενον can refer back to the subject of φωτίζει, i.e. to τὸ φῶς represented by the relative pronoun ὅ. The participle without the article thus expresses what happens simultaneously with the action of the verb, and how the action occurs. In BLASS-DEBRUNNER this is called an adverbial use of the participle [3]), and the translation is thus: "He (i.e. Logos) was the true light, which enlightens every man when it (light) enters the world". Freely rendered the verse goes thus: Logos was the true light, which enlightens every man by coming into the world.

This grammatical interpretation of v. 9 has significance in determining the thought content. Thus it is impossible here to separate light's enlightening work from its coming [4]). In other words, both φωτίζει and ἐρχόμενον characterize the coming of Jesus [5]).

What provides the thought-model for this coming of light? It would be natural to interpret light against the background of ideas of Messiah's light [6]). Since Logos in John is the light, it is more

---

[1]) Thus R. E. BROWN, *John*, 9-10, with criticism of BURNEY, SCHLATTER, BULTMANN, WIKENHAUSER.

[2]) See especially R. SCHNACKENBURG, *Johannesevangelium*, 230-31.

[3]) F. BLASS and A. DEBRUNNER, *Grammatik des neutestamentlichen Griechisch*, 11. Aufl., Göttingen 1961, 260, especially 418,5.

[4]) Cf. that C. H. DODD, *The Interpretation*, 201 f., thinks that φωτίζει refers to the general revelation as background for the special revelation in the coming of Christ.

[5]) Cf. R. E. BROWN, *John*, 28, who refers to the Messianic passage of Isaiah ix 2.

[6]) See p. 121, note 1.

probable that the thought-model behind v. 9 is the coming of the primordial light, with the lawgiving of Moses.

Several references in John support this view. In John x 35 f. the term ὁ λόγος τοῦ θεοῦ seems to be used of the Torah given at Sinai, and this idea provide the background for the saying regarding Jesus' being sent into the world [1]). And in John xii 46 ff. it is stated that Jesus' coming as light brings ὁ λόγος and ἐντολή from God. These expressions are also understood easiest in the light of Torah [2]). And in several other places, John transfers the Torah's function to Jesus, and uses terminology which usually belongs together with the Torah. For examp e, it is stated in Jewish sources that the Torah gives life to the world, and thus in John vi 33 that Jesus as the bread from heaven gives life to the world [3]). On this basis it is sensible to understand Logos' and light's coming in v. 9 against the background of the lawgiving of Moses as a thought-model.

In addition, there are several likenesses between the ideas bound up in the Torah in Judaism and ideas in John i 4-9. It has already been shown that Jewish texts where primordial light from the creation (Gen. i 3) came into appearance at the lawgiving, are a thought-parallel to primordial light in John i 4-5, which appeared with the coming of Jesus v. 9. Also, as stated, the word דבר is identified with the light and the Torah in Jewish texts, and even with the Torah as a creative instrument [4]). Thus in John, Logos is identified with light, and Logos is the creative instrument, John i 3 ff. Furthermore, the Torah is life [5]) and accordingly in John i 4, life is in Logos. Further, ideas directly connected with the lawgiving at Sinai illuminate John i 9. At the lawgiving, Moses brought the primordial light down from heaven [6]), and according to John i 9 primordial light makes its appearance at the coming of Jesus. As

---

[1]) N. A. DAHL, *Current Issues*, 133 f.

[2]) E. HIRSCH, *Studien zum vierten Evangelium*, Tübingen 1936, 99, sees that John xii 49-50 alludes to the lawgiving at Sinai, but he draws the wrong conclusion that the words from οἶδα to ἐστιν for this reason are an added gloss. Cf. R. BULTMANN, *Johannes*, 263, note 7. R. E. BROWN, *John*, 491-92 finds Deuteronomic ideas and terminology in John xii 48-50.

[3]) See P. BORGEN, *Bread from Heaven*, 148-54.

[4]) Gen. R. I:7; III:1-3.

[5]) See references in A. SCHLATTER, *Der Evangelist Johannes*, Stuttgart 1930, 158-59, commenting upon John v 39. Cf. P. BORGEN, *Bread from Heaven*, 148-49, 165 ff.

[6]) See above, p. 121, note 1. Cf. S. AALEN, *Die Begriffe "Licht" und "Finsterniss"*, Oslo 1951, 273, note 3.

the lawgiving of Moses was for all men ¹), so in John i 9 the light
shines for every man when it comes. Of particular note here is
Sap. Sal. 18:4, where it says that the law's light will be given
to the world: τὸ ·· νόμου φῶς τῷ αἰῶνι δίδοσθαι ²). It is also note-
worthy that according to Jewish thought, the coming of the Torah
made possible walking in the light ³). In a similar way we find that
Jesus' coming as the light makes it possible for men to walk in the
light, John viii 12 f., xii 35 ff., cf. xii 46 ff.

Thus there are very good grounds for concluding that the conception of logos-light's coming in John i 9 has as a model the conception of Torah-light's coming with Moses.

However, in John i 6-9 weight is laid on John's coming. Thus we
find the aorist forms ἐγένετο and ἦλθεν referring to John in
vv. 6-7, whereas the present φωτίζει is used of light's enlightening
function. Since φωτίζει and the participle ἐρχόμενον both refer to
the incarnation, it is therefore the actual enlightening function
which the incarnation effects that is in mind, and not the punctual
aspect of the event in itself.

John's appearance signified a marked event in salvation-history.
Thus it is understandable that it must be made clear that he is not
the light itself. It is therefore possible, but unnecessary, to see any
polemic against a baptism-sect in v. 8 ⁴). In contrast to the fact
that John was not the light, the true light's singularity stands out:
it was Logos-light of Gen. i 3, "and God said, 'Let there be light' ".

Jewish source-material is also of interest with regard to John's
function. In John v 33 ff., it is John's service as a witness which is
more closely defined. He was the kindled lamp which burnt and
lit up. As background one can refer to the idea that Moses lit a lamp
for Israel and took light from the law's light, Syr. Baruch 17:1-

---

¹) S. AALEN, *op. cit.*, 295 f.

²) S. AALEN, *ibid.*, 194. One version of Test. Levi 14:4 has even a close
phraseological parallell to the words of John i 9.

³) Mek. Ex. 13:18; cf. Sifre Num. 6:25, § 41; Ex. R. 36:3; Midr. Ps. 27,
§ § 1-3. Concerning Torah as the light of the world, see S. AALEN, *op. cit.*,
289, and J. JERVELL, *Imago Dei, FRLANT*, N.F. 58, Göttingen 1960,
100 f. In John iii 19 ff. we find the thought that the coming of the light
unmasks men. Cf. S. AALEN, *op. cit.*, 233-36; 321-24.

⁴) R. BULTMANN, *Johannes*, 29 and R. E. BROWN, *John*, 28 find polemic
against a baptism-sect, so also R. SCHNACKENBURG, *Johannesevangelium*,
226 ("warscheinlich"); John i 6 is interpreted differently by C. K. BARRETT,
The Gospel according to St. John, London 1958, 132 f; E. HAENCHEN, *op. cit.*,
328 f.

18:2 [1]). And without actually referring to the creation account, in
Midr. Ps. 36 § 6 it is stated that the many men from Moses down to
the sons of the Hasmoneans who saved Israel, were as lamps which
had been extinguished again. Therefore one ought to pray that God
Himself would give light [2]). Seen against this background, it is
understandable that John's witness to the light had a significance
in salvation history: he was the lamp, not the light itself.

PRIMORDIAL LIGHT AND NIGHTFALL IN PRIMORDIAL TIME: JOHN i 4-5.

Having considered John's and primordial light's entry into history, John i 6-9, we can turn to primordial light and nightfall in
primordial time, vv. 4-5. Once again we are up against grammatical
problems. This time it is the sentence division between vv. 3-4.
Here we shall follow Nestle's text which begins a new sentence with
ἐν αὐτῷ in v. 4. Among the many considerations of this problem,
we can rely upon that of K. HAACKER. He demonstrates that creation formulas of a similar type to that in John i 3 emerge, if the full
stop is placed before ἐν αὐτῷ, v. 4 [3]). Verse 4 therefore deals with
the ideas of Life and light in relation to Logos and mankind from
the creation onwards (v. 3). Verse 5a gives a general depiction in
the present of the relation between light and darkness, and thereafter in v. 5b, a description of an event in the past in aorist form,
that is the assault of darkness against light.

Verse 5b καὶ ἡ σκοτία αὐτὸ οὐ κατέλαβεν provides a good point
of departure for a consideration of the thoughts contained in the
verses. The debate among scholars has centered around the term
καταλαμβάνειν, "grasp", either (a) to accept or (b) to seize with power
and overcome in an undesirable or hostile manner. Scholars such
as BULTMANN, WIKENHAUSER and HAENCHEN think that καταλαμβάνειν here means to grasp in the sense of receiving and accepting:
"and the darkness did not receive it (light)". They stress particularly that the thought here is parallel to that expressed in the phrase
οὐκ ἔγνω, v. 10, and οὐ παρέλαβον in v. 11. All these give expression to

---

[1]) See also 3 Petirat Mosheh, 71 ff.

[2]) See S. AALEN, op. cit., 186-87 and reference to John v 35 on page 187,
note 1. Such a subordinate lamp is John also according to F. NEUGEBAUER,
"Miszelle zu Joh v, 35", Zeitschrift für die neutestamentliche Wissenschaft,
LII, 1961, 130, who interprets John v 35 against the background of LXX
Ps. cxxxii 17, as the lamp of Messiah.

[3]) See survey of research in R. SCHNACKENBURG, Johannesevangelium,
215-17; K. HAACKER, "Eine formgeschichtliche Beobachtung zu Joh i 3 fin",
Biblische Zeitschrift, N. F. 12, 1968, 119-21.

the idea that wisdom is not accepted by men [1]). On the other hand, scholars have argued that the verb καταλαμβάνειν in i 5 must be understood in the same sense as in xii 35 [2]). In xii 35 it is clear that the term is taken from daily life and describe as nightfall which comes upon man by surprise. The verb therefore means to seize or surprise one in an undesirable or hostile manner. In support of this interpretation it could also be noted that the expression in John i 5 and xii 35 presents a common formula for an unexpected und undesired nightfall, a formula which is well attested outside the N.T. [3]).

In the light of our analysis of John i 1-18 an additional factor can be used to strengthen this interpretation. The structure used for John i 1-18 makes it natural to divide vv. 4-9 into two parts: vv. 4-5, light in primordial time, and vv. 6-9, what happened at John's and light's entries into history. Thus, the phrases used in connection with the coming of Jesus οὐκ ἔγνω v. 10, and οὐ παρέλαβον, v. 11, are not parallels to v. 5b, which refers to primordial time, not the later entry of light in history.

The event to which v. 5b refers, seems to be the Fall, either connected with Adam, or with Adam and the sin of the first generations. In Jewish sources there are three particular lines of thought on the Fall which are of interest in understanding John i.

The first line of thought maintains that primordial light became removed, concealed or weakened, because of sin. So it is stated in Chag. 12a that God let primordial light shine in Adam but then concealed it (גנז, reserve, conceal) because of the sinful Flood and Babel-building generations [4]). Also in place here is the idea that sunshine and length of days were lessened because of Adam's Fall.

The second line of thought, in a similar way maintains that the sins of Adam and the first generations led directly to darkness and night. The idea here can be developed to the extent that darkness and night grew, but the eventuality of complete darkness was averted by God's goodness and Adam's repentance [5]).

---

[1]) R. BULTMANN, *Johannes*, 28 ("die Finsternis hat es nicht erfasst"); Cf. E. KÄSEMANN, *op. cit.*, 79; E. HAENCHEN, *op. cit.*, 322.

[2]) A. SCHLATTER, *Johannes*, 9; M.-E. BOISMARD, *Le Prologue de Saint Jean, Lectio Divina* 11, 33-38; C. H. DODD, *The Interpretation*, 36. 107; R. E. BROWN, *John*, 8.

[3]) See especially A. SCHLATTER, *Johannes*, 9.

[4]) Cf. Lev. R. XI:7. Cf. that sin gradually caused the Shekina to be removed, Gen. R. XIX:7.

[5]) Gen. R. XI:2 and XII:6. Abodah Zarah 8a. E. PREUSCHEN, *Die apo-*

Generally speaking, these two lines of thought see the darkness as a consequence of sin and thereby a punishment [1]).

The third line of thought does not regard the darkness only as a punishment, but identifies sin and darkness. This identification is found particularly in the Dead Sea Scrolls where the spirits of light and darkness, and the children of light and darkness are mentioned. The idea is also found without this mythological dualism in Syr. Baruch 17-18, where Adam's darkness is contrasted to the light of the law [2]).

In John there are places where darkness can be understood as a result of disbelief and sin, for example in xii 35, but there are also places where sin and darkness are closely connected or identified, John iii 19 ff. In John i 5b it is stated that nightfall seeks to overcome the light of day, and darkness here seems to be identified with man's sin [3]). Jewish texts support the hypothesis that John here is referring to Adam's Fall, and eventually the first generation's Fall as well, particularly as we find sin and darkness identified in Syr. Baruch 17-18, where Adam's darkness is mentioned.

According to John i 5b light was not overcome by darkness—but nightfall must have led to a new situation. Since John i 9 and xii 46 talk about the coming of light with the coming of Jesus, it follows by virtue of the fact, that primordial light, which mankind had according to John i 4, was removed from them. And since light's coming brought back life, viii 12, it follows that the original life, mentioned in John i 4, was lost. Thereby the train of thought in John follows precisely that of Jewish interpretative traditions, which consider light and life among the things lost at the Fall, brought back at a later moment of time in history, or in the coming aeon [4]).

---

kryphen gnostischen Adamschriften, Giessen 1900, 30-32. Cf. S. AALEN, *op. cit.*, 199. 265-66.

[1]) Gen. R. II:3 identifies the sinful generations with the primordial chaos in Gen i 2. Cf. Apocryphon Johannis 73:16-18, where the Deluge is depicted as darkness. See O. BETZ, "Was am Anfang geschah", *Abraham unser Vater* (OTTO MICHEL Festschrift), Leiden 1963, 38.

[2]) See for example I QS 3:25 and I QM; Test. Napht. 2:10; 1 Enoch 108:1; Philo, Quest. in Gen. ii:82. Cf. S. AALEN, *op. cit.*, 178 ff. and N. A. DAHL, "Begrepene 'Lys' og 'mörke' i jödedommen", *Norsk teologisk tidsskrift*, 53, 1952, 80 f.

[3]) Concerning light and darkness in John, see for example R. SCHNACKEN-BURG, *Johannesevangelium*, 223 ff.

[4]) Gen. R. XII: 6; Tanchuma B. Bereshit 18. J. JERVELL, *Imago dei*, 113 ff. See also Chag. 12a.

Thus we have already touched on the interpretation of John i 4 and 5a, but some points must be added. One could attempt an understanding of the general saying in v. 5a, καὶ τὸ φῶς ἐν τῇ σκοτίᾳ φαίνει, against the background of ideas in the Dead Sea Scrolls: how God created man, and the spirits of light and darkness are depicted there [1]). In John, however, light and darkness are not two equal religious-ethical powers. In fact, in John i 4 it is said only of light that it was with men in the beginning [2]). On this essential point, John follows the traditions which let Adam, and thereby mankind, have light as their original possession, with the ensuing Fall and darkness. The general saying in v. 5a, that light shines in the darkness, tells thereby of the possibility of the Fall in primordial time as well as in the later coming of light, but does not state that light and darkness are equal powers in men.

CONCLUSION

(1) We have attempted to show that the structure of the Prologue of John must primarily be understood on the basis that it is meant to be an exposition of Gen. i 1 ff. The question of poetry or prose is therefore of subordinate significance.

(2) John i 1-8 seems to draw on learned Jewish exegesis, wherein Logos, דבר and light, אור are connected on the basis of Gen. i 3.

(3) John i 4-9 should be understood against the background of Jewish traditions of primordial light which was followed by darkness in primordial time, thus to reappear later in history, or in the coming aeon.

(4) The participle ἐρχόμενον in John i 9 seems to refer back to the subject for φωτίζει, and both words depict light's, i.e. Jesus' coming.

(5) Since Logos in John is the light, the lawgiving at Sinai seems to provide a thought-model behind the coming of light in John i 9. With the lawgiving, the light of the Law shone upon all men, just as light in John i 9 enlightens every man.

(6) Therefore it is possible to understand vv. 6 ff. in terms of John, as a witness and lamp, introducing the salvation-history situation which prepared the coming of light in history.

---

[1]) I QS 3.

[2]) Detailed discussion of light and darkness in the Dead Sea Scrolls and in the Johannine writings in R. E. BROWN, "The Qumran Scrolls and the Johanninne Gospel and Epistles", *Catholic Biblical Quarterly*, XVII, 1955, 403-419; 559-574.

(7) καταλαμβάνειν in John i 5b means "seize", "overcome", in an undesirable or hostile manner. The conception of nightfall in this verse can be understood against the background of Jewish conceptions of the removal of light, and the coming of the darkness of night with Adam's and the first generation's sin. John seems to say implicitly that light and life were removed at the Fall, in order to be brought back into the world by the coming of Jesus.

(8) Even though an understanding of the Targum schema a), b), c) / c), b), a) in John i 1-18 can be attempted on the basis of theories of a source reworked and supplemented by the evangelist, we have tried to show that Jewish traditions and a closer analysis of the Prologue of John make such analysis unnecessary, at least in verses 4-9. Therefore it would seem to be a viable hypothesis that John i 1-18 in entirety can be treated as a composition of the evangelist himself, wherein elements from different traditions are woven together.

This study is a partial study of John i 1-18 and will naturally lead to corresponding investigations of the ideas in vv. 3 and 10-13, respectively, of Logos' creation of the world, and coming to its work of creation with the coming of Jesus; and in vv. 1-2 and 14-18, respectively, of the existence of Logos and God before the creation, and the epiphany at the coming of Jesus, when Logos became flesh. As soon as these enquiries have been carried out, the relation between John i 1-18 and the gospel as a whole can be taken up in entirety. Meanwhile, this study concludes with the more limited field indicated by the title, "Logos was the true Light."

THE WEDDING AT CANA (JOHN II 1-11):
A PENTECOSTAL MEDITATION?

JOSEPH A. GRASSI
Madison, New Jersey

The Jewish feast of Pentecost lies in the background of the great outpouring of the Spirit in Acts i-ii that opens Luke's narrative. It is our purpose here to point to similarities between Acts chaps. i and ii and the opening sign at Cana in John ii 1-11; we will also try to show how the meaning of the Jewish Pentecost may help to bring out the full significance of the first sign of Jesus at Cana in Galilee.

We will not be concerned here to try to reach to the original historical setting of the sign at Cana [1]). Likewise, we will assume, as many authors [2]) have pointed out, a double meaning in the narrative pointing to the messianic age and the gift of the Spirit. Our concern will only be to point out how the covenant background of the feast of Weeks together with similarities to Acts i and ii help to bring out the symbolism of Jesus' first sign.

Originally the feast of Pentecost marked the end of the harvest. It was called the feast of Weeks by the Jews, and marked the end of a period of seven weeks after the beginning of the harvest season. However, in the post-exilic period, the feast gradually took on the characteristics of a celebration of the covenant and the giving of the Torah. This is shown in the intertestamental literature. In the book of Jubilees, Pentecost is the most important Jewish feast. It retains its character as a harvest festival, but becomes the day when the great covenants of the past took place. Noah, e.g., went out of

---

[1]) F. E. WILLIAMS has suggested that John ii 1-11 may be a dramatization of Luke v 33-39 in its themes of fasting, new and old wine. Cf. "Fourth Gospel and Synoptic Tradition, Two Johannine Passages", *JBL* 86 (1967), pp. 311-319. Others, especially D. M. DERRETT have sought the original historical event in the light of Jewish custom and law. Cf. "Water into Wine", *BibZeit* 7 (1963), 80-97.

[2]) Cf. R. BROWN, in the *Anchor Bible, The Gospel According to John* (N.Y. 1966), pp. 97-111.

the ark at this time and God made a covenant with him (vi 1-17). Abraham also made a covenant with God at the time of this feast (xxiv 20); likewise, the patriarchs Isaac (xxii 1) and Jacob (xliv 1-4). Pentecost is described as a feast when all the people should renew the covenant:

.... for this reason it is ordained and written in the heavenly tablets that they should celebrate the feast of weeks in this month once a year to renew the covenant each year. (vi 17)

In view of the extensive use of Jubilees by the Qumran community, J. T. MILIK [1]) dates Jubilees before 100 B.C.

In the Qumran community, a close connection was made between Pentecost and the covenant. According to the Manual of Discipline, new members took their "final vows" after a year of instruction and an additional year of probation (ch. vi). At this time all the members of the community renewed their covenant to keep the law of Moses with all their heart (1 QS 2:19). A number of considerations make it most probable that this annual renewal of the the covenant took place at Pentecost: (1) MILIK states, "Our oldest manuscripts of the Damascus Covenant place the renewal of the covenant in the third month of the year" [2]). (2) The book of Jubilees, which was the community's guide book calendar calls for a renewal of the covenant year by year by all the people at the feast of Pentecost (vi 17, cited above).

Rabbinic tradition likewise links the giving of the Law and Pentecost, although the first evidence is about the middle of the second century. The Seder Olam Rabba [3]) states that the Ten Commandments were given on the sabbath day of the feast of Weeks. In the Talmud [4]) a century later, Rabbi Eleazar ben Pedath said that Pentecost was the day on which the Torah was given. These rabbinic references, while late, may be drawn from a earlier tradition.

In the New Testament there are three direct references to Pentecost. These are in Acts ii, the initial great outpouring of the Spirit on Pentecost day; Acts xx 16, where Paul hastens to Jerusalem for the feast; and 1 Cor. xvi 8 where Paul wants to stay at Ephesus

---

[1]) *Ten Yars of Discovery in the Wilderness of Judea*, p. 32.
[2]) *Ibid.* p. 117.
[3]) STRACK and BILLERBECK, *Kommentar zum N.T. aus Talmud und Midrash*, Vol. 2, p. 601.
[4]) *Pes. 68b*

until Pentecost. There are some indications that Christians thought of Pentecost in terms of the celebration of the giving of the New Torah through the resurrection of Christ. In Acts, ch. ii, the sound of a mighty wind, the flames of fire, the voices understood in many languages all remind us of the account of the giving of the covenant in Exodus xix. Yet E. LOHSE [1]) reminds us that the references are not strong enough to conclude definitely that Luke is thinking in terms of a new revelation like that of Sinai.

With this background of Pentecost as a Jewish and possibly a Christian feast of the covenant we can now go to the text of John ii 1-11 with an eye on the corresponding opening sign in Acts ii. *"On the third day* there was a marriage at Cana in Galilee . . ."* (John ii 1). The reference to the third day has been interpreted in various ways: it may mark the completion of the first seven days after the witness of John the Baptist (i 19-28), or it may be the 3rd day after the call of Philip and Nathaniel. However, with Pentecost in mind, the three days before the giving of the Torah and covenant on Sinai have a very special place in Jewish tradition. They are called the "days of bounding" to commemorate the order that no one was to approach the holy mountain during this time, and that no one was to engage in marital relations. It was a time of prayer and preparation. It was on the third day that Moses went up to the mountain (Ex. xix 16). The resurrection of Jesus on the third day may be related to the third day on the mountain as the inauguration of a new covenant.

"At Cana in *Galilee* . . ." The first sign of Jesus takes place in Galilee. This may be of significance, for the Pentecostal account in Acts ii does point out that the first recipients of the Spirit were Galileans: "Are not all these who are speaking Galileans? (ii 7).

"The *mother of Jesus* was there" (John ii 1). The only other place in the New Testament where the precise expression, "the mother of Jesus" is used is in Acts i 14, "All these with one accord devoted themselves to prayer together with the women and Mary, the *mother of Jesus,* and with his brethren". In the symbolic sense of John ii 3, the mother of Jesus appears to be a representative figure of the Church [2]) which implicitly asks for the new wine of the

---

[1]) KITTEL, *Theological Dictionary of the N.T.*, vol. vi, p. 49.

[2]) Cf. BROWN, pp. 108-109. Also E. J. KILMARTIN, "The Mother of Jesus was there", *SciEccl* 15 (1963) pp. 213-226. R. J. DILLON writes, "In the retrospect of the final age, Mary becomes the representative of the faithful

Spirit as she says to Jesus, "They have no wine". In Acts i 14, during the preparatory "days of bounding", Mary the mother of Jesus, the brethren and the twelve pray together for the gift of the Spirit. Corresponding to the wine at Cana, the effects of the Spirit are likened to those of new wine by the crowd when they remark, "They are filled with new wine" (ii 13). The brethren of Jesus also find a place close to the Cana story: "After this he went down to Capernaum with his mother and his *brethren* and his disciples: and there they stayed for a few days" (ii 12).

"When the wine failed, the mother of Jesus said to him, 'They have no wine' " (ii 3). The Torah was frequently called "wine" in view of its effects on men [1]). The old wine was come to an end [2]). It must be renewed. The account in Acts also has the underlying theme of one period that is drawing to a close: "When the day of Pentecost had come ... (ii 1). It is now truly the feast of the completion of the harvest, the time of fulfillment. Peter announces that the prophecies of Joel concerning the last days have been fulfilled (ii 17).

"And Jesus said to her, "O woman, what have you to do with me? My hour has not yet come" (ii 4). Jesus' reference to his *hour* gives the important key that the whole story has a deeper meaning that can only be understood after the *hour* of Jesus, which is his death and glorification (cf. John vii 6, 8, 30; viii 20; xii 23; xiii 1). It is only then that the Spirit will be given as we see in John vii 39, "Now this he said about the Spirit, which those who believed in him were to receive; for as yet the Spirit had not been given, because Jesus was not yet glorified".

"His mother said to the servants, 'Do whatever he tells you' " (ii 5). These words belong to the covenant background of the Pentecost feast of the Torah. When Moses ascended Mt. Sinai, God instructed him to tell the people to listen to his voice and keep the covenant.When Moses told this to the people they all answered together, "Everything the Lord has said, we will do" (Ex. xix 3-8). At Cana the emphasis is on obedience to the words of Jesus and his

---

remnant of Israel. "They have no wine" is an expression of the craving of the faithful Israel for the riches of the new age." Cf. "Wisdom Tradition and Sacramental Retrospect in the Cana Account (Jn 2:1-11)", *CBQ* 24 (1962), p. 291.

[1]) Exod. R. 25, 7.

[2]) C. H. DODD brings out the contrast between the Torah and Christ in *Interpretation of the Fourth Gospel* (Cambridge, 1958), pp. 56-57.

commands. Jesus' word is the new Torah that must be obeyed. The writer carefully notes Jesus' commands and the exact obedience: "Jesus said to them, 'Fill the jars with water'. *And they filled them up to the brim"* (ii 7). He then tells them to draw out some and bring to the steward. The text notes, *"So they took it"* (ii 8b). In the fourth gospel, obedience to Jesus' words is a sign of belonging to the new covenant: "He who has my commandments and keeps them, he it is who loves me" (xiv 21). Cf. also xiv 23; xv 14. The Spirit only comes through following Jesus and obeying his word. Likewise, in Acts ii, Luke points out that the Spirit comes on the gathered assembly as a result of obedience to Jesus' command to gather together in his name in Jerusalem after his ascension. The last words of Jesus in Luke carry this injunction: "Behold I send the promise of my Father upon you; but stay in the city, until you are clothed with power from on high" (xxiv 49). The precept is repeated in Acts i 4. Both Luke and Acts point out how the disciples carefully obeyed his command: in Acts i 12 they return from Mount Olivet to Jerusalem to an upper room where they wait and pray for the coming of the Spirit; in Luke xxiv 52, they return to Jerusalem.

"Now six stone jars were standing there, for the Jewish rites of purification, each holding two or three measures. Jesus said to them, 'Fill the jars with water'. And they filled them to the brim" (ii 6-7). These two verses have a strong emphasis on filling or completion. The number six, of course, is a familiar symbol of incompletion in the bible. The jars themselves can hold an enormous quantity of water, but they are still far short of their capacity. At Jesus' order they are filled. The execution of the command is carefully noted: "they filled them *to the brim"*. Jesus brings them to overflowing capacity. The Greek of v. 6 literally reads that the jars held from two to three measures. The work of Jesus is to fulfil the Father's design to give the Spirit without any measure: "It is *not by measure* that he gives the Spirit" (iii 34). The Pentecostal account in Acts also emphasizes this filling by the Spirit: the Spirit fills the house where they were gathered together (ii 2); "They were all filled with the Holy Spirit" (ii 4); they were filled or drunk with new wine (ii 13); it is the outpouring of the Spirit on all flesh (ii 17) ; it is an overflowing gift that goes out from the disciples to believers in the crowd; Peter tells them that if they repent and believe, they will receive the gift of the Spirit (ii 38).

In the Cana account, v. 9, the steward did not know where the new wine had come from. Jelus also tells Nicodemus that no one really knows where the Spitir is from. It is like wind which comes and goes and no one knows where it is from (iii 8).

In Acts ii, a sound like a strong wind of unknown source suddenly fills the house (v. 2). It has visible effects on men causing them to speak in tongues praising God; however, the source cannot be verified and the crowd remains bewildered.

"You have kept the good wine until now" (ii 10). The good wine has been reserved and kept for the messianic times. It is a familiar theme in the prophets that the last times will be characterized by a superabundance of good wine (Amos ix 13-14; Jer. xxxi 12). In the Acts of the Apostles, when some mock the disciples as being filled with new wine, Peter announces that the coming of the Spirit is actually the fulfillment of the prophet Joel who had declared that a great outpouring of the Spirit had been reserved for the last days (ii 16-17).

"This, the first of his signs, Jesus did at Cana in Galilee, and manifested his glory; and his disciples believed in him" (ii 11). The reference to the manifestation of his glory is another link with the Exodus account of the giving of the Law. When Moses went up to receive the stone tablets, the writer states that the glory of the Lord settled upon Mt. Sinai and all the Israelites saw it as a consuming fire on the mountain top (xxiv 16-17). The Cana account closes with the brief statement, "and his disciples believed in him". This is also the conclusion of the Pentecost narrative in Acts. The author refers to the early pentecostal community as "all those who believed" (ii 44).

We may conclude then that there is considerable evidence that the wedding at Cana has a deep symbolic meaning in the mind of the evangelist as he thinks of Jesus' word as a new Torah. It has many aspects of a Pentecostal meditation, with some striking similarities to the description of the great outpouring of the Spirit at Pentecost in Acts ii. The old wine has run out. The disciples, the brethren, and the mother of Jesus ask for the new wine of the Spirit. This is given through obedience to Jesus' word as the nucleus of the New Covenant. Through Jesus, God gives the Spirit without measure to believers. Filled to the brim with the Spirit, they manifest his glory and bring the overflowing gift to others.

THE SOURCE ANALYSIS OF THE FOURTH GOSPEL
A GROWING CONSENSUS?

BY

ROBERT KYSAR
Minnesota

Some seven years ago DWIGHT MOODY SMITH published his article, "The Sources of the Gospel of John: An Assessment of the Present State of the Problem" [1]), in which he reviewed the work of HEINZ BECKER, WILHELM WILKENS, and SIEGFRIED SCHULZ endeavoring to penetrate behind the fourth gospel to the sources utilized by the evangelist. He concluded his essay by suggesting a number of trends which seemed to betray an emerging consensus in the source criticism of the fourth gospel: First, John did not use the synoptic gospels, even though he may have drawn some of his material from a tradition having some points of contact with the synoptic oral tradition; second, some interest in the genre of johannine *Reden* seemed to be arising; and third, the fundamentally semitic background of the johannine tradition seemed agreed upon, thanks in part to the discoveries at Qumran [2]). While SMITH's observations concerning the degree of consensus in Fourth gospel source criticism were accurate, it is instructive that he did not at the time of the publication of his article propose that an actual consensus was emerging among the critics as to which johannine passages are most likely to have been taken from a source and which originated from the hand of the evangelist. In the time which has elapsed since SMITH's observations, we have had more opportunity to appropriate the contributions of the works he considered, and more important we have had new efforts at the task of the source critical study of the fourth gospel [3]). For those

---

[1]) DWIGHT MOODY SMITH, "The Sources of the Gospel of John: An Assessment of the Present State of the Problem", *New Testament Studies* 10 (63-64), pp. 336-351.

[2]) *Ibid.*, pp. 349-351.

[3]) For a history of the efforts to do source criticism of the fourth gospel cf. BENJAMIN BACON, *The Fourth Gospel in Research and Debate* (New York: Moffat, Yard, and Co., 1910); JAMES MOFFATT, *Introduction to the Literature of the New Testament*(New York: Scribner and Sons, 1911); WILHELM

reasons, it is the proposal of this paper that we attempt to go further in seeking the consensus SMITH spoke of—that we seek a consensus, at least of a preliminary kind, among the critics with regard to the passages they isolate. Such an effort appears necessary, if the critical study of John is to proceed. For with some sort of beginning for the source analysis of the gospel, it would then be possible to make some still more valuable studies on the basis of that generally agreed upon source analysis: Redaction criticism could then proceed in the manner which has been so richly rewarding in the study of the synoptics [1]. Significant conclusions regarding the *Sitz im Leben* of the evangelist and consequently some conclusions with regard to the history of the community in that period in which he wrote could be ventured [2]. The investigation of the proposed sources with the resultant hypotheses regarding the history of the johannine tradition would be an obvious benefit of such a consensus.

This paper will attempt to assess the degree of this consensus by looking at nine major source theories as they apply to a selected chapter of the gospel. Chapter six has been selected for a number of reasons, but primarily because it offers a single chapter in which both narrative and discourse material appear. Moreover, the chapter offers johannine material which in some cases has obvious synoptic contacts and in other cases drastically non-synoptic pericopes. The source theories applied to this chapter represent the most valuable contributions to the question since (and including) the monumental work of RUDOLF BULTMANN. After a brief introduction to the source theories, a visual representation of the agreement and divergence among them will be followed by some conclusions.

BOUSSET, "Ist das vierte Evangelium eine literarische Einheit ?" *Theologische Rundschau,* 12 (1909), pp. 1-12; PAUL FEINE, JOHANNES BEHM, WERNER GEORG KÜMMEL, *Introduction to the New Testament* (New York: Abingdon Press, 1966), pp. 142-154; WILBERT FRANCIS HOWARD, *The Fourth Gospel in Recent Criticism and Interpretation*, revised by C. K. BARRETT (London: The Epworth Press, 1955); JOACHIM JEREMIAS, "Johanneische Literarkritik", *Theologische Blätter,* 20 (1941), pp. 33046; RUDOLF SCHNACKENBURG, *The Gospel According to St. John* (New York: Herder and Herder), vol. I, pp. 48-52, 59-72.

[1] For example, ROBERT FORTNA, "Source and Redaction in the Fourth Gospel's Portrayal of Jesus' Signs", *Journal of Biblical Literature,* 89 (1970), pp. 151-166.

[2] For example, J. LOUIS MARTYN, "Source Criticism and Religionsgeschichte in the Fourth Gospel", *Jesus and Man's Hope* (A *Perspective* Book published by Pittsburgh Theological Seminary), vol. I, pp. 247-273.

It is the assumption of this study that such a sampling of the degree of consensus among the theories might be suggestive of the sort of consensus to be found should the theories as applied to the entire gospel be compared as they have been here in the case of chapter six.

The nine theories in the order in which they appear in the under-lining scheme below are: First, BULTMANN's proposal of a *semeia* and *Offenbarungsreden* sources. As is well known, BULTMANN proposed the evangelist constructed his gospel utilizing these two sources plus a passion source and a miscellany of other sources and traditions; the gospel then underwent an alleged redaction at the hands of an orthodox ecclesiastical figure [1]). Following the lead of his teacher, HEINZ BECKER attempted to reconstruct the gnostic *Offenbarungsreden* source utilized by the evangelist; his method to do so was primarily *Religionsgeschichte*, since he tried to establish the source by finding gnostic parallels for johannine logia [2]). The third and most recent source theory considered here is that of ROBERT FORTNA, who reconstructed a "signs gospel" from his careful analysis primarily of aporias appearing in the fourth gospel [3]). Since FORTNA's proposed source is an exclusively narrative source and BECKER's exclusively sayings material, they are supplementary for our purposes. WILHELM WILKENS proposed four stages to the development of the fourth gospel: (1) a *Grund-evangelium* (2) to which were added seven discourses which consti-tuted a second source, (3) the result being then revised into a "passion narrative", and (4) finally redacted [4]). The fifth source

---

[1]) RUDOLF BULTMANN, *Das Evangelium des Johannes*, 16th ed. with Erganzungsheft (Göttnigen: Vandenhoeck und Ruprecht, 1962). For a useful summary and critique cf. DWIGHT MOODY SMITH, Jr., *The Composition and Order of the Fourth Gospel: Bultmann's Literary Theory* (New Haven: Yale University, 1965).

[2]) HEINZ BECKER, *Die Reden des Johannesevangeliums und der Stil der gnostischen Offenbarungsrede*, (Göttingen: Vandenhoeck und Ruprecht, 1956). For a critical review cf. SMITH, "The Sources of the Gospel of John: An Assessment of the Present State of the Problem", pp. 343 ff.

[3]) ROBERT FORTNA, *The Gospel of Signs. A Reconstruction of the Narrative Source Underlying the Fourth Gospel*, Society of New Testament Studies Monograph Series, 11 (Cambridge: The University Press, 1970. For a critical review cf. ROBERT KYSAR, *Perspective*, 11 (1970); pp. 334-336 and SMITH, *Journal of Biblical Literature*, 89 (1970), pp. 498-501.

[4]) WILHELM WILKENS, *Die Entstehungsgeschichte des vierten Evangeliums* (Zollikon: Evangelischer Verlag, 1958). For critical reviews cf. J. M. ROBIN-SON, "Recent Research in the Fourth Gospel", *Journal of Biblical Literature*, 78 (1959), pp. 242-246; and C. K. BARRETT, "Die Entstehungsgeschichte

theory utilized here is that of WILHELM HARTKE, whose proposal
calls for a separation of a signs source which had been expanded
into a ur-John before the evangelist revised the work to produce
its present form [1]). EDWIN BROOME's elaborate source hypothesis
isolates seven probable sources: A collection of independent
sayings beginning with ἀμήν, ἀμήν (S1), logia of a Greek character
without the introductory expression found in S1 (S2), logia which
show a definite Aramaic origin (S3), the EGO EIMI sayings (S4),
the seven signs (S5), independent anecdotes about Jesus (S6), and
a passion source (S7) [2]). In the course of applying his hypothesis
to chapter six we will have occasion to use only his proposed
S1, S4, and S5. OCTAVE MERLIER isolates in *formgeschichtliche*
manner four types of discourse material in John and proposes that
the evangelist made clear use of some sort of source (oral or
written) in the appearances of the first type of sayings, namely,
dialogues which, MERLIER contends, were contained in an anonymous collection of logia. Beyond this logia source, MERLIER proposes that there was an account of the life, death and resurrection
of Jesus "treated in a 'johannine manner' " which a redactor
harmonized with the collection of sayings. Discourses of edification
and preaching were then added to the gospel, followed by a final
redaction which produced the present work [3]). It is only that first
alleged collection of logia which we shall investigate below. The
work of SIEGFRIED SCHULZ's *Themageschichte* constitutes our
eighth source theory. For our purposes we will invoke those theme
traditions which SCHULZ develops around *Bildworte* and *Bildrede*

---

des vierten Evangeliums", *Theologische Literaturzeitung*, 84 (1959), pp.
828-829. WILKENS' article, "Evangelist und Tradition im Johannesevangelium", *Theologische Zeitschrift*, 16 (1960), pp. 81-90, has also been utilized
and is cited ETJ below.

[1]) WILHELM HARTKE, *Vier urchristliche Parteien und ihre Vereinigung
zur apostolischen Kirche*, (Berlin: Akademie Verlage, 1961). For critical
reviews cf. PAUL VIELHAUER, "Einleitung in das Neue Testament (Fort-
setzung)", *Theologische Rundschau*, 31 (1966), pp. 193-231; G. BERTRAM,
Theologische Literaturzeitung, 89 (1964), pp. 837-842; and J. N. BIRDSALL,
Journal of Theological Studies, 14 (1963), pp. 473-476.

[2]) EDWIN C. BROOME, Jr. "The Sources of the Fourth Gospel", *Journal
of Biblical Literature*, 63 (1944), pp. 107-121.

[3]) OCTAVE MERLIER, *Le quatrième Évangile: La question Johannique XI*.
Études Neo-Testamentaires, 2. (Paris: Presses Universitaires de France,
1961). For critical reviews cf. SCHNACKENBURG, *The Gospel According to Saint
John*, vol. I, pp. 61-62; and J. T. FORESTELL, *Theological Studies*, 23 (1962),
pp. 649-652.

and the EGO EIMI logia [1]). Finally, M. E. BOISMARD's distinction
between the "first" and later stratum of the fourth gospel will be
applied along with the other proposals [2]). Where other consensus
can be suggested by reference to less elaborate and explicit source
hypotheses, such will be done by means of notes.

It is instructive to note several things about the source theories
here examined. First, it is important that they emerge from a
variety of methods. The traditional methodology of source criticism
has been utilized by BULTMANN and FORTNA. HARTKE has applied
the same method somewhat revised, however, by his ambitious
effort to retain an encyclopedic history of tradition perspective.
Traditional source criticism with a special interest in Aramaisms
characterizes the hypothesis of BROOME. WILKENS and BOISMARD
both depart from source criticism by claiming that their efforts
are designed only to describe the stages of composition through
which the gospel went, all at the hands of the same evangelist; and
hence their work does not purport to be source analysis at all.
While BECKER's work is clearly *Religionsgeschichte*, SCHULZ calls
his method *Themageschichte*, and MERLIER's efforts seem to be in
the tradition of *Formgeschichte*. That such a variety of methodolo-
gies characterizes the nine theories we propose to compare is important, since if any consensus of significance is achieved, it will mean
that such consensus has emerged from a considerably wide range
of methods. Hence, one can argue that the degree of consensus is
that much more valuable, since it has not been the effect of similarly applied methods. A second observation is necessary when
considering the comparison of these nine theories, namely, the
variance of degree of specificity and exactitude attempted by each
out of his methodology. While the source criticism of FORTNA, for
instance, allows and even requires him to delineate carefully between
the source and the evangelist (sometimes excluding single words

---

[1]) SIEGFRIED SCHULZ, *Komposition und Herkunft der Johanneischen Reden*,
Beiträge zur Wissenschaft vom Alten und Neuen Testament (Stuttgart: W.
Kohlhammer, 1960), and *Untersuchungen zur Menschensohn-Christologie im
Johannesevangelium* (Göttingen: Vandenhoeck und Ruprecht, 1957). For
critical reviews cf. ROBINSON, "Recent Research in the Fourth Gospel",
pp. 247-250.

[2]) M. E. BOISMARD, "L'évolution du thème eschatologique dans les
traditions johanniques", *Revue Biblique*, 68 (1961), pp. 507-525. For a
critical review cf. SCHNACKENBURG, *The Gospel According to Saint John*,
vol. I, pp. 70-71.

or short phrases from the proposed source), WILKENS' method necessitates that he do no more than mark off larger passages which represent the earliest stage of the gospel. Such variety does hinder the comparison of the hypotheses but must be accepted as the consequence of the important variety of methods involved.

The abbreviations used in the underlining to designate the theories are:

bs — BULTMANN's *semeia* source

bo — BULTMANN's *Offenbarungsreden* source

 f — FORTNA's signs gospel

go — BECKER's gnostic *Offenbarungsreden*

wg — WILKENS' *Grundevangelium*

wr — WILKENS' *Reden* (allegedly used in expanding the *Grundevangelium*)

hz — HARTKE's signs source

hv — HARTKE's ur-John

 sl — BROOME's collection of Aramaic sayings

s4 — BROOME's collection of EGO EIMI sayings

s5 — BROOME's signs source

 m — MERLIER's anonymous logia collection

sb — SCHULZ's *Bildworte-reden* tradition

ss — SCHULZ's Son of Man tradition

boi — BOISMARD's "first strata" of the gospel

In the underlining scheme, the first line indicates BULTMANN's source hypotheses. The second line is utilized for FORTNA's sign gospel in the narrative material and BECKER's *Offenbarungsreden* in the discourse sections of the chapter. The third marks off WILKENS' *Grundevangelium* and *Reden* sources, while the fourth line is reserved for HARTKE's signs and ur-gospel proposals. The fifth line is a conglomerate representation of the theories of BROOME, MERLIER, SCHULZ, and BOISMARD. Where there is agreement among any or all of these theories as to the attribution of a passage to sources, the underlining will combine the appropriate symbols; the notes in the margin will indicate the meaning of such combinations.

Μετὰ ταῦτα ἀπῆλθεν ὁ Ἰησοῦς πέραν τῆς θαλάσσης τῆς Γαλιλαίας
bsbsbsbsbsbsbsbsbsbsbsbsbsbsbsbsbsbsbsbsbsbsbsbsbsbsbsbsbsbsbsbsbsbsbsbsbsbsbs
ffffffffffffffffffffffffffffffffffffffffffffffffffffffffffffffffffffffffffffffffffffffffffffffffffffffffffffffffffffffffff
wgwgwgwgwgwgwgwgwgwgwgwgwgwgwgwgwgwgwgwgwgwgwgwgwgwgwgwgwgwgwgwgwgwgwgwgwgwg
hzhzhzhzhzhzhzhzhzhzhzhzhzhzhzhzhzhzhzhzhzhzhzhzhzhzhzhzhzhzhzhzhzhzhzhzhzhzhzhzhzh
s5s5s5s5s5s5s5s5s5s5s5s5s5s5s5s5s5s5s5s5s5s5s5s5s5s5s5s5s5s5s5s5s5s5s5s5s5s5s5s5s5s5s5s5s5s5s5s5
τῆς Τιβεριάδος. 2 ἠκολούθει δὲ αὐτῷ ὄχλος πολύς, ὅτι ἑώρων τὰ σημεῖα
bsbsbsbsbsbsbsbsbsbsbsbsbsbsbsbsbsbs
ffffffffffffffffffffffffffffffffffffffffffffffffffffffffff
wgwgwgwgwgwgwgwgwgwgwgwgwgwgwgwgwgwgwgwgwgwgwgwgwgwgwgwgwgwgwgwgwgwgwg
hzhzhzhzhzhzhzhzhzhzhzhzhzhzhzhzhzhzhzhzhzhzhzhzhzhzhzhzhzhzhzhz
s5s5s5s5s5s5s5s5s5s5s5s5s5s5s5s5s5s5s5s5s5s5s5s5s5s5s5s5s5s5s5s5s5s5s5s5s5s5s5s5s5s5s5s5s5s5s5
ἃ ἐποίει ἐπὶ τῶν ἀσθενούντων. 3 ἀνῆλθεν δὲ εἰς τὸ ὄρος Ἰησοῦς, καὶ
bsbsbsbsbsbsbsbsbsbsbsbsbsbsbsbsbsbsbsbsbs
ffffffffffffffffffffffffffffffffffffffffffffffffffffffffffffffffffffffffffff
wgwgwgwgwgwgwgwgwgwgwgwgwgwgwgwgwgwgwgwgwgwgwgwgwgwgwgwgwgwgwgwg
hzhzhzhzhzhzhzhzhzhzhzhzhzhzhzhzhzhzhzhzhzhzhzhzhzhzhzhzhzhzhzhzhzhz
5s5s5s5s5s5s5s5s5s5s5s5s5s5s5s5s5s5s5s5s5s5s5s5s5s5s5s5s5s5s5s5s5s5s5s5s5s5s5s5s5s5
ἐκεῖ ἐκάθητο μετὰ τῶν μαθητῶν αὐτοῦ. 4 ἦν δὲ ἐγγὺς τὸ πάσχα, ἡ
bsbsbsbsbsbsbsbsbsbsbsbsbsbsbsbsbsbsbsbsbs
ffffffffffffffffffffffffffffffffffffffffffffffffffffffffffffffff
wgwgwgwgwgwgwgwgwgwgwgwgwgwgwgwgwgwgwgwgwgwgw
hzhzhzhzhzhzhzhzhzhzhzhzhzhzhzhzhzhzhzhzhzhzhzhzhzhzhzhzhzhzhzhzhzhz
s5s5s5s5s5s5s5s5s5s5s5s5s5s5s5s5s5s5s5s5s5s5s5s5s5s5s5s5s5s5s5s5s5s5s5s5s5s5s5s5s5s5s5s5
ἑορτὴ τῶν Ἰουδαίων. 5 ἐπάρας οὖν τοὺς ὀφθαλμοὺς ὁ Ἰησοῦς καὶ θεασά-
bsbsbsbsbsbsbsbsbsbsbsbsbsbsbsbsbsbsbsbsbsbsbsbsbsbsbsbsbsbsbsbs
ffffffffff   ffffffffffffffffffffffffffffffffffffffffffffffffffffffffffffffffff
wgwgwgwgwgwgwgwgwgwgwgwgwgwgwgwgwgwgwgwgwgwgw
hzhzhzhzhzhzhzhzhzhzhzhzhzhzhzhzhzhzhzhzhzhzhzhzhzhzhzhzhzhzhzhzhzhz
s5s5s5s5s5s5s5s5s5s5s5s5s5s5s5s5s5s5s5s5s5s5s5s5s5s5s5s5s5s5s5s5s5s5s5s5s5s5s5s5s5s5s5
μενος ὅτι πολὺς ὄχλος ἔρχεται πρὸς αὐτόν, λέγει πρὸς Φίλιππον· πόθεν
bsbsbsbsbsbsbsbsbsbsbsbsbsbsbsbsbsbsbsbsbsbsbsbsbsbsbsbsbsbsbsbsbsbs
fffffffffffffffffffffffffffffffffffffffffffffffffffffffffffffffffffff   ffffffffff
wgwgwgwgwgwgwgwgwgwgwgwgwgwgwgwgwgwgwg   wgwg
hzhzhzhzhzhzhzhzhzhzhzhzhzhzhzhzhzhzhzhzhzhzhzhzhzhzhzhzhzhzhzhzhzhzhzh
s5s5s5s5s5s5s5s5s5s5s5s5s5s5s5s5s5s5s5s5s5s5s5s5s5s5s5s5s5s5s5s5s5s5s5s5s5s5s5s5s5s5s5s5s5

v. 1: WILKENS argues that the locale in Galilee is traditional and is less
sure of the reference to τῆς Τιβεριάδος (ETJ).

vs. 2-3: HAENCHEN claims that these verses betray the theology of the
Vorlage (*loc. cit.*) [1]).

v. 5: FORTNA suggests that the signs gospel originally read τοῖς μαθηταῖς
αὐτοῦ instead of πρὸς Φίλιππον (pp. 57-58). WILKENS' suggestion is similar
(ETJ).

---

[1]) These citations of Haenchen are to his yet unpublished and incomplete
commentary on the Gospel of John circulated privately. For other indications
of HAENCHEN's somewhat ambiguous position with regard to the sources
for the fourth gospel cf. "History and Interpretation in the Johannine
Passion Narrative", *Interpretation*, 24 (1970), pp. 198-219 (especially p. 207,
n. 24); "Johanneischen Probleme", *Zeitschrift für Theologie und Kirche*,
56 (1959), pp. 19-54, also found in *Gott und Mensch* (Tübingen: J. C. B.
Mohr, 1965), pp. 78-113; " 'Der Vater, der mich gesandt hat' ", *New Testament Studies*, 9 (1963), pp. 208-216, also printed in *Gott und Mensch*, pp. 68-77.

136 ROBERT KYSAR

ἀγοράσωμεν ἄρτους ἵνα φάγωσιν οὗτοι; 6 τοῦτο δὲ ἔλεγεν πειράζων

αὐτόν· αὐτὸς γὰρ ᾔδει τί ἔμελλεν ποιεῖν. 7 ἀπεκρίθη αὐτῷ ὁ Φίλιππος·

διακοσίων δηναρίων ἄρτοι οὐκ ἀρκοῦσιν αὐτοῖς, ἵνα ἕκαστος βραχύ τι

λάβῃ. 8 λέγει αὐτῷ εἷς ἐκ τῶν μαθητῶν αὐτοῦ, Ἀνδρέας ὁ ἀδελφὸς

Σίμωνος Πέτρου· 9 ἔστιν παιδάριον ὧδε ὃς ἔχει πέντε ἄρτους κριθίνους

καὶ δύο ὀψάρια· ἀλλὰ ταῦτα τί ἐστιν εἰς τοσούτους; 10 εἶπεν ὁ Ἰησοῦς·

ποιήσατε τοὺς ἀνθρώπους ἀναπεσεῖν. ἦν δὲ χόρτος πολὺς ἐν τῷ τόπῳ.

ἀνέπεσαν οὖν· οἱ ἄνδρες τὸν ἀριθμὸν ὡς πεντακισχίλιοι. 11 ἔλαβεν οὖν

v. 7: Again WILKENS doubts that the disciple was named in the *Grund-evangelium* (ETJ). HAENCHEN calls the content of v. 7 clearly "traditional" (*loc. cit.*).

v. 9: FORTNA has some doubt that the name Σίμωνος appeared in the signs gospel (p. 58).

v. 9: WILKENS is not certain that the source referred to the one who had the fragments of food as a "boy" (ETJ).

τοὺς ἄρτους ὁ Ἰησοῦς καὶ εὐχαριστήσας διέδωκεν τοῖς ἀνακειμένοις,
bsbsbsbsbsbsbsbsbsbsbsbsbsbsbsbsbsbsbsbsbsbsbsbsbsbsbsbsbsbsbsbsbsbsbsbsbsbsbsbsbsbsbsbsbsbsbsbsbs
fffffffffffffffffffffffffffffffffffffffffffffffffffffffffffffffffffffffffffffffffffffffffffffffffffffffffffffffffffffffffffffffffffffffffffffffffffffff
wgwgwgwgwgwgwgwgwgwgwgwgwgwgwgwgwgwgwgwgwgwgwgwgwgwgwgwgwgwgwgwgwgwgwgwg
hzhzhzhzhzhzhzhzhzhzhzhzhzhzhzhzhzhzhzhzhzhzhzhzhzhzhzhzhzhzhzhzhzhzhzhzhzhzhzh
s5s5s5s5s5s5s5s5s5s5s5s5s5s5s5s5s5s5s5s5s5s5s5s5s5s5s5s5s5s5s5s5s5s5s5s5s5s5s5s5s5s5s5s5s5s5s5s5s
ὁμοίως καὶ ἐκ τῶν ὀψαρίων ὅσον ἤθελον. 12 ὡς δὲ ἐνεπλήσθησαν, λέγει
bsbsbsbsbsbsbsbsbsbsbsbsbsbsbsbsbsbsbsbsbsbsbsbsbsbsbsbsbsbsbsbsbsbsbsbsbsbsbsbsbsbsbsbsbsbsbsbsbs
fffffffffffffffffffffffffffffffffffffffffffffffffffffffffffffffffffffffffffffffffffffffffffffffffffffffffffffffffffffffffffffffffffffffffffffffffffffff
wgwgwgwgwgwgwgwgwgwgwgwgwgwgwgwgwgwgwgwgwgwgwgwgwgwgwgwgwgwgwgwgwgwgwgwg
hzhzhzhzhzhzhzhzhzhzhzhzh
s5s5s5s5s5s5s5s5s5s5s5s5s5s5s5s5s5s5s5s5s5s5s5s5s5s5s5s5s5s5s5s5s5s5s5s5s5s5s5s5s5s5s5s5s5s5s5s5s
τοῖς μαθηταῖς αὐτοῦ· συναγάγετε τὰ περισσεύσαντα κλάσματα, ἵνα
bsbsbsbsbsbsbsbsbsbsbsbsbsbsbsbsbsbsbsbsbsbsbsbsbsbsbsbsbsbsbsbsbsbsbsbsbsbsbsbsbsbsbsbsbsbsbsbsbs
fffffffffffffffffffffffffffffffffffffffffffffffffffffffffffffffffffffffffffffffffffffffffffffffffffffffffffffffffffffffffffffffffffffffffffffffffffffff
wgwgwgwgwgwgwgwgwgwgwgwgwgwgwgwgwgwgwgwgwgwgwgwgwgwgwgwgwgwgwgwgwgwgwgwg
s5s5s5s5s5s5s5s5s5s5s5s5s5s5s5s5s5s5s5s5s5s5s5s5s5s5s5s5s5s5s5s5s5s5s5s5s5s5s5s5s5s5s5s5s5s5s5s5s
μή τι ἀπόληται. 13 συνήγαγον οὖν, καὶ ἐγέμισαν δώδεκα κοφίνους
bsbsbsbsbsbsbsbsbsbsbsbsbsbsbsbsbsbsbsbsbsbsbsbsbsbsbsbsbsbsbsbsbsbsbsbsbsbsbsbsbsbsbsbsbsbsbsbsbs
fffffffffffffffffffffffffffffffffffffffffffffffffffffffffffffffffffffffffffffffffffffffffffffffffffffffffffffffffffffffffffffffffffffffffffffffffffffff
wgwgwgwgwgwgwgwgwgwgwgwgwgwgwgwgwgwgwgwgwgwgwgwgwgwgwgwgwgwgwgwgwgwgwgwg
s5s5s5s5s5s5s5s5s5s5s5s5s5s5s5s5s5s5s5s5s5s5s5s5s5s5s5s5s5s5s5s5s5s5s5s5s5s5s5s5s5s5s5s5s5s5s5s5s
κλασμάτων ἐκ τῶν πέντε ἄρτων τῶν κριθίνων ἃ ἐπερίσσευσαν τοῖς
bsbsbsbsbsbsbsbsbsbsbsbsbsbsbsbsbsbsbsbsbsbsbsbsbsbsbsbsbsbsbsbsbsbsbsbsbsbsbsbsbsbsbsbsbsbsbsbsbs
fffffffffffffffffffffffffffffffffffffffffffffffffffffffffffffffffffffffffffffffffffffffffffffffffffffffffffffffffffffffffffffffffffffffffffffffffffffff
wgwgwgwgwgwgwgwgwgwgwgwgwgwgwgwgwgwgwgwgwgwgwgwgwgwgwgwgwgwgwgwgwgwgwgwg
s5s5s5s5s5s5s5s5s5s5s5s5s5s5s5s5s5s5s5s5s5s5s5s5s5s5s5s5s5s5s5s5s5s5s5s5s5s5s5s5s5s5s5s5s5s5s5s5s
βεβρωκόσιν. 14 Οἱ οὖν ἄνθρωποι ἰδόντες ὃ ἐποίησεν σημεῖον ἔλεγον
bsbsbsbsbsbsbsb
fffffffffffffffffffffff.....fffff   ffffffffffffffff   ffffffffffff
wgwgwgwgwgwgwgwgwgwgwgwgwgwgwgwgwgwgwgwgwgwgwgwgwgwgwgwgwgwgwgwgwgwg
hzh   hzhzhzhzhzhzhzhzhzhzhzhzhzhzhzhzhzhzhzhzhzhzhzhzhzhzhzhz
s5s5s5 s5s5s5s5s5s5s5s5s5s5s5s5s5s5s5s5s5s5s5s5s5s5s5s5s5s5s5s5s5s5s5s5s5s5s5s5s5s5s5s
ὅτι οὗτός ἐστιν ἀληθῶς ὁ προφήτης ὁ ἐρχόμενος εἰς τὸν κόσμον. 15 Ἰησοῦς
fffffffffffffffffffffffffff   ffffffffffffffffffff
wgwgwgwgwgwgwgwgwgwgwgwgwgwgwgwgwgwgwgwgwgwgwgwgwgwgwgwgwgwgwgwgwgwg
hzhzhzhzhzhzhzhzhzhzhzhzhzhzhzhz   hzhzhzhz
s5s5s5s5s5s5s5s5s5s5s5s5s5s5s5s5s5s5s5s5s5s5s5s5s5s5s5s5s5s5s5s5s5s5s5s5s5s   s5s5s5s5s

vs. 12-13: FORTNA contends that vs. 12-13b (through οὖν) read either as indicated here or as follows: καὶ ἔφαγον (πάντες) καὶ ἐχορτάσθησαν. (pp. 59-60, 238). HAENCHEN asserts that v. 12 has been taken over from the *Vorlage* (loc. cit.).

v. 14: Between vs. 13 and 14 FORTNA proposes that the signs gospel included τοῦτο τέταρτον ἐποίησεν σημεῖον ὁ Ἰησοῦς καί (p. 105). HAENCHEN finds evidence in this verse for the use of the *Vorlage* (loc. cit.).

v. 15: FORTNA's reconstruction of the signs gospel suggests vs. 15 ff. constituted an interlude which included the walking on water and a miraculous landing. The portion of 15b which is underlined here is preceded by καὶ ἀποταξάμενος αὐτοῖς ἀπῆλθεν ὁ Ἰησοῦς . . . (pp. 64-65).

οὖν γνοὺς ὅτι μέλλουσιν ἔρχεσθαι καὶ ἁρπάζειν αὐτὸν ἵνα ποιήσωσιν

βασιλέα, ἀνεχώρησεν πάλιν εἰς τὸ ὄρος αὐτὸς μόνος. 16 Ὡς δὲ ὀψία

ἐγένετο, κατέβησαν οἱ μαθηταὶ αὐτοῦ ἐπὶ τὴν θάλασσαν, 17 καὶ ἐμβάντες

εἰς πλοῖον ἤρχοντο πέραν τῆς θαλάσσης εἰς Καφαρναούμ. καὶ σκοτία

ἤδη ἐγεγόνει καὶ οὔπω ἐληλύθει πρὸς αὐτοὺς ὁ Ἰησοῦς, 18 ἥ τε θάλασσα

ἀνέμου μεγάλου πνέοντος διηγείρετο. 19 ἐληλακότες οὖν ὡς σταδίους

εἴκοσι πέντε ἢ τριάκοντα θεωροῦσιν τὸν Ἰησοῦν περιπατοῦντα ἐπὶ

τῆς θαλάσσης καὶ ἐγγὺς τοῦ πλοίου γινόμενον, καὶ ἐφοβήθησαν. 20 ὁ δὲ

λέγει αὐτοῖς· ἐγώ εἰμι· μὴ φοβεῖσθε. 21 ἤθελον οὖν λαβεῖν αὐτὸν εἰς τὸ πλοῖον, καὶ εὐθέως ἐγένετο τὸ πλοῖον ἐπὶ τῆς γῆς εἰς ἣν ὑπῆγον.

bsbsbsbsbsbsbsbsbsbsbsbsbsbsbsbsbsbsbsbsbsbsbsbsbsbsbsbsbsbsbsbsbsbsbsbsbsbsbsbsbsbsbsbsbsbsbsbsbsbsbs
ffffffffffffffffffffffffffffffffffffffffffffffffffffffffffffffffffffffffffffffffffffffffffffffffffffffffffffffffffffffffffffffffffffffffffffffffffff
wgwgwgwgwgwgwgwgwgwgwgwgwgwgwgwgwgwgwgwgwgwgwgwgwgwgwgwgwgwgwgwgwgwgwg
hzhzhzhzhzhzhzhzhzhzhzhzhzhzhzhzhzhzhzhzhzhzhzhzhzhzhzhzhzhzhzhzhzhzhzhzhzhzhzhzhzh
s5s5s5s5s5s5s5s5s5s5s5s5s5s5s5s5s5s5s5s5s5s5s5s5s5s5s5s5s5s5s5s5s5s5s5s5s5s5s5s5s5s5s5s5s5s5s5s5s5s5s5s

22 Τῇ ἐπαύριον ὁ ὄχλος ὁ ἑστηκὼς πέραν τῆς θαλάσσης εἶδον ὅτι

bsbsbsbsbsbsbsbsbsbsbsbsbsbsbsbsbsbsbsbsbsbsbsbsbsbsbsbsbsbsbsbsbsbsbsbsbsbsbsbsbsbsbsbsbsbsbsbsb
ffffffffffffffffffffffffffffffffffffffffffffffffffffffffffffffffffffffffffffffffffffffffffffffffffffffffffffffffffffffffffffffffffffff
wgwgwgwgwgwgwg

hvhvhvhvhvhvhvhvhvhvhvhvhvhvhvhvhvhvhvhvh
s5s5s5s5s5s5s5s5s5s5s5s5s5s5s5s5s5s5s5s5s5s5s5s5s5s5s5s5s5s5s5s5s5s5s5s5s5s5s5s5s5s5s5

πλοιάριον ἄλλο οὐκ ἦν ἐκεῖ εἰ μὴ ἕν, καὶ ὅτι οὐ συνεισῆλθεν τοῖς μαθηταῖς

bsbsbsbsbsbsbsbsbsbsbsbsbsbsbsbsbsbsbsbsbsbsbsbsbsbsbsbs   bsbsbsbsbsbsbsbsbsbsbsbsbsbsbsbsbsbsbsbsbsbs
ffffffffffffffffffffffffffffffffffffffffffffffffffffffffff   ffffffffffffffffffffffffffffffffffffffffffffffffffffffffffffffff

hvhvhvhvhvhvhvhvhvhvhvhvhvhvhvhvhvhvhvhvhvhvhvhvhvhvhvhvhvhvhvhvhvhvhvhvhvh
s5s5s5s5s5s5s5s5s5s5s5s5s5s5s5s5s5s5s5s5s5s5s5s5s5s5s5s5s5s5s5s5s5s5s5s5s5s5s5s5s5s5s5s

αὐτοῦ ὁ Ἰησοῦς εἰς τὸ πλοῖον ἀλλὰ μόνοι οἱ μαθηταὶ αὐτοῦ ἀπῆλθον. 23

bsbsbsbsbsbsbsbsbsbsbsbsbsbsbsbsbsbsbsbsbsbsbsbsbsbsbsbsbsbsbsbsbsbsbsbsbsbsbs
ffffffffffffffffffffffffffffffffffffffffffffffffffffffffffffffffffffffffffffffffffffffffffff

hvhvhvhvhvhvhvhvhvhvhvhvhvhvhvhvhvhvhvhvhvhvhvhvhvhvhvhvhvhvhvhvhvhvhvhvhvhv
s5s5s5s5s5s5s5s5s5s5s5s5s5s5s5s5s5s5s5s5s5s5s5s5s5s5s5s5s5s5s5s5s5s5s5s5s5s5s5s5s5s5s5s

ἄλλα ἦλθεν πλοιάρια ἐκ Τιβεριάδος ἐγγὺς τοῦ τόπου ὅπου ἔφαγον τὸν

wgwgwgwgwgwgwgwgwgwgwgwgwgwgwgwgwgwgwgwgwgwgwgwgwgwgwgwgwgwgwg
hzhzhzhzhzhzhzhzhzhzhzhzhzhzhzhzhzhzhzhzhzhzhzhzhzhzhzhzhzhzhzhzh
s5s5s5s5s5s5s5s5s5s5s5s5s5s5s5s5s5s5s5s5s5s5s5s5s5s5s5s5s5s5s5s5s5s5s5s5s5s5s5s5s5s5s5

ἄρτον εὐχαριστήσαντος τοῦ κυρίου. 24 ὅτε οὖν εἶδεν ὁ ὄχλος ὅτι Ἰησοῦς

wgwgw   wgwgwgwgwgwgwgwgwgwgwgwgwgwgwg
hzhzhz   hzhzhzhz
s5s5s5s5s5s5s5s5s5s5s5s5s5s5s5s5s5s5s5s5s5s5s5s5s5s5s5s5s5s5s5s5s5s5s5s5s5s5s5s5 s5 s

οὐκ ἔστιν ἐκεῖ οὐδὲ οἱ μαθηταὶ αὐτοῦ, ἐνέβησαν αὐτοὶ εἰς τὰ πλοιάρια

wgwgwgwgwgwgwgwgwgwgwgwgwgwgwgwgwgwgwgwgwgwgwgwgwgwgwgwgwgwgwgwgwgwgwg
zhzhzhzhzhzhzhzhzhzhzhzhzhzhzhzhzhzhzhzhzhzhzhzhzhzhzhzhzhzhzhzhzhzhzhzhz
s5s5s5s5s5s5s5s5s5s5s5s5s5s5s5s5s5s5s5s5s5s5s5s5s5s5s5s5s5s5s5s5s5s5s5s5s5s5s5s5s5s5s5

καὶ ἦλθον εἰς Καφαρναούμ ζητοῦντες τὸν Ἰησοῦν. 25 καὶ εὑρόντες

bsbsbsbsbsbsbs
ffffffffffffffffffffffffff
wgwgwgwgwgwgwgwgwgwgwgwgwgwgwgwgwgwgwgwgwgwgwgwgwgwgwgwgwgwgwgwg
hzhzhzhzhzhzhzhzhzhzhzhzhzhzhzhzhzhzhzhzhzhzhzhzhzhzhzhzhzhzhzhzh
s5s5s5s5s5s5s5s5s5s5s5s5s5s5s5s5s5s5s5s5s5s5s5s5s5s5s5s5s5s5s5s5s5s5s5s5s5s5s5s5s5s5s5

v. 22 ff.: FORTNA marks the remainder of the underlined portion of the chapter in parentheses, indicating that there is less certainty of its inclusion in the original signs gospel (pp. 67-70).

v. 23: HARTKE prefers the textual reading ἐπελθόντων οὖν τῶν πλοίων (א) and attributes it to the Z source (p. 53).

v. 24: HARTKE contends that the most likely reading of the Z source here was καὶ ἰδόντες ὅτι οὐκ ἦν ἐκεῖ ὁ . . . (א * syᶜ) (p. 53).

αὐτὸν πέραν τῆς θαλάσσης εἶπον αὐτῷ· ῥαββί, πότε ὧδε γέγονας; 26
bsbsbsbsbsbsbsbsbsbsbsbsbsbsbsbsbsbsbsbsbsbsbsbsbsbsbsbsbsbsbsbsbsbsbsbsbsbsbsbsbsbsbsbsbsbsbsbsbsbs
fffffffffffffffffffffff fffffffffffffffffffffffffffffffffffffffffffffffffffffffffffffffffffffffffffffffffffffffffffffffffffff
wgwgwgwgwgwgwgwgwgwgwgwgwgwgwgwgwgwgwgwgwgwgwgwgwgwgwgwgwgwgwgwgwgwgwgwgwgwg
hzhzhzhzhzhzhzhzhzhzhzhzhzhzhzhzhzhzhzhzhzhzhzhzhzhzhzhzhzhzhzhzhzh
s5s5s5s5s5s5s5s5s5s5s5s5s5s5s5s5s5s5s5s5s5s5s5s5s5s5s5s5s5s5s5s5s5s5s5s5
ἀπεκρίθη αὐτοῖς ὁ Ἰησοῦς καὶ εἶπεν· ἀμὴν ἀμὴν λέγω ὑμῖν, ζητεῖτέ

wgwgwgwgwgwgwgwgwgwgwgwgwgwgwgwgwgwgwgwgwgwgwgwgwgwgwgwgwgwgwgwgwgwgwgwgwgwg
slslslslslslslslslslslslslslslslslslslslslslslslslslslslslslslslslslslslslslslslslslslslslslslslslslslslslslslslslslslslsls
με οὐχ ὅτι εἴδετε σημεῖα, ἀλλ᾽ ὅτι ἐφάγετε ἐκ τῶν ἄρτων καὶ ἐχορτάσθητε.

wgwgwgwgwgwgwgwgwgwgwgwgwgwgwgwgwgwgwgwgwgwgwgwgwgwgwgwgwgwgwgwgwgwgwgwgwgwg
slslslslslslslslslslslslslslslslslslslslslslslslslslslslslslslslslslslslslslslslslslslslslslslslslslslslslslslslslslslslsls
27 ἐργάζεσθε μὴ τὴν βρῶσιν τὴν ἀπολλυμένην, ἀλλὰ τὴν βρῶσιν τὴν
bobobobobobobobobobobobobobobobobobobobobobobobobobobobobobobobobobobobobobobobobobob
gogogogogogogogogogogogogogogogogogogogogogogogogogogogogogogogogogogogogogogogogogogogogogog
wgwgwgwgwgwgwgwgwgwgwgwgwgwgwgwgwgwgwgwgwgwgwgwgwgwgwgwgwgwgwgwgwgwgwgwgwgwg

ssssssssssssssssssssssssssssssssssssssssssssssssssssssssssssssssssssssssssssssssssssssssssssssssssssssssssssss
μένουσαν εἰς ζωὴν αἰώνιον, ἣν ὁ υἱὸς τοῦ ἀνθρώπου ὑμῖν δώσει· τοῦτον
bobobobobobobobobobobobobobobo
gogogogogogogogogogogogogog
wgwgwgwgwgwgwgwgwgwgwgwgwgwgwgwgwgwgwgwgwgwgwgwgwgwgwgwgwgwgwgwgwgwgwgwgwgwg

ssssssssssssssssssssssssssssssssssssssssssssssssssssssssssssssssssssssssssssssssssssssssssssssssssssssssssssss
γὰρ ὁ πατὴρ ἐσφράγισεν ὁ θεός. 28 εἶπον οὖν πρὸς αὐτόν· τί ποιῶμεν

wgwgwgwgwgwgwgwgwgwgwgwgwgwgwgw   wrwrwrwrwrwrwrwrwrwrwrwrwrwrwrwrwrwr
                                      hvhvhvhvhvh
sssssssssssssssssssssssssssssssssssssssss   mmmmmmmmmmmmmmmmmmmmmmmm
ἵνα ἐργαζώμεθα τὰ ἔργα τοῦ θεοῦ; 29 ἀπεκρίθη Ἰησοῦς καὶ εἶπεν αὐτοῖς·

wrwrwrwrwrwrwrwrwrwrwrwrwrwrwrwrwrwrwrwrwrwrwrwrwrwrwrwrwrwrwrwrwrwrwrwrwrw
hvhvhvhvhvhvhvhvhvhvhvhvhvhvhvhvhvhvhvhvhvhvhvhvhvhvhvhvhvhvhvhvhvhvh
mmmmmmmmmmmmmmmmmmmmmmmmmmmmmmmmmmmmmmmmmmmmmmmmmmmmmmmmmmmmmm
τοῦτό ἐστιν τὸ ἔργον τοῦ θεοῦ, ἵνα πιστεύητε εἰς ὃν ἀπέστειλεν ἐκεῖνος. 30

wrwrwrwrwrwrwrwr wrwrwrwrwrwrwrwrwrwrwrwrwrwrwrwrwrwrwrwrwrwrwrwrwrwrwrwrwrw
hvhvhvhvhvhvhvhvhvhvhvhvhvhvhvhvhvhvhvhvhvhvhvhvhvhvhvhvhvhvhvhvhvhvh
mmmmmmmmmmmmmmmmmmmmmmmmmmmmmmmmmmmmmmmmmmmmmmmmmmmmmmmmmmmmmm
εἶπον οὖν αὐτῷ· τί οὖν ποιεῖς σὺ σημεῖον, ἵνα ἴδωμεν καὶ πιστεύσωμέν

wrwrwrwrwrwrwrwrwrwrwrwrwrwrwrwrwrwrwrwrwrwrwrwrwrwrwrwrwrwrwrwrwrwrwrwrwrw
hvhvhvhvhvhvh hzhzhzhzhzhzhzhzhzhzhzhzhzhzhzhzhzhzhzhzhzhzhzhzhzhzhzhzhzhzhz
mmmmmmmmmmmmmmmmmmmmmmmmmmmmmmmmmmmmmmmmmmmmmmmmmmmmmmmmmmmmmm

v. 26: FORTNA writes after v. 25, "The source may have continued here
with material which is now buried in the rest of ch. 6, notably in the episode
with Peter in vi 67 ff." (p. 238; cf. pp. 195-196).

σοι; 31 τί ἐργάζῃ; οἱ πατέρες ἡμῶν τὸ μάννα ἔφαγον ἐν τῇ ἐρήμῳ,

wrwrwrwrwrwrwrwrwrwrwrwrwrwrwrwrwrwrwrwrwrwrwrwrwrwrwrwrwrwrwrwrwrwrwrwr wrwrw
hzhz   hvhvhvhvhvhvhvhvhvhvhvhvhvhvhvhvhvhvhvhvhvhvhvhvhvhvhvhvhvhvhvhvh
mmmmmmmmmmmmmmmmmmmmmmmmmmmmmmmmmmmmmmmmmmmmmmmmmmmmmmmmmmmmmmmmm
καθώς ἐστιν γεγραμμένον· ἄρτον ἐκ τοῦ οὐρανοῦ ἔδωκεν αὐτοῖς φαγεῖν.

wrwrwrwrwrwrwrwrwrwrwrwrwrwrwrwrwrwrwrwrwrwrwrwrwrwrwrwrwrwrwrwrwrwrwrwrwrw
hvhvhvhvhvhvhvhvhvhvhvhvhvhvhvhvhvhvhvhvhvhvhvhvhvhvhvhvhvhvhvhvhvhvhvh
mmmmmmmmmmmmmmmmmmmmmmmmmmmmmmmmmmmmmmmmmmmmmmmmmmmmmmmmmmmmmmmmmm
32 Εἶπεν οὖν αὐτοῖς ὁ Ἰησοῦς· ἀμὴν ἀμὴν λέγω ὑμῖν, οὐ Μωϋσῆς

wrwrwrwrwrwrwrwrwrwrwrwrwrwrwrwrwrwrwrwrwrwrwrwrwrwrwrwrwrwrwrwrwr wrwrw
hzhzhzhzhzhzhzhzhzhzhzhzhzhzhzhzhzhzh
mmmmmmmmmmmmmmmmmmmmmmmmmmmmmmmmmmmmmmmmmmmmmmmmmmmmmmmmmmmmmmmmmm
δέδωκεν ὑμῖν τὸν ἄρτον ἐκ τοῦ οὐρανοῦ, ἀλλ' ὁ πατήρ μου δίδωσιν ὑμῖν

wrwrwrwrwrwrwrwrwrwrwrwrwrwrwrwrwrwrwrwrwrwrwrwrwrwrwrwrwrwrwrwrwrwrw

mmmmmmmmmmmmmmmmmmmmmmmmmmmmmmmmmmmmmmmmmmmmmmmmmmmmmmmmmmmmmmmmmm
τὸν ἄρτον ἐκ τοῦ οὐρανοῦ τὸν ἀληθινόν· 33 ὁ γὰρ ἄρτος τοῦ θεοῦ ἐστιν
bobobobobobobobobobobobobobobobobob

wrwrwrwrwrwrwrwrwrwrwrwrwrwrwrwrwrwrwrwrwrwrwrwrwrwrwrwrwrwrwrwrwr

mmmmmmmmmmmmmmmmmmmmmmmmmmmmmmmmmmmmmmmmmmmmmmmmmmmmmmmmmmmmmmmmm
ὁ καταβαίνων ἐκ τοῦ οὐρανοῦ καὶ ζωὴν διδοὺς τῷ κόσμῳ. 34 εἶπον οὖν
bobobobobobobobobobobobobobobobobobobobobobobobobobobobobobobobobobobo

wrwrwrwrwrwrwrwrwrwrwrwrwrwrwrwrwrwrwrwrwrwrwrwrwrwrwrwrwrwrwrwrwrwrw

mmmmmmmmmmmmmmmmmmmmmmmmmmmmmmmmmmmmmmmmmmmmmmmmmmmmmmmmmmmmmmmmm
πρὸς αὐτόν· κύριε, πάντοτε δὸς ἡμῖν τὸν ἄρτον τοῦτον. 35 εἶπεν αὐτοῖς

wrwrwrwrwrwrwrwrwrwrwrwrwrwrwrwrwrwrwrwrwrwrwrwrwrwrwrwrwrwrwrwrwr wrw

mmmmmmmmmmmmmmmmmmmmmmmmmmmmmmmmmmmmmmmmmmmmmmmmm   ms4sbboims4sb
ὁ Ἰησοῦς· ἐγώ εἰμι ὁ ἄρτος τῆς ζωῆς· ὁ ἐρχόμενος πρὸς ἐμὲ οὐ μὴ
bobobobobobobobobobobobobobobobo   bobobobobobobobobobobobobobobobo
gogogogogogogogogogogogogogogog   gogogogogogogogogogogogogogogogo
wrwrwrwrwrwrwrwrwrwrwrwrwrwrwrwr   wrwrwrwrwrwrwrwrwrwrwrwrwrwrwr

ms4sbboims4sbboims4sbboims4sbboims4sbboims4sbboims4sbboims4sbboims4sbbo
πεινάσῃ, καὶ ὁ πιστεύων εἰς ἐμὲ οὐ μὴ διψήσει πώποτε. 36 Ἀλλ' εἶπον
bobobobobobobobobobobobobobobobobobobobobobobobobobobobobobobobobobobobo
gogogogogogogogogogogogogogogogogogogogogogogogogogogogogogogogogogogog
wrwrwrwrwrwrwrwrwrwrwrwrwrwrwrwrwrwrwrwrwrwrwrwrwrwrwrwrw

ms4sbboims4sbboims4sbboims4sbboims4sbboims4sbboims4sbboims4sb   mboimboimboi

v. 33: BULTMANN proposes this saying followed v. 35 in the sayings source (p. 168, n. 1).

v. 35: The underlining of this verse represents the continuation of MERLIER's source (m), BROOME's S4 (s4), SCHULZ's *Bildworte-reden* tradition (sb), and the beginning of those verses which BOISMARD isolates as the first "strata" of the gospel (boi).

ὑμῖν ὅτι καὶ ἑωράκατέ με καὶ οὐ πιστεύετε. 37 πᾶν ὃ δίδωσίν μοι ὁ

gogogogogogogogogogogogog
wrwrwrwrwrwrwrwrwrwr
hzhzhzhzhzhzhzhzhzhzhzhzhzhzhzhzhz
mboimboimboimboimboimboimboimboimboimboimboimboimboimboimboimboimboimboi
πατὴρ πρὸς ἐμὲ ἥξει, καὶ τὸν ἐρχόμενον πρός με οὐ μὴ ἐκβάλω ἔξω, 38
bobobobobobobobobobobobobobobobobobobobobobobobobobobobobobobobo
gogogogogogogogogogogogogogogogogogogogogogogogogogogogogogogogogogogog
wrwrwrwrwrwrwrwrwrwrwrwrwrwrwrwrwrwrwrwrwrwrwrwrwrwrwrwrwrwrwrwrwrwrwrw

mboimboimboimboimboimboimboimboimboimboimboimboimboimboimboimboimboimboi
ὅτι καταβέβηκα ἀπὸ τοῦ οὐρανοῦ οὐχ ἵνα ποιῶ τὸ θέλημα τὸ ἐμὸν ἀλλὰ

wrwrwrwrwrwrwrwrwrwrwrwrwrwrwrwrwrwrwrwrwrwrwrwrwrwrwrwrwrwrwrwrwrwrw

mboimboimboimboimboimboimboimboimboimboimboimboimboimboimboimboimboimboi
τὸ θέλημα τοῦ πέμψαντός με. τοῦτο δέ ἐστιν τὸ θέλημα τοῦ πέμψαντός

wrwrwrwrwrwrwrwrwrwrwrwrwrwrwrwr wrwrwrwrwrwrwrwrwrwrwrwrwrwrwrwrw

mboimboimboimboimboimboimboimboimboimboimboimboimboimboimboimboimboimboi
με, 39 ἵνα πᾶν ὃ δέδωκέν μοι μὴ ἀπολέσω ἐξ αὐτοῦ, ἀλλὰ ἀναστήσω

wrwrwrwrwrwrwrwrwrwrwrwrwrwrwrwrwrwrwrwrwrwrwrwrwrwrwrwrwrwrwrwrwrwrw

mboimboimboimboimboimboimboimboimboimboimboimboimboimboimboimboimboimboi
αὐτὸ ἐν τῇ ἐσχάτῃ ἡμέρᾳ. 40 τοῦτο γάρ ἐστιν τὸ θέλημα τοῦ πατρός

wrwrwrwrwrwrwrwrwrwrwrwrwrwrwrwrwrwrwrwrwrwrwrwrwrwrwrwrwrwrwrwrwrwrw

mboimboimboimboimboimboimboimboimboimboimboimboimboimboimboimboimboimboi
μου, ἵνα πᾶς ὁ θεωρῶν τὸν υἱὸν καὶ πιστεύων εἰς αὐτὸν ἔχῃ ζωὴν αἰώνιον,

wrwrwrwrwrwrwrwrwrwrwrwrwrwrwrwrwrwrwrwrwrwrwrwrwrwrwrwrwrwrwrwrwrwrw

mboimboimboimboimboimboimboimboimboimboimboimboimboimboimboimboimboimboi
καὶ ἀναστήσω αὐτὸν ἐγὼ ἐν τῇ ἐσχάτῃ ἡμέρᾳ. 41 Ἐγόγγυζον οὖν οἱ

wrwrwrwrwrwrwrwrwrwrwrwrwrwrwrwrwrwrwrwrwrwrwrwrwrwrwrwr   wrwrwrwrwrwrwrwr

mboimboimboimboimboimboimboimboimboimboimboimboimboimboimboimboimboimboi

v. 37: BECKER believes vs. 48, 47, possibly 51a, 44 and 45b preceded in that order v. 37 in the source (p. 130).

v. 37c: BULTMANN has this passage following v. 45 in his hypothetical source (p. 172).

v. 41 ff.: WILKENS believes that vs. 41-46 represents a traditional block of logia which originally would have followed vs. 47-51b before they were incorporated into the Grundevangelium (pp. 94-98).

Ἰουδαῖοι περὶ αὐτοῦ ὅτι εἶπεν· ἐγώ εἰμι ὁ ἄρτος ὁ καταβὰς ἐκ τοῦ

wrwrwrwrwrwrwrwrwrwrwrwrwrwrwrwrwrwrwrwrwrwrwrwrwrwrwrwrwrwrwrwrwrw

mboimboimboimboimboimboimboimboimboimboimboimboimboimboimboimboimboi
οὐρανοῦ, 42 καὶ ἔλεγον· οὐχ οὗτός ἐστιν Ἰησοῦς ὁ υἱὸς Ἰωσήφ, οὗ ἡμεῖς

wrwrwrwrwrwrwrwrwrwrwrwrwrwrwrwrwrwrwrwrwrwrwrwrwrwrwrwrwrwrwrwrwrw

mboimboimboimboimboimboimboimboimboimboimboimboimboimboimboimboimboi
οἴδαμεν τὸν πατέρα καὶ τὴν μητέρα; πῶς νῦν λέγει τόι ἐκ τοῦ οὐρανοῦ

wrwrwrwrwrwrwrwrwrwrwrwrwrwrwrwrwrwrwrwrwrwrwrwrwrwrwrwrwrwrwrwrwrw

mboimboimboimboimboimboimboimboimboimboimboimboimboimboimboimboimboi
καταβέβηκα; 43 ἀπεκρίθη Ἰησοῦς καὶ εἶπεν αὐτοῖς· μὴ γογγύζετε

wrwrwrwrwrwrwrwrwrwrwrwrwrwrwrwrwrwrwrwrwrwrwrwrwrwrwrwrwrwrwrwrwrw

mboimboimboimboimboimboimboimboimboimboimboimboimboimboimboimboimboi
μετ' ἀλλήλων. 44 Οὐδεὶς δύναται ἐλθεῖν πρός με ἐὰν μὴ ὁ πατὴρ ὁ
bobobobobobobobobobobobobobobobobobobobobobobobobobobobobobobobobo
gogogogogogogogogogogogogogogogogogogogogogogogogogogogogogogogogog
wrwrwrwrwrwrwrwrwrwrwrwrwrwrwrwrwrwrwrwrwrwrwrwrwrwrwrwrwrwrwrwrwrw

mboimboimboimboimboimboimboimboimboimboimboimboimboimboimboimboimboi
πέμψας με ἑλκύσῃ αὐτόν, κἀγὼ ἀναστήσω αὐτὸν ἐν τῇ ἐσχάτῃ ἡμέρᾳ. 45
bobobobobobobobobobobobob
gogogogogogogog
wrwrwrwrwrwrwrwrwrwrwrwrwrwrwrwrwrwrwrwrwrwrwrwrwrwrwrwrwrwrwrwrwrw

mboimboimboimboimboimboimboimboimboimboimboimboimboimboimboimboimboi
ἔστιν γεγραμμένον ἐν τοῖς προφήταις· καὶ ἔσονται πάντες διδακτοὶ

wrwrwrwrwrwrwrwrwrwrwrwrwrwrwrwrwrwrwrwrwrwrwrwrwrwrwrwrwrwrwrwrwrw
hvhvhvhvhvhvhvhvhvhvhvhvhvhvhvhvhvhvhvhvhvhvhvhvhvhvhvhvhvhvhvhvhvh
mboimboimboimboimboimboimboimboimboimboimboimboimboimboimboimboimboi
θεοῦ· πᾶς ὁ ἀκούσας παρὰ τοῦ πατρὸς καὶ μαθὼν ἔρχεται πρὸς ἐμέ. 46
bobobobobobobobobobobobobobobobobobobobobobobobobobobobobobobobobo
gogogogogogogogogogogogogogogogogogog   gogogogogogogogog
wrwrwrwrwrwrwrwrwrwrwrwrwrwrwrwrwrwrwrwrwrwrwrwrwrwrwrwrwrwrwrwrwrw
hvhv
mboimboimboimboimboimboimboimboimboimboimboimboimboimboimboimboimboi
οὐχ ὅτι τὸν πατέρα ἑώρακέν τις, εἰ μὴ ὁ ὢν παρὰ τοῦ θεοῦ, οὗτος ἑώρακεν

wrwrwrwrwrwrwrwrwrwrwrwrwrwrwrwrwrwrwrwrwrwrwrwrwrwrwrwrwrwrwrwrwrw
hvhvhvhvhvhvhvhvhvhvhvhvhvhvhvhvhvhvhvhvhvhvhvhvhvhvhvhvhvhvhvhvhvh
mboimboimboimboimboimboimboimboimboimboimboimboimboimboimboimboimboi

vs. 44-45: BULTMANN's reconstruction of the *Offenbarungsreden* has these verses following v. 47 (pp. 171-172).

144   ROBERT KYSAR

τὸν πατέρα. 47 ἀμὴν ἀμὴν λέγω ὑμῖν, ὁ πιστεύων ἔχει ζωὴν αἰώνιον. 48

bobobobobobobobobobobobobobobobob
gogogogogogogogogogogogogogogogog
wrwrwrwrwrwrwr   wrwrwrwrwrwrwrwrwrwrwrwrwrwrwrwrwrwrwrwrwrwrwrwrwrwr
hvhvhvhvhvhvhvh
mboimboimboimboimboimboimboimboimboimboimboimboimboimboimboimboimboimboi

Ἐγώ εἰμι ὁ ἄρτος τῆς ζωῆς. 49 οἱ πατέρες ὑμῶν ἔφαγον ἐν τῇ ἐρήμῳ

bobobobobobobobobobobobobobo
gogogogogogogogogogogogogogo
wrwrwrwrwrwrwrwrwrwrwrwrwrwrwrwrwrwrwrwrwrwrwrwrwrwrwrwrwrwrwrwrwrwrwrwrw

mboimboimboimboimboimboimboimboimboimboimboimboimboimboimboimboimboimboi

τὸ μάννα καὶ ἀπέθανον· 50 οὗτός ἐστιν ὁ ἄρτος ὁ ἐκ τοῦ οὐρανοῦ κατα-

wrwrwrwrwrwrwrwrwrwrwrwrwrwrwrwrwrwrwrwrwrwrwrwrwrwrwrwrwrwrwrwrwrwrwrwrw

mboimboimboimboimboimboimboimboimboimboimboimboimboimboimboimboimboimboi

βαίνων, ἵνα τις ἐξ αὐτοῦ φάγῃ καὶ μὴ ἀποθάνῃ. 51 ἐγώ εἰμι ὁ ἄρτος ὁ

wrwrwrwrwrwrwrwrwrwrwrwrwrwrwrwrwrwrwrwrwrwrwrwrwrwrwrwrwrwrwrwrwrwrwrwrw

mboimboimboimboimboimboimboimboimboimboimboimboim   msbmsbmsbmsbmsbms

ζῶν ὁ ἐκ τοῦ οὐρανοῦ καταβάς· ἐάν τις φάγῃ ἐκ τούτου τοῦ ἄρτου,

wrwrwrwrwrwrwrwrwrwrwrwrwrwrwrwrwrwrwrwrwrwrwrwrwrwrwrwrwrwrwrwrwrwrwrwrw

msbmsbmsbmsbmsbmsbsbmsbmsbmsbmsbmsbmsbmsbmsbmsbmsbmsbmsbmsbmsbmsbmsbmsbm

ζήσει εἰς τὸν αἰῶνα· καὶ ὁ ἄρτος δὲ ὃν ἐγὼ δώσω ἡ σάρξ μού ἐστιν ὑπὲρ

wrwrwrwrwrwrwrwrwrwrwrwrwrwrwrwrwrwrwrwrwrwrwrwrwrwrwrwrwrwrwrwrwrwrwrwrw

bmsbmsbmsbmsbmsbm   mmmmmmmmmmmmmmmmmmmmmmmmmmmmmmmmmmmmmmmmmmmmmmmmm

τῆς τοῦ κόσμου ζωῆς. 52 Ἐμάχοντο οὖν πρὸς ἀλλήλους οἱ Ἰουδαῖοι

wrwrwrwrwrwrwrwrwrwrwr

mmmmmmmmmmmmmmmmmmmmmmmmmmmmmmmmmmmmmmmmmmmmmmmmmmmmmmmmmmmmmmmmm

λέγοντες· πῶς δύναται οὗτος ἡμῖν δοῦναι τὴν σάρκα φαγεῖν; 53 εἶπεν

mmmmmmmmmmmmmmmmmmmmmmmmmmmmmmmmmmmmmmmmmmmmmmmmmmmmmmmmmm   mslssm

v. 47b: BULTMANN contends 47b followed v. 48 in the source. (p. 170)
BECKER concurs with this reconstruction, inserting εἰς ἐμέ between ὁ πιστεύων
and ἔχει Ἐωὴν . . . (p. 130).
v. 51: BOISMARD contrasts vs. 51-58 with 35-50. The second represents
the first strata, while 51-58 is of the second strata.
v. 53: The underlining here represents the continuation of MERLIER
(m), BROOME's Sl source (sl), and SCHULZ's proposed Son of Man theme
tradition (ss).

οὖν αὐτοῖς ὁ Ἰησοῦς· ἀμὴν ἀμὴν λέγω ὑμῖν, ἐὰν μὴ φάγητε τὴν σάρκα

mslssmslssmslssmslssmslssmslssmslssmslssmslssmslssmslssmslssmslssmslssmslssm
τοῦ υἱοῦ τοῦ ἀνθρώπου καὶ πίητε αὐτοῦ τὸ αἷμα, οὐκ ἔχετε ζωὴν ἐν

mslssmslssmslssmslssmslssmslssmslssmslssmslssmslssmslssmslssmslssmslssmslssm
ἑαυτοῖς.

mslssmslss

MERLIER's proposed logia source continues uninterrupted and without support from the other theories vs. 54-58. The only other sources detected for the remainder of the chapter are the attribution of v. 59 by WILKENS to his *Reden* expansion of the *Grundevangelium*, v. 62 by SCHULZ to the Son of Man tradition, and v. 66 by HARTKE to the signs source. None of these are supported by other proposals.

A perusal of the underlining makes a number of observations possible. First, there is obviously an area of general agreement among the theories which can be summarized as follows: (1) vs. 1-15 [1]), 16-21 [2]), and 22-25 (excluding πότε ὧδε γέγονας at v. 25) are generally agreed to be evidence of the use of a signs or miracle

---

[1] E. E. JOHNSTON similarly finds evidence for the fourth evangelist's use of his own peculiar source in these verses; he argues this from a comparison of the johannine account of the feeding with the synoptic version and concludes "... that, for at least this part of the story, John had access to a source—oral or written..." (p. 152). "The Johannine Version of the Feeding of the Five Thousand: An Independent Tradition?," *New Testament Studies*, 8 (1961/2), pp. 151-154. That John was dependent upon a nonsynoptic *Urschrift* is evident throughout the gospel, thinks S. MENDNER, but especially in vi 1-20. "Zum Problem 'Johannes und die Synoptiker'", *New Testament Studies*, 4 (1958), pp. 282-307.

[2] Others who would concur with the attribution of vs. 1-21 to some sort of signs source include SCHNACKENBURG, *The Gospel According to Saint John*, vol. I, p. 65 (SCHNACKENBURG concludes, on the one hand, "It is difficult to point to written sources among the traditions upon which the evangelist worked," but suggests, on the other hand, "The use of a written 'σημεῖα-source' may be maintained with some probability", p. 72), and REGINALD H. FULLER who would exclude from the source and attribute to the evangelist the allusion to the "feast of Jews" in v. 4, and the qualification of the prophet as the one who was to come into the "world" in v. 14. *Interpreting the Miracles* (Philadelphia: Westminster Press, 1963), pp. 88-89.

source. (2) These verses are commonly claimed to be from some sort of a *Vorlage*: 27a, 35b (beginning with ἐγώ εἰμι), 37b (beginning with καὶ τὸν ἐρχόμενον), 44a, b (but excluding κἀγὼ ἀναστήσω κτλ.), 45b (beginning with πᾶς ὁ ἀκούσας), and 47b (beginning with ὁ πιστεύων)-48. (3) There is general agreement as to a number of passages where the evangelist has inserted his own material: v. 1, τῆς Τιβεριάδος, v. 24, εὐχαριστήσαντος τοῦ κυρίου, vs. 52-59 (excepting v. 53, the proposals of MERLIER throughout the passage, and WILKENS on v. 59), [1]) vs. 60-65 (excepting SCHULZ at v. 63), and vs. 66-71 (HARTKE dissenting at v. 66). (4) Generally, it is obvious that there is much greater agreement on the narrative portion of the chapter than the discourse passages, and it would appear that our critics agree that the method of the evangelist was to insert short sayings from a source (e.g., vs. 27, 35b, 37b, 44, 48, 46b-48, and 53) into longer and more complex discourses of his own composition [2]).

In addition to the consensus attained on the above mentioned points, it is possible to suggest a number of points at which *considerable* agreement, if not consensus, seems to prevail. First, that a source (s) has been utilized at the following verses has considerable support from the critics: vs. 28b-31, 46, and 52. Second, that v. 6 was not part of the original signs source seems to have notable support [3]).

---

[1]) SCHNACKENBURG proposes that an "eucharistic homily" linked with Ps. lxxviii 24 lies behind vs. 31-58, or at least 51-58 (*Ibid.*, p. 73). However, GEORG RICHTER argues on the basis of an alleged aporia caused by a shift in the meaning of "bread from heaven" that the literary disunity of vs. 31-58 is due to the fact that 51b-58 was a later insertion into the chapter. "Zur Formgeschichte und literarischen Einheit von Joh. vi 31-58", *Zeitschrift für die Neutestamentliche Wissenschaft*, 60 (1969), pp. 21-55. And DEKKER maintains that, because of the inconsistent use of the expressions "the Jews" and "crowd" here and elsewhere in the gospel, chapter 6 was added to the original gospel (written by a Jewish-Christian) by a non-Jewish Christian redactor. "Grundschrift und Redaktion im Johannesevangelium", *New Testament Studies*, 13 (1966), pp. 66-80.

[2]) This observation is not unrelated to the conclusion C. H. DODD drew regarding the allusive presence of traditional sayings material tucked away in the johannine discourses. *Historical Tradition in the Fourth Gospel* (Cambridge: The University Press, 1963), pp. 430 ff. Cf. BENT NOACK, *Zur Johanneischen Tradition* (København: Rosenkilde og Bagger, 1954), section 3.

[3]) The only assistance given our search for a consensus by the statistical analysis of MacGREGOR and MORTON is their observation that there is a break between vs. 1-21 and 22-71. They attribute the former to their pro-

It is evident then from the brief examination of the source theories proposed for chapter six that a growing consensus as to the sources utilized by the fourth evangelist is emerging [1]). The evidence obtained from this survey is sufficient to suggest that a substantial agreement might indeed exist among the critics with regard to the entire gospel and that such consensus needs to be examined and utilized in further johannine studies. It is imperative that the critical study of this gospel attempt to employ the work of others upon which there can be some concurrence, lest our work become hopelessly mired down in repetitious research.

---

posed "J$_1$ Source" and the latter to "J$_2$." *The Structure of the Fourth Gospel* (Edinburgh: Oliver and Boyd, 1961), pp. 93-135.

[1]) This is not to deny the existence of the sizable body of scholars who continue to maintain that source analyses of the fourth gospel of any kind are fruitless and impossible speculation. Notable examples of this group are EDUARD SCHWEIZER, who in spite of suggesting evidence for a source at ii 12 and iv 46-54, declares, "I am opposed to the separation of sources as attempted by Bultmann in his commentary being particularly skeptical of the separation of a sayings source" ("Orthodox Proclamation. The Reinterpretation of the Gospel by the Fourth Evangelist", *Interpretation*, 8 [1954], p. 396, n. 27; cf. *Ego Eimi* . . .: *Die religionsgeschichtliche Herkunft und theologische Bedeutung der johanneischen Bildreden, zugleich ein Beitrag zur Quellenfrage des vierten Evangeliums*, FRLANT n.s. 38 [Göttingen, 1939]), FRANCIS WILLIAMS ("Fourth Gospel and Synoptic Tradition. Two Johannine Passages", *Journal of Biblical Literature*, 86 [1967], pp. 311-319, especially p. 319), C. K. BARRETT (*The Gospel According to St. John* [London: SPCK, 1958], p. 17), and E. RUCKSTUHL (*Die literarische Einheit des Johannesevangelium: Der gegenwartige Stand der einschlagigen Forschungen*, Studia Friburgensia n.s. 3. [Freiburg in der Schweiz, 1951]). It is my suggestion that those who are in general convinced of the effectiveness of source analyses of the fourth gospel seek the consensus of the present scholarly work and proceed in their work on the basis of that consensus, notwithstanding the circle which stands opposed to the entire enterprise.

THE FOURTH GOSPEL AND THE SAMARITANS

JAMES D. PURVIS

Boston

A number of studies have appeared in recent years relating the Fourth Gospel to Samaria and the Samaritans, and to a type of Christian thought which may have developed at an early time in Samaria [1]. These have included suggestions ranging from proposals that the Gospel was dependent upon Christological traditions which developed in Northern Palestine and which drew upon a Moses theology and eschatological concepts which were current in that region [2], to theories that the Gospel was produced by Samaritan Christians [3], or that it was a missionizing tract designed to appeal to and win coverts from the Samaritans [4]. Some of these studies have been of a tentative, probing nature; others have been more assertive in their proposals. All have agreed in maintaining that traditions preserved in Samaritan literature are helpful in understanding either the background of the Fourth Gospel or the audience to which it may have been addressed.

Although some scholars in the past had noted connections

---

[1] John BOWMAN, "The Fourth Gospel and the Samaritans," *BJRL*, 40 (1958), 298-308; *Samaritanische Probleme: Studien zum Verhältnis von Samaritanertum, Judentum und Urchristentum* (Stuttgart, 1967); "The Identity and Date of the Unnamed Feast of John 5:1", in Hans GOEDICKE (ed.), *Near Eastern Studies in Honor of William Foxwell Albright* (Baltimore, 1971), pp. 43-56; George W. BUCHANAN, "The Samaritan Origin of the Gospel of John," in Jacob NEUSNER (ed.), *Religions in Antiquity: Essays in Memory of E. R. Goodenough* (Leiden, 1968), pp. 149-175; Edwin D. FREED, "Samaritan Influence in the Gospel of John," *CBQ*, 30 (1968), 580-597; "Did John Write His Gospel Partly to Win Samaritan Converts?" *Novum Testamentum*, 12 (1970), 241-256; Wayne E. MEEKS, "Galilee and Judea in the Fourth Gospel," *JBL*, 85 (1966), 159-169; *The Prophet-King: Moses Traditions and the Johannine Christology* (Leiden, 1967), pp. 216-257; 286-319; Charles H. H. SCOBIE, "The Origins and Development of Samaritan Christianity," *New Testament Studies*, 19 (1972-73), 390-414, esp. 401-408.

[2] So MEEKS, *Prophet-King*, see esp. pp. 314-319.

[3] So BUCHANAN, "Samaritan Origin of the Gospel of John."

[4] So BOWMAN, "Fourth Gospel and the Samaritans," esp. p. 302; FREED, esp. in "Did John Write His Gospel Partly to Win Samaritan Converts?"

between the Fourth Gospel and Samaria [5]), these were mostly limited to comments on the story of the Samaritan woman of iv 1-42, and one or two other passages. Given the volume of interpretive literature on the Fourth Gospel, it must be said that until recently Johannine scholars have largely ignored the Samaritans. For that matter, with one exception (John BOWMAN), Samaritanologists have largely ignored the Fourth Gospel, or have not been inclined to regard Samaritan materials as useful in understanding its background [6]).

The purpose of this paper is to examine this recent phenomenon of Johannine/Samaritan studies: to determine why these connections have been made, what validity they might have, and what additional observations need yet be offered. In the opinion of the writer, a good case can be made for viewing Samaria as the locale where a number of the Johannine traditions originally developed. Also, traditions preserved in Samaritan literature may be regarded as helpful (if they are used critically) in understanding the background of the Johannine Christology. At the very least, the Samaritan traditions need to be appreciated for what they reveal of the heterogeneity of Palestinian intellectual history during the Roman period, for it was out of this matrix that Johannine Christianity appears to have emerged.

I. The Availability of Samaritan Texts

There are a number of reasons why Samaritan traditions have been consulted recently in Fourth Gospel studies. Not the least of these has been the availability of Samaritan texts. In this regard, two recent publications by John MACDONALD have played an important role: the *Memar Marqah*, Aramaic text and English translation (1963); and *The Theology of the Samaritans* (1964) [7]). A third and more recent publication, *The Samaritan Chronicle No. II* (1969), has also added to the availability of Samaritan texts [8]). The texts

---

[5]) Notably, Hugo ODEBERG, *The Fourth Gospel: Interpreted in its Relation to Contemporaneous Religious Currents in Palestine and the Hellenistic-Oriental World* (Uppsala, 1929), pp. 173-190.

[6]) See, for example, John MACDONALD, *Theology of the Samaritans* (London, 1964), pp. 421, 450.

[7]) *Memar Marqah: The Teaching of Marqah*, vol. I: *The Text*; Vol. II: *The Translation, Beihefte zur Zeitschrift für die alttestamentliche Wissenschaft*, 84 (Berlin, 1963).

[8]) *Beihefte zur Zeitschrift für die alttestamentliche Wissenschaft*, 107 (Berlin, 1969). See also another portion of this chronicle published by MACDONALD,

MACDONALD has published or cited have been available for some time, although not necessarily in useful editions or in English translations, but have not been generally known or readily accessible to non-Samaritanologists. In addition to making these texts more accessible, MACDONALD's publications have had the added value of making scholars aware of the existence of yet other texts, some of which are found in obscure places [9]. Of all of these texts, the writings of Marqah have been drawn upon most extensively (in some cases exclusively) for comparative studies. There are both advantages and disadvantages to be noted in this: on the one hand, Marqah has an abundance of traditions which invite comparisons with elements in the Fourth Gospel; on the other hand, early Samaritan theology appears to have been more complex than would be indicated from this one source.

Marqah, the classical theologian of Samaritanism, lived in an important period of Samaritan history (4th century, C.E.) and contributed significantly to the sect's literature and liturgy. The major work attributed to him, the *Memar Marqah*, or Teaching of Marqah, is especially rich in the traditions it preserves concerning Moses and Joseph. Although Marqah also contains traditions con-

---

under the title, "The Beginnings of Christianity According to the Samaritans," with commentary by A. J. B. HIGGINS, in *New Testament Studies*, 18 (1971-72), 54-80.

[9] Of particular importance are (1) The *Defter*, the oldest part of the Samaritan liturgy, as well as other liturgical materials: see A. E. COWLEY, *The Samaritan Liturgy*, vol. I: *The Common Prayers*; vol. II: *The Text of the Samaritan Liturgy* (Oxford, 1909); M. HEIDENBEIM, *Bibliotheca Samaritana*, II. *Die samaritanische Liturgie* (Leipzig, 1885); Paul KAHLE, "Die zwölf Marka-Hymnen aus dem 'Defter' der samaritanischen Liturgie," in *Opera Minora* (Leiden, 1965), pp. 162-212; John MACDONALD, "*Annual of the Leeds University Oriental Society*, (2, 1959-61), 54-73; see also the large number of Samaritan liturgical texts which have been privately printed in recent years for the use of the Samaritan community in Ḥolon, Israel which are available from the scribe-editor-publisher, Avraham Ṣadaqa, Box 2590, Tel Aviv; (2) the *Asaṭir*, a midrashic collection in the form of a chronicle: see Moses GASTER *The Asatir: the Samaritan Book of the 'Secrets of Moses'* (London, 1927); Z. BEN HAYYIM, "spr ʾsṭyr, ʿm trgym wpryrwš," *Tarbiz*, 14 (1943), 104-125; 174-190; 15 (1944), 71-87; (3) the *Book of Joshua*: see T. G. JUYNBELL, *Chronicon Samaritanum, arabice conscriptum, cui titulus est Liber Josuae* (Leiden, 1848); O. T. CRANE, *The Samaritan Chronicle or Book of Joshua* (New York, 1890); this work is not to be confused with the texts published by Moses GASTER in *ZDMG*, 62 (1908), 209-279, 494-549, which he called "Das Buch Josua in hebräische-samaritanischer Rezension;" that work represented the Joshua portion of the chronicle-tradition published recently by John MACDONALD as *Samaritan Chronicle No. II*, see note 8; (4) medieval Samaritan treatises and essays (see note 18); (5) Samaritan chronicles (see note 18).

cerning the *Taheb*, most of what is known about that Samaritan eschatological figure is learned from other, and later sources [10]). It is evident that there have been divergent strains in Samaritan theology over the long period of that sect's history, and that some of these pre-dated Marqah's work. It is not precisely clear how he related to these, although his work may have been synthetic. One thing is clear, however, and that is that Marqah was not a representative of that branch of Samaritanism which glorified Joshua [11]). That stream of thought is reflected in the Samaritan *Book of Joshua* as well as in some other sources [12]). Although the *Taheb* is related to Moses in the *Memar Marqah* [13]), it has been asserted that that figure was related to Joshua in other Samaritan circles (frequently identified as Dosithean) [14]). At any rate, we have in the Samaritan materials available to us (Marqah and others) a wealth of traditions concerning Joseph, Moses, Joshua, and the *Taheb*, as well as Abraham and Jacob—all of which are, or should be, grist for the Johannine scholar's mill.

There are, however, several caveats which need to be offered in

---

[10]) Especially from the 14th century hymn the *Shira Yetima*, by Abisha‘ ben Phinehas. See HEIDENHEIM, *Die samaritanische Liturgie*, pp. 85-99; Adalbert MERX, *Der Messias oder Taheb der Samaritaner, Beihefte zur Zeitschrift für die alttestamentliche Wissenschaft*, 17 (Giessen, 1909); John BOWMAN, "Early Samaritan Eschatology," *Journal of Jewish Studies*, 6 (1955), 63-72; Moses GASTER, *Samaritan Oral Law and Ancient Traditions*, vol. I: *Samaritan Eschatology* (London, 1932), pp. 221-277.

[11]) On this, see the comments in J. D. PURVIS, "Samaritan Traditions on the Death of Moses," in G. W. E. NICKELSBURG (ed.), *Studies on the Testament of Moses, Septuagint and Cognate Studies*, 4 (Society of Biblical Literature, 1973), pp. 93-117, esp. p. 96, III.

[12]) See A. D. CROWN, "Some Traces of Heterodox Theology in the Samaritan Book of Joshua," *BJRL*, 50 (1967), 178-198. See also his "New Light on the Inter-Relationships of the Samaritan Chronicles from some Manuscripts in the John Rylands Library," *BJRL*, 54 (1972) 282-313, esp. 308-311.

[13]) As correctly noted by MEEKS, *Prophet-King*, pp. 248-249.

[14]) See MERX, "Der Messias oder Taheb der Samaritaner," pp. 41, 43, 49; CROWN, "Heterodox Theology," 185-186; "Dositheans, Resurrection and a Messianic Joshua," in *Antichthon*, I (1967-1968); cf. also Abram SPIRO, "Stephen's Samaritan Background," Appendix V of J. MUNCK, *Acts of the Apostles (Anchor Bible)*, revised by W. F. ALBRIGHT and C. S. MANN (Garden City, New York, 1967), pp. 290-291, and BOWMAN, "The Identity and Date of the Unnamed Feast of John 5:1," pp. 45-47. H. G. KIPPENBERG, however, has suggested that glorification of Joshua was related to an anti-Dosithean polemic: see *Garizim und Synagoge, Traditionsgeschichtliche Untersuchungen zur samaritanischen Religion der aramäischen Periode* (Berlin, 1971), pp. 321-323. See also MEEKS, *Prophet-King*, pp. 252-254, for a brief discussion of the Joshua-*Taheb*.

reference to the use of Samaritan texts. With the exception of their Pentateuch (and perhaps Targum) all of the Samaritan literary and liturgical texts post-date the 4th century C.E. Moreover, even the earliest of these (Aramaic) texts are preserved in medieval and modern manuscripts. Anyone familiar with the history of the Samaritan scribal tradition is aware of the liberties which have been taken by copyists and authors in their use of materials. As one Samaritan scholar has noted, "most Samaritan writings show a constant process of adaptation and editorial manipulation" [15]. Marqah may be taken as an example, inasmuch as he is the Samaritan writer who has been and who will probably continue to be the most frequently cited for comparative purposes. The critical edition of the *Memar* edited by MACDONALD is based on 18th and 19th century manuscripts. The oldest known manuscript of the *Memar* is no older than the 14th century. It has been called to my attention that virtually all of the passages dealing with such eschatological subjects as the *Taheb* and the future resurrection are lacking in the older manuscript [16]. This is mentioned not to cast negative judgment on MACDONALD's edition (for the later texts could be superior to the earlier text), but to point out the complexity of text-critical problems in Samaritan literary works; with Marqah, so with others. We are dealing with the literary products of a living religion with a long history. Also, while priority is often given to Marqah for reconstructing early Samaritan theology, there are a number of pseudonymous texts found in medieval manuscripts (such as the Aramaic *Asaṭir* and the Arabic *Book of Joshua*) which in origin could have been as old as Marqah's writings, although they are now badly preserved [17]. Again, there are a number of medieval Samaritan Arabic treatises and later Hebrew texts which may very well have drawn upon older traditions [18]. All of which is to say that a Samar-

---

[15] T. H. GASTER, "Samaritans," *Interpreters Dictionary of the Bible*, Vol. R-Z (New York, 1962), p. 195.

[16] I am indebted to Professor Stanley ISSER, State University of New York at Binghamton, for calling this to my attention.

[17] The Samaritan *Book of Joshua* is preserved in a manuscript copied from a 13th century Arabic chronicle, which claimed to be based on older sources. See CROWN, "Inter-relationships of the Samaritan Chronicles," 286-293. The *Asaṭir* is preserved in an Aramaic text which Ben-Ḥayyim dates to the 9th-12th centuries on philological grounds, See *spr 'styr*, 14, 107-110.

[18] Most of the medieval Samaritan Arabic treatises remain unpublished. Some of these are cited or referred to by MACDONALD, *Theology of the Samaritans, passim*. GASTER published translations of eschatological parts of these

itan tradition is not necessarily useful for comparative purposes because it is found in a writing thought to be early, or necessarily useless because it is found in a writing known to be late. What is important is that the tradition be treated critically.

The problem, briefly stated, is this: given the nature of the materials in which the Samaritan traditions are preserved, how can these be employed critically in the reconstruction of the early theology of the sect? This is a difficult but not a hopeless problem. Certainly the first step is a careful reconstruction of the early history of that sect, i.e. during the Hellenistic and Roman periods, and the determination of those factors which would have contributed to its intellectual life. In this, our major sources are non-Samaritan Jewish and Christian texts and archaeological data. The only scholar to have undertaken a comprehensive study of the

---

in his *Samaritan Eschatology*. For a useful catalogue of the unpublished medieval and modern texts, see Edward ROBERTSON, *Catalogue of the Samaritan Manuscripts in the John Rylands Library, Manchester*, vol. II: *The Gaster Manuscripts* (Manchester, 1962).

It is extremely difficult to assess the antiquity of traditions preserved in the Samaritan chronicles, although two of these preserve materials which may be useful for early comparative studies: the 14th century chronicle of Abuʾl Fataḥ, and the so-called *Samaritan Chronicle No. II*, published by MACDONALD. For Abuʾl Fataḥ, see Edward VILMAR, *Abulfathi Annales Samaritani*. (Gotha, 1856). The earliest portions of the chronicle were translated by R. Payne SMITH, "The Samaritan Chronicle of Abuʾl Fataḥ," in M. HEIDENHEIM (ed.) *Deutsche Vierteljahrsschrift für englisch-theologische Forschung und Kritik*, vol. II (Gotha, 1863), pp. 304-333, 431-459. See also the two annotated priest-lists, the *Tolidah* and the *šalšalat*: John BOWMAN, *Transcript of the Original Text of the Samaritan Chronicle Tolidah* (Leeds, 1955): M. GASTER, "The Chain of Samaritan High Priests," in *Texts and Studies* (London, 1925-28), vol. I, pp. 483-502; vol. II, pp. 131-138. See also the 19th century chronicle published by ADLER, which contains some unique materials: E. N. ADLER and M. SÉLIGSOHN, "Une nouvelle chronique samaritaine," in *Revue des Études juives*, 44 (1902), 188-222; 45 (1902), 70-98, 223-254; 46 (1903), 123-146.

An interesting body of Samaritan literature is that associated with the birth of Moses: (1) a 14th century poem by Jacob the *rabban* of Damascus (T. H. GASTER, "A Samaritan Poem about Moses," in A. BERGER, *et al.*, *The Joshua Bloch Memorial Volume: Studies in Booklore and History* (New York, 1960), pp. 115-139); (2) a 14th century acrostic poem by Abdullah ben Salamah (COWLEY, *Samaritan Liturgy*, pp. 746-753); (3) a 16th century Arabic treatise, the *Maulid an-Nashi*, by Ismâ'il ar-Rumaihi of Damascus (S. J. MILLER, *The Samaritan Molad Mosheh* (New York, 1949), pp. 56-203; (4) the 19th century Aramaic *Molad Mosheh* of Phinehas ben Isaac (MILLER, *op. cit.*, pp. 232-353). There are also some 12-13th century poems on the birth of Moses attributed to Ghazal al-Duwaik. See GASTER, *Samaritan Eschatology*, p. 71; MACDONALD, *Theology of the Samaritans*, pp. 45-46.

Aramaic Samaritan traditions from the perspective of early Samaritan history has been H. G. KIPPENBERG, in *Gerizim und Synagoge: Traditionsgeschichtliche Untersuchungen zur samaritanischer Religion der aramäischen Periode* (1971) [19]. KIPPENBERG has suggested that Samaritan theology developed at an early time around several distinct groups within that community, specifically priests and laymen, with the latter group including teachers of the Pentateuch, elders, and judges. The development of the synagogue led to the ascendancy of the lay teacher over the priests, and also to the development and proliferation of sectarian movements. KIPPENBERG is able to relate specific traditions in the Aramaic literature with one or another of these groups, and also offer suggestions concerning the fusion of priestly and lay traditions, as, for example, in Marqah.

In addition to KIPPENBERG's work, the historical-critical studies of John BOWMAN and his student A. D. CROWN are sometimes helpful in appreciating the complexity of Samaritan thought. BOWMAN has maintained that Samaritan theology developed from early times down to the late middle ages in a dialectic between a priestly orthodoxy and a lay (supposedly Dosithean) heterodoxy; and that divergent streams of religious thought are evident in various medieval texts [20]. Although BOWMAN's Hegelian dialectic is not beyond criticism, his observations concerning the conflicting nature of various Samaritan traditions certainly have validity. Also, these traditions appear to have polarized around priestly and lay movements, as both KIPPENBERG and BOWMAN have maintained, although it is not at all clear to what extent the lay movements may be identified as Dosithean [21]. BOWMAN has himself been involved

---

[19] *Religionsgeschichtliche Versuche und Vorarbeiten*, 30 (Berlin, 1970).

[20] BOWMAN, "The Importance of Samaritan Researches," *Annual of the Leeds University Oriental Society*, 1 (1959-1959), 43-54; "Pilgrimage to Mount Gerizim," in M. Avi-Yonah, *et al., Eretz Israel*, vol. VIII (Jerusalem, 1964), pp. 17-28. BOWMAN's thesis, which receives its fullest expression in "Pilgrimage to Mount Sinai" is that Dositheanism represented a lay movement which began to gain ascendancy over the orthodox Samaritan priesthood in the time of Baba Rabbah, with the synagogue as its institutional base. The two movements remained in tension until the 14th century when an accomodation was made between the two, producing a new orthodoxy and a new liturgy.

[21] BOWMAN's work suffers from a lack of documentation. His observations concerning the nature of Dositheanism appear to be derived almost exclusively from Abu'l Fataḥ, and most particularly from Abu'l Fataḥ's account of the Dosithean sub-sects, many of which differed radically from one another.

in Samaritan/Johannine researches, suggesting *inter alia* that the Gospel may have been written "to make a bridge between Samaritans and Jews in Christ" [22]. Most recently, he has suggested that the type of Samaritanism to which the Gospel would have made its appeal was that of the Dosithean variety [23]. This is an observation which should not be overlooked. BOWMAN has been aware of the variety of Samaritan traditions and the complexity of Samaritan thought, more so than many of the scholars who have been engaged in Johannine/Samaritan studies. In fact, if a general negative criticism could be leveled against these studies it would be that many references to Samaritan traditions have tended to operate under the tacit assumption that early Samaritan thought was fairly uniform. This is an assumption which cannot be taken for granted.

II. *The Fourth Gospel and Samaria*

There are several considerations concerning the Fourth Gospel which would necessitate a close examination of Samaria and the type of religious thought which developed there. The first and most obvious of these is that the Samaritans are mentioned in the Gospel and are generally presented in a favorable light (iv 1-42) [24]. In addition to having visited Samaria early in his career (iv 1-42), Jesus is also said to have retreated at a later time to a locale identified as Ephraim (xi 54) [25]. There are also geographical texts in the Fourth Gospel suggesting that John the Baptist may have been active in Samaria (iii 23) [26].

These observations have long been noted, although not a great

---

The most vulnerable part of his thesis is the connection between Dositheanism and the Joshua traditions.

[22] "The Fourth Gospel and the Samaritans," p. 302.

[23] "Identity and Date of the Unnamed Feast in John 5:1," pp. 45-47; cf. also BOWMAN, *Samaritanische Probleme: Studien zum Verhältnis von Samaritanertum, Judentum und Urchristentum* (Stuttgart, 1967), pp. 55, 76.

[24] Something to be noted also in Luke-Acts; see Luke ix 52; x 33-37; xvii 16; Acts i 8; viii 1-25.

[25] On this locale, see Raymond BROWN, *The Gospel According to John (i-xiii) (Anchor Bible)* (Garden City, N.Y., 1966), p. 441; cf. also, FREED, "Samaritan Influence in the Gospel of John," 581.

[26] At Aenon near Salim. So W. F. ALBRIGHT, "Recent Discoveries in Palestine and the Gospel of John" in W. D. DAVIES and D. DAUBE (eds.), *The Background of the New Testament and its Eschatology* (Cambridge, 1956), pp. 159-160. For this and alternative possibilities see BROWN, *Ibid.*, p. 151. See also M-É. BOISMARD, "Aenon près de Salem (Jean III, 23)," *Revue Biblique*, 80 (1973), 218-229.

deal has been made of them. A notable exception was the suggestion offered by H. HAMMER (1913) that Jesus and his disciples were Samaritans, a view which could hardly be entertained seriously and which has accordingly been assigned to the limbo of scholarly foot-notes [27]). Similar to this was the novel suggestion of Georges ORY (1956) that John the Baptist—whom he identified as the original Christian messiah—was none other than the Samaritan herisiarch Dositheus [28]). This thesis seems to have evaded even the footnotes of Fourth Gospel studies.

More recently it has been suggested that there are several additional considerations which would indicate the importance of Samaria for Johannine studies. One of these has been that Samaria (and with it Galilee) may play a more important role in this Gospel than had previously been recognized. This has been most clearly articulated by Wayne MEEKS, who has pointed out that the northern locales fulfill a "symbolic function" in John in which their significance far exceed the relatively small attention they are given in the narrative [29]). This relates closely to another observable phenomenon in the Gospel: that the Jews are represented as Jesus's enemies (so v 18, 41, 52; vii 1, 11, 13; viii 48, 57; ix 18; xviii 12, 38; xix 7, 12, 20, etc.), and are contrasted with believing members of the Israelite —not exclusively or necessarily Jewish— nation [30]). Also, concurrent with the recent accessibility of Samaritan texts, it has been pointed out that a number of distinctive elements of John's Gospel, especially its Christology, may be clarified by reference to Samaritan traditions. Germane also to these considerations are the recent suggestions that the speech of Stephen of Acts vii may provide important data on early Samaritan Christianity [31]).

---

[27]) *Traktat von Samaritanermessias: Studien zur Frage der Existenz Jesu* (Bonn, 1913). HAMMER's work is cited by Paul KAHLE, "Untersuchungen zur Geschichte des Pentateuchtextes," *TSK* 88 (1915), 399-439.

[28]) "Jean le Baptiseur," *Cahiers Renan*, 3/10 (1956), 1-24; "La Samarie, patrie d'un Messie," *Ibid.*, 3/11 (1956), 1-16.

[29]) MEEKS, "Galilee and the Fourth Gospel;" *The Prophet-King*, pp. 313-318.

[30]) BUCHANAN, "The Samaritan Origin of the Gospel of John," 158-166.

[31]) Abram SPIRO, "Stephen's Samaritan Background," in J. MUNCK, *The Acts of the Apostles (The Anchor Bible)*, Revised by W. F. ALBRIGHT and C. S. MANN (Garden City, N.Y., 1967), Appendix V, pp. 285-300. See also R. SCROGGS, "The Earliest Hellenistic Christianity," in Jacob NEUSNER (ed.), *Religions in Antiquity: Essays in Memory of E. R. Goodenough* (Leiden, 1968), pp. 176-206, esp. pp. 182-197; SCOBIE, "Origins and Development of Samaritan Christianity," esp. 391-400.

Samaritans, Galileans, and Jews

If one were to judge the relative significance in John of Galilee, Samaria, and Judah by purely quantitative measurements, Judah would emerge as the most important and Galilee and Samaria as subordinate and less significant. This would be due to the fact that John records no less than three visits of Jesus to Jerusalem and devotes the greater part of his narrative to events which allegedly transpired in Judah. But this quantitative consideration could easily obscure the relative significance of the northern and southern locales in the Gospel. What is important to note is that Jerusalem plays an important role in John for negative reasons. It is the place of judgment and rejection. This is particularly clear in John's treatment of the proverb that "a prophet has no honor in his own country" (iv 44-45). The Synoptics explain Jseus's use of this saying in reference to his rejection in Galilee. But John states that after Jesus cited this proverb he went into Galilee where the Galileans welcomed him (iv 45), just as the Samaritans had previously done (iv 39-42). There is no mass rejection in either Galilee or Samaria in the Fourth Gospel, but only in Jerusalem. It is clear that to John, Jesus' *patris*, his native land, was not the territory in which he was raised (Galilee), much less Samaria, but Judah— the spiritual home of the Jewish people [32]). As Wayne MEEKS has noted, "The journeys to Jerusalem in John symbolize the coming of the redeemer to 'his own' and his rejection by them, while the emphasized movement from Judea to Galilee (especially iv 43-54) symbolizes the redeemer's acceptance by others, who thereby become truly 'children of God,' the real Israel" [33]). Although MEEKS emphasizes the welcoming by the Galileans in this dialectic, and suggests that "Samaria has a somewhat smaller role than Galilee in this Gospel" [34]), it may be argued that acceptance of Jews in Samaria (iv 39-42) plays a more important role than the welcoming in Galilee (iv 43-54). The Galileans were Jews, but the Samaritans were not, although they believed themselves to be Israelites. The confession of the believing Samaritans ("we know that this is the Savior of the world," iv 42) seems particularly significant in the theme of Jesus's rejection by his own and acceptance by others.

---

[32]) MEEKS, "Galilee and Judea in the Fourth Gospel," 163-166.
[33]) *Ibid.*, 165
[34]) *Ibid.*, 166

There seems also to have been a conscious attempt in the Fourth Gospel to relate the Galileans to the Samaritans rather than to the Judaeans, to whom one might expect them to have been related due to a common faith ("Jewish" rather than "Samaritan"). To John, the Galilean Jews were much closer to the non-Jewish Samaritans than to their Jewish brethren in Jerusalem, as judged in reference to the theme of acceptance/rejection. This may account for the use of the term "Israelite" rather than "Jew" in Jesus's statement concerning Nathaniel ("an Israelite, indeed, in whom is no guile," i 47). "Israelite" was the term used by Samaritans to distinguish themselves from Jews. John's use of the term for a Galilean suggests that he also wished to make a distinction. Galilean Jews such as Nathaniel were not to be confused with Judaean Jews such as those who vilified and rejected Jesus. The confession of the Israelite Nathaniel, "Rabbi, you are the Son of God! You are the King of Israel" (i 49), stands in marked contrast to the statement of the Jerusalemite Jews, "We have no king but Caesar" (xix 15). The use of "Israelite" to indicate a northern Palestinian (as distinct from a Judaean) was not unusual in Palestine in the first century, as has been pointed out by George BUCHANAN [35]). The term was so used by the Samaritans of themselves, and sometimes by Jews in reference to the descendents of the *gôlâh* of northern Israel (the so-called "lost tribes"). That the term was used in John i 47 to tie the believing Jews of the Galilee to the Samaritans is further suggested by Jesus's statement to Nathaniel, "You will see heaven opened, and the angels ascending and descending upon the son of man" (i 51). This is an obvious allusion to the story of Jacob's experience at Bethel (Genesis xxviii 10-17), which was used by the biblical writers as an aetiological legend for the founding of the northern cultic center at Bethel, and by the Samaritans as a tradition relating the Patriarchs to their cultic center at Mt. Gerizim (which they identified with Bethel).

Although the significance of Samaria and Galilee in the Fourth Gospel, as pointed out by MEEKS and BUCHANAN, has not generally been recognized, the anti-Jewishness of this Gospel has not been overlooked. This has usually been explained by the Patristic testimony relating the Fourth Gospel to the gentile Christian community at Ephesus. A Gospel in which Jesus was rejected by Jews to be

---

[35]) "Samaritan Origin of the Gospel of John," pp. 158-159.

accepted by others, and in which the term "Jew" was used oppro-
briously, would certainly have been received favorably in non-
Jewish Christian circles. There is no reason then to doubt the
Patristic evidence linking the promulgation and use of this Gospel
to the gentile churches of the Roman province of Asia. But there
is also internal evidence, topographic and other, to suggest that the
origins of the Gospel (or a number of its traditions) may have been
Palestinian. These have long been noted; the growing awareness in
recent years of the rich complexity of Palestinian Judaism during
the first century has added to the suggestions linking this Gospel
to Palestine [36]). But what is one to make of the anti-Jewishness of
an alleged Palestinian Gospel? This question may be clarified by
viewing the negative attitude of the Fourth Gospel towards Judaeans in the context of its positive attitude towards Samaritans and
Galileans. In this Gospel, Jesus is not rejected by Jews to be accepted by Gentiles, but accepted by Israelites (i.e. Samaritans and
Galileans) to be rejected by Jews. This would have had special
significance for gentile Christians who later made use of this Gospel.
But the origins of these Gospel traditions would more likely be
found amongst those Palestinians, Christians of Galilean and Samaritan background, who are cited for having received and welcomed
Jesus. MEEKS has accordingly argued that the geographical symbolism of the Fourth Gospel tends to support the suggestion made
some time ago by Karl KNUDSIN that a number of the traditions
in John took shape in Christian communities in Galilee and Samaria
which were engaged in missionizing propaganda [37]). BUCHANAN,
working independently of MEEKS but coming to a similar conclusion,
has suggested that John's Gospel was a product of the Christian
church in Samaria. He has further suggested that Samaria may have
been the territory entrusted to the spiritual care of the Apostle John
in that distribution of responsibilities which assigned Paul and
Barnabas to the gentiles and James, Peter, and John to the circum-
cised (Gal. ii 7-9) [38]).

There seems to be good reason, then, for affirming that Samaria
played an important role in the development of the Fourth Gospel,
either as the place where some of the Johannine traditions devel-

---

[36]) On this, see especially, BUCHANAN, *Ibid.*, pp. 149-156.
[37]) MEEKS, "Galilee and Judea in the Fourth Gospel," 168-169; *Prophet-
King*, pp. 314-316.
[38]) BUCHANAN, "Samaritan Origin of the Gospel of John," pp. 173-175.

oped (following MEEKS), or as the center from which the Gospel itself emanated (so BUCHANAN). Needless to say, the former position could be more easily assimilated into contemporary Johannine scholarship than the latter, if only because it is concerned with a more limited issue. The testing of either hypothesis is, however, dependent upon the satisfactory demonstration of at least two things: first, that the theology of the Gospel accords with what can otherwise be learned about the theology of the early Christian church in Samaria; and second, that elements of the Gospel may be clarified by reference to theological traditions which were entertained by the people of that region (i.e., the Samaritans).

Christianity in Samaria

Unfortunately, not a great deal is known about the early history of Christianity in Samaria. Although the author of Luke-Acts regarded the evangelization of the region as an important stage in the expansion of Christianity (compare Acts i 8 and viii 4-25), and the apostolic mission in Samaria seems to have been anticipated in his gospel (Luke ix 5-156; x 33-37; xvii 16), he reported little about the character of the Samaritan church. He did indicate, however, that in-roads in conversion were made among the followers of Simon Magus, with Simon himself being drawn to Christianity (xiii 9-13), and that the church in Samaria was generally supportive of the position of the church of Antioch in its disagreement with some Jewish Christians (so xv 3). The early experience of Christianity with Simonianism in Samaria may account for the attention of the Church Fathers to the Samaritan sects, especially those of Simon and Dositheus (who was related to Simon either as teacher or disciple) [39]. Except for a consideration of the heresies and an occasional reference to a bishop of Neapolis, little else is learned about Samaritan Christianity from Patristic sources [40]. Judging from the

---

[39] On these, see especially MONTGOMERY, The Samaritans, the Earliest Jewish Sect: Their History, Theology and Literature (Philadelphia, 1907; reprinted, New York, 1968), pp. 252-265; N. SCHMIDT, "Sects (Samaritan)," in James HASTINGS, Encyclopaedia of Religion and Ethics (New York, 1928), vol. XI, pp. 343-345; S. KRAUSS, "Dosithée et les Dosithéens," Revue des Études juives, 42 (1901), 27-42; J. THOMAS, Le Mouvement Baptiste en palestine et Syrie (Gembloux, 1935), passim; M. BLACK, The Scrolls and Christian Origins (New York, 1961), pp. 56-74. See also the forthcoming essay by Stanley ISSER, "The Samaritans and their Sects," in the Cambridge History of Judaism, vol. II.

[40] MONTGOMERY, Samaritans, pp. 98-124.

edicts of the Byzantine rulers against the Samaritans, it is evident that Christianity did not supersede main-line Samaritanism in central Palestine [41]). The writings of Justin Martyr may give us some clues to the character of early Samaritan Christianity, inasmuch as he was a native of Neapolis, but Justin seems to have known more about Judaism and Greek philosophy than he knew about the theology of Samaritanism. There are, in fact, many indications that Samaria was strongly Hellenized during the Greek and Roman periods [42]). It must be kept in mind that the movement centered at Mt. Gerizim was only one component of the religious complex of Samaria and that Samaritan Christianity probably drew followers from a number of religious backgrounds.

It has recently been suggested that Stephen was a Samaritan Christian. If this could be substantiated, the speech of Stephen in Acts vii would provide an extremely important set of data by which to judge the alleged Samaritan or Samaritan Christian background of the Fourth Gospel.

The arguments for the Samaritan background of Stephen's speech have been set forth by Abram SPIRO, and summarized with supporting and dissenting opinions by C. H. H. SCOBIE [43]). These will not be repeated here, except to note those points at which the argument has or does not have validity. On the whole it may be said that a tentative case has been made for the Samaritan background of Stephen, although not all of the suggestions offered merit consideration. First of all, as SPIRO has pointed out, Stephen was said to have been a native of Samaria by the 14th century Samaritan Chronicler Abu'l Fath [44]). Also, there are portions of Stephen's speech which agree with readings of the Samaritan Pentateuch [45]). This phenomenon in itself may not be as important as has been suggested, inasmuch as these readings could simply reflect use of non-Masoretic Palestinian textual tradition (of which the Samaritan

---

[41]) *Ibid.*, esp. pp. 110-124.

[42]) See the writer's comments on this subject in the essay "The Samaritans, in the forthcoming *Cambridge History of Judaism*, vol. I.

[43]) See note 31.

[44]) The Samaritan tradition also notes that Simon Magus was buried in front of Stephen's home. VILMAR, *Abulfathi Annales Samaritani*, Arabic section, p. 159.

[45]) Specifically, Acts vii 4 (a reading known also from Philo); vii 5 (probably incorrectly identified as a Samaritan reading); vii 32; vii 37 (which probably reflects the reading of Deut. xiii 18f of Exodus xx in the Samaritan redaction).

Pentateuch was itself a redaction) [46]). What does seem to be important is that the speech of Stephen reflects a Samaritan view of
history, from Abraham to Solomon [47]). What is especially significant in this is Stephen's condemnation of the Jewish nation from
the time of Solomon on as a people who had resisted the Holy
Spirit. The offense of Solomon had been in building a temple, "a
house made with hands", unlike the tabernacle which Moses had
built after a divine pattern, and which Joshua brought into the land.
"*Our fathers,*" i.e. the Israelite nation as a whole, had this tabernacle from Moses in the wilderness and under Joshua in Canaan.
But Solomon erred in building a temple, and the nation which followed him was a stiff-necked people resisting God's spirit—"As
your fathers did, so do you" (vii 51). We see here virtually the same
distinction between Israel ("our fathers") and Judah ("*your fathers*")
as has been noted in John's Gospel. A distinction is made between
the faithful Israel and the unfaithful Jews. Moreover, in this case
the source of the distinction is precisely that which the Samaritans
claimed—the illegitimacy of the Jerusalem sanctuary. As for the
Samaritans, so too for Stephen: the Jerusalem temple was of the
wrong kind ("made with hands"), of the wrong pattern, and in the
wrong place [48]). Still this is not a full espousal of the Samaritan
claim (i.e., Gerizim and not Jerusalem), but only a utilization of
part of it (not Jerusalem). This calls to mind the discussion in John

---

[46]) This textual tradition of the Pentateuch had also been in use at Qumrân, and is known from other sources. See J. D. PURVIS, *The Samaritan
Pentateuch and the Origin of the Samaritan Sect* (Cambridge, Mass., 1968),
pp. 78-87; F. M. CROSS, "The Evolution of a Theory of Local Texts," In
Septuagint and Cognate Studies, 2 (Society of Biblical Literature, 1972), pp.
108-126; "Contributions of the Qumrân Discoveries to the Study of the
Biblical Text," *IEJ*, 16 (1966), 81-95.
[47]) The claim of Stephen that Jacob was buried at Shechem (vii 16) may
be a Samaritanism, although most Samaritan traditions on the burial of the
Patriarch agree with the Jewish tradition relating to Hebron. According to
MACDONALD, some Samaritan traditions locate the cave of Machpelah at
Gerizim: *Theology of the Samaritans*, p. 329. Much less certain is SPIRO's un-
documented claim that early Samaritan theology emphasized Abraham (so
too, supposedly, Stephen) more so than Moses: "Stephen's Samaritan Background," pp. 291-293. Emphasis upon Abraham does appear, however, to
have been characteristic of the Hellenized Samaritans of the time of Antio-
chus IV. See PURVIS, "Samaritans," forthcoming in *Cambridge History of
Judaism*, vol. I. This attitude could possibly have belonged to a stream of
Samaritan thought in the 1st century, but this is not certain.
[48]) SPIRO: " . . . made by hands, of the wrong material, and in the wrong
'place.' " *Ibid.*, p. 295.

iv in which the Samaritan woman raised the question of the legitimate place of worship ("Our fathers worshipped on this mountain, but you [Jews] say that in Jerusalem is the place where men ought to worship," iv 20), to which Jesus replied that in the coming hour a spiritual worship would be established which would render both cultic centers unimportant. The speech of Stephen may reflect a similar understanding (cf. vi 14).

Stephen's view of Moses and the Law is more difficult to assess. On the one hand, his representation of Moses (vii 35-38) is near poetic [49]; on the other, it was said of Stephen that he not only spoke against the temple, but also against the Law (so vi 13). There may in fact have been some downgrading of Moses in the speech, if not of the law itself: Moses is represented as having been important because he promised that God would raise up a prophet like himself (vii 37, after Deut. xviii 15); Moses delivered living oracles, but the nation (all of the nation, "our fathers," vii 39) refused to obey him and lapsed into idolatry (vii 39-43); and Moses spoke with "the angel" rather than directly with God (vii 35, 38), with the Law having been delivered by angels (vii 53). The use of angels is a familiar motif in Samaritan literature. They are usually associated with the glorification of important events (e.g. the birth and death of Moses and the receiving of the Law), but sometimes function to safeguard the transcendence of God [50]. If Stephen's use of the motif was to downgrade both Moses and the Law, by separating each from God by at least one stage, this was quite the opposite of the Samaritan usage of angels. Also, in Samaritan traditions on the receiving of the Law at Sinai (e.g., in Marqah) angels are in attendence but the Law is received by Moses from God.

If Stephen was a Samaritan, and the evidence inclines in that direction, we may receive some previously unrecognized information about Samaritan Christianity: for Christians of that region, Jesus

---

[49]) As pointed out by SCROGGS, "The Earliest Hellenistic Christianity," p. 184. SPIRO points out that vii 35-38 is similar to a Samaritan hymn, which he does not identify (the essay suffers from poor documentation): "Stephen's Samaritan Background," p. 286. The section is, in fact, stylistically similar to many of the poetic encomia to Moses in the *Memar Marqah* and the liturgy. SPIRO may have been referring to the long poem on Moses ("This is he who ... /This is he who ... , etc.) in the *Moulid an-Nashiᶜ*. MILLER, *The Samaritan Molad Mosheh*, pp. 38-40.

[50]) So Numbers xxii 20 and xxiii 4, where SP reads *mlᵓk ᵓlhym* (MT = *ᵓlym*). Also, the Samaritan Targum sometimes uses "angels" or "angel of God" as a surrogate for the Divinity: So Gen. viii 1, 24; ix 6; xvi 22.

was compared with Abraham and Moses as being the fulfillment
of the revelation-tradition associated with them in particular, rather
than the family of David of Jerusalem (although David himself was
not denigrated). The temple of Jerusalem was viewed as theologically non-viable, just as it had been illegitimate in the first place.
And, finally, the Jewish nation was viewed as being at enmity with
God, disobeying his Law and killing his prophets, especially Jesus
the Righteous One. The view of Moses and the Law is not altogether
clear from what survives of Stephen's speech, but it is strongly
suggested that Jesus was greater than Moses (as the fulfillment of
the promise is greater than the promise, vii 37) and greater than
the Law, inasmuch as it was delivered only by angels (against the
position of Samaritanism) and the people were unable to keep it
(so vii 53). We shall see that these views are remarkably similar to
those encountered in the Fourth Gospel.

Johannine Christology and Samaritan Traditions

What were the sources of the Johannine Christology? For whom
would this theological understanding of Jesus have had a clear but
special meaning? Those who have turned to Samaria for answers to
these questions have done so out of the conviction that the messiahship of Jesus as it was represented in John was of a non-Davidic
type for which Jewish sources give us scant information. It has been
pointed out, for example, that Jesus was not identified by John as
being of Davidic descent, or of the tribe of Judah, although he was
called a Jew; that his Galilean origins were regarded by his contemporaries as suggesting that he could not be the messiah, at least
not by their understanding of messiahship (vii 26-31, 40-44, cf. i 46);
and that he willingly accepted the messianic title from a Samaritan
woman (iv 25-26) but was equivocal before Pilate when the Roman
governor asked if he were "king of the Jews" (xviii 33-36). It has
also been noted that this Gospel identifies Jesus as the prophet (so
vi 14, cf. iv 19, ix 17, a prophet), an eschatological figure distinct
from the Christ (see esp. vii 40-41; cf. i 21, 25), while also identifying
him with the Christ—however as a Christ-figure called the Savior
of the world (iv 29, 42) and the Son of God (xi 27), but not the son
of David. The utilization of Samaritan traditions has led some
scholars to conclude that one or another of the eschatological models
which developed in northern Palestine may have provided the
background for John's understanding of the non-Davidic, Prophet-

Christ (so BUCHANAN, BOWMAN, FREED), or that the Gospel represents a consolidation of eschatological traditions of differing provenance, Jewish and Samaritan (so MEEKS) [51]).

A number of Samaritan eschatological figures—or supposed Samaritan eschatological figures—have been proposed for the alleged model of the Johannine Christology, not all of which may be clearly identified from Samaritan texts. BUCHANAN has suggested two: the one a royal figure modeled after Joseph, supposedly the Messiah ben Joseph or ben Ephraim otherwise known from medieval Jewish sources [52]); the other a prophetic figure modeled after the old northern Israelite prophet Elisha [53]). Of the two, a stronger case is made for the prophet Elisha model, although both present difficulties in regard to the Samaritan traditions.

The kingship of Jesus is represented in the Fourth Gospel, according to BUCHANAN, in two titles: the "Son of God," which is equated with King of Israel (in i 49), and the "son of Joseph" (i 45; vi 42), which, it is suggested, is used in lieu of "son of David" as a royal title. Both point, BUCHANAN claims, to a Samaritan messianic figure, the Messiah ben Joseph. This interpretation is based on the Jewish tradition of the Messiah ben Ephraim, who is represented in some late sources as a warrior-forerunner of the Davidic Messiah who would be from Galilee and lead the tribes of Ephraim, Benjamin and part of Gad in a triumphal battle in which he would die. BUCHANAN suggests that the Samaritan origin of this messianic type may be seen in traditions preserved in Marqah concerning Joseph the King, although this position is not developed by a study of the Samaritan texts themselves.

There are several difficulties with this thesis. First of all, it is not at all clear that "son of Joseph" has any other than a patronymic function in the Fourth Gospel. In one of the two texts BUCHANAN cites the function is clearly patronymic (vi 42). Second, "son of Joseph" is not known to have been one of the titles of any of the Samaritan eschatological figures, although the designation could have been used of any non-priestly member of the Samaritan

---

[51]) *Prophet-King*, p. 318: "It is quite clear that the gospel as it stands is the product of the consolidation of traditions of differing provenance. While Jesus fulfills the expectation of a prophet-king like Moses, he is also the 'Messiah' awaited by the Judaeans—though not the Bethlehemite son of David they expect."

[52]) "Samaritan Origins of the Gospel of John," pp. 159-160.

[53]) *Ibid.*, pp. 166-172.

community. There are several considerations, however, which would cause us to look closely at the figure of Joseph in Samaritan thought. For example, Joseph is given the Aramaic title *malkâh* in Marqah[54]; the *Taheb* is sometimes described as having a warrior function in his coming which is related to the blessing of Joseph in Deut. xxxiii 17 [55]); and there is at least one text in which some connection or similarity is noted between Joseph and the *Taheb* [56]). An examination of these traditions in the context of Samaritan thought reveals, however, that (1) the socalled kingship of Joseph was not analogous to the kingship of David in either historical or eschatological associations (so that "son of Joseph" would not have been a Samaritan royal eschatological title comparable to "son of David" in Jewish eschatology), and (2) that Joseph does not appear to have served as the model of an eschatological figure for the Samaritans [57]).

The kingship of Joseph was understood in Marqah in several ways: first, in reference to Joseph's position of political leadership while vizier under Pharaoh in Egypt; second, as representative of the high status of the Samaritan community (the descendants of Joseph); third, as representing the claim of the Samaritan people to territorial rights in Samaria by virtue of Joseph's burial near Mt. Gerizim. In the third instance, the Aramaic title *malkâh* as used of Joseph clearly has the meaning of owner or possessor rather than ruler, as has been pointed out by H. G. KIPPENBERG (Joseph— "Der Besitzer des Garizim") [58]).

> Where is there the like of Joseph, illumined, wise, possessing the spirit of God. He possessed the place. Therefore his bones were born by the prophet who was the faithful one of the Lord's house. There is none like *Yôsēf malkâh* and there is none like *Mōšē Nebi'âh*. Each of them possessed high status; Moses possessed prophethood, Joseph possessed the Goodly Mount. There is none greater than either of them [59]).

KIPPENBERG is probably correct in his suggestion that the Joseph traditions were originally nurtured by the Samaritan laity rather

---

[54]) The relevant texts from Marqah are gathered in KIPPENBERG, *Garizim und Synagoge*, pp. 254-269. On Joseph in the chronicles, see PURVIS, "Samaritan Traditions on the Death of Moses," p. 107.

[55]) See MACDONALD, *Theology of the Samaritans*, p. 366.

[56]) *Memar Marqah* IV. 12 (MACDONALD's edition: I., text, pp. 110-111; II., translation, pp. 185-186.

[57]) *Contra* A. D. CROWN; see "Some Traces of Heterodox Theology," 185-186.

[58]) *Garizim und Synagoge*, pp. 257-265.

[59]) *Memar Marqah, loc. cit.*

than by the priests (the descendants of Aaron), or the scribes (the teachers of Moses). Joseph would have served that segment of the Samaritan community as an archetypal figure to compare (or possibly contrast) with such figures as Joshua, who had established the Tabernacle on Gerizim and ruled after the settlement in Canaan; or Moses who was not only prophet but also the one who had political leadership of the nation. The title *melek* was sometimes applied to Moses (infrequently) and to Joshua (especially in the Chronicles, e.g., the *Book of Joshua* and MACDONALD's *Chronicle II*). If there was any competitiveness between Moses and Joseph in regard to kingship, this was leveled out with Moses receiving the title Prophet and Joseph King (as may be seen in the text cited above). The situation appears to have been somewhat different with Joshua. Joshua is called *melek* in some traditions, as Joseph is in others. In each case, the *melek* is associated with Moses: in Marqah, Moses reestablishes Joseph's kingship; in the *Book of Joshua* and *Chronicle II*, Joshua establishes the kingdom in the land of Cannaan by virtue of being Moses's chosen successor. But Joshua is also related to Joseph, inasmuch as he brought his remains into Canaan and buried them near Gerizim. A. D. CROWN has noted that texts which glorify Joseph and Moses together do not as a rule magnify Joshua [60]. My research on Samaritan traditions on the death of Moses tends to support this. There seems to have been an early alignment of Joseph and Moses in some Samaritan circles and Moses and Joshua in others. The writer is inclined to attribute the Moses-Joshua linkage to the Samaritan priesthood, inasmuch as Joshua is said to have established the Tabernacle on Gerizim, and the Joseph-Moses linkage to the Samaritan laity, the descendants of Joseph and the lay teachers of the Torah.

It is generally recognized that Moses served as an eschatological model in the development of Samaritan thought, and it is frequently asserted that Joshua also did. The same cannot be said of Joseph, at least not on the basis of the Samaritan texts which have been preserved [61]. The text of Marqah which compares the *Taheb* to Joseph (part of which is cited above) does not represent the *Taheb* after

---

[60] CROWN, *loc. cit.*

[61] I cannot agree with the position of A. D. CROWN that the *Taheb* of orthodox, priestly Samaritan circles was modeled after Joseph, or that this figure was contrasted with a *Taheb* of Dosithean, heterodox circles modeled after Joshua.

the analogy of Joseph, but rather compares Joseph, Moses, and the *Taheb* in reference to what each possessed or will possess, in contrast to the humble beginnings represented in the tent-dwelling Abraham. If Joseph served the Samaritan community or any part of it as a model for future political leadership it was as a wise and righteous leader who would rule under a foreign, Pharaoh-like sovereign. This is the only type of political order the people of Samaria have known from the Persian period to modern time, although the Joseph-Pharaoh paradigm has been too frequently realized due to tyrannical overlordship. The ideal model is here one of a secular, this-worldly order. The rule of Joseph did not provide the Samaritan community with an archetypal kingdom for eschatological development as did the kingdom of David in the Jewish tradition. When the idea of a "second kingdom" developed in Samaritan thought, it was with the understanding of the restoration of a period of Divine Favor (the *Raḥûtâh*), an alleged period in the early history of the sect associated with Moses and Joshua [62]. Given these considerations, and also the fact that "son of Joseph" has a clear patronymic function in at least one of its two appearances in the Fourth Gospel (so vi 42), it does not appear that the author of this Gospel drew upon a Samaritan tradition of a Messiah ben Joseph based on Joseph *malkâh*.

BUCHANAN's thesis that Jesus is also presented in the Fourth Gospel after an Elisha-model has much to commend it, but not on the basis of Samaritan sources. Just as the Samaritans have disavowed any historical relationship with the northern Israelite kings, they have also denied any spiritual affinities with the northern prophets mentioned in the Jewish scriptures. Elijah and Elisha are both mentioned in the Samaritan chronicles, but not with any respect. Elijah, for example, is said to have been a house-guest of the widow of Zarephath and to have caused the death of her son

---

[62] There seem to have been two traditions in early Samaritan thought concerning the end of the *Raḥûtâh*. According to one tradition, the *Raḥûtâh* ended with Moses's death; according to the other it extended through Joshua time to the time of Eli ,with whom it came to an end. The story in Josephus, *Antiquities* XVIII.85-89 concerning Pilate's suppression of a *Taheb*-claimant and his following relates to the former of traditions, for it is stated that the alleged *Taheb* took his group to Gerizim to uncover the sacred vessels which Moses had hidden. On these two traditions, see PURVIS, "Samaritan Traditions on the Death of Moses," p. 96. On the hidden vessels and Moses, see especially Marilyn COLLINS, "The Hidden Vessels in Samaritan Tradition," *JSJ*, 3 (1973), 97-116.

by eating all the food of the household [63]). Both Elijah and Elisha are said to have been false prophets, after the model of Deuteronomy xviii 20-22 [64]), with Elijah being called *hakkôšāp* (the sorcerer) and Elisha *hamm^e'ônēn* (the soothsayer), probably after Deut. xviii 10[65]). It may be, however, that traditions concerning Elijah and Elisha as popular folk heroes circulated in northern Palestine quite independently of the Samaritan movement centered at Gerizim, and that these sources were drawn upon in the development of the Fourth Gospel tradition. BUCHANAN has made a good case for an Elisha-Jesus typology in John, but if any segment of the Samaritan community had at any time entertained an Elisha-*Taheb* typology this was expunged in the development of Samaritan thought.

The term most frequently encountered in Samaritan texts for the eschatological agent is the *Taheb*, a title which allows several translation-interpretations: the "restorer," the "returning one", or the "repentant" (from the root *tûb/šûb*). Late medieval and modern interpretations suggest the double meaning, the returning one (i.e., a figure like Moses) who will be the restorer (i.e., of the *Rahûtâh*). Also, in the late traditions, the figure is associated with the Divine promise to Moses in Deut. xviii 18-22 ("I will raise up for them a prophet like you from among their brethren, etc."). It has been said that at his appearance the *Taheb* will recover the sacred vessels which have been hidden in a cave on Mt. Gerizim, and that he will have with him the rod of Moses and a container of Manna. Such is the understanding of the contemporary Samaritan community concerning this figure [66]). This is the interpretation which Moses GASTER learned earlier in this century from the priests at Nablus, and which he applied consistently in his treatment of Samaritan eschatology. He assumed that this view had prevailed from ancient to modern times [67]). James MONTGOMERY also represented the *Taheb* as a

---

[63]) MACDONALD, *Samaritan Chronicle No. II*, pp. 163-164.
[64]) *Ibid.*, p. 168.
[65]) *Ibid.*, pp. 170-171.
[66]) So my conversations with Samaritans.
[67]) So in *Samaritan Eschatology*, pp. 221-277. See also *The Samaritans: Their History, Doctrines, and Literature*. Schweich Lectures, 1923 (London, 1925) pp. 90-91. GASTER did suggest that there may have been a strand of Samaritan thought which related the *Taheb* to Joshua rather than Moses, but this seems mostly to have been a concession to A. MERX. This point of view was not developed in GASTER's treatment of Samaritan eschatology. See GASTER's review of MERX's *Der Messias oder Ta'eb der Samaritaner*, in *Studies and Texts*, I, pp. 638-648, esp. pp. 647-648.

Moses-like eschatological prophet in his classical study of the Samaritans (1907), although he noted considerations which contributed to the difficulty of interpretation and mentioned several alternative theories (which he rejected) [68].

If we may speak of a prevailing point of view concerning the *Taheb*, it would be that this was a prophetic type modeled after Moses. In this, the opinions of MONTGOMERY and GASTER have played an important role. Also, it is also a well-known fact that Deut. xviii 18-22 is found among the interpolations in the Samaritan Tenth Commandment (in Exodus xx but not Deut. v), and it has been assumed that its presence there is due to the same sort of sectarian motivation which caused the inclusion of Deuteronomic passages relating to the building of an altar on Mt. Gerizim (Deut. xxvii 2-3a, 4-7; xi 30, with the Samaritan reading of Gerizim rather than Ebal in xxvii 4, and the reading Shechem in xi 30). Consequently, even the most casual references to the messianic expectation of the Samaritan woman of John iv seem to operate on the tacit assumption that for her and her co-religionists the "messiah" would have been a Mosaic eschatological prophet [69].

There is, however, another interpretation concerning the *Taheb* which may have relevance for Johannine studies: That is the view that early Samaritan eschatology anticipated a Joshua-like *Taheb*. This opinion had been entertained by Adalbert MERX in the 19th century, but was rejected by MONTGOMERY and virtually ignored by Moses GASTER. It has recently been revived by John BOWMAN and A. D. CROWN [70]. BOWMAN has maintained that Samaritan "messianism" developed in lay, Dosithean circles, and that priestly Samaritans had no doctrine of the *Taheb* prior to the 14th century. The Dosithean eschatology, BOWMAN claims, is best represented in the Samaritan *Book of Joshua*, in which Joshua is represented as the prototype of the Samaritan savior [71].

It has been asserted that the Joshua *Taheb* is known from non-

---

[68] MONTGOMERY, *The Samaritans*, pp. 243-250.

[69] Compare the many commentaries on John iv. On this assumption, see esp. SCOBIE, "Development of Samaritan Christianity," 404; FREED, "Did John Write His Gospel Primarily to Win Samaritan Converts?" 245. FREED even offers the inaccurate statement that the Mosaic *Taheb* "developed as the fifth article of the Samaritan creed." The so-called fifth article of faith was rather the confession concerning the Day of Judgment.

[70] See above, note 14.

[71] "Identity and Date of the Unnamed Feast of John 5:1," p. 46.

Samaritan Christian sources, specifically from an account preserved
in Photius concerning a dispute amongst the Samaritans in the 6th
century reported by Bishop Eulogius of Alexandria [72]. According
to this tradition, the position of some Dosithean Samaritans that
Dositheus was (i.e., had been) the *Taheb* was contravened by the
claim of other Samaritans that the *Taheb* was Joshua. It is not clear
whether this refers to a belief in a coming *Taheb* like Joshua, or to a
non-eschatological view that the *Taheb* had already appeared in
history as Joshua. The latter interpretation has been argued by
KIPPENBERG and is probably correct [73]. In addition to the Eulogius
tradition, A. D. CROWN has suggested that the Joshua-like *Taheb* is
also known from Justin Martyr, or, that the Joshua-Jesus typology
in Justin (a native of Samaria) was dependent upon an older Samaritan Joshua-*Taheb* typology [74]. Samaritan traditions relating to
the alleged Joshua *Taheb* are no less obscure. In fact, specific literary
references are virtually non-existent [75]. The theory is based primarily on the understanding of the function of the *Taheb* as a
restorer of the period of the tabernacle-worship on Mt. Gerizim.
Inasmuch as this period was a time during which Joshua is said to
have ruled as king (according to the *Book of Joshua* and *Chronicle
II*), it would appear, according to this theory, that the model after
which the *Taheb* was understood was not Moses but Joshua. This
is a plausible thesis, but there is little evidence, outside of its own
logic, to support it. Also, if any segment of the ancient Samaritan
community did hold to a view of a Joshua-like *Taheb* it would more
likely have been the priestly community (contra BOWMAN and
CROWN), and not a lay movement such as the Dositheans. Joshua
is represented as having established the tabernacle and his work is
seen in *Chronicle II* and the *Book of Joshua* as having been hand-in-
glove with the priesthood. Emphasis upon Joshua would more likely
have been anti-Dosithean than Dosithean, as KIPPENBERG has maintained [76]), whether such an emphasis was historical (so KIPPENBERG)
or eschatological (so MERX, BOWMAN, and CROWN).

[72]) On which, see MONTGOMERY, *Samaritans*, p. 245.

[73]) *Garizim und Synagoge*, p. 322.

[74]) "New Light on the Inter-Relationships of Samaritan Chronicles," 309.
Cf. also other Christian traditions relating to the Joshua-Jesus typology and
Deut. xviii 18-22, as noted by KIPPENBERG, *loc. cit.*

[75]) An interesting text from a 16th century Arabic treatise citing an
alleged teaching of Marqah was cited by MERX, on which, however, see
MEEKS, *Prophet-King*, p. 253.

[76]) *Garizim und Synagoge*, pp. 321-327.

Bowman has recently related the alleged Joshua *Taheb* to John's gospel by suggesting that the unnamed feast of John v 1 ff. was *Purîm* and that the visit to Samaria of John iv 1 ff. coincided with the Samaritan minor feast of *ṣammût happesah*. Just as the Samaritan woman supposedly saw Jesus as the coming Joshua "who would restore the Temple on Mt. Gerizim, recapture the land and divide it among the Samaritans as the true Israel" [77]), the story in John v supposedly points to Jesus as a Joshua-like figure through whom the remembrance of Amalek would be eradicated (Exodus xvii 14)—i.e. through him and not through Esther or Mordecai. The statement of John v 46, "for he [Moses] wrote of me," refers, Bowman claims, to Exodus xvii 14 ("Write this as a memorial in a book and recite it in the ears of Joshua, that I will utterly blot out the remembrance of Amalek from under heaven"), and not to Deut. xviii 18. Bowman notes that this Joshua-Jesus typology in reference to Amalek is found also in Justin Martyr and the Epistle to Barnabas [78]). On the latter point Bowman is certainly correct, but it may not be said that he has made a strong case for the Joshua-Jesus typology in either John iv or John v.

The Joshua *Taheb* concept itself remains an enigma. As Samaritan eschatology developed it was with the understanding that the *Taheb* would restore the *Raḥûtâh*, a period associated historically (at least in some circles) with Joshua. And yet it was not Joshua who served as the archetypal model of the *Taheb*, but Moses, or so we must judge from the extant sources relating to the *Taheb*. This was undoubtedly due to the eschatological significance which came to be attributed to Deut. xviii 18-22/Exodus xx in the Samaritan community and to the preëminence of Moses in Samaritan thought. But the association of the *Taheb* with Moses rather than Joshua would also have been due to the original use of Joshua in some Samaritan circles (priestly) as a *non-eschatological model*, i.e., as a model leader for the *restoration in history* of the old priestly order. Later, with the loss of Samaritan confidence in future history, the function of the Joshua restorer would have been transferred to the eschatological *Taheb*, but not with the identification of the *Taheb* as Joshua. By that time the identification of the *Taheb* with Moses seems to have been secure.

There remains then one other figure for whom the Samaritan

---

[77]) "Identity and Date," p. 49.
[78]) *Ibid.*, pp. 50-51; 55.

theological understanding might have provided a background for the Johannine Christology: Moses. Moses was not only important in but central to Samaritan theology. It has long been noted that the rôle of Moses in Samaritan thought is analogous in many respects to the role of Jesus in Christian thought [79]. These similarities have recently been underscored by MACDONALD, who has suggested that Samaritanism was influenced by Christian theology in its development, and especially by the Johannine Christology [80]. It has been suggested that the influence might have been in the other direction, but the only one to have done so in a systematic fasion has been Wayne MEEKS. MEEKS has, however, argued that it was not exclusively a Samaritan view of Moses which lay behind the Johannine Christology, but a type of Moses-piety known from both Jewish and Samaritan sources, howbeit to a great extent from Samaritan materials [81]. It was, moreover, within a polemical context that the Johannine Christology developed, with the Gospel tradition responding to a community which "put its trust in Moses as a supreme prophet, God's emissary and revealer, and the defender in the heavenly court of the true Israelites who trusted in him" [82]. The Gospel did not seek to represent Jesus as a new Moses, but rather indicate that he fulfilled those functions elsewhere attributed to Moses and in such a superior and exclusive manner that he preempted Moses of those functions and reduced him to a witness to Jesus comparable to the witness of John the Baptist [83].

According to MEEKS, those aspects of the Moses-piety which were particularly important as archetypal models for the Johannine Christology were the themes of Moses as prophet and king (or prophet-king). Central in these was the understanding that Moses had ascended into heaven and was enthroned as God's earthly regent when he received the Torah. Although Jewish traditions relating to this are not abundant (Philo and medieval aggadah), Samaritan

---

[79] See, for example, John MACDONALD, "The Samaritan Doctrine of Moses," *Scottish Journal of Theology*, 13 (1960), 149-162. Moses's role in Samaritan theology is also analogous to that of Muhammad in Islam. See MONTGOMERY, *Samaritans*, pp. 225-232; T. H. GASTER, "Samaritans," p. 145. Most recently, see MACDONALD, *Theology of the Samaritans*, 147-222.

[80] MACDONALD, *Theology of the Samaritans*, pp. 147-222, 450.

[81] *Prophet-King*, pp. 216-257.

[82] *Ibid.*, p. 295. MEEKS's description is here a letter-perfect representation of classical Samaritan Mosaism. On the polemical character of the Gospel, see also pp. 297-301.

[83] *Ibid.*, p. 319.

sources provide ample witness to this understanding of Moses.

But for the Fourth Gospel, Jesus was the unique prophet-king, with Moses being reduced to a mere mediator of spiritual gifts which had superior countertypes in Jesus, e.g., the bread from heaven and the Torah. Jesus was the one sent from God through whom (in contrast to Moses) had come Grace and Truth. Above all, Jesus was the one who had come from God, and no one had ascended into heaven, not even Moses (as the Moses-piety contended), "but he who descended from heaven, the Son of Man" (iii 13, cf. vi 62) [84]. Meeks finds the theme of descent/ascent of the heavenly messenger lacking in the Moses traditions, and suggests that the Johannine Christology was here dependent upon gnostic mythology for which parallels may be found in Mandaean sources [85]. In this, Meeks appears to have overlooked an important aspect of Samaritanism in the 1st century, *viz.* Samaritan sectarian movements represented by such figures as Simon and Dositheus. In addition to the Mosaism of the Gerizim-based Samaritans there were other movements in Samaria which utilized a gnostic or quasi-gnostic vocabulary (see, for example, Simon in Acts viii 9-10).

Meeks's treatment of Samaritan tradition in respect to the Fourth Gospel may be commended in two respects: first, he has accurately represented the view of Moses as prophet-king in the Samaritan sources he has treated; second, he has proffered a plausible thesis that this understanding of Moses provided the model for the Johannine understanding of Jesus, with Jesus replacing Moses. Meeks is on much less certain ground, however, in his suggestion that to John Jesus was the Mosaic eschatological prophet, and that this eschatological understanding was related to both Samaritan Mosaism and the Johannine Christology [86]. Why would the Fourth Gospel have sought to identify Jesus as the prophet like Moses when it sought in every other way to demonstrate Jesus's superiority to Moses? Although Jesus is referred to at least five times in this Gospel as a prophet, nowhere is Deut. xviii 18-22 cited to indicate that he is a prophet like Moses [87]. This is not to deny that Moses served as a model for John's understanding of Jesus,

---

[84]) *Ibid.*, pp. 298-301.
[85]) *Ibid.*, p. 297.
[86]) *Ibid.*, pp. 45-47, 246-254.
[87]) As pointed out by C. Goodwin, and cited in Buchanan "Samaritan Origins of the Fourth Gospel," p. 171, note 1.

but to call into question the idea that the Mosaic eschatological prophet served as a model. Indeed, it may be questioned whether the idea of the Mosaic eschatological prophet was an essential component of *early* Samaritan Mosaism.

It is frequently asserted that the Moses-model for an eschatological figure was of great antiquity in the Samaritan community because of the interpolation of the passage from Deut. xviii 18-22 in Exodus xx in the Samaritan biblical text. There are two difficulties in this assertion. The first is that this passage is not necessarily a *sectarian* reading. The second is that the Samaritan text of Deut. xxxiv 10 has been clearly manipulated to assert that there will *not again arise a prophet in Israel like Moses* [88]). This may suggest early opposition in some Samaritan circles to a Mosaic eschatological prophet, with the reading designed to avert an eschatological interpretation of Deut. xviii 18-22. The Deut. xviii 18-22/Exodus xx texts could at any rate have been divested of eschatological significance by virtue of the fact that as Moses's chosen successor Johua was the *historical* prophet like Moses (see Numbers xxvii 18-23; Deut. xxxi 14-15, 23; Joshua i 1-17 in the MT and *Chronicle II*; Samaritan *Book of Joshua*, Chapters 2, 7-11).

It has been assumed for too long that the inclusion of Deut. xviii 18-22 in the Samaritan text of Exodus xx was a sectarian addition reflecting a peculiar or distinctive tenet of that faith. There are three sets of additions to Exodus xx in the Samaritan Pentateuch. The first is concerned with Gerizim and is clearly sectarian (following Exodus xx 17, from Deut. xxvii 2-3a, 4-7, and xi 30, with the Samaritan reading ʾēlôn môreʾ mûl šeḵem in xi 30, and the reading Gerizim rather than Ebal in xxvii 4). The second reading is found within Exodus xx 19, and is an addition to the response of the people based on Deut. v 24 (21)-27(24). The third set of readings follows Exodus xx 21, indicating God's response to the people based on Deut. v 28(25)-31(28), interrupted by an addition paralleling Deut xviii 18-22. The second and third sets are not sectarian additions, but interpolations based on the statements in Deut. v 24(21), 28(25), and xviii 17 that these words were spoken at the time of the giving of the law at Mt. Horeb. As such, the readings are consistent with expansionistic character of the Samaritan text in general, a characteristic known also from a non-Masoretic

---

[88]) *wlʾ qm ʿwd nbyʾ bysrʾl kmšh* (MT = *wlʾ qm nbyʾ ʿwd bysrʾl kmšh*).

Palestinian textual type found at Qumrân [89]). The addition of Deut. xviii 18-22 in Exodus xx was, then, a way of filling out the text by making it agree with Deut. xviii 17, not a sectarian addition such as the interpolations of Deut. xxvii 2-3a, 4-7, and xi 30. That these were of a different type is indicated by the fact that the latter passages were interpolated in the Ten Commandments of Deut.v in the Samaritan Pentateuch, whereas the Deut. xviii 18-22 passage was not. The inclusion of the prophet like Moses passage in Exodus xx would certainly have contributed to the Samaritan eschatological speculation of a Mosaic *Taheb*, but the concept itself does not account for the origin of the reading. In fact, there is evidence that Samaritan Mosaism had little eschatology associated with it in early times: so Deut. xxxiv 10 in the Samaritan text; so also Rabbinic traditions which identified Samaritanism as a Sadducean type sect with no doctrine of a resurrection [90]). Eschatological concepts appear to have developed initially among the Samaritan sects [91]), and to have become popular enough to have been accepted by the community as a whole by the time of Marqah. In these, the figure of Moses seems to have predominated as the model for the *Taheb*, based no doubt on the eschatological interpretation of Deut. xviii 15, 18-22/Exodus xx, but the coming of an eschatological prophet like Moses was not a *sine qua non* of early Samaritan Mosaism.

Is Jesus represented as the prophet like Moses (Samaritan or otherwise) in the Fourth Gospel? Jesus is called the prophet in John (vi 14), and some Johannine passages have been cited as perhaps containing allusions to Deut. xviii 15, 18-22 [92]), but it would be more accurate to describe John's portrayal of Jesus as a prophet *like but unlike* Moses. Jesus was greater than Moses (i 17; vi 49-58; ix 24-40) [93]), just as he was greater than Abraham (viii 53-59) and Jacob (iv 12-14). In contrast to this, Samaritan traditions relating the *Taheb* to Moses do not represent the eschatalogical Moses-like

---

[89]) See Purvis, *The Samaritan Pentateuch and the Origin of the Samaritan Sect*, pp. 71-73, 78-87.

[90]) Montgomery, *Samaritans*, pp. 175-176, 186-188.

[91]) Some of the sects, however, held to the older, more conservative Samaritan views. The Dositheans appear to have had branches and/or subsects which denied the resurrection of the dead. See Montgomery, *Samaritans*, pp. 252-265.

[92]) See, for example, Meeks, *Prophet-King*, pp. 45-46.

[93]) *Ibid.*, pp. 287-301.

figure as being superior to his prototype. If anything, they suggest that he will be inferior to Moses [94]).

It is at this point that the polemical character of the Johannine Christology, as pointed out by MEEKS, needs to be stressed. The Fourth Gospel appears to have drawn upon the Moses typology in its understanding of Jesus but for the purpose of demonstrating the superiority of Jesus. This Moses-piety was espoused by the Samaritan community as well as by some Jews. The Gospel traditions could thus have addressed themselves to the Samaritans, but certainly not for the purpose of making converts (FREED) or making "a bridge between Samaritans and Jews in Christ" (BOWMAN). The writer is inclined to think that the author of the Fourth Gospel was involved in a polemic with Samaritan Mosaism, and not only that, but also in a polemic with a heterodox branch of the Samaritan community which was engaged in the promotion of a particular figure as the Mosaic eschatological prophet. It is known from both Samaritan and non-Samaritan sources that Dositheus was regarded by his followers as the prophet like Moses [95]), and that he brought into being a major Samaritan sect which endured for a considerable time. Also, the Samaritan prophet put to death by Pontius Pilate associated his work with Moses (*Antiquities* XVIII, 85-87), and there may have been some Mosaic associations with Simon Magus [96]). Is it not possible that the author of the Fourth Gospel consciously avoided the use of Deut. xviii 18-22 because of the use of this passage by some followers of Samaritan pretenders to the *Taheb* status [97]) ? In this case, Jesus would not only have been greater than Moses, but greater also than any near contemporary figure who was represented by his followers as a prophet like Moses.

---

[94]) As correctly noted by MONTGOMERY, *Samaritans*, pp. 244- 245.

[95]) Compare Origen, *Contra Celsum* I. 57: "And after the time of Jesus, Dositheus the Samaritan also wished to persuade the Samaritans that he was the Christ predicted by Moses."

[96]) Stanley ISSER has called to my attention that the title the "Standing One" (*ho hestōs* = Aram *qā'êm*) used by both Simon and Dositheus, and usually interpreted as an expression of divinity, was also used in Samaritan Mosaism to signify Moses's standing before God (so the Targum to Deut. v 28; of Exodus xxxiii 21; *Memar Marqah* IV, 12). On the understanding of this term for Divinity, see MONTGOMERY, *Samaritans*, p. 215; KIPPENBERG, *Garizim und Synagoge*, pp. 374- 349.

[97]) Or, possibly, non-Samaritan pretenders to the prophet like Moses status. Was Theudas the sorcerer (*góēs*) of this type? Compare Acts v 36 and Josephus, *Antiquities* XX, 97-99.

III. *The Fourth Gospel and the Samaritans*: *A Tentative Proposal*

To summarize to this point: a good case can be made for viewing the development of the Johannine Christology in a Palestinian Christian Community which regarded itself as alienated from the spiritual traditions of Jerusalem and which regarded Jesus as a Jew who had been rejected by his own people. There is sufficient evidence to identify Samaria, or perhaps Samaria-Galilee, as the locale in which this community was centered. As such, it drew upon the theological traditions current in that region for the expression of its understanding of Jesus, making use of a Moses-piety popular also among the Samaritans, but displacing Moses with Jesus who, as prophet-Christ, was superior to Moses. The community would thus have found itself as much at enmity with Gerizim-based Samaritanism as it was with Jerusalem-based Judaism. It makes little sense, therefore, to suggest that the Gospel of John was a missionizing tract designed to win Samaritan converts or to unite Samaritans and Jews in Christ. The aims of the Gospel were essentially self-serving to the community which produced it, to reinforce belief in Jesus as the Christ through whom one might have life (xx 31). The Christ Jesus was, was not a royal figure after a Davidic model, but the king of Israel after the model of Moses the prophet—a king of the celestial realms, a king whose kingship was not of or from this world (xviii 33-37). But this Jesus was not a prophet like Moses, but a figure in every way superior to Moses. It does not appear that this community made use of Samaritan eschatological traditions which might have anticipated a coming Joseph-like or Joshua-like figure. Indeed, it is not at all clear that these figures served as eschatological models in early Samaritan thought, it being more likely that they were prototypes for ideal rule and priestly restoration within history. The Johannine community may, however, have made use of an Elisha model in the signs attributed to Jesus. If it did, it was relying on traditions which developed independently of the Samaritan community centered at Gerizim.

It is further suggested that the representation of Jesus as greater than Moses reflects not only a polemic with Samaritan (or a Samaritan-like) Mosaism, but also a polemic with a northern Palestinian sectarian movement engaged in the promotion of a particular figure as the Mosaic eschatological prophet. The hints received from the

Gospel suggest that the heresiarch was the leader of a baptizing sect, a wonder-worker, and someone who claimed that he was a divine being. Christian and Samaritan traditions relating to sectarian movements in Samaria would indicate that the most likely candidates for this unnamed prophet-*magus* would be Simon, Meander, and Dositheus. The writer is inclined to identify him with Dositheus, although Acts viii 9-24 would suggest Simon. This position is proffered here as a tentative proposal. It is suggested that the following considerations in the Fourth Gospel reflect this polemic.

1. *The Downgrading of John the Baptist in Samaria (iii 22-36)*: It is to be noted that the Fourth Gospel carefully locates two discussions with John the Baptist in which his inferiority to Jesus is stressed, one in Bethany beyond the Jordan (i 27); the other in Samaria (at Aenon near Salim, iii 22). In the latter account, the superiority of Jesus is based on his heavenly origin: "He who comes from above is above all; he who is of the earth belongs to the earth, and of the earth he speaks; he who comes from heaven is above all" (iii 31). There is no reason to doubt that the John of these accounts was the John the Baptist known from Josephus and the Synoptic Gospels. But these accounts would not only have served the interests of a Christian community desirous of stressing its superiority over the followers of John, but also *vis-à-vis* the claims of any other baptizing sect, especially in Samaria (the locale of the last of these discussions). Samaritan traditions indicate that the largest of their sects, the Dositheans, was such a baptizing movement: the first convert to the sect was said to have uttered the confession, "My faith is in thee, Yahweh, and in Dusis thy prophet" while immersed in water (evidently the baptismal formula), and it was said that the Dositheans performed all their prayers in water [98]). The words attributed to John: "He who comes from above is above all, etc." (iii 31), would have been particularly important in a polemic with a community which claimed its founder was a divine man. It is reported that Simon claimed to be the "Power of God which is called Great" (Acts viii 10) [99]), and Origen included both Simon and

---

[98]) VILMAR, *Abulfathi Annales Samaritani*, Arabic section, pp. 151-157. See MONTGOMERY, *Samaritans*, p. 257.

[99]) Compare the ascription to God in the opening line of the *Memar Marqah*: "Great is the Mighty Power who endures forever" (*rb ḥylh rbh*

Dositheus in his list of those heretics who claimed to be Sons of God or the Power of God (contra *Celsum* I. 57) [100]). To this list of Samaritan heretics should also be added Meander, who was allegedly a disciple of Simon (Justin, I Apology 26), a baptist (Irenaeus, *Against Heresies* I, 23, 5), and one who claimed that "he himself is the person who has been set forth from the invisible beings as a savior, for the deliverance of men" (Irenaeus, *loc. cit.*). Thus while John iii 22-26 speaks in particular of Jesus and John the Baptist, it may point beyond John to others or to one in particular, the founder of a baptizing sect who claimed to be the Divine Power. The response of the Fourth Gospel was here, as elsewhere, that Jesus was the unique Son of God, the only one who had come from heaven (compare iii 31 and iii 13). The inference is clear: all others who made this claim were imposters. The hypothesis that this would apply not only to John (if such a claim had been made for John) but also to Dositheus is strengthened by the fact that John and Dositheus were equivalent names. That the Johannine material on John the Baptist represented an anti-Dosithean polemic was noted some time ago by Georges ORY, although his case was clouded by the contention that John and Dositheus were historically identical individuals [101]).

2. "*You are right in saying, 'I have no husband;' for you have had five husbands, and he whom you now have is not your husband; this you said truly.*" (*iv* 17-18): It has long been recognized that this statement may contain a reference to the historical experience of the Samaritan nation, and an allusion to and negative judgment on its contemporary spiritual condition. As such, the text would allow several interpretations, not only in respect to the five previous husbands, but to the present (non-legitimate?) husband. One such interpretation would be that the text involves a play-on-words with the Hebrew/Aramaic *ba'al*, master, lord; a word used in ancient times for husband as well as for the Cannaanite storm-god, and also for the Hebrew God Yahweh (compare Hosea ii 16-17). According to II Kings xvii 29-34, the Assyrians colonized Samaria

---

dmmn l'lm). On the use of this epithet in the Samaritan community, see esp. KIPPENBERG, *Garizim und Synagoge*, pp. 328-349.

[100]) Also included in this brief catalogue were the Jewish leaders Judas the Galilean and Theudas. Compare Acts v 33-39; *Antiquities* XVIII, 3-10, 23-25; XX, 97-99.

[101]) See above, note 28.

with Mesopotamians from five districts who brought their native gods with them into Palestine. The list of II Kings xvii 30-31 enumerates seven such pagan deities, although Josephus's account suggests that five gods were brought by the five groups (*Antiquities* IX, 288). These could have been the five husbands, *be'ālim*, alluded to in iv 18a. But who or what was the present *ba'al* (husband) who was not truly Samaria's *ba'al* (lord, divinity)? It is sometimes suggested that this was Yahweh, as he was allegedly imperfectly worshipped by the Samaritans [102]. Yahweh may be referred to in iv 22 ("You worship what you do not know"), but the present husband of iv 18b seems rather to have been someone else—a being the Samaritan people had temporarily espoused as lord, but in a relationship which could only be described as illicit. The woman was not said to have been a faithless wife—which would be the understanding if the *ba'al*/husband was meant to be understood as Yahweh. It is the husband who is singled out: "he whom you now have is not your husband;" i.e., he has no right or claim to be your husband (*ba'al*, lord). We are reminded of Justin Martyr's claim of the wide-spread acceptance of Simon Magus as a divine being by the people of Samaria (I Apology 26). That the husband who was not a true husband was a false teacher was suggested by Jerome [103], who identified this person as Dositheus.

It will be noted that meetings at wells in the Pentateuchal traditions are closely associated with marital themes [104], and especially with the right matching of mates: Rebekah for Isaac in Genesis xxiv 10-14; Rachel for Jacob in Genesis xxix 1-12; and Zipporah for Moses in Exodus ii 16-21. If John iv 18b is correctly interpreted as meaning that the false teacher of Samaria is not Samaria's true husband (*ba'al*, master, lord) then the implication of the meeting at the well is clear: Jesus is or should be acknowledged as such. The writer could not take this beyond an implication, however, for his story would not allow him to extend his metaphor that far. But he could represent the Samaritan woman as believing that *he* was the Christ, and the people of Samaria as acknowledging that *he* was the Savior of the world (iv 20, 42), thus

---

[102] See BROWN, *Gospel According to John (i-xii)*, p. 171.
[103] See ODEBERG, *Fourth Gospel*, p. 179.
[104] As noted by J. BLIGH, and cited by BROWN, *Gospel According to John (i-xii)*, p. 171. See also BOISMARD, "Aenon près de Salem," 223-226.

undercutting the claims of the followers of such Samaritan figures as Dositheus, Meander, and Simon.

3. *"The Jews answered him, 'Are we not right in saying that you are a Samaritan and have a demon?' Jesus answered, "I have not a demon, but I honor my Father and you dishonor me' "* (*viii* 48-49); Two things are to be noted in this: first, Jesus had said something which caused his adversaries (Jews) to feel justified in calling him a Samaritan and in accusing him of being demon-possessed; second Jesus denied that he had a demon. What had caused this double-charge to be leveled? Why did Jesus respond as he did?

The most obvious answer to the first question is that Jesus had said that the Jews were "not of God" (viii 47), and were not Abraham's children (viii 39), (hence the Samaritan charge), and he had previously said that he was a spiritual being whose genesis was "not of this world" (viii 23) (hence the charge of demon possession). He also affirmed that there would come a time when men would know who he really was—"then you will known that I am he" (viii 28)—a statement which could easily be interpreted as an affirmation of divinity [105]). Considering that Simon and Dositheus were both reported in Christian sources as having claimed divinity for themselves, and of representing themselves as the earthly embodiments of the Celestial Power (not of this world) [106]), Jesus's claim of a heavenly origin could also have been a cause of his having been called a Samaritan. The charges of his being demon-possessed and also being a Samaritan were not necessarily two distinct and un-related charges. Jesus was making a claim for himself which was also being made by some prophets of Samaria, who were probably thought (by the Jews) to be demon-possessed. It is interesting to note in this connection that Patristic sources relate the claims of the false prophets of Samaria to the work of demons.

The wicked demons were not satisfied with saying before the appearance of Christ that there had been so-called sons of Zeus. After he had appeared and lived among men, when they learned how he had been predicted by the prophets . . . [they] put forward others, Simon and Meander of Samaria, who by doing mighty works of magic deceived and are still deceiving many [107]).

[105]) On which, see C. H. DODD, *The Interpretation of the Fourth Gospel* (Cambridge, 1968), pp. 93-96.
[106]) This was said especially of Simon, and also, less frequently of *Dositheus*. The *Recognitions of Clement* II. 10-11 claims that Simon usurped the title of the "Standing One" from Dositheus, his teacher.
[107]) Justin Martyr, *I Apology* 56. See above, *Constitutions of the Holy Apostles* VI. 2, 7 and 9; Origen, *Contra Celsum* VI. 11.

The accusation of Jesus being demon-possessed was not limited to the Fourth Gospel (see Mark iii 22-30; Matt. ix 34; xii 24-37; Luke ix 15-26). What is distinctive here is that the charge was tied into the charge of being a Samaritan. The two accusations received one reply because they were one charge: not because the Jews believed all Samaritans to be demon possessed, but rather some Samaritans—i.e., those who made claims for themselves such as Jesus was making for himself [108]). R. H. STRACHAN rightly observed in this double-charge and its reply a reference to the wonder-workers of Samaria: "It is regarded as sufficient that Jesus should repel both epithets by saying, 'I have not a devil.' He is no false prophet of the Dositheus type. 'I seek not mine own glory' " [109]).

4. *"Jesus said to her, 'I am the resurrection and the life, he who believes in me, though he die, yet shall he live, and whoever lives and believes in me shall never die. Do you believe this?' She said to him, 'Yes, Lord; I believe that you are the Christ, the Son of God, he who is coming into the world.' "* (xi 26-27):

And a man, Meander, also a Samaritan, of the town Capparetaea, a disciple of Simon, and inspired by devils, we know to have deceived many while he was in Antioch by his magical art. He persuaded those who adhered to him that they should never die, and even now there are some living who hold this opinion of his.

(Justin Martyr, *I Apology* 26).

He [Meander] gives, too, as he affirms, by means of that magic which he teaches, knowledge to this effect, that one may overcome those very angels that made the world; for his disciples obtain the resurrection by being baptized into him, and can die no more, but remain in the possession of immortal youth.

(Irenaeus, *Against Heresies* I. 23, 5).

From the Samaritans one Dositheus arose and asserted that he was the prophesied messiah; there are Dositheans to this day who originate from him; they both preserve books by Dositheus and certain myths about him to the effect that he did not taste death, but is still alive somewhere.

(Origen, *Commentary on John* XIII. 27).

The raising of Lazarus was the most dramatic of Jesus's signs. It was said by John to have been performed in order that those who witnessed it would believe that Jesus had been sent from God

---

[108]) This was perceived by C. K. BARRETT, *The Gospel According to St. John* (London, 1955), p. 290.
[109]) *The Fourth Gospel: Its Significance and Environment* (London, 1947), p. 214.

(so xi 42). It was, moreover, a dramatic action verifying Jesus's claim that he was the Resurrection and the Life (xi 25). The statement of Jesus and the response of Lazarus's sister Martha, as cited above, were precipitated by Jesus's earlier statement, "Your brother shall rise again," and Martha's reply, "I know that he will rise in the resurrection at the last day" (xi 23-24). But as the Resurrection, Jesus can give life now to the dead, and eternal life to the living. Belief that Jesus was the Christ was for Martha belief in this. The Christ is "the Son of God, who is coming into the world," who could say "whoever lives and believes in me shall never die." Although this confession of faith was given by a Jewess, the messianic view it espouses bears little resemblance to traditional Jewish messianism. It bears a great deal of resemblance, however, to the claims of the wonder-workers of Samaria such as Meander, and perhaps also Dositheus (although it was not said of him that he conferred the eternal life he had). The superiority of Jesus over the Samaritan *magi* was demonstrated in that he could not only bestow eternal life, but even raise a man who had been dead for four days, and thus reveal the glory of God (xi 39-40).

5. *The Signs*: The Samaritan prophets were represented in the New Testament (Acts viii 9-11) and Patristic literature as magicians. The author of the Fourth Gospel drew upon a source which magnified Jesus through seven signs which he performed. It would not be inaccurate to say that Jesus was represented in these signs as a *magus*-like figure, although early Christian communities would have eschewed the *magus* label because of its negative connotations (cf. Acts xiii 6, 8) [110]). The magician worked for his own gain and glory, but Jesus glorified his Father through his signs. In so doing he not only verified his contention that he had come from God, but demonstrated his true and unique claim to that status over any pretender or false-prophet [111]), Samaritan or other.

---

[110]) See Morton SMITH's comments on "The Relation of 'Magician' to *Theîos anēr* and 'Son of God,'" in *Clement of Alexandria and a Secret Gospel of Mark* (Cambridge, Mass., 1973), pp. 227-229.

[111]) *Concluding note*: It is possible that the contemporary false prophets of Samaria are alluded to in the figurative discourse on the Good Shepherd (x 1-18): the strangers (*hoi allótrioi*,the aliens or enemies, x 5), thieves, and robbers (*kléptai kai lēstaí*, x 8, 10), and the hireling (*ho misthōtós*, x 12-13). This was suggested by J. WELLHAUSEN, on which see ODEBERG, *Fourth Gospel*, pp. 328-329 (refutation with some concession). MEEKS has noted that the motif of the good shepherd was one aspect of the Moses piety (*Prophet-*

King, pp. 307-313), and that the theme of the sheep hearing the shepherds voice may be related to the mission of the prophet like Moses (*Ibid.*, pp. 66-67, 312). The blanket condemnation of Jesus's predecessors as thieves and robbers (x 8) would make a great deal of sense in the context of those who had claimed to be Mosaic prophets but who were rather magicians. The textual difficulties of this verse (readings which eliminate "all," "before me") could well be the result of the failure to perceive this, and the mistaken notion that this was an allusion to Judaism's prophets, sages, and teachers.

THE BELOVED DISCIPLE IN
THE GOSPEL OF JOHN
Some Clues and Conjectures

PAUL S. MINEAR
Guilford

Johannine scholars are familiar with the search for the identity of the beloved disciple and no less familiar with the multiple frustrations encountered in that search. The role of this disciple is too important to permit abandoning the search; the evidence is too baffling to permit a confident solution. Each hypothesis leaves us with a series of conjectures, none of which can command consensus. I suggest that there are two lessons to be learned from the fact that every search ends in impasse.

First of all, our inability to grasp the intention of the Evangelist is a measure of the distance between his thought-processes and ours. We must assume that he knew what he was trying to convey by his references to this particular figure. If his intention escapes us, we must conclude that our minds move to different rhythms. We can also assume that his immediate audience understood his references to the beloved disciple better than we do. If so, the author and his first audience must have shared certain attitudes, a definite apperceptive mass, that created a resonance to his intentions which has since been lost. Where we desire to distill from each set of data certain dependable historical inferences, his desire probably moved in a quite different direction. Therefore, in listening in on this conversation we should lay aside our preoccupations and become more alert to what was important to them.

In the second place, we should learn something from the author's curious refusal to name this particular disciple. It is surely not accidental that, in every context where this disciple remains unnamed, other disciples are carefully identified by name. The same silence characterizes John's references to Jesus' mother. She appears on several occasions; but though other women are named, she is never named. If we knew only this Gospel, we would never have learned her name. Why this intentional hiding of the name? We infer that these participants had a "halo" of symbolic meanings for the Evangelist. We infer that in conveying these symbolic meanings he considered the descriptive epithets (e.g., mother, beloved) to be more significant than a name would have been. Presumably those same epithets were more evocative to his readers as well. Their reactions are almost the opposite of those of the modern exegete. We want to identify this disciple in order to solve the problem of the authorship of the Gospel (xxi 24) and thus to establish its precise place in the literary history of the period. In that original dialogue, much greater attention was given to the distinctive nuances of those descriptive phrases. In this essay our goal is to recover some of the nuances in that dialogue [1]).

In that endeavor the first essential is to have a clear picture of John's audience.

John's Audience

I will proceed on the assumption that John's audience was composed mainly of Jews and that the major components in that audience were those groups which Professor J. Louis MARTYN has called "conversation partners". Some of these partners were believers who, by remaining within the synagogues, had become subject to multiple pressures because of their conviction that they could simultaneously be disciples of both Moses and Jesus. Of these, probably some kept their discipleship to Jesus secret because of the hostility of fellow-Jews (MARTYN, *History and Theology in the Fourth Gospel*, N.Y., Harper and Row, 1968, p. 105) John kept his eye on both the secret and the avowed followers of Jesus. Other partners had already broken away from the synagogue, either on their own volition or by force. John also wished to appeal to rank-and-file members of the synagogue, the common folk who had not yet accepted Jesus as the Messiah (*ibid.*, p. 101). To reach them he had to carry on a debate with the rulers of the synagogues, the "Jamnia-trained loyalists" who sooner or later adopted the policy

---

[1]) Among possible nuances which I consider too doubtful to explore in this essay are these two. (1) John may have wished to stress this feature of the disciple's vocation: that, like his Lord, he wanted to come not in his own name, but in that of his Lord (v 43), so that those who believed through his witness might have life in that name alone (xx 31). (2) Or he may have wished to make a point similar to one found in the Apocalypse: i.e., Jesus promised to every faithful witness a name that is hidden, a name tantamount to eternal life and membership in the Holy City (Rev. ii 17; iii 5, 12).

of expelling from the synagogues any Jew who accepted Jesus.

Because of this multiple audience, the Evangelist had to speak to his readers on various levels. For all his hearers, however, a key problem was their own personal relation to the synagogue. His Gospel was therefore designed to shape the subsequent conversations between those readers and their Jewish neighbors, both before and after any formal separation of church from synagogue. These wider conversations, according to Prof. MARTYN, oscillated around three continuing issues: "the technical question of Jesus' messiahship; the correct interpretation of his signs; the relation between him and the towering figure of Judaism, Moses" (ibid., p. 91). Thus the character of this audience determined the basic agenda. The nature of that agenda was such as to focus attention on opposing interpretations of Scripture; this, in turn, would focus attention upon possible correlations between the Scriptural traditions about Moses and the Christian traditions about Jesus. The Christian witness that Scripture had been fulfilled in and by Jesus would be cogent only when presented by Jewish believers attesting to what they had seen and heard of Jesus in the context of God's covenant-promises to Moses [2]).

The Moses-Benjamin Typology

Whether we think of synagogue laymen or their technically trained leaders, we can be confident that both groups "knew well some form of the hope for the Prophet-Messiah like Moses who would perform signs" (MARTYN, op. cit., p. 101). The boundary between synagogue and church was crossed when Jews accepted Jesus as this Prophet-Messiah. The Jamnia loyalists denied that Jesus met the specifications of this typology, insisting that any such matching of a person with those specifications could be decided only by rabbis competently trained in midrashic interpretation of Scripture (MARTYN, op. cit., p. 105). But John defended his faith in Jesus as that prophet like Moses, and aimed his defence at an audience composed of four segments: members in his own church,

---

[2]) In a later study MARTYN traces several stages in the history of the Johannine school, corresponding to at least three stages in the developing alienation between church and synagogue. I have been unable to correlate my conjectures with his, although I believe that such a correlation might strengthen both his history of the Johannine community and my analysis of Johannine typology. Cf. MARTYN's essay in Ephemerides Theologicae Lovaniensis, 1976.

secret believers in the synagogues, unbelieving laymen in the synagogues, and the Jamnia loyalists. In what follows here I do not try to prove the presence of this typology in the Gospel, since Johannine specialists have adequately documented that thesis [3]). Rather, I will advance a supplementary hypothesis concerning the role of Benjamin in that Mosaic portrait.

The basis for the expectation of the coming of a prophet like Moses is provided by the book of Deuteronomy; and in the development of that expectation two passages were central: xviii 15-22 and xxxiv 1-12. In the Deuteronomic prototype, as in the Johannine antetype, the climax is reached in a Passion Story in which the prophet's death is understood as necessary to God's design. "The days approach when you must die" (Deut. xxxi 14, 16). Within the context of the Passion Story both prophets are seen as mediators of a covenant, obedience to which marks the difference between life and death (Deut. xxx 20). A basic form for conveying this covenant is a series of farewell discourses (Deut. xxix-xxxiii; John xiii-xvii) in which, although many unrelated items appear, one may note many subtle correspondences. In both, the prophet summons God's people to gather together as a people in the presence of their God. "You stand this day all of you before the Lord your God" (Deut. xxix 10). Prominent in both accounts is the poignant testimony to the community's dullness and ignorance (Deut. xxxii 28). In the Deuteronomic scenario, the whole nation is represented in and by "the heads of your tribes", the twelve patriarchs named as a way of stressing the presence of "all Israel" (xxix 10; xxxi 30; xxxiii 5, 21). It is almost certain that the Gospel views the twelve tribes, or the whole of Israel, as present in the twelve disciples. Against the prospect of death, both prophets consecrate the people to God and assure them of God's blessing, guidance and love (Deut. xxxiii 1-3). They are entrusted with a law and a mission which continue the work of the prophet-king (Deut. xxxiii 4). The people are reminded of the signs by which each prophet had authenticated his role as God's spokesman, intercessor, mediator and judge (Deut. xxix 2 f.; xxxiv 11; John xx 30). The whole narrative conveys an assurance

---

[3]) J. L. MARTYN, op. cit.; W. A. MEEKS, The Prophet-King, 1967; T. F. GLASSON, Moses in the Fourth Gospel, 1963; H. M. TEEPLE, The Mosaic Eschatological Prophet, 1957; F. HAHN, Christologische Hoheitstitel, 1963; J. JEREMIAS, art. "Moses", in KITTEL, Theological Dictionary of the New Testament.

that God intends to gather his people from their exile (Deut. xxx 4; John xi 52); yet there is also the promise that nations other than Israel will ultimately be included in the redemptive work of the prophet (Deut. xxix 13 f.; John xvii 20; xx 29). It is of course easy for modern Gentile readers to remain oblivious to these correspondences; but it was more difficult for ancient Jewish readers to do so, granted their loyalty to Moses and their familiarity with Deuteronomy.

I believe that it is more than coincidental that both farewell discourses reach their climax when the narrator adopts a tradition with a separate form, a form that expressed emotional intensity as well as liturgical sonority. In Deuteronomy xxxiii this form is that of a blessing pronounced by Moses on each of the twelve tribes consecutively. This blessing represents Moses' intercession for those from whom he will soon be separated; it is his assurance of God's continuing love for his people and his dependable care for all "who are consecrated to him". By John's day, this farewell blessing would have exerted a contemporaneous power, inasmuch as Jews believed that at death Moses had been translated to heaven. In John's Gospel, there is a similar shift from table conversations to the "highpriestly" prayer, a prayer representing Jesus' intercession for his disciples both before and after his own glorification. Moreover, in praying for these twelve, Jesus prayed for the elect people of God, manifesting his unity with them and indicating their share in his glory and life. Thus both prophets fulfilled a vocation to share with God's people whatever gifts they had themselves received. It is these significant and far-reaching parallels that induce us to concentrate attention upon Deuteronomy xxxiii and John xvii, the latter as an appropriate climax to the earlier dialogue.

In that dialogue the Evangelist chooses the speakers with some care. Of course the whole group of disciples on occasion speaks as a single chorus, and here there is no need to distinguish one from another (e.g., xvi 29). There are other occasions when Thomas (xiv 5) or Philip (xiv 8) or the second Judas (xiv 22) serve as interlocutors. Yet because they quickly disappear we may assume that the Evangelist's interest in them was quite perfunctory. But his interest in three disciples is far from perfunctory. Two of these are named: Judas and Simon Peter. With them the Synoptic accounts have made us familiar. The third is unnamed: the beloved disciple, first introduced in xiii 23. To his role there is no parallel in the Synoptics. And yet John shows continuing interest in him. Why?

The far-reaching correspondences between the two farewell discourses, to which we have called attention, impels us to explore the Deuteronomic tradition for possible answers. I think that we find such an answer in Deuteronomy xxxiii 12, in Moses' blessing of Benjamin, and especially in the three descriptions of this patriarch. First of all, he is "the beloved of the Lord". We recall earlier traditions indicating that Benjamin had been the best-loved son of Jacob-Israel. According to Gen. xliv 30 Jacob's life was so "bound up in the lad's life" that the death of son would be the death of father. Jubilees xliii 11 demonstrates the fact that this conception of the bond between Jacob and Benjamin was still alive in John's day. Benjamin was also the best-loved brother of Joseph, and was the only son of Jacob not implicated in the betrayal of Joseph. This might possibly correspond to the fact that alone among the Twelve the beloved disciple did not deny his discipleship during Jesus' trial and crucifixion (John xviii 15; xix 26). The Deuteronomic blessing proves that generations after the patriarchal period, this whole tribe could be revered as "the Lord's beloved". At least among the rabbis this phrase was a way of distinguishing Benjamin from all other patriarchs (*Jewish Encyclopedia* III, 24) [4]).

The more conventional this description had become in John's milieu, the more he could assume that Jewish readers would understand his use of that epithet. The allusion, to be sure, is not verbally precise. In John the usual phrase is "the disciple whom Jesus loved". Yet John used the verb for *love* five times (four times agapaō- xiii 23; xix 26; xxi 7, 20 and once phileō- xx 2), and in John Jesus is the most frequent referent for the term *lord* (kurios). The first reference to this beloved one comes very near the beginning of the farewell discourse; he remains a prominent character thereafter until the very end of the Gospel. It is significant that the *first* description of the patriarch in Deuteronomy xxxiii 12 becomes the *most frequent* identification in John of this disciple. We suggest that in the minds of Jewish Christians this mnemonic tag would serve

---

[4]) Also, in what Charles identified as the original version of the Testament of Benjamin, we find this significant claim: "(I shall be called) one beloved of the Lord and a doer of the good pleasure of his mouth". (T.B xi 1) This text is not, however, the one preferred by M. DE JONGE, *Testamenta XII Patriarcharum*, Leiden, 1970, p. 85.

to link the two figures and their two stories. More than this, it would remind all living members of the tribe of Benjamin that a special relationship had linked them to Jesus during the days of his Passion and that a special promise had been given to them after his Ascension.

The blessing of Benjamin has a second feature, related to the first in synonymous parallelism.

NAB: Benjamin is the beloved of the Lord
     who shelters him all the day.
RSV: He dwells in safety by him,
     He encompasses him all the day long.
NEB: The Lord's beloved dwells in security,
     The high God shields him all the day long.

The translations vary, but they agree on the underlying thought. As a mark of his love, God provides for Benjamin a secure shelter, an assurance of continuing protection "all the day long" [5].

Other tribes might fall away, might be lost in exile or dispersion; but not this tribe. For the sake of its "head", God assures the tribe of his permanent presence. This assurance of the Lord's presence and protection is also basic to John's portrait of the beloved disciple. He shares, of course, in the destiny accorded all the disciples in the intercessory prayer; but in addition he has a promised destiny that distinguishes him from the others. It is the Lord's intention that this disciple should "wait until I come" (xxi 22, 23 NEB). That promise is immediately misunderstood, but, as usual in this Gospel, the misunderstanding is designed to call attention to a hidden meaning, to a deeper truth. The surface content of the promise seemed to refer to the physical death of this disciple, and some listeners were thus deceived by that surface. Jesus explicitly rejects that meaning. Yet exegetes have been baffled in their search for any other but the plain meaning. For instance, C. K. BARRETT, who is no mean interpreter of the Gospel, is impelled to give up the search and to conclude that the popular understanding of the saying must have been its only original meaning, John's disavowal notwithstanding. "Jesus did *not* say to him that this disciple was not to die" (xxi 23) (C. K. BARRETT, *The Gospel According to St. John*,

---

[5] S. R. DRIVER (I.C.C. *Deuteronomy*, p. 403) interprets this security as "freedom from the fear of death". The writer of the Testament of Benjamin (xi 4) gives another version: "He shall be a chosen one of God forever".

London, SPCK, 1955, p. 488). I think that this dilemma can be resolved if Jesus' promise to this disciple is viewed as the echo of Moses' promise to Benjamin: "The Lord shelters him all the day". The vocation of this disciple in and through his descendants will be continued and guarded by the Lord until the Lord comes. We call attention to the fact that the pivotal verb in the promise is *menein* (to abide), which in John has a wide range of weighty connotations. For example, in xii 34 there is a similar misunderstanding of a prophecy concerning the Messiah, in which the point at issue is a double meaning in this same verb. No one would claim that in that verse the misunderstanding was in fact the original intention. There, too, the problem is created by a confusion between physical death and divine abidingness. One other observation must be made about the double meaning of this promise in John xxi 22, 23. If, in his picturing of this individual disciple, John was also thinking about his prototype, the patriarchal head of the tribe, and if therefore he was assuring the Christian heirs of this tribe of their participation in the Advent of Christ, the misunderstanding which he imbedded intentionally in the text would call attention to precisely that corporate promise. The Gospel fuses the promise of Parousia with the promise of Jesus (and Moses) to this patriarchal community. Moses had promised to "establish you this day as his people . . . as he swore to your fathers" (Deut. xxix 13). Included within this promise was "life, blessing, length of days", an assured dwelling of God with this elect community (Deut. xxx 20; xxxii 47). John's thinking may also have been "communal" in his promise to the beloved disciple. And when, in listening to his Gospel, his audience was reminded of Moses' farewell discourse, that reminder would have carried a sense of security in a dangerous world in which the promise to the beloved disciple would hold much the same meaning as "God shelters him all the day". To an early Christian "all the day" would mean the same as "until I come". To link these two promises, Moses' and Jesus', may not be fully convincing, but it is at least preferable to the flat denial that John xxi 23 means what it says.

In the third assurance in his blessing of Benjamin, Moses included a clause that is clearly intended to carry a meaning parallel to the first two; yet the precise meaning remains problematic. In part, the problem is how to construe the antecedents to the pronominal subjects:

RSV: he (God) encompasses him (Benjamin) all the day long,
　　　　and makes his (God's) dwelling between his (Benjamin's) shoulders.
NAB: who (God) shelters him all the day,
　　　　while he (Benjamin?) abides securely at his (God's?) breast.
NEB: the High God shields him all the day long,
　　　　and he (Benjamin) dwells under his (God's) protection.

The question is whose dwelling is made between whose shoulders. Then there is a further anatomical ambiguity. *Shoulders* is clearly metaphorical, but to what does the metaphor refer? In the picture of God dwelling between Benjamin's shoulders, RSV agrees with some rabbinic exegesis which saw those as mountains in the territory of Benjamin and God's dwelling as the temple built between two of those mountains.

"The divine presence is always in the West, in the territory of Benjamin". (Midrash Rabbah Num II, 10; *Testament of Benjamin* ix 2-5; STRACK-BILLERBECK, *Kommentar zum N.T.*, III, p. 286.)

The choice of this dwelling place signified God's love for Benjamin and his assurance of security [6]).

This reading of the text would seriously threaten our conjectured typology.

The result is quite different if we follow the lead of the NAB and NEB translators. Here it is Benjamin who abides securely between the Lord's shoulders, a difficult but not impossible metaphor [7]).

In this case the parallelism with the first two clauses in Deut. xxxiii 12 is clearer, and the points of contact with the Johannine symbolism become striking indeed. Three times the Evangelist repeats the phrase "lying close to the breast of Jesus", twice in the first scene and once in the last (xiii 23, 25; xxi 20). This is his way of identifying this disciple to his readers, a tag that would enable them to link the Passion Story directly to their prior knowledge of this figure. In this reading of the matter, John has found in Deuteronomy the assurance that because Benjamin was beloved by the Lord, the Lord assured him of two basic things: long-term security and intimate knowledge of the Lord's will and way. To be sure, the Deuteronomic shoulders (LXX ŌMŌN) is not the same

---

[6]) This interpretation is favored by S. R. DRIVER and others (*op. cit.*, p. 404).

[7]) S. R. DRIVER recognizes the possibility of this interpretation and he mentions scholars who support it. He rejects it because of the incongruous idea of Benjamin, pictured as a reclining man (sic), dwelling between Jehovah's shoulders (*ibid.*).

as the Johannine *kolpō* (xiii 23) or *stethos* (xiii 25; xxi 20), but the phrase adopted by NEB carries a number of the right overtones: "close to Jesus". Such closeness, in the three Johannine contexts, connotes affection, familiarity, trust, intimacy of shared knowledge and intention, permanent friendship. Where there is such a wide range of potential connotations it is hazardous to pin an author down to one. Yet if we conclude that the Johannine school shared that understanding of the Mosaic blessing, this conclusion would strengthen our conjecture that the Johannine picture of the beloved disciple is an instance of haggadic midrash on the Mosaic farewell—enigmatic, to be sure, but no more of an enigma than Deut. xxxiii 12.

If one follows this course, then he arrives at a set of correspondences that is too complete to be accidental. All three features in Moses' blessing recur in the Johannine portrait; more than this, every key phrase which John used to identify this disciple is an echo of Deuteronomy xxxiii 12. This set of coincidences appears, in turn, within a wider complex of images: Jesus as a prophet like Moses; the comparable Passions and farewell addresses; the presence of the Twelve as representatives of the separate tribes and of all Israel; the special roles assigned to selected patriarchs and disciples; the pervasive presence of symbolic, haggadic and typological patterns of thought; the instinctive ways in which listeners would identify themselves with the head of their own community.

Having weighed the evidence provided by Deuteronomy, we should now look more closely at varying Johannine contexts to see how this subtle reference to Benjamin may have affected John's address to his immediate audiences.

The Johannine Contexts

The role of the beloved patriarch in the Johannine scenario comes clearly to the surface in the final chapter of the Gospel. We have already examined the parallelism between Moses' assurance of "freedom from the fear of death" for Benjamin, and Jesus' promise that this disciple will wait until he comes. There is, we believe, some connection between the conception of "all the day" and "until I come", and also some connection between the *waiting* for Jesus and the *abiding* in the presence of Jesus (cf. i 32 f., 39 f.; v 38; vi 27, 56; viii 31, 35; xii 24, 34, 46; xiv 10, 17, 25; xv 4-16). We believe that John designed the misunderstanding of Jesus' promise in xxi 21, 23 to call attention to these hidden connections.

Let me add here that the account of the fishing trip stresses the unique ability of this disciple to discern secrets hidden from others, a gift which is the mark of a prophet. It is fitting that the disciple loved by Jesus should be the first to recognize Jesus' presence as Lord. Love and insight are related. It is in his possession of this prophetic vision and witness that he is distinguished from Peter. In his power to identify his *glorified* Lord there may be a contact with a rabbinic tradition that Benjamin was untainted by sin (Shab. 55b) and that accordingly his corpse was not exposed to corruption by worms (BB 17a).

We should not overlook the care with which the Evangelist makes this disciple a dependable witness to all that had happened (xxi 24). Confidence in the Gospel is thus linked to confidence in this disciple who had been present at the Supper, had been warned of the betrayal in advance, had probably gained special access to the trial, had been present beneath the cross, had received the gift of a "mother" and could certify to the emptiness of the tomb. If, as some have cogently argued, this Gospel was written not to supplement but to replace other accounts, it is likely that the signature of this particular disciple is a mark of competition between the Johannine and other Christian communities, each with its favorite Gospel. If, as seems certain, the debate between believing and non-believing Jews centered in the interpretation of those events in which this disciple was present, this Gospel would carry special force not simply because of his presence, but also because of Jesus' own underwriting of his testimony. The Lord authenticated this Benjamin as "a doer of the good pleasure of his mouth" (T.B. xi 1).

Such a line of reasoning may prompt various conjectures concerning the impact of this story, in John 21, on John's conversation partners in the synagogues. Jewish readers would probably sense a sharp contrast between this open and direct testimony to Jesus and that of "secret disciples" like Nicodemus. This disciple had been willing to make his oath of allegiance in public and in writing; he had done so as a true representative of the true Israel. We recall that according to the Genesis narrative it was immediately before the birth of Benjamin that God had blessed Jacob, had given him the name Israel and had promised that from him would spring "a nation and a company of nations" (Gen. xxxv 9-12). It is clear that John stressed the truths to which this prophetic disciple was

privy; but in doing this the narrative is implicitly sympathetic to
Jews who did not have ready access to the living witness of such a
prophetic revealer. Since the basic truths remained hidden even
from a disciple like Peter until a prophet had revealed them to him,
readers would be helped to understand the bewilderment and lack
of faith of their Jewish neighbors. They would be helped to appreciate even the hostility of the "Jamnia loyalists", since the
fulfilment of Scripture had taken place in ways that were understandably obscure even to trained interpreters. The assurance of
Jesus to the beloved disciple would, however, extend beyond this
"sympathetic understanding" of Israel's hostility. The promise to
this "second Benjamin" would convey a promise that Israel as a
whole would ultimately share in the consummation, even in spite
of its present hostility. He whom Jacob-Israel loved is also loved
by Jesus. Jewish believers in Jesus could therefore have confidence
in the ultimate salvation of their people, a confidence that would
undergird their obligation to continue the witness of this Benjamin
to Israel, whatever the cost.

Such conjectures would become even more attractive if we should
posit not only a Jewish-Christian audience for John, but also a
Benjaminite-Christian audience. Now the position of this disciple
in knowing the mind of the Lord (xiii 23) and in conveying an
authoritative tradition about him would be strategic in affirming
the priority and prestige of that community over other Christian
groups. If that were true, the contrast between Peter and this
disciple, in John xxi, might reflect a corresponding suspicion of the
Petrine community on the part of this Benjaminite community [8]).
However, such conjectures become, at best, extremely tenuous.

Shifting now from the last appearance of this disciple to the first,
we note that the Johannine introduction of the disciple anticipates
the later episodes. He held a special position at the farewell supper,
where Jesus recognized that his hour had come (xiii 1) and where
he waged his final conflict with the Devil. Here the spotlight shifts
back and forth among the three representatives of Israel, the three
types of Jewish response to Jesus. The blackest light falls upon
Judas as a tool of Satan, a Jewish disciple who betrayed his Master.

---

[8]) It is not impossible that Paul's self-identification with the tribe of
Benjamin (Rom. xi 1; Phil. iii 5) reflects not only the current prestige of that
tribe but also the recognized status of a Benjaminite church. In neither
text is such an identification necessary to establish Paul's standing as a Jew.

He stands in the lowest echelon of the Johannine cast, much more culpable than secret believers and more culpable even than unbelievers in the synagogues. Simon Peter represents quite a different type: well-meaning, but dull and slow, if not stupid. He requires help from others to know what is going on; he cannot fathom the foot-washing (xiii 6, 7) nor grasp the intent of Scripture (xiii 18). His lack of the gift of prophecy makes him dependent on the disciple who had it. This latter, i.e., the unnamed disciple, was in a position to ask Jesus and to relay his reply (xiii 25). It is significant that the position of this disciple vis-à-vis Jesus paralleled precisely the position of Jesus vis-à-vis God, for the phrase *en tō kolpō* in xiii 25 is equivalent to the phrase *eis ton kolpon* of i 18 (a fact obscured in the RSV). In both places the phrase suggests intimacy of vision and knowledge that qualifies a person to mediate divine grace and truth. The beloved Son relies on the beloved disciple. When the hour comes for the Son to go to his father, for loving his own until the end (xiii 1), Jesus trusts this disciple to convey to the others the mystery of Judas' rebellion as evidence of the power of his love. Yet it is not until Chapter xxi that this mystery will become clear, as the love of the glorified Lord is again recognized by this prophet. The scene in Chapter xiii is extremely rich in symbolism which resists reduction to clumsy prose. But enough has been said here to suggest that these three types of disciples would be of keen interest to believers within John's church; they would help them to detect various kinds of treason and incomprehension among themselves and also to understand various responses to their witness among their Jewish neighbors.

Now we shift to the role of the beloved disciple in the arrest and trial of Jesus. It is possible, of course, that the reference in xviii 15 to another disciple introduces a wholly different actor. Thus whatever inference may be drawn from this chapter must remain tentative. It seems to me, however, that the balance of evidence favors identification with the beloved disciple (cf. R. E. BROWN, *The Gospel According to John*, N.Y., Doubleday, 1966, I, xciv). Arguing from that assumption, we note that here, as in Chapter xiii, the three types of discipleship are again presented. Judas returns, assisting the soldiers who have come to arrest Jesus. Peter is here, drawing a rebuke from Jesus over his sword-play and later denying his membership in the band of disciples. Here, too, is Caiaphas, whose prophecy concerning the death of one man "for the people" is in process of fulfillment—a telling detail for all Jewish readers, whether or not they were members of the church. It is this high priest who consequently shows a direct interest in learning more about Jesus' disciples (xviii 19). That discussion gives Jesus an opening for underscoring his habit of teaching wherever Jews came together and to stress the corresponding candor with which he expected his disciples to give their own witness (vs. 21) "Ask them".

Unfortunately, Peter refuses to speak or to act so openly. Such courage is left to one disciple alone. This disciple was not only a Jew, but a Jew who was known to the high priest and perhaps even a familiar friend. (That is the implication of *gnostos* in several passages in the LXX: II K. x 11; Ps. lv 13; Job xix 14.) The degree of knowledge and the possibility of friendship were such that this man had easy access to the inner court of the high priest. Yet he, unlike Peter, was quite willing to accept the charge of guilt by association, for he entered those precincts *with Jesus*, the arrested and accused prophet. Even more than this, it was on *his* appeal to the doorkeeper that Peter was admitted. He shows no trace of Galilean reticence or Petrine fear. *Persona grata* bravely takes his stand beside *persona non grata*. Peter's denial is shown to be all the more shameful in view of the forthright testimony of both the beloved Son and his beloved disciple. The same contrast makes their behavior all the more courageous and persuasive.

The thrust of the story is clear: handed over to the Jews, this prophet was executed as "the king of the Jews" in response to the demands of the Jews. Yet the same story differentiates at least six types of Jew: Judas, Caiaphas, officers from the chief priests and Pharisees, Jesus, Simon Peter, and the disciple who was in good standing with both the priestly and the disciplic circles. This last person is at home in Jerusalem and Judea. (His appearances, except for the final one, were limited to this region, traditionally assigned to Benjamin.) He had full right to be present at the table, in the Garden for the arrest, and inside the highest ecclesiastical court. His courage and openness stand in sharpest contrast to the double-dealing of Judas and the double-talk of Peter. It is to such a disciple that Jesus directs those who wish to learn more about himself and his teaching. "They know what I said" (vs. 21). In such a command, quite apart from its accuracy as a word of Jesus, we may detect the Evangelist's own commendation of this particular disciple as a mediator between Jews in the churches and Jews in the synagogues, a man whom every believer should emulate and to whose testimony every non-believer should pay heed. In reading this Gospel each Jewish reader came in touch with this man's tested and dependable disclosure. Like Jesus, he might be struck by Jewish officers (vs. 22 f.), but no more than in the case of Jesus would such a blow be evidence of bearing false witness.

Not only was this disciple a witness to the Supper, the betrayal and denial and trial; he also was the only male disciple placed by any Evangelist at the crucifixion (xix 25-37). This surely bespeaks his courage in being present as the soldiers were carrying out their grim duty. It also qualifies him to verify the fact that Jesus had in fact died on the cross, whenever the rumor that he had not actually died should appear. He was also in a position to testify to the fulfilments of Scripture in the piercing of Jesus' side and in the failure to break his bones (v. 36, 37), details which themselves reflect highly midrashic modes of thought. Those modes would presumably have been useful in debates with synagogue exegetes of John's day. In any case, the figure of the beloved disciple is here linked to various Jewish debates over the circumstances surrounding Jesus' death. He who could testify to the certainty of Jesus' death could also give the most convincing testimony to the emptiness of the grave (xx 8) and the presence of the risen Lord (xxi 7). He could join in the corporate Christian affirmation, "we have beheld his glory" (i 14).

It is highly significant that from the cross Jesus gave two commands to persons who, though unnamed, were closest to him. The original significance of those commands is difficult to recover with assurance (cf. R. E. Brown, *Biblical Reflections on Crises Facing the Church*, N.Y., Paulist, 1975, p. 102). The prophet Jesus here discloses to this mother the fact that this particular disciple is now her son; he has been given to her as her son, in lieu of Jesus himself. Is Jesus here restoring to Rachel her son Benjamin? Does Mary represent Jacob-Israel, with the midrashic corollary that this man is Jacob's best-loved son [9]?

---

[9] The two chief characters in this episode have this in common: the Evangelist never names them. In view of John's habit of naming all other important actors in the story, we take this fact as evidence of symbolic overtones. If Jewish readers have now linked this disciple to Benjamin, this episode would impel them to associate this "mother" with Rachel, Jacob's best-loved wife, whose prayers to God during the exile had, according to the rabbis, alone secured God's promise to restore Israel.

If so, for this woman to accept this son, as she evidently did, would require an act of obedience to such a prophetic disclosure. And such an act would carry a strong implicit appeal to John's conversational partners in the synagogues: "Hear, O Israel. This faithful Christian believer is your own brother. Listen to his testimony. In him lies the fulfilment of God's covenants with Jacob and with Moses, your own true destiny."

The interpretation of Jesus' word to this son must accord with the interpretation of the word to his mother. This disciple is called upon to recognize this new two-sided relationship and is commanded to obey the duties implicit in it. Henceforth he becomes son to this mother, to the mother of Jesus. The revelation seem to have been immediately understood and accepted by these two (vs. 27). But again, the interpretation is far from transparent to twentieth century readers. If Mary in any sense represents Israel, and the disciple, Benjamin, this command demonstrates Jesus' concern for his people in a way which no disciple should ignore. The crucifixion produces a redefinition of sonship and motherhood, of the relation of the individual to the community, and of Israel to the church. This redefinition of Israel is probably related to the announcement of the Risen Lord in xx 17, that Jesus' Father has now become the Father of all disciples and that they have therefore now become brothers. So, too, in xix 27 the implication is this: disciples of this Messiah must acknowledge in Israel their own mother and must take care of her in their own home; Israel in turn must recognize these disciples as its own sons and accept their home as God's intention for itself. That such a revelation should be located at the cross may suggest the conviction that this is the only place where such a rapprochement between synagogue and church can take place, here where the King of the Jews dies, as the high priest himself had said, "for the people". In dying, the beloved son embraced in his love this disciple and this mother, and thus he accomplished their mutual acceptance. In blessing this Benjamin, who alone was left of his mother's children, Jesus was blessing this Rachel (Gen. xliv 20). As this prophet like Moses was lifted up, demonstrating his love for his people, "all his holy ones were in his hand; they followed at his feet" (Deut. xxxiii 3). It is probably significant that it was not until after Jesus has so united the new mother with her new son that he could say "It is finished".

Even more enigmatic is the role of the beloved disciple at the

tomb on Easter morning. It is clear that a negative picture is again
assigned to Peter in contrast to the positive picture of his rival.
What is the meaning of their race tomb-ward and of one disciple's
greater speed? Or the meaning of Peter's precedence in entering
the tomb? Or the meaning of the precise disposition of the linen
cloths? What did the beloved disciple see and believe on this
occasion? I must confess to a high degree of bewilderment. The clues
to a satisfactory answer are largely absent. There is an implicit
contrast between the overt disciples in xx 1-10 and the covert
disciples who were responsible for the anointing and burial (xix 38 f.).
The two men running to the tomb were able to corroborate the
discovery of Mary Magdalene that this was the tomb in question
and that it was empty (cf. MINEAR, "We don't Know Where",
Interpretation, 30, 1976, pp. 125-139). They did not yet understand
the Scriptural prophecies concerning resurrection. They did not yet
know "where" the body had been laid (xx 13) (cf. Joshua's comparable reflections on Israel's ignorance concerning the grave of
Moses. Ass. Moses, xi 4 f., on the basis of Deut. xxxiv 6). Not yet
did they grasp any new mandate, for "they went back to their
homes" (vs. 10). Peter and his comrade shared a notable lack of
understanding; yet the author discerned a difference between them.
It has been difficult, however, for modern readers to grasp the
precise points of contrast between these two followers. If we had
a more complete knowledge of John's conversational partners and
of their midrashic modes of argument, we might move toward
greater clarity. All that we can do is to hazard various guesses.
Had the "partners" in those synagogues and churches developed
strong antipathies to Peter as a Galilean fisherman and spokesman
for the church? Had he provoked an antagonism among the synagogue leaders which eventuated in his own martyrdom? (xxi 18).
Had Peter turned away from a patient and forgiving mission to
the synagogues because of this antagonism? In contrast to Peter's
disaffection, did some other Christian leader mount a new campaign
to reach the synagogues? Did that leader place a renewed accent
upon Jesus' love for Israel, his fulfilment of God's promises to
Moses? Did that leader find that, given this specific audience,
witnesses other than Peter could give a more persuasive testimony
concerning the decisive events that had taken place in Jerusalem,
in the territory of Benjamin? If this other witness were identified
as "beloved of the Lord" would auditors in the synagogue detact

an allusion to Moses' blessing of Benjamin? I believe that all this is possible, and even probable. We need to recall that although many Johannine scholars accept Mosaic typology as a basic component of Johannine christology, the presence of that typology remains implicit rather than explicit, even after we consider such texts as i 17; iii 14; v 45 f.; vii 19, 22 f.; ix 28 f. That being so, we should not expect the Benjaminite connection of the beloved disciple to be more explicit. In this case the implicit fulfilment of God's promise to Moses in Deut. xviii 15, 18 serves as an appropriate corollary to the implicit fulfilment of Moses' promise to Benjamin in Deut. xxxiii 12. What is a prophet without his people?

Such speculation has merit, but it remains speculation. What is less speculative has already been presented:

1. The portrait of Jesus as fulfilling God's promise of a prophet like Moses.
2. The appeal to Scripture and to the signs as a way of validating this typology.
3. The origin of the Gospel in a situation of conflict between churches and synagogues, whether that conflict was past, present or anticipated.
4. The claim that the Gospel represents the true testimony of a disciple distinguished from other disciples as "beloved of the Lord" (xxi 24).
5. The care with which the Gospel locates the presence of this disciple within the crucial stage of Jesus' mission: farewell discourses, the Supper, arrest, trial, crucifixion, burial, empty tomb, glorification.
6. The assurance of a permanent role for this disciple as a son of Jesus' mother and as one who would abide until Jesus' return.

In the hypothesis that the Evangelist's picture of the beloved disciple was in part shaped to conform to the picture of Benjamin in Deut. xxxiii 12, we have taken a step beyond these assured conclusions. How long a step? Is it too long? Specialists in Johannine and rabbinic studies are likely to give differing answers. Nonetheless, I believe that the hypothesis I have advanced is worth a sustained testing. Should it survive this scrutiny, if only as a *possible* reading of the Gospel, it would have far-reaching implications for many aspects of Johannine studies: e.g., the provenance of the Gospel; its role in the conflicts between churches and synagogues; its stress upon the work which John the Baptist and Jesus did *in Judea*; the hermeneutical attitudes of the Evangelist toward Scripture, together with our own hermeneutical attitudes toward his work; the typological and midrashic character of his vocabulary and thought; his ecclesiology and eschatology. Over the centuries the search for the beloved disciple has been so intense and so wide-ranging that it is an act of consummate audacity to suggest a new thesis for consideration. Yet no one is wholly content with the present solutions of the riddle, and the issue is of such central importance that it would be wrong to call off the search entirely. That search requires the careful reexamination of every clue, however fanciful at first sight [10]).

---

[10]) In preparing the final draft of this essay I have profited from comments of Professors B. S. CHILDS, J. L. MARTYN and R. E. BROWN.

ASIDES IN THE GOSPEL OF JOHN

BY

JOHN J. O'ROURKE
Philadelphia

Everyone admits that there are asides or editorial comments in Jn, although there is not universal agreement as to their number or extent [1]). Moreover, some claim that a number of these already existed in the sources used by the evangelist and were taken over bodily by him [2]). It is proposed to examine here what is the most systematic study of these asides, that of M. C. TENNEY, accepting for the moment his tenfold classification of their types: 1) translations, 2) asides indicating time and place, 3) indications of customs, 4) reflections showing the identity of the author, 5) memories of the disciples, 6) explanations of situations or actions, 7) enumerations or summaries, 8) identifications of persons, 9) notes on the

---

[1]) Among the commentaries consulted were R. E. BROWN, *The Gospel according to John i-xii* (*AB* 29; Garden City, N.Y.: Doubleday, 1966), *The Gospel according to John xiii-xxi* (*AB* 29A; 1970) (the pagination is successive in the two volumes; thus only the pages will be cited; R. BULTMANN, *The Gospel of John*, translated by G. R. BEASLEY-MURRAY *et al.* (Oxford: Blackwell, 1971); B. LINDARS, *The Gospel of John* (*New Century Bible*; London: Gliphants, 1972; L. MORRIS, *The Gospel according to John: The English Text with Introduction, Exposition and Notes* (*NICNT*: Grand Rapids, Eerdmans, 1971); J. N. SANDERS, *The Gospel according to St. John*, edited and completed by B. A. MASTIN (*HNTC*; New York: Harper & Row, 1968) (comments on cc. 16-21 are actually MASTIN's but reference will be made to Sanders); A. WIKENHAUSER, *Das Evangelium nach Johannes*, 3rd ed. (*RNT* 4; Regensburg: Pustet, 1961).

[2]) Such are found occasionally in R. T. FORTNA, *The Gospel of Signs: A Reconstruction of the Narrative Source Underlying the Fourth Gospel* (*SNTSMS*; Cambridge: Cambridge University, 1970); in the hypothetical sources based on BULTMANN in D. MOODLY SMITH, *The Composition and Order of the Fourth Gospel: Bultmann's Literary Theory* (New Haven and London: Yale University, 1965); in H. M. TEEPLE, *The Literary Origin of the Gospel of John* (Evanston: Religion and Ethics Institute, 1974.) Various theories of composition are outlined and critiqued in R. KYSER, *The Fourth Evangelist and His Gospel* (Minneapolis: Augsburg, 1975); cf. also his review of TEEPLE, *Origins* in *JBL* 93 (1974) 308-312. In the present article "evangelist" means whoever produced that actual gospel which we have; the purpose of the article is not to defend or to attack any theory of composition.

knowledge of Jesus, 10) theological discussions [3]). The criterion for determining the presence of such asides is this: Their omission would not affect greatly the flow of the narrative, but is should be noted that some asides may be important for the achievement of an important goal of the evangelist [4]), as, for example, his remarks about fulfillment [5]).

TENNEY lists eight examples of translational asides in i 38, 41, 42; iv 25; ix 7, xix 13, 17; xx 16 [6]). To these can be added v 2's ἡ ἐπιλεγομένη Ἑβραϊστὶ בוטא [7]) although these words could be placed under some other heading.

TENNEY finds locations of time and place in i 28, vi 4, 59; vii 2; viii 20; ix 14; x 22-23; xi 18, 30; xix 14, 31, 42. However, viii 20 is better classified as a theological reflection [8]); xi 30's ἀλλ᾽ἦν ἔτι ἐν τῷ τοπῷ ὅπου ὑπήντησεν αὐτὴ ἡ Μάρθα does not seem to be an aside because it heightens the narrative; ἦν δὲ νύξ in xiii 30 [9]), if an aside, is perhaps better classified as a theological reflection [10]).

TENNEY gives as an indication of a custom iv 9. xix 40's καθὼς ἔθος ἐστὶν τοῖς Ἰουδαίοις ἐνταφιάζειν [11]) is such.

As a reference to the author [12]) he lists i 14b, 16; xiii 23; xix 35; xxi 23, 24-25. Apparently he considers ὃν ἠγάπα ὁ Ἰησοῦς the aside in xiii 23 and καὶ ἐκεῖνος οἶδεν ὅτι ἀληθῆ λέγει the aside in xix 35. Though these may be asides, they cannot be classified as references

---

[3]) M. C. TENNEY, "The Footnotes of John's Gospel," *Bibliotheca Sacra* 117 (1960) 350-364; he notes, 351, "In attempting to simplify the analysis ...the classifications have been kept to a minimum number..."

[4]) TENNEY, "Footnotes" 350; see BROWN, *John* cxxxvi.

[5]) Cf., s.v., J. J. O'ROURKE, "John's Fulfillment Texts," *Sciences Ecclésiastiques* 19 (1967) 433-443.

[6]) TEEPLE, *Origins* 144, considers this as characteristic of his "S" but he ascribes the last three to "R" in his breakdown of the gospel into chapters and verses.

[7]) BROWN, *John* 205 f. is not clear about this; words are in FORTNA, *Gospel of Signs* 240, MOODY SMITH, *Reconstruction* 41. What should be the form of the name is of no concern to this study; for the question see M. M. METZGER, *A Textual Commentary on the Greek New Testament* (New York and London: United Bible Societies, 1971) 208.

[8]) BROWN, *John* 339, does not consider this an aside; MORRIS, *John* 144 does. At the very least οὔπω ἐληλύθει ἡ ὥρα αὐτοῦ is; see BULTMANN, *John* 284.

[9]) Considered as redactorial by WIKENHAUSER, *Johannes* 254.

[10]) See BULTMANN, *John* 482 f.

[11]) Not so indicated by BROWN, *John* 932; LINDARS, *John* 593 is doubtful. BULTMANN, *John* 680, states: "for the non-Jewish reader it is added that this corresponds to the Jewish mode of burial."

[12]) In accepting this classification I am not accepting any theory of authorship or composition.

to the author; the former is an identification of a person and the latter an explanation. On xix 35 the note is not to be limited to καὶ ἐκεῖνος οἶδεν ὅτι ἀληθῆ λέγει but should include καὶ ἀληθινὴ αὐτοῦ ἐστιν ἡ μαρτυρία and ἵνα καὶ ὑμεῖς πιστεύσητε. [13])

As references to recollections of disciples he lists ii 22 [14]); viii 27; x 6; xii 16; xiii 28; xx 9. He does not consider ii 17 as such, but it seems to be one [15]). However, viii 27's οὐκ ἔγνωσαν ὅτι τὸν πατερα αὐτοῖς ἔλεγεν is better classified as an explanation. In x 6 Tenney limits the aside to ἐκείνη δὲ οὐκ ἔγνωσαν τίνα ἦν ἃ ἐλάλει αυτοῖς; however, the preceding words ταύτην τὴν παροιμίαν εἶπεν αὐτοῖς ὁ 'Ιησοῦς also seem to be part of the aside [16]) and it should accordingly be classified as an explanatory note of which the words following are part. xiii 28 together with the following verse should be classified as an enumeration or summary [17]).

Tenney finds explanatory notes in ii 9, 24-25; iv 2; [18]) vi 23, 71; vii 5, 39; xi 51; xii 6; xix 36; xx 30-31; xxi 7, 8, 19. He considers only οἱ δὲ διάκονοι ᾔδεισαν οἱ ἠντληκότες τὸ ὕδωρ [19]) as the aside in ii 9, but the preceding words καὶ οὐκ ᾔδει πόθεν ἐστίν should be included [20]). iii 24 [21]) and iv 44 [22]) are also explanatory notes. vii 22's οὐχ ὅτι ἐκ τοῦ Μωϋσέως ἐστὶν ἀλλ' ἐκ τῶν πατέρων seems an obvious example [23]). As has been already noted, viii 27 belongs under this class. ix 22-23 should also be considered as such an aside since it repeats the content of the preceding verses [24]). xi 5, "For Jesus loved Martha and her sister Mary and Lazarus", is also

---

[13]) Thus BROWN, *John* 932 but 936, "Probably editorial." Without hesitation thus SANDERS, *John* 412; WIKENHAUSER, *Johannes* 335.

[14]) As will be seen later this goes with part of ii 21 to form a theological reflection.

[15]) Thus BULTMANN, *John* 124.

[16]) Thus seemingly BULTMANN, *John* 375.

[17]) TENNEY, "Footnotes," 364 gives only xiii 28, but 356 seems to imply xiii 29 also.

[18]) TEEPLE, *Origins* 177 finds this a later gloss; there is no textual support for this view.

[19]) TENNEY, "Footnotes" 357.

[20]) BROWN, *John* 97; WIKENHAUSER, *Johannes* 72.

[21]) Thus BROWN, *John* 150; MORRIS, *John* 238. LINDARS, *John* 165 allows the possibility; likewise SANDERS, *John* 133.

[22]) iv 43 is included in the note by BROWN, *John* 186 f.; MORRIS, *John* 222; SANDERS, *John* 149; WIKENHAUSER, *Johannes* 115.

[23]) Thus WIKENHAUSER, *Johannes* 157; cf. BROWN, *John* 310.

[24]) Thus BROWN, *John* 370, 380; BULTMANN, *John* 335; WIKENHAUSER, *Johannes* 190. Opposed is LINDARS, *John* 347.

one [25]). Likewise xi 3 is an explanation breaking the course of the narrative [26]). xi 13 is possibly such an aside [27]). xi 33 is another example [28]). Perhaps τοῦ διάβολος ἤδη βεβληκότες εἰς τὴν καρδίαν ἵνα παραδοῖ αὐτὸν 'Ιούδας Σίμωνος 'Ισκαριώτου in xiii 2 should be considered an explanatory note [29]). ὁ παραδιδοὺς αὐτόν in xviii 5 of itself would be an indication of a person [30]), but if the words εἱστήκει δὲ καὶ 'Ιούδας and μετ'αὐτῶν are part of the aside, the whole remark is an explanatory note; certainly these words do not add anything to the narrative and they are actually redundant in the context of xviii 3-11 [31]). xviii 28's καὶ αὐτοὶ οὐκ εἰσῆλθεν εἰς τὸ πραιτώριον ἵνα μὴ μιανθῶσιν ἀλλὰ φάγωσιν τὸ πάσχα [32]) seems to be an explanatory note; some would include the preceding words ἦν δὲπ ρωΐ [33]) as part of the aside. Perhaps xix 20 is also such a comment, for it contains little that is essential to the narrative [34]). xix 37 should be included with xix 36 and the verses constitute a theological reflection. xx 30-31 should rather be classified as an enumeration and summary. Perhaps another explanatory note is οὐδεὶς δὲ ἐτόλμα τῶν μαθητῶν ἐξετάσαι αὐτόν, σὺ τίς εἶ, εἰδότες ὅτι ὁ Κύριός ἐστιν in xxi 12 [35]).

As enumerations and summaries TENNEY lists ii 11; iv 54; xxi 14. As has been noted, iii 28-29 and xx 30-31 should be included here.

For him identifications of persons are found in vii 50; xi 2 [36]); xviii 10, 14, 40. To these should be added perhaps i 24's καὶ ἀπε-

---

[25]) Thus SANDERS, *John* 265. BROWN, *John* 433, "seems"; cf. 420.

[26]) Thus SANDERS, *John* 266; seemingly so BROWN, *John* 420.

[27]) Thus SANDERS, *John* 266; seemingly in accord is BROWN, *John* 420.

[28]) Thus BROWN, *John* cxxxvi, 466, 468 f.

[29]) Perhaps this is the view of SANDERS, *John* 305; WIKENHAUSER, *Johannes* 249.

[30]) Thus BROWN, *John* 805, 810 who does not consider the same expression in xviii 2 an aside. MORRIS, *John* 743, considers it an aside in both verses.

[31]) BULTMANN, *John* 638 and n. 1, would not agree, but his argument is not convincing, for what was once in a source can later be used as an aside.

[32]) For BULTMANN, *John* 656 it is a "comment." FORTNA, *Gospel of Signs* 243 places this in parentheses.

[33]) Thus MORRIS, *John* 762 f.

[34]) Perhaps thus MORRIS, *John* 807; WIKENHAUSER, *Johannes* 33. Contra is BROWN, *John* 897. FORTNA, *Gospel of Signs* 243 places in parentheses.

[35]) Thus WIKENHAUSER, *Johannes* 350.

[36]) TENNEY, "Footnotes" 359 has xi 21, but 364 correctly has xi 2.

σταλμένοι ἦσαν ἐκ τῶν Φαρισαίων [37]); perhaps all of i 44 [38]); xi 6's ὁ λεγόμενος Δίδυμος, xii 4's ὁ μέλλων αὐτὸν παραδιδόναι [39]); part of xiii 23 as was noted earlier; xiv 22's οὐκ ὁ Ἰσκαριώτης [40]); perhaps xviii 13's ἦν γὰρ πενθερὸς τοῦ Καϊαφᾶ, ὃς ἦν ἀρχιερεὺς τοῦ ἐνιαυτοῦ ἐκείνου [41]); perhaps ὁ δὲ μαθητὴς ἐκεῖνος ἦν γνωστὸς τῷ ἀρχιερεῖ in xviii 15 [42]); xviii 16's ὁ γνωστὸς τοῦ ἀρχιερέως [43]), perhaps συγγενὴς ὢν οὗ ἀπέκοψεν τὸ ὠτίον in xviii 26 [44]); xxi 38's ὢν μαθητὴς τοῦ Ἰησοῦ κεκρυμμένος δὲ διὰ τὸν φόβον τῶν Ἰουδαίων [45]); xix 39's ὁ ἐλθὼν πρὸς αὐτὸν νυκτὸς τὸ πρῶτον [46]); xx 2's ὃν ἐφίλει Ἰησοῦς [47]); xx 24's ὁ λεγόμενος Δίδυμος [48]), xxi 2's use of the same words [49]); xxi 2's ὁ ἀπὸ Κανὰ τῆς Γαλιλαίας [50]); xxi 20's ὃν ἠγάπα ὁ Ἰησοῦς [51]) and ὃς καὶ ἀνέπεσεν ἐν τῷ δείπνῳ ἐπὶ τὸ στῆθος αὐτοῦ καὶ εἶπεν, τίς ἐστιν ὁ παραδιδούς σε [52]).

According to TENNEY indications of Jesus' knowledge are found in vi 6, 64; xii 37-43; xiii 11 [53]). However, xii 37-43 should rather be considered a theological reflection, under which classification he places it also.

For TENNEY theological reflections are found in iii 16-21 [54]),

---

[37]) Thus BROWN, John 44, 51, 71. FORTNA, Gospel of Signs 235 has in presumed gospel.

[38]) MOODY SMITH, Reconstruction 39 has in source; likewise, FORTNA, Gospel of Signs 242.

[39]) Thus BROWN, John 447.

[40]) Thus BROWN 637, but 641 "may Be."

[41]) BROWN, John 821 "not clear"; FORTNA, Gospel of Signs 242 has in source.

[42]) MOODY SMITH, Reconstruction 48 has in source; likewise, FORTNA, Gospel of Signs 242.

[43])

[44]) MOODY SMITH, Reconstruction 48 has in source; likewise, FORTNA, Gospel of Signs 243.

[45]) Thus apparently BROWN, John 932; LINDARS, John 592; WIKENHAUSER, Johannes 336.

[46]) Thus BROWN, John 932, 946; LINDARS, John 592 "may be a gloss."

[47]) Thus BROWN, John 979; SANDERS, John 417.

[48]) Thus BROWN, John 1018; SANDERS, John 100 n. 2 MOODY SMITH, Reconstruction 50 f. brackets xx 24-28.

[49]) Thus BROWN, John 1066; SANDERS, John 442.

[50]) Thus BROWN, John 1066.

[51]) LINDARS, John 638 "may be a gloss."

[52]) Thus BROWN, John 1101; MORRIS, John 877.

[53]) TENNEY, "Footnotes," 364.

[54]) TENNEY, "Footnotes" 361 considers this as "likely." It is accepted as an aside by SANDERS, John 129; MORRIS, John 228. BROWN, John 149 does not consider it such. WIKENHAUSER, Johannes 91 takes no firm position.

31-36 [55]); xiii 37-43 [56]). To these should be added i 2 perhaps [57];) i 6-8 [58]), 9 [59]), 12b-13 [60]), 14b as noted above; i 15 [61]), 16 as was noted above; i 17-18 [62]); ii 21-22's ἐκεῖνος δὲ ἔλεγεν περὶ τοῦ ναοῦ τοῦ σώματος αὐτοῦ. ὅτε οὖν ἠγέρθη ἐκ νεκρῶν ἐμνήσθησαν οἱ μαθηταὶ αὐτοῦ ὅτι τοῦτο ἔλεγεν καὶ ἐπίστευσαν τῇ γραφῇ καὶ τῷ λόγῳ ὃν εἶπεν ὁ Ἰησοῦς [63]).

καὶ νῦν ἐστιν in iv 23 and v 25 are words that clearly are a theological reflection inserted into the narrative because in the total context of the Gospel the hour does not arrive until the Passion (see vii 30; viii 20 contrasted with xii 23); moreover, in the context of the Gospel Jesus had not disassociated himself from worship in the Temple in Jerusalem (see vii 10-viii 58; x 22-39), nor had the Spirit yet been sent (see xiv 16, 26; xv 26; xvi 7) [64].

Other examples of theological reflections are vii 30's ὅτι οὔπω ἐληλύθει ἡ ὥρα αὐτοῦ [65]); viii 35's ὁ δὲ δοῦλος οὐ μένει ἐν τε οἰκίᾳ εἰς

---

[55] TENNEY, "Footnotes," 361 considers this as "likely." It is considered an aside by MORRIS, *John* 243; SANDERS, *John* 135; WIKENHAUSER, *Johannes*, 35, 100. BROWN, *John* 159 does not consider it such. C. H. DODD, *The Interpretation of the Fourth Gospel* (Cambridge: Cambridge University, 1955) 308 is diffident about the question here and elsewhere.

[56] Thus also BROWN, *John* 483 f.; LINDARS, *John* 437-439; MORRIS, *John* 603-606.

[57] Thus BULTMANN, *John* 35 and n. 2.

[58] Thus BROWN, *John* 3, 9; BULTMANN, *John* 16; WIKENHAUSER, *Johannes* 38, 443.

[59] Thus BROWN, *John* 6, 9.

[60] Thus BROWN, *John* 3, 11; BULTMANN, *John* 17; WIKENHAUSER, *Johannes* 38, 46.

[61] Thus BROWN, *John* 3, 15; LINDARS, *John* 96; BULTMANN, *John* 16; WIKENHAUSER, *Johannes* 38, 46.

[62] Thus BROWN, *John* 3, 16 f. BULTMANN, *John* 17 considers i 17 as certainly such and i 18 as probably such.

[63] Thus MORRIS, *John* 201; WIKENHAUSER, *Johannes* 81. TENNEY, "Footnotes," 355, 364 considers only ii 22 as the aside and under a different classification, as was noted above. BROWN, *John* 123 hesitates regarding ii 21 but cxxxvi accepts it as part of the aside.

[64] R. SCHNACKENBURG, *The Gospel according to John* Vol. 1, translated by K. SMYTH (*HTCNT*; New York: Herder and Herder, 1968) 436 ff. should have developed his thought in this way since Jesus was in Samaria the Spirit had yet to be sent. M. J. LANGRANGE, *Évangile selon Saint Jean*, 8th ed. (*EB*; Paris: Gabalda, 1948) 113 f. comments: "La reprise ἔρχεται ὥρα est corrigée ou plutôt précisée (*contradictée in adjecte*) par καὶ νῦν ἐστι (*sic*) comme dans Jo. v, 25...ce qui prouve bien que c'est du style de Jo... L'heure viendra, et ce futur sera maintenu par προσκυνήσουσι, mais c'est déjà maintenant puisque l'œuvre est commencée." This is a rather tortured conclusion.

[65] Thus apparently LINDARS, *John* 295.

τὸν αἰῶνα; ὁ υἱὸς μένει εἰς τὸν αἰῶνα [66]); xii 14b-16 [67]); xiii 1 [68]);
xviii 9's ἵνα πληρωθῇ ὁ λόγος ὃν εἶπεν ὅτι οὓς δέδωκάς μοι οὐκ ἀπώλεσα
ἐξ αὐτῶν οὐδένα: [69]) xix 24's ἵνα ἡ γραφὴ πληρωθῇ ἡ λεγούσα διεμερί-
σαντο τὰ ἱμάτιά μου ἑαυτοῖς καὶ ἐπὶ τὸν ἱμάτιόν μου ἔβαλεν κλῆρον [70]);
xix 28's ἵνα τελειωθῇ ἡ γραφὴ λέγει Διψῶ [71]). Other possible examples
are xiii 3 [72]) and καὶ μετὰ τὸ ψωμίον τότε εἰσῆλθεν εἰς ἐκεῖνον ὁ Σατανᾶς
in xiii 27 [73]).

As was noted earlier ii 24-25; vii 39; viii 20; xi 51-52 and xix
36-37 [74]) should be included under this heading.

The following table will graphically show their distribution
according to types. These occurrences which appear as doubtful
asides will be marked with a question mark.

ype	1	2	3	4	5	6	7	8	9	10
2	?									x
6-8										x
9	?									x
12b-13										x
14b				x						
15										x
16			x							
17-18										x
24	?							x		
28		? x								
38			x							
41		x								
42		x								

Type		1	2	3	4	5	6	7	8	9	10
i	44		?						x		
ii	9b						x				
ii	11							x			
ii	17				x						
ii	21-22										x
ii	23-25										x
iii	16-21										x
iii	24						x				
iii	31-36										x
iv	2						x				
iv	9				x						
iv	23										x
iv	25		x								

[66]) BROWN, John 355 "seems such."
[67]) BROWN, John 455 admits such for xii 16 but hesitates about the rest;
likewise LINDARS, John 424 f. TENNEY, "Footnotes" 354, 364 admits only
xii 16 and put it under a different class, as was noted earlier. WIKENHAUSER,
Johannes 228 considers it all an aside.
[68]) Thus BROWN, John 563 f.; MORRIS, John 613; WIKENHAUSER, Johannes
249.
[69]) Thus BROWN, John, cxxxvi, 805; MORRIS, John 809, WIKENHAUSER,
Johannes 332.
[70]) Thus BROWN, John 897; MORRIS, John 809; WIKENHAUSER, Johannes
332.
[71]) Thus WIKENHAUSER, Johannes 333. For BULTMANN, John 674 it is
such in the source. BROWN, John 898 seemingly does not consider it such,
but see 929 f.
[72]) See WIKENHAUSER, Johannes 250. BROWN, John 548, 564 definitely
thinks otherwise.
[73]) Seemingly thus MORRIS, John 627. BROWN, John 587 disagrees but
admits that others hold differently.
[74]) Thus WIKENHAUSER, Johannes 335; SANDERS, John 413; MORRIS,
John 832. For BULTMANN, John 677 it is such already in the source.

Type	?	1	2	3	4	5	6	7	8	9	10
iv 44							x				
iv 54								x			
v 2				x							
v 25											x
vi 4	?			x							
vi 6									x		
vi 23	?						x				
vi 59					x						
vi 64b									x		
vi 71							x				
vii 2	? [75]			x							
vii 5							x				
vii 22							x				
vii 30											x
vii 39											x
vii 50									x		
viii 20											x
viii 27								x			
viii 35											x
ix 7				x							
ix 14				x							
ix 22-23							x				
x 6							x				
x 22-23							x				
xi 2								x			
xi 3							x				
xi 5								x			
xi 13							x				
xi 16									x		
xi 18					x						
xi 51-52											x
xii 4								x			
xii 6							x				
xii 14b-16										x	
xii 33							x				
xii 37-43										x	
xiii 1										x	
xiii 2	?						x				
xiii 3	?										x
xiii 11									x		
xiii 23										x	

Type	?	1	2	3	4	5	6	7	8	9
xiii 27										
xiii 28-29						x				
xiii 30										
xiv 22										x
xviii 5b	?						x			
xviii 9										
xviii 10b	?									x
xviii 13	?									x
xviii 14										x
xviii 15	?									x
xviii 16										x
xviii 26	?									x
xviii 28								x		
xviii 40										x
xix 13					x					
xix 14a						x				
xix 17					x					
xix 20	?							x		
xix 24										
xix 28										
xix 31					x					
xix 35								x		
xix 36-37										
xix 38								x		
xix 39										x
xix 40							x			
xx 2										x
xx 9								x		
xx 16					x					
xx 24					x					
xx 30-31									x	
xxi 2										x
xxi 7										x
xxi 7								x		
xxi 8	?							x		
xxi 12	?							x		
xxi 14									x	
xxi 19								x		
xxi 20 [76]										x
xxi 20 [77]										x
xxi 23							x			
xxi 24-25							x			

Unfortunately the different classifications are not altogether mutually exclusive. Thus vi 59 could also be considered an enumeration or summary; xii 14b-16 is a mixture of theological reflections

---

[75] TENNEY, "Footnotes" 353 shares this hesitation.
[76] ὃν ἠγάπα ὁ Ἰησοῦς.
[77] ὃς καὶ ἀνέπεσεν ... ὁ παραδιδούς σε.

and a remembrance of disciples; xiii 1 could be considered an explanation; xiii 3 could be considered a reference to Jesus' knowledge; xiii 30's ἦν δὲ νύξ could be classified as an indication of time; xviii 15 could come under explanations as could xix 31; xix 35 could be considered a theological reflection; xx 9 could be considered an explanation as could xxi 23; xxi 24-25 could be considered also as a mixture of an explanation and a summary.

As can be seen the asides are not evenly distributed among those chapters in which they are found [78]) and there are none in chapters xv-xvii, which are entirely presented as words of Our Lord. However, there does appear some connection with the amount of narrative in a given chapter and the likelihood of the appearance of asides as will be shown in the following table:

Chapter	Number of Verses	Asides per Verse [79])	Percentage of Narrative [80])
i	51	.176-.274	.553
ii	25	.200	.666
iii	36	.083	.202
iv	54	.111	.415
v	47	.042	.201
vi	71	.056-.084	.380
vii	52	.096-.115	.343
viii	48	.062	.245
ix	41	.073	.385
x	42	.047	.174
xi	57	.122	.500
xii	50	.100	.437
xiii	38	.158-.210	.368
xiv	31	.032	.052
xviii	40	.125-.250	.548
xix	42	.262-.286	.655
xx	31	.161	.611
xxi	25	.320-.400	.564

Based en the number of asides c. xxi stands out from the rest of the Gospel, and this criterion could be indicative of another author at work. This is another argument to be added to those for holding

---

[78]) TENNEY, "Footnotes" 351 says that they "are evenly distributed"; however, 362 he more correctly speaks of "random occurrence."

[79]) The range in some chapters results from taking the minimum and maximum number of asides as indicated by the presence or absence of a question mark in the first table.

[80]) The percentages are derived for the finite verbs in narrative against the number of verbs in each chapted as given in J. J. O'ROURKE, "The Historic Present in the Gospel of John," *JBL* 93 (1974) 586 f.

that the last chapter was not written by the one who gave most of the form to the preceding chapters. However, the criterion of asides per verse has to be used cautiously, since the asides differ from one another at times considerably by their length.

While it may be impossible to derive the sources of Jn or to discern the stages of composition, if there was more than one—which seems certain with regard to Jn xxi compared to the rest of the Gospel—it is also impossible to determine whether or not a given aside already existed as such in a source which was then taken over without change into the Gospel as we now have it [81]). This seems as true of the theological reflections as it does of the other types of asides. However, καὶ νῦν ἐστιν in iv 23; v 25 seem to be from the final stage of redaction.

[81]) See notes 71 and 74 above.

THE IDENTITY AND FUNCTION OF THE 'ΙΟΥΔΑΙΟΙ IN THE FOURTH GOSPEL

BY

JOHN ASHTON

Oxford

Within the past decade have appeared in the pages of this journal two important articles by Malcolm Lowe on the identity of οἱ 'Ιουδαῖοι in early Christian literature.[1] It is the first of these, focused primarily on the Fourth Gospel, that furnished the starting-point of the following reflections.

There are in fact three questions that arise in connection with the Johannine 'Ιουδαῖοι; two belong to exegesis, the third to history. The first asks who they are, the second what role or function they fulfil, the third why the evangelist regards them with such hostility. Always a puzzle, this third question has become even more teasingly problematic in recent years, as scholars have come to recognize the fundamental Jewishness of the Johannine group.[2] The three questions are obviously closely linked, and in spite of the fact that the third takes us out of the realm of textual understanding into that of historical explanation, it hangs upon the answers to the other two because it cannot be correctly formulated without them. This article is written in the first place as an exegetical study in the belief that there are still some strands left to be unravelled in this densely

---

[1] "Who were the 'Ιουδαῖοι?", *NT* 18 (1976) 101-130; "'Ιουδαῖοι of the Apocrypha", *NT* 23 (1981) 56-90.

[2] Hence the *prima facie* absurdity of any theory that sees the Gospel as a *Missionsschrift* written with the aim of gaining Jewish converts. So W. C. van Unnik, "The Purpose of St. John's Gospel", *Studia Evangelica* I [= *Texte und Untersuchungen* 73] (Berlin, 1959) 382-411, reprinted in W. C. van Unnik, *Sparsa Collecta* I *Supplements to Novum Testamentum* 29 (Leiden, 1973) 35-63; J. A. T. Robinson, "The Destination and Purpose of St. John's Gospel", *NTS* 6 (1959/60) 117-131. K. Bornhäuser some years earlier had provided a better basis of discussion by distinguishing six possible references of 'Ιουδαῖοι, five of which he detected in the Gospel: *Das Johannesevangelium: eine Missionsschrift für Israel* (Gütersloh, 1928). As the most widely appropriate rendering of the term, Bornhäuser proposed "die Fanatiker der Tora" (p. 140).

woven skein. But in disentangling the first two questions I hope to expose the third more clearly.

If the Gospel were indeed the *ungenähter Leibrock* Strauss thought it to be this programme could be carried through quite straightforwardly. Here I assume that Strauss was wrong; and I shall be arguing that certain passages of particular difficulty are best explained as the result of a process of redaction. (Which means utilizing some arguments of a historical kind to help in elucidating what are essentially exegetical questions.) This can be illustrated from the very first occurrence of 'Ιουδαῖοι in the Gospel, at Jn. 1:19, which is an example of a relatively late editorial insertion.[3] From the interpreter's point of view this instance is not very important: the most that can be said is that the introduction of the 'Ιουδαῖοι thus early bestows a somewhat hostile flavouring on the interrogation of John by the priests and Levites. Other passages present more problems.

I. IDENTITY

Lowe sets out to tackle the first of our questions, concerning the identity of the 'Ιουδαῖοι. His answer, shorn of frills, is that they were inhabitants of the province of Judea, not Jews, but Judeans.

This solution has on the whole been poorly received by professional *Neutestamentler*. Hartwig Thyen's verdict is milder than some others. He concedes that "M. Lowe im ganzen wohl zutreffend urteilt, daß die Wendung οἱ 'Ιουδαῖοι fast überall mit 'die Judäer' und nicht mit 'die Juden' zu übersetzen ist." But then he adds, unsurprisingly, that "für Johannes ist Judäa nicht eine beliebige geographische Provinz. Als Gottes und seines Gesandten 'Eigentum' ist Judäa vielmehr eine eminent theologische Provinz."[4] In fact Lowe himself acknowledges this possibility, or something like it, in an anticipatory summary of his conclusions with a curiously self-contradictory ring to it: "We shall see that the everyday meanings suffice, so that there is no need to see in John's Gospel some fantastic allegorical meaning of the word (though its author may have intended to convey an allegorical meaning too)."[5] Since it is the "allegorical meaning" that most interpreters of the Gospel,

---

[3] See R. T. Fortna, *The Gospel of Signs* (Cambridge, 1970), p. 170.

[4] "'Das Heil kommt von den Juden'", *Kirche, Fs. G. Bornkamm*, ed. D. Lührmann and G. Strecker (Tübingen, 1980), p. 179.

[5] "'Ιουδαῖοι", p. 110.

Bultmann above all, regard as the most important (the Jews standing as a living symbol of human obduracy and incomprehension
when confronted by the revelation of Jesus) one can readily understand why Lowe's discussion has not been accorded the close attention it deserves. But if what Thyen admits to be his "generally very
pertinent" observations are allowed, why should not future
translators adopt his suggestion and substitute 'Judeans' for 'Jews'
in all except possibly the four instances in which, according to
Lowe's own admission, this rendering does not quite work?[6] Since
the negative charge attached to the term 'Ιουδαῖοι within the Gospel
is conferred *by the Gospel itself*, why should it not be carried by 'Judeans' just as well as by 'Jews'? Of course the modern reader would
have to re-adjust his ideas and re-align his responses, but this is
surely Lowe's central point: if the evangelist was in fact referring
to the inhabitants of Judea (and their official leaders or representatives) and not to Jews in general, then it is wrong to continue to
use a totally misleading rendering in versions that are consequently
bound to be misinterpreted. (And who can say that, given the
power of suggestion over the human mind, the repeated association
of 'Jews' with animosity towards Jesus does not continue to instil
a certain anti-Semitism in many less sophisticated readers despite
all the determined disavowals by leading Christian churchmen?)

This is Thyen's answer, in his own words: "es sprechen alle
Anzeichen dafür, daß 'die Juden' seines Evangeliums die Vertreter
desjenigen 'Judentums' sind, das sich nach der Katastrophe des
jüdischen Krieges unter Führung des Lehrhauses von Jabne
regeneriert und in eben dem Maß, in welchem dessen moralischer
Autorität als deren Folge mehr und mehr auch rechtliche
Kompetenz zuwächst, zur normativen Kraft wird. Und weil diese
angesichts der Verwüstungen des Krieges nahezu unglaubliche
Regeneration des Judentums unter judäisch-pharisäischer Führung
erfolgte ..., ist die 'falsche' Übersetzung 'die Juden' am Ende tat-
sächlich die allein richtige." [7] So to Lowe's conclusion, which I
have suggested contains an inner contradiction, Thyen responds
with a paradox: the 'erroneous' translation is actually the only
correct one!

---

[6] Jn. 4:9 (bis), 22; and possibly 18:20.
[7] "Heil", p. 180.

In this case contradiction and paradox are both the offspring of confusion. Thyen bundles the three questions I have distinguished into the same bag. One must first separate out the question concerning the identity of the Ἰουδαῖοι (which belongs to the straightforward *story* level)[8] from that concerning the role and function of the Ἰουδαῖοι within the Gospel conceived as a complex web of meaning (which belongs on the level of allegory or theology). Alternatively, and perhaps more simply, one could say that whereas Lowe is interested in reference Thyen is more preoccupied with sense.[9] For the moment, following Lowe, we may stick with the first question.

The root difficulty is obvious enough: in translating Ἰουδαῖοι into a modern language like English or German one is forced to choose between alternative renderings. The English word 'Jews' suggests race and/or religion, but not (except in certain Arab circles) nationality, for which we now have the word 'Israeli'. 'Judeans' on the other hand can only refer to natives or inhabitants of Judea. In the original Greek both references are equally possible, and in Josephus (the contemporary author whose usage is most relevant to this issue) equally common. So here is a case where, as happens not infrequently, *any* translation involves a falsification. In three instances in the Fourth Gospel, 7:1, 11:7 and 11:54 (the last not picked out by Lowe) the rendering 'Judeans' is more immediately appropriate because in all three the Ἰουδαῖοι in question are directly linked with Judea. (Even the RSV hesitates over the first of them). But it would seem odd to reserve the rendering 'Judeans' for these three instances alone, when the Gospel employs the same word throughout. So what are we to say to Lowe's rather sweeping proposals?

Rites and festivals

Because of the sheerly linguistic difficulty there may be no completely satisfactory answer to this question; nevertheless a number of points may be made. In the first place we may turn to a consideration of the 'neutral' passages, from which the hostile over-

---

[8] This is what J. Louis Martyn called the *einmalig* level, see J. Louis Martyn, *History and Theology in the Fourth Gospel* (New York/Evanston, 1968), p. 9.

[9] From the opening paragraph of his article Lowe uses the words 'meaning' and 'reference' indiscriminately, as if they had the same meaning. The relevance and importance of the Fregean distinction will be defended *infra*.

tones typical of the Fourth Gospel are missing, starting from those in which the term τῶν 'Ιουδαίων is used to qualify a feast. These are 2:13; 6:4; 11:55 (Passover); 5,1 (unspecified, but also Passover); 7:2 (Tabernacles); and 19:42 (Preparation). To these must be added 2:6 (κατὰ τὸν καθαρισμὸν τῶν 'Ιουδαίων). In these cases, says Lowe, the various Greek terms should be rendered "Judean feast/Passover/rites of purification/day of Preparation."[10] Earlier, in a note, he had made a more modest claim for the last two passages, saying simply, "*It is conceivable* that ὁ καθαρισμὸς τῶν 'Ιουδαίων (Jn 2:6) and ἡ παρασκευὴ τῶν 'Ιουδαίων (Jn 19:42) have similar connotations (and should thus be rendered analogously)";[11] and he would presumably say the same of Jn 19:40, a remark upon burial customs. Now the trouble with Jn. 2:6 is that it alludes to an episode in Cana in Galilee; so by including this Lowe has exposed himself to an easy rejoinder. Klaus Wengst for one pounces upon this phrase and tosses it back at Lowe with this rather dismissive comment: "Mag Lowe für die zitierten Wendungen noch Möglichkeiten für eine — freilich nicht überzeugende — Argumentation finden, für 2,6 etwa ist sein Verständnis schlechterdings ausgeschlossen."[12]

Now Lowe's arguments, it seems to me, are not to be so lightly brushed aside. The point he is making is that in the Greco-Roman world in which John is writing religious customs and beliefs were associated with the regions and nations from which they originated. (I leave aside his intriguing suggestion that the reason for adding τῶν 'Ιουδαίων when mentioning the feasts is "to explain why people are faced with a journey to Judea":[13] for Jn. 2:6 at any rate this will not work.) Lowe thinks that at the period when they originated, "when Judaism was merely the religion of Judea in the strict sense," such phrases would have meant "feast/Passover of the Judeans". And "it is conceivable that such phrases continued somewhat inaccurately to have the same meaning at least long enough for the main author of John's Gospel to have understood them in this way."[14]

---

[10] "'Ιουδαῖοι", p. 129.
[11] "'Ιουδαῖοι", pp. 117-118, n. 54 [my italics].
[12] *Bedrängte Gemeinde und verherrlichter Christus* (Neukirchen-Vluyn, 1981), p. 39.
[13] "'Ιουδαῖοι", p. 116.
[14] "'Ιουδαῖοι", p. 117.

Lowe offers rather weak support for his suggestion that John knew these phrases, or something like them, from the Septuagint—ἐν πάσαις ταῖς ἑορταῖς οἴκου Ἰσραηλ (Ez. 45:17) is the nearest parallel he can find; but this does not invalidate his central contention that when Judea was still a country with a national identity the primary reference of ἑορτὴ τῶν Ἰουδαίων will have been to a feast of the Judeans. Wayne Meeks, commenting on an earlier proposal[15] that since the term Ἰουδαῖοι in the Fourth Gospel is primarily geographical it should be translated 'Judeans' rather than 'Jews', observes that "no choice may be necessary, for ancient authors in the age of syncretism tend to identify a cultic community either by its principal deity ... or by its place of origin ... When pagan authors speak of *Ioudaioi*, as they usually do when referring to the people we call Jews, the term denotes the visible, recognizable group with their more or less well-known customs, who have their origin in Judea but preserve what we would call their 'ethnic identity' in the diaspora."[16] This is an interesting and valuable observation, although the identification of a cultic community by its place of origin is not confined to "the age of syncretism". When in England people refer to a religious custom of Poles or Pakistanis they are implying that the custom in question originated in Poland or Pakistan. In fact one could often substitute "as is done in Poland" or "as the custom is in Pakistan" without changing the sense. Of course we are once again confronted with the awkward fact that 'Judeans' has a much more restricted denotation than Ἰουδαῖοι. And at least in the context of a wedding-feast in Galilee it would certainly seem odd to speak of *Judean* rites of purification. But this oddity derives from the limitation of the English word and does not affect the Greek. In the innumerable instances in which Josephus, by a variety of expressions, refers to the traditions, laws or customs of his own people, one would often be hard put to it to specify whether the primary reference is to Jews (of the diaspora) or Judeans.[17] In such cases it is a grave mistake

---

[15] By C. J. Cuming, "The Jews in the Fourth Gospel", *ExpT* 60 (1948/9) 290-292.

[16] "'Am I a Jew?' Johannine Christianity and Judaism", *Christianity, Judaism and Other Greco-Roman Cults. Studies for Morton Smith*, ed. J. Neusner (Leiden, 1975), p. 182.

[17] In *A.J.* XIII 397, for instance, the primary reference of τὰ πάτρια τῶν Ἰουδαίων ἔθη might be to Judeans (cf. XVIII 196), but in general Josephus was deeply conscious that the customs of which he was so proud, grounded in the law,

to attempt to adjudicate, as it were, between two conflicting claims, because the claims do not in fact conflict. The whole point of continuing to identify the customs of a particular group of immigrants or their descendants by the name of their nation of origin (whether one uses the adjective 'Polish' or the noun 'Poland') is that their practices have not changed: however long the group may have lived in their host country they can still be singled out by the customs which they share with 'the folks back home'—the Poles of Poland or the Pakistanis of Pakistan. Only if Poland or Pakistan ceased to exist would this natural association become problematic. This is of course what happened to Judea, but *not until after the Bar Cochba rebellion*, that is to say well after the publication of the Fourth Gospel.[18] We should therefore be on our guard against reading into the text of the Gospel a dissociation which did not exist at the time it was composed.

The foregoing discussion, focused as it is upon a handful of passages in the Gospel that are really on the periphery of our concerns (all involving the so-called 'neutral' usage of ᾿Ιουδαῖοι) may seem inordinately long. But this is a case in which it is easier to accept the premises than the conclusion: even in the isolated instance of purification rites practised in Galilee but identified as a custom τῶν ᾿Ιουδαίων (Jn. 2:6) there is no reason to deny that an implicit allusion to *Judea* is part of the meaning. But what is true is that the translator is put in an impossible position. Meeks' observation that ''no choice may be necessary'' does not apply to him, since he cannot avoid the anachronistic dissociation between the racial and religious meaning of 'Jews' and the national and regional meaning of 'Judeans'. So while there is some reason for dissatisfaction with Lowe's proposed rendering of these passages (''Judean feast'' etc.) this stems from the inadequacy of the English language rather than from any real weakness in his arguments.

---

were practised by Jews everywhere: ταῦτα πράττομεν οὐ μόνον ἐπ' αὐτῆς ᾿Ιουδαίας, ἀλλ' ὅπου ποτὲ σύστημα τοῦ γένους ἐστὶν ἡμῶν ... (*Ap.* I 32. Cf. *Ap.* II 277; *A.J.* XIV 65 f.; XV 50 etc.).

[18] One of the last contemporary examples of the local reference might be the expression οἵ ποτε ᾿Ιουδαῖοι that occurs in a 2nd century inscription from Smyrna (*IGRR* IV 1431.29 = *CII* 742). This is probably an allusion to Judean émigrés rather than (as used to be thought) to Anatolian converts from Judaism. Cf. A. J. Kraabel in *JJS* 33 (1982), p. 455. (I owe this reference to Dr. Peter Hayman.)

King of the Ἰουδαῖοι

The next phrase I want to discuss, ὁ βασιλεὺς τῶν Ἰουδαίων, poses similar problems for the translator, but takes us closer to the heart of the Gospel. In the Fourth Gospel Jesus is addressed as βασιλεὺς τοῦ Ἰσραήλ on two occasions, first by Nathanael (1:49), secondly by the crowd as he enters Jerusalem (12:13). This is an honorific title, appropriately put on the lips of people acknowledging Jesus' Messiahship. Βασιλεὺς τῶν Ἰουδαίων has a different ring and is not a natural way of speaking for native Jews. Lowe concludes that it would mean King of Judea in the strict sense for Palestinian Jews, but that Pilate, whose prefecture included Idumea and Samaria, might have had a larger area in mind. Obviously the real question is not what *Pilate* meant (how could we know?) but what the phrase means in the context of the Passion-narrative. This cannot be determined without a full exegesis. Here I simply want to argue that Lowe's suggested rendering, "King of Judea", does convey at least part of the meaning.

In a brief section headed, like this one, *King of the Ἰουδαῖοι*, Lowe cites among others Diodorus (who calls Aristobulus ὁ τῶν Ἰουδαίων βασιλεύς in *Lib. Hist.* XL, ii), but not, surprisingly, Josephus. This author employs a number of different expressions when speaking of the kings of Israel or Judah. In the section of the *Antiquities* in which he needs to distinguish between the two kingdoms (Books VIII-IX) he never qualifies βασιλεύς by τῶν Ἰουδαίων but always by Ἱεροσολύμων or τῶν Ἱεροσολυμιτῶν[19] as opposed to τῶν Ἰσραηλιτῶν. In Book VII his terminology fluctuates: David is called King of the Israelites and of the Hebrews, but also ὁ τῶν Ἰουδαίων βασιλεύς and βασιλεὺς τῆς Ἰουδαίας.[20] In the second half of the work Josephus speaks of an inscription in the temple of Jupiter Capitolinus in Rome reading "From Alexander, the King of the Ἰουδαῖοι",[21] and later of course the same title is given to Herod.[22]

In general it must be said that Josephus' usage does not bear out Lowe's contention that one possible reference of Ἰουδαῖοι is to Judeans *as opposed to* other Jews. Nothing in his account of the history

---

[19] Or occasionally ὁ τῶν δύο φυλῶν βασιλεύς: VIII 246, 298; cf. VIII 274; IX 4, 142. From Amaziah (IX 186) the two tribes merge into one (Judah).

[20] Israelites: VII 76, 120. Cf. VI 368 (Saul); Hebrews: VII 105, 128, 131; τῶν Ἰουδαίων: VII 72 (cf. *B.J.* VI 438); τῆς Ἰουδαίας: VII 101.

[21] XIV 36. There is some dispute about the name, but not about the title.

[22] XV 409; XVI 291, 311; cf. XIV 280.

of the two kingdoms gives any backing to the idea that 'Ιουδαῖοι could be an appropriate term for distinguishing the inhabitants of the southern kingdom from those of the north. In the case of the royal title, only when the danger of ambiguity is passed is Josephus prepared to call Herod King of the 'Ιουδαῖοι.[23] Of course there is no question of Herod's sovereignty extending beyond the confines of his own kingdom (Judea, in whatever extension is envisaged by the context); so it could still be argued that at least the primary reference of the term is to the citizens of Judea. And on the *story* level at which Lowe conducts his enquiry there is an even stronger case for saying that the people crying out for Jesus to be crucified can only be those natives of Judea to whose compassion and sense of nationhood Pilate appeals unavailingly when he asks them, "Shall I crucify your king?" (Jn. 19:15).

"Salvation is from the 'Ιουδαῖοι"

Most of the preceding discussion has been conducted on the small but relatively open and uncluttered terrain shared by philologists and exegetes—a piece of common ground free from bogs and hidden hollows. What follows is more contentious, not just in the sense that views diverge more sharply, but in the sense that arguments concerning the pre-history of the Gospel text often have the appearance of taking place in separate rooms, or perhaps in a single private den, reserved for exegetes and filled with the smoke of theological *parti pris*, where as in a game of stud poker one's most important cards are concealed from the eyes of the other players. If, like Bultmann, you put all your cards on the table, you risk having them swept aside by your opponent with scarcely a glance, so calmly confident is he of the superiority of his own hand.

In an article of a scope as restricted as this one there can be no question of a detailed defense of all the positions on which it is based. Here I assume not only that the Gospel as we have it was not composed *d'un seul jet* (the proofs of this leap to the eye) but that the attempt to discern different layers is both legitimate and fruitful. As Wellhausen sagely remarked long ago, the difficulty of the enterprise does not remove the reasons that made it necessary to

---

[23] Once, in a rhetorical appeal to the noble example of Jehoiachin, Josephus calls him βασιλεὺς 'Ιουδαίων (*B.J.* VI 103). But this is an instance of an exception that proves the rule.

embark on it in the first place.[24] I believe it can be shown (and of
course there is nothing novel in such a contention) that the majority
of the passages in which the term Ἰουδαῖοι has the meaning most
characteristic of the evangelist (that of a hostile group unable and
unwilling to accept the revelation of Jesus) belong to a relatively
late stratum, dating at the very earliest from the period immediately preceding the expulsion of the Johannine Christians from the
synagogue.

If this is so then Jesus' uncompromising assertion, to the
Samaritan woman, that "Salvation is from the Ἰουδαῖοι" (Jn.
4:22)—incidentally one of the passages Lowe finds hardest to fit in
with his own thesis—constitutes a challenge as well as a crux. In
fact there can be few phrases in the Gospel more capable of laying
bare an exegete's basic presuppositions than this one: it sends the
commentators flying in all directions. Some of course ignore the
difficulty,[25] others evade it. Bultmann, characteristically, dismisses
it as a gloss ("schon 1:11 zeigte, daß der Evangelist die Juden nicht
als das Eigentums- und als Heilsvolk ansieht"[26]—though surely
this is not what is implied by the expression ἐκ τῶν Ἰουδαίων!).
Bauer sees it as an example of a source somehow holding its own
against the evangelists's general intention.[27] Thyen, who adopts the
phrase for the title of his article, attempts, unsuccessfully in my
view, a harmonizing exegesis along salvation-historical lines. Of
these three different ways of tackling the problem Bauer's seems to
me the most promising, but it requires some modification because
it is *a priori* unlikely (and certainly not to be assumed) that an in-
telligent author will incorporate into his own finished work a dictum with whose general tenor he is in radical disagreement.

---

[24] "Wenn er [*sc.* the attempt to distinguish different strata in the Gospel] nur
schlecht gelingt, so ist das kein Beweis gegen das Vorhandensein der Gründe, die
ihn notwendig machen" (*Das Evangelium Johannis* [Berlin, 1908], p. 7).

[25] E.g. Bernard, who blandly remarks: "The evangelist is not forgetful of the
debt which Christianity owes to Judaism" (I, p. 148).

[26] *Johannesevangelium*, p. 139, n. 6. Thyen ("Heil", p. 169, n. 30) cites the even
harsher dismissal of J. Kreyenbühl: "Eine der abgeschmacktesten und un-
möglichsten Glossen ..., die jemals einen Text nicht nur entstellt, sondern in sein
gerades Gegenteil verkehrt haben."

[27] Rejecting the idea of a glossator operating under the influence of Paul, he
says, "Eher möchte man glauben, daß die Urform einer von Johannes in seinem
Sinne bearbeiteten Geschichte, in der sich Jesus vom jüdischen Standpunkt mit
den Samaritern auseinandersetzt, durchbricht" (*ad. loc.*). In alluding to this opinion of Bauer, Thyen contents himself with no other comment than an exclamation
mark!

Nevertheless even Birger Olsson, who is more insistent than most upon the principle of integral interpretation, admits that the passage "has a pre-history" and that "the author who gave the narrative its present form had at his disposal different kinds of material, each with its own 'history'."[28]

The positive attitude towards the ʾΙουδαῖοι implied in the saying under discussion is not, *pace* Thyen, easily reconcilable with the hostility displayed by the evangelist elsewhere. Even the single appellation ʾΙουδαῖος applied unequivocally to Jesus in Jn. 4:9 gathers *ipso facto* favourable associations which accord ill with the negative overtones it acquires later.[29]

On examining the episode of Jesus' encounter with the Samaritan woman for itself one can see that it is not an original unity; the profound discussion of the significance of living water has been superimposed upon an earlier, simpler story, whose main focus of interest is the relationship between Samaritans and ʾΙουδαῖοι. This story (4:4-10, 16-19) is continued in 4:20-26; "denn das Motiv von V. 5-9 wiederholt sich hier ja auf höherem Niveau."[30] This transposition onto a higher level is surely to be attributed to the evangelist or someone close to him: in particular the conjunction of spirit and truth (4:23) is typical of a work in which spirit is rarely named without some reference to word. So probably the best solution is that of Klaus Haacker,[31] who argues that the salvation phrase, far from being spatchcocked between repetitions

---

[28] *Structure and Meaning in the Fourth Gospel* (Lund, 1974), p. 119.

[29] Colin Hickling argues that in the first four chapters, in material taken over from the tradition, the Gospel displays "a generally affirmative attitude towards Judaism"; whereas "a different stance prevails in much of the remainder of the gospel, particularly in material likely to be owed either directly to the redactor or to tradition which he has extensively developed"; C. J. A. Hickling, "Attitudes to Judaism in the Fourth Gospel", *L'Evangile de Jean*, ed. M. de Jonge (Louvain, 1977) 347-354 (this quote pp. 351 f.).

[30] Bultmann, *Johannesevangelium*, p. 128.

[31] "Gottesdienst ohne Gotteserkenntnis. Joh 4.22 vor dem Hintergrund der jüdisch-samaritanischen Auseinandersetzung", *Wort und Wortlichkeit, Fs. E. Rapp* I, ed. B. Benzing *et al.* (Meisenheim am Glan, 1976) 110-126. This is easily the most penetrating of the spate of articles that have appeared on this subject in recent years. See I. de la Potterie, "'Nous adorons, nous, ce que nous connaissons, car le salut vient des Juifs'. Histoire de l'exégèse et interprétation de Jn 4, 22", *Biblica* 64 (1983) 74-115. De la Potterie himself has no time for source or redaction criticism: "le recours à des couches littéraires différentes qu'ont voulu pratiquer quelques critiques, ne sert à rien. Il pose plus de problèmes qu'il n'en résout" (pp. 85 ff.).

of the theme of worship, was an integral element of the source. This
he reconstructs as follows:

[19] The woman said to him, "Sir, I perceive that you are a prophet.
[20] Our fathers worshiped on this mountain; and you say that
Jerusalem is the place where men ought to worship." [21] Jesus said
to her, ... [22] "You worship what you do not know; we worship what
we know, for salvation is from the Jews." ... [25] The woman said
to him, "I know that Messiah is coming (he who is called Christ);
when he comes, he will show us all things." [26] Jesus said to her, "I
who speak to you am he."

Haacker marshalls an impressive case in favour of the thesis that
the phrase under discussion harks back to a debate between Jews
and Samaritans, probably centred upon Gn. 49:8-12, Jacob's blessing on Juda (which understandably posed problems for Samaritan
interpreters): [32] "Diese Hypothese wird zur Gewißheit, wenn man
bedenkt, daß der Judaspruch in Gn. 49 im Rahmen des *Jakobssegens*
steht. An '*unseren Vater Jakob*', mit dessen Namen der Ort der
Handlung verbunden war, hatte die samaritanische Frau im
Gespräch mit Jesus zuvor erinnert und sich danach noch einmal auf
'unsere Väter' berufen. Die Antwort Jesu in V. 22 trifft ins
Schwarze, wenn ihre Spitzenaussage ausgerechnet aus Gn. 49
geschöpft ist." [33]

Even if *Gewißheit* seems too strong a claim for Haacker's thesis,
and the details of his reconstruction must in the nature of things remain in doubt, his explanation of the present state of the text
(*überlieferungskritisch*, as he points out, rather than *literarkritisch*) is
powerful and convincing. The missionary thrust into Samaria
reflected in this story will obviously have preceded (by how long it
is impossible to say) the angry encounters between the Johannine
group and the Jewish authorities illustrated in the Gospel from ch.
5 onwards. [34] It is worth bearing in mind that as we know from
Josephus, although the Samaritans were in certain circumstances
prepared to identify themselves as Ἰουδαῖοι, they would desist from

---

[32] "Die samaritanische Chronik II bezieht die Stelle wie der jüdische Chronist
auf David und Salomo—und beugt damit wohl bewußt einer eschatologischen
(messianischen) Auslegung vor" ("Gottesdient", p. 121).

[33] "Gottesdienst", pp. 122 f.

[34] This is not to endorse Raymond Brown's view that the wave of theological
speculation reflected in ch. 5 was actually precipitated by the admission of
Samaritan converts into the Johannine group. See *The Community of the Beloved
Disciple* (London, 1979), pp. 36 ff.

doing so as soon as the *religious* differences had been brought out into the open.[35] And that the contrast between Samaritans and Jews
at this point is predominantly religious can hardly be contested.
Nonetheless the passage does cohere more easily than Lowe himself
has spotted with his general view that 'Ιουδαῖοι is to be translated
'Judeans'. After all, the immediate context is the opposition between two sacred mountains, Gerizim and Sion, and when
Jerusalem is explicitly mentioned it is natural to take the 'Ιουδαῖοι
that follows as referring in the first place to the people of that
region—the Judeans. If it be objected that such a rendering cannot
but distort the sense of the passage as a whole, then one must
reiterate that this is not a problem for the interpreter but for the
translator, handicapped as he is by the conceptual distinction between Jews and Judeans with the Greek word alone neither contains nor imposes. (The same can be said of the other passage that
causes Lowe problems: ''I have always taught ... in the temple,
where all 'Ιουδαῖοι come together'' (Jn. 18:20): although the
primary reference here must be a broad one to Jews from all parts
of the world comming to worship in Jerusalem, it would be patently
absurd to leave the Judeans out!)

How then is the assertion that ''salvation is from the Ju-
deans/Jews'' to be interpreted in the light of the Gospel as we know
it, and how would such an integral reading differ from that implied
in the original context? If, as I have suggested, the passage recalls
a missionary thrust from south to north in the early days of the
Johannine community, then one might suppose that this mission
did in fact originate in Judea. (Ch. 1 similarly reflects an even
earlier mission further north, designed to persuade the people of
Galilee that Jesus was the Messiah.) Whatever additional meanings
the term 'Ιουδαῖοι acquired from its usage in the Fourth Gospel
there is then no need to reject an original association with Judea in
the dictum ''salvation is from the 'Ιουδαῖοι''. Quite simply, Judea
is conceived as the country of origin of Jesus the Messiah (Jn. 1:41;
4:25) and *as such* the source of salvation.

Lowe asserts (it is another occasion of difficulty for him) that
''Jesus' supposedly Judean origin ... is hardly in evidence
anywhere in John's Gospel (except conceivably at Jn. 4:44)''.[36]

---

[35] *A.J.* XI 340-344; cf. Lowe, '''Ιουδαῖοι'', p. 125, n. 75.
[36] '''Ιουδαῖοι'', p. 125, n. 77.

This is not so, since the Prologue too, as Wayne Meeks has shown, evinces the same basic conviction that Judea is Jesus' ἴδια πατρίς, the place where he truly belongs but can no longer find a home.[37] Meeks points out that the verb μένειν, so much part of the evangelist's developed theology, is used of Jesus' sojourns in Galilee (1:39f.; 2:12; 7:9), Samaria (4:40), Transjordan (10:40) and Ephraim, when "he no longer went about openly among the Judeans" (11, 54), but never of his visits to Judea and Jerusalem.[38] There is thus evidence, strongly supported in Ch. 4 itself, of a movement from Judea to Galilee and (less significantly for the Gospel as a whole) Samaria. Such a movement is more than just a historical echo of Jesus' various journeys: it indicates a passage, a transplantation even, of a message (a gospel in the original sense) from the place where it first sprang up to a more welcoming soil.

This is not the place to argue in detail how the antipathy between north and south is reflected elsewhere in the Gospel. (The evidence is well laid out by Meeks.) But there is no reason to suppose that it was motivated from the outset by especially deep theological concerns. Indeed the passage which best illustrates it, Jn. 7:40-52 (from which the term Ἰουδαῖοι is significantly absent), is a fairly simple, synoptic-type controversy story, centred straightforwardly upon the messianic claims characteristic of the foundation charter of the community (if that is not too pretentious a title for the signs source), the twin titles of 'prophet' and 'Messiah'.

By the time the Gospel was completed, the word Ἰουδαῖοι had acquired, all too evidently, much more sinister connotations. But the evangelist never repudiated the basic tradition that the original home (πατρίς, ἴδια) of the Messiah/Saviour was Judea. This is shown by his readiness both to preface his work with a hymn testifying to this truth and to build some of his most profound theological reflections into a simple account of an early mission in Samaria.

Judeans in Galilee?

The only other texts that present difficulties for Lowe's argument occur close together towards the end of Ch. 6 (verses 41 and 52).[39]

---

[37] "Galilee and Judea in the Fourth Gospel", *JBL* 85 (1966) 159-169. Thyen gives further support for this view: "Heil", p. 171 n. 38.

[38] "Galilee", p. 167.

[39] Most observers of the Johannine Jews have some difficulty in squeezing these two instances into their general theories; for the Ἰουδαῖοι in ch. 6 are neither Ju-

Lowe affirms that in the following chapter, where the Gospel speaks of Jesus' fear of the Judeans, the opening words, ''after this'' refer to a confrontation between Jesus and 'Ιουδαῖοι in the synagogue at Capernaum (Jn. 6:59). ''Thus the text as it stands forces us to understand these to have been Judeans too *in some sense*''.[40] This is perhaps acceptable at the level of integral interpretation (though one is entitled to ask, Judeans in what sense?), but almost ever since the advent of critical exegesis dangerous cracks have been detected in the bridge between Chs. 6 and 7,[41] and few scholars would be happy with an argument resting on this ramshackle structure alone. (In any case if there were Judeans in Galilee in any numbers, Jesus would scarcely have been able to evade them by staying there!) Of course there is no reason why *Jews* should not have been in Galilee; indeed, in the broad sense the Galileans had just as good a title to the name 'Ιουδαῖοι as their fellow-Jews further afield in the diaspora.[42] All the same, if Lowe is right in his contention that elsewhere in the Gospel 'Ιουδαῖοι refers to Judeans, some explanation must be sought for the shift of reference in this single passage.

One possible explanation is that Ch. 6, or at least this section of it, was composed at a time when the regional connotations of 'Ιουδαῖοι had become faded or blurred—sufficiently at any rate to allow the evangelist to employ the term in a setting in which, as soon as one's attention is drawn to the geographical oddities, it can be seen to be about as much in place as a hornet in a bee-hive.[43] And if the incongruity slips past most readers unobserved, this

---

deans in any obvious sense, nor religious authorities, nor even uniformly hostile, since they bicker among themselves (γογγύζειν, 6:33; μάχεσθαι, 6:52) about how to take the words of Jesus. See the comparative table drawn up by U. C. von Wahlde on pp. 49 f. of an article yet to be considered: ''The Johannine 'Jews': A critical survey'', *NTS* 28 (1981/2) 33-60. An exception is J. W. Bowker, who makes these texts the corner-stone of his theory that the one section of Judaism ''which almost always appears as taking up a position of unquestioning and invariable opposition to Jesus ... is not the Jews, it is the Pharisees'': ''The Origin and Purpose of St. John's Gospel'', *NTS* 11 (1964/5) 398-408. Why I disagree with this view (quoted from p. 400) will emerge later.

[40] '''Ιουδαῖοι'', p. 120 (my italics).
[41] E.g. Wellhausen, *Evangelium*, pp. 28, 34.
[42] See for example Jos. *B.J.* II 232 (a particularly clear instance): ... πόλλων ἀναβαινόντων 'Ιουδαίων ἐπὶ τὴν ἑορτὴν ἀναιρεῖταί τις Γαλιλαῖος. More generally see *B.J.* II 195 ff.
[43] Such a suggestion would fit in well with Barnabas Lindars' thesis, argued on totally other grounds, that ch. 6 did not belong to the first edition of the Gospel but to the second: *Behind the Fourth Gospel* (London, 1971), pp. 47-50.

might be because the evangelist has succeeded in foisting upon the
Judeans those qualities of blindness and obduracy which make
them the obvious candidates at any point in the story where interlocutors with just such characteristics are required—even though
their internal dissensions here jar somewhat with the stereotype.
Here we can refine slightly upon Lowe's assertion that even the
'Ιουδαῖοι operating in Galilee were "in some sense" Judeans.
Within the Gospel as a whole their role of uncomprehending ques-
tioners is roughly that which is associated with the Judeans
elsewhere, most pertinently in the preceding chapter.

In view of the other unusual features of the passage in which they
occur we may prefer to leave these two instances in Ch. 6 out of account. If we opt for this course then we can see that wherever
'Ιουδαῖοι is used of actual human beings with a role to play in the
narrative, these are natives or inhabitants of Judea. But to say this
is to say very little: the nature and significance of the role they play
is left undefined, and the reasons for assigning it to them unex-
plored. Nor, I suspect, would Lowe himself be satisfied with such
a conclusion. For he is anxious to, as it were, contain the infection,
to argue that without further specification 'Ιουδαῖοι not only can but
must refer to Judeans; and at the close of his article he speaks of
"the Palestinian use of 'Ιουδαῖοις to distinguish Judeans from
Galileans etc."[44] as the one that is characteristic of the gospels in
general. Such a usage, if established, would indeed be singular: it
would be like using the word 'Poles' to *distinguish* the inhabitants of
Poland from Poles living abroad. Here it is not enough to show that
the term is constantly employed to refer to natives of the country
concerned—which in any case is a fact too obvious to require proof,
possibly even a tautology. One would need, surely, *separate words*
(poles apart) for natives and expatriates, which is what we do not
have.[45] In the whole of his long article I have detected only one

---

[44] "'Ιουδαῖοι", p. 130.

[45] Unsurprising in itself, the ambivalence of the Greek word reflects an identical
ambivalence in the Aramaic word יהודי —one that had existed at least since the
5th century. Thus in transcribing the phrase חרי יהודיא —'freemen of the
Jews'/'Jewish freemen' (Cowley, 30:19), the copyist made a significant slip,
writing instead חרי יהוד —'freemen of Judea'/'Judean freemen' (Cowley 31:18),
obviously without noticing the difference. This establishes the local reference. But
later in the same letter the writer (Yedoniah) speaks on behalf of יהודיא כל בעלי
יב —'Jews, citizens of Elephantine' (30:22/31:22; cf. line 26 of both documents).
Similarly (to take but one further example) one can contrast יהודין זי יב (20:2) with
יהודיא די ביהוד (Ezra 5:1).

isolated instance (which Lowe labels 'instructive') of such a use, and that is Jos. *A.J.* XVII 254 ff., in which, as he says, "Josephus states first that many Galileans, Idumeans and people from Jericho and Perea had come to Jerusalem to celebrate Pentecost, where they were joined by αὐτοὶ 'Ιουδαῖοι. Since all had come to a Jewish festival, and the Jewish areas of Palestine were precisely Galilee, Perea, Judea and Idumea, αὐτοὶ 'Ιουδαῖοι here indisputably signifies *the Judeans in the strict sense''*. But as Lowe admits, "later in the same passage he relates how the Romans attacked the 'Ιουδαῖοι, now meaning *the whole crowd*,"[46] which makes it clear that the word itself does not carry the required specification.[47] Much more typical of Josephus' usage is his distinction between οἱ ἐν τῇ 'Ιουδαίᾳ κατοικοῦντες and αἱ τρεῖς τοπαρχίαι προσκείμεναι (A.J. XIII 50) or between two groups of 'Ιουδαῖοι, the first οἱ ἐν τῇ 'Ιουδαίᾳ and the second οἱ ἐν 'Αλεξανδρίᾳ κατοικοῦντες (A.J. XIV 113).

But if 'Ιουδαῖοι has a broader extension than either 'Jews' or 'Judeans' we should even so be grateful to Lowe for alerting us to the dangerously misleading inaccuracy of what he calls "the current mistranslations".

Authorities

Before addressing the second big question, that of role or function, we may strive for a little more precision in the first. If Jesus' adversaries are Judeans, what kind of Judeans are they? Lowe does not bother with this extra refinement; and when others wonder out loud whether it is perhaps the authorities rather than the general populace who are held in the evangelist's sights, it is of Jewish rather than of Judean authorities that they do the wondering. In fact this neat distinction between the Jewish people (with whom on the whole the evangelist had no quarrel) and their official representatives (the real target of his resentment) is for many not a complementary but an alternative way of clearing the Fourth Gospel from the ugly suspicion of anti-Semitism. Thus Urban C. von Wahlde, who has industriously collated the views of a large number of earlier commentators, concludes: "although a current trend in scholarship is to see the Johannine Jews as comprising both the common people and the authorities, upon close examination we

---

[46] "'Ιουδαῖοι", p. 105, n. 14.
[47] Here it is given by the little word αὐτοί!

found that there is little or no reason for seeing the Johannine Jews as common people except for the case of 6.41,52''.[48] (A further hint of certain peculiarities in the use of the term in this chapter.)

There is no need to contest von Wahlde's findings that with this couple of exceptions every instance of what he calls the characteristic Johannine usage involves a reference to Jewish (or Judean) authorities. Unfortunately however this result is not itself of any great moment. For what John writes, usually at any rate, is not οἱ ἄρχοντες, or some equivalent expression like οἱ ἐν τέλει, but simply οἱ Ἰουδαῖοι, and this in spite of the fact that such terms as ἄρχοντες, ἀρχιερεῖς, and even Φαρισαῖοι are known and available to him. Like many others, including Lowe, von Wahlde fails to distinguish between sense and reference. Long ago Bultmann had pointed out that in the Fourth Gospel "die verschiedenen Typen von Reichen und Armen, Zöllnern und Dirnen, Heilung such-enden Kranken und wißbegierigen Fragern sind verschwunden. Nur wo der vom Evangelisten benutzte Stoff es erfordert, begegnen einzelne Personen".[49]

He drew the correct conclusion that the Jews in the Fourth Gospel have a symbolic role and that this is one of the features that set it apart from the other three. To insist, with however painstaking a precision, on the *reference* of the term is still to fall short of the *sense*.

This distinction, which is important for my argument at this point, is not quite the same as the well-known Fregean distinction,[50] though it can be explained by starting from Frege's most famous example, that of the morning-star and the evening-star, which both have the same reference (the planet Venus) but, obviously, different senses. One can answer the question, "What is the morning-star?" satisfactorily by saying, "it is actually a planet," and the further question, "Which planet?" by "the planet

---

[48] "Johannine 'Jews'" cf. n. 39, p. 54.

[49] *Johannesevangelium*, p. 59, n. 5.

[50] G. Frege, "Über Sinn und Bedeutung", *Zeitschrift für Philosophie und philosophische Kritik* 100 (1892) 25-50 [ET in *Translations from the Philosophical Writings of Gottlob Frege*, ed. P. Geach and M. Black (Oxford, 1952) pp. 56-78]. The word *Bedeutung* means 'meaning', which makes it a very clumsy tool for the use to which Frege puts it: 'reference' is vastly more apt. Frege applied the term to sentences as well as to proper names, and reached the curious conclusion that all sentences with the same truth-value (*Wahrheitswerth*), i.e. true or false, have the same *Bedeutung*.

Venus''. And the same two answers would serve equally well to identify the evening-star. But what (though he does not say so) is presumably the source of Frege's example, a couplet attributed to Plato in the *Greek Anthology*,[51] shows that the simple business of identification may be a long way from giving a full understanding of the *meaning* of the two terms. In fact in some contexts one could give a perfectly proper answer to the question, "What does 'morning-star' mean?" without mentioning the planet Venus at all. Such a precise identification is certainly irrelevant to an understanding of the Greek couplet.

Similarly the question asked by both Lowe and von Wahlde falls outside the realm of exegesis and in any case is incapable of eliciting the *kind* of answer exegesis requires. For the Fourth Gospel is not an unpretentious and impartial record of events concerning certain individuals and groups: it is a work of literature, and since this is so what really counts towards understanding the various characters is a knowledge of their role or function within the whole.[52]

In works of pure literature, like the majority of plays and novels, one can *identify* the characters simply by consulting a list of the *dramatis personae*. Who is Oswald? Steward to Goneril. In the case of the gospels, which resemble 'historical' plays or novels in this respect, the matter is more complex. They derive much of their material, and most of their characters, from outside their own world of discourse (an obvious possible exception is the beloved disciple in John).[53] So it is certainly legitimate to attempt to answer the question, "Who were the ʼΙουδαῖοι?" as Lowe does, by appealing to external as well as to internal evidence. But we can no more understand the gospels by answering this and similar questions of *reference* than we can understand a play of Shakespeare by scanning the list of *dramatis personae*. Exegesis demands a total reading: the *sense* we attach to the characters (Hamlet's indecisiveness,

---

[51] Ἀστὴρ πρὶν μὲν ἔλαμπες ἐνὶ ζωοῖσιν Ἑῷος·
νῦν δὲ θανὼν λάμπεις Ἕσπερος ἐν φθιμένοις.

(*Anth. Graec.* VII 670)

[52] There is no reason why what is obviously true of individual characters (Judas the traitor, Thomas the doubter) should not also apply to groups and gatherings. The specific role and function of several specific characters in John has been studied by Eva Kraft, "Die Personen des Johannesevangeliums", *Evangelische Theologie* 16 (1956) 18-32.

[53] One may also wonder whether characters such as Nathanael, Nicodemus and Lazarus have been invented *ad hoc* by the evangelist.

Macbeth's ambition, Othello's jealousy) proceeds from and is justified by a reading of the work in question.[54]

Here, however, the interests of the exegete by no means co-incide with those of the historian.[55] Of course the gospels furnish evidence—of a kind—for a historian asking general questions about the reference of various terms (Scribes, Pharisees, chief-priests, 'Ιουδαῖοι) at the time of their composition. But here history and in-terpretation must be allowed to go their separate ways. The wilful obduracy of the 'Ιουδαῖοι of the Fourth Gospel does not prove that this is how the real 'Ιουδαῖοι actually behaved, any more than the portrayal of Richard III in Shakespeare's play of that name is reliable evidence for the character of the historical Richard. Cer-tainly the historian has a right to stake a claim in this territory and his claim must be respected; but with this proviso the exegete too must be permitted to work his own lode. In a work of literature, especially one with as urgent a rhetoric as that of the Fourth Gospel, the important question concerns the role or function of the various characters: this is what I have called *sense*.

II. FUNCTION

Bultmann writes of the symbolic function of the Jews in one of those gleaming little cameos of compressed insight that stud the pages of his commentary.[56] Given that he soars high above the *story* level which is as far as any question concerning identity or reference can reach,[57] what he has to say can scarcely, as far as it goes, be

---

[54] Not that one can sum up any of these characters in a word. Even personages of a size to spark off bright new adjectives (Pickwick, Quixote, Tartuffe) always elude the grasp of the wordmakers.

[55] The relationship between exegesis and history exhibits a kind of master/slave dialectic which brooks no merging of roles. I hope to develop this point elsewhere.

[56] Bultmann's masterly treatment of the central question still leaves room on the periphery for two other problems: (a) the *untypical* usages (discussed in the first part of this article; (b) the employment of different terms (discussed in what follows).

[57] Theoretically one could ask about the sense (function) of the 'Ιουδαῖοι without budging from the *story* level, because the distinction between sense and reference does not overlap with that between the *story* and what is variously thought of as the allegorical, symbolic or theological meaning of the Gospel. On the lower level the function of the 'Ιουδαῖοι is to display the surprising unreceptiveness to Jesus' message of his own people in his own lifetime. On the higher level (which, follow-ing the basic insight of Clement of Alexandria, I prefer to think of as the spiritual meaning of the Gospel), it is hard to see any point at all in questions restricted to reference.

faulted; nor, in my view can it be put more succinctly. Accordingly I quote it here for the sake of completeness:

> The term οἱ 'Ιουδαῖοι, characteristic of the Evangelist, gives an overall portrayal of the Jews, viewed from the standpoint of Christian faith, as the representatives of unbelief (and thereby, as will appear, of the unbelieving "world" in general). The Jews are spoken of as an alien people, not merely from the point of view of the Greek readers, but also, and indeed only properly, from the stand-point of faith; for Jesus himself speaks to them as a stranger and correspondingly, those in whom the stirrings of faith or of the search for Jesus are to be found are distinguished from the "Jews", even if they are themselves Jews. In this connection therefore even the Baptist does not appear to belong to the "Jews". This usage leads to the recession or to the complete disappearance of the distinctions made in the Synoptics between different elements in the Jewish people; Jesus stands over against the Jews. Only the distinction between the mass of the people and its spokesmen occasionally proves to be necessary for the Evangelist's presentation of his theme; but this, characteristically, is often drawn in such a way that the 'Ιουδαῖοι, who are distinguished from the ὄχλος, appear as an authoritative body set over the Jewish people. Οἱ 'Ιουδαῖοι does not relate to the empirical state of the Jewish people, but to its very nature (Wesen).[58]

What then can be added? About the role of the Jews as such, nothing at all. But since we are now concerned with sense or meaning, and since meaning, as de Saussure taught the structuralists, is conveyed by contrasts or oppositions (not always binary), one can still put questions about those other actors (aside from the ὄχλος and the ἄρχοντες to whom Bultmann alludes) who appear now and then alongside the Jews, either supporting them or blending with them or even elbowing them aside. I am thinking of such terms as Φαρισαῖοι, ἀρχιερεῖς and, most mysterious of all, κόσμος.

Important though their role is, the Jews are not ubiquitous in the Fourth Gospel, and it is worth asking why. Why in particular, when they play such an important part in the Passion narrative, does Jesus not name them at all in his urgent warnings to his disciples the previous evening?

Pharisees

It is widely held nowadays that 'Pharisees' in this Gospel (and most pertinently in chs. 7 and 9) is virtually a synonym for 'Jews' and belongs to the same level of redaction.[59] (Even Bultmann

---

[58] The Gospel of John (Oxford, 1971), pp. 86 f.; Johannesevangelium, p. 59.

[54] E.g. Wengst: "beide Begriffe erscheinen als Einheit, sie explizieren sich gegenseitig." An inspection of all the relevant texts shows that "das Judentum als einheitliche, pharisäisch bestimmte Größe auftritt" (Bedrängte Gemeinde, p. 42). Notwithstanding my reservations I find Wengst's discussion careful and thorough.

thinks this about ch. 9). Thus Martyn mentions but does not examine the opinion of Wellhausen and Spitta that 9:18-23 were added by the evangelist to his source.[60] But like Ernst Bammel, I believe that "the Pharisees-passages reflect controversies between the Christian community and shades of opinion within the Jewish world. They represent old valuable tradition."[61] What we have in 9:18 is not just a shift in nomenclature but a radical hardening of attitudes. In fact the blind man himself, whose cure foreshadows and symbolizes his conversion, is not present at the interrogation of his parents that leads to the sentence of excommunication. One senses at this point that the decision has already been taken, the rift is inevitable. Not so in the earlier conversation between the Pharisees and the blind man: the Pharisees debate among themselves on familiar subjects along familiar lines. What the blind man eventually says of Jesus, ὅτι προφήτης ἐστίν, v. 17, constitutes a relatively modest claim, one that had been made for Jesus from a very early stage. The same is true, of course, of 'Messiah', but by now this had evidently gathered a lot more weight. The Pharisees make a brief reappearance at the end of the chapter, in a conclusion (9:40-41) which as it stands is a brilliant example of Johannine irony. Originally however the question they put to him (Μὴ καὶ ἡμεῖς τυφλοί ἐσμεν;) could have been a genuine plea for enlightenment.

I have already mentioned the little controversy story at the end of ch. 7. Its true beginning is in 7:32, where the chief priests and Pharisees (an alliance yet to be elucidated) send out officers (ὑπηρέται) to arrest Jesus. This discussion too is conducted on a relatively low level, arising out of claims already made for Jesus in the signs-source. At the opening of the following chapter (8:12-20) the Pharisees are still present. Here the subject matter is richer, since Jesus brings up the topic of his Father (neither term nor topic occurs in ch. 7); but whatever interpretation one puts on this passage there is a natural break at 8:20. The Jews of 8:22 *can* be identified with the Pharisees of 8:13, but such an identification, on the level of integral interpretation, is no reason for refusing to recognize separate strata at this point. Besides, the debate here (on

---

[60] *History* (cf. n. 8), p. 13, n. 31.

[61] "'John did no miracle': John 10:41'", *Miracles*, ed. C. F. D. Moule (London, 1965) 179-202. This fine article deserves more widespread recognition. (This quote, p. 197).

the conditions of legally admissible testimony) is an ordinary rabbinical-style argument, very unlike the refutation by riddle, typically Johannine, that follows.

The one passage that might be thought perhaps to tell against the distinction I have been advocating between Jews and Pharisees occurs in ch. 12: ὅμως μέντοι καὶ ἐκ τῶν ἀρχόντων πολλοὶ ἐπίστευσαν εἰς αὐτόν, ἀλλὰ διὰ τοὺς Φαρισαίους οὐχ ὡμολόγουν ἵνα μὴ ἀποσυνάγωγοι γένωνται (12:42). This verse is odd in more ways than one. In general, chs. 11 and 12 present a rather different view of the 'Ιουδαῖοι from the rest of the Gospel. Apart from 11:8, 54, two of the three passages where the 'Ιουδαῖοι can only be Judeans, they are presented in a sympathetic light: 11:19, 31, 36, 45; 12:9, 11. So there is already some doubt about the level of redaction of these chapters. At 12:42 the Pharisees, in distinction from the authorities, are credited with the power of dismissal from the synagogue, whereas earlier (11:46; 12:19) they are tacitly assumed to be identical with those same authorities. Bammel says of the mention of the Pharisees here and at 3:1, "this is redaction level", without further explanation.[62] Presumably the passage was written after the composition of ch. 9 (to which it unambiguously alludes) had been completed; but it is puzzling (and possibly a weak point in my argument) that the evangelist has not written διὰ τοὺς 'Ιουδαίους at this point or, as elsewhere, διὰ τὸν φόβον τῶν 'Ιουδαίων (cf. 7:13; 9:22; 20:19). One possible explanation, though not one that can figure as part of the exegesis, is that the writer was thinking directly of the Pharisees at Yavneh.

However these passages are finally interpreted we must distinguish here between two separate theses. First there is the general thesis that in the great majority of instances commonly accepted as 'typical' the term 'Ιουδαῖοι occurs in passages that which suggest that the rift between Christians and Jews is either imminent or has already taken place. Secondly there is the thesis that the Pharisee passages, or at any rate the most important of them, reflect an earlier stage in the history of the Johannine community, when real debate with the leaders of the parent community was still possible and still in fact going on. The latter thesis nicely coheres with the former but is not required to establish it.

---

[62] I think Bammel is right, and that it belongs to the level of redaction at which, as we shall see in the next section, the Pharisees are assigned a role in the planning and preliminaries of Jesus' arrest.

Passion-narrative

In considering the role of the Ἰουδαῖοι in the Passion-narrative we may best begin with the story of the arrest, which is as close as the Fourth Gospel ever gets to the synoptic tradition. The first verse for examination, 18:3, contains no explicit mention of the Ἰουδαῖοι. (They are waiting in the wings). It is convenient to set out John and the corresponding passage in Mark in parallel columns. (It is to be noted that in Mark and Matthew the arrest follows immediately upon the account of the prayer in the Garden, which John of course omits.)

Mk. 14:43 (= Mt. 26:47)	Jn. 18:3
καὶ εὐθὺς ... παραγίνεται ὁ Ἰούδας εἷς τῶν δώδεκα, καὶ μετ' αὐτοῦ ὄχλος μετὰ μαχαιρῶν καὶ ξύλων παρὰ τῶν ἀρχιερέων καὶ τῶν γραμματέων καὶ τῶν πρεσβυτέρων.	ὁ οὖν Ἰούδας λαβὼν τὴν σπεῖραν καὶ ἐκ τῶν ἀρχιερέων καὶ ἐκ τῶν Φαρισαίων ὑπηρέτας ἔρχεται ἐκεῖ μετὰ φανῶν καὶ λαμπάδων καὶ ὅπλων.

These texts are different enough to make any theory of direct dependence unlikely, but close enough to point back to a common tradition. Since apart from two exceptions stemming from the Matthean redaction (Mt. 21:45; 27:62) the curious conjunction of ἀρχιερεῖς and Φαρισαῖοι is confined to John, we may suppose that it is the evangelist or one of his school who has substituted Φαρισαῖοι for the γραμματεῖς and/or πρεσβύτεροι he presumably inherited. Leaving aside the σπεῖρα (what was a Roman cohort doing here?), we may notice the presence of the ὑπηρέται, who figure in an earlier story of an (attempted) arrest, a story in which, as here, they were sent by οἱ ἀρχιερεῖς καὶ οἱ Φαρισαῖοι (7:32; cf. 7:45). What is more, it was these same 'chief priests and Pharisees' who according to John engineered Jesus' arrest and execution in the first place. Here too there is a fairly close parallel, this time in Matthew:

Mt. 26:3 (cf. Mk. 14:1; Lk. 22:2)	Jn. 11:47-53
Τότε συνήχθησαν οἱ ἀρχιερεῖς καὶ οἱ πρεσβύτεροι τοῦ λαοῦ εἰς τὴν αὐλὴν τοῦ ἀρχιερέως τοῦ λεγο-	Συνήγαγον οὖν οἱ ἀρχιερεῖς καὶ οἱ Φαρισαῖοι συνέδριον ... εἷς δέ τις ἐξ αὐτῶν Καϊαφᾶς, ἀρχιερεὺς ὢν τοῦ ἐνιαυτοῦ ἐκείνου, εἶπεν αὐτοῖς

μένου Καϊαφᾶ, καὶ συνεβουλεύ-
σαντο ἵνα τὸν Ἰησοῦν δόλῳ
κρατήσωσιν καὶ ἀποκτείνωσιν.

... ἀπ' ἐκείνης οὖν τῆς ἡμέρας
ἐβουλεύσαντο ἵνα ἀποκτείνωσιν
αὐτόν.

John has expanded an inherited tradition to include Caiaphas'
famous prophecy. And once again he has replaced πρεσβύτεροι (or
whatever) by Φαρισαῖοι. In this case, obviously, there is no room for
the ὑπηρέται who for John are the natural agents of the Sanhedrin
(named only here in this Gospel). This is also true of 11:57.

At the arrest of course, the chief priests and Pharisees are not
physically present. The chief priests will play an important part in
the subsequent drama; not so the Pharisees, who now drop out of
the story altogether. They have made so to speak positively their
last appearance, and so they bow out, leaving the stage to the
'Ιουδαῖοι who, along with the ἀρχιερεῖς who represent them (19:21),
are the true villains of the Passion story.

In 18:12 the narrative takes a new turn: the talking over, the arrest is effected: ἡ οὖν σπεῖρα καὶ ὁ χιλίαρχος καὶ οἱ ὑπηρέται τῶν
'Ιουδαίων συνέλαβον τὸν Ἰησοῦν καὶ ἔδησαν αὐτόν (Jn. 18:12—there is
no synoptic parallel to this verse).

Are we to conclude from the evidence so far presented that John
makes no distinction between the chief priests and Pharisees on the
one hand and the 'Ιουδαῖοι on the other, that he uses the two terms
equivalently and indifferently? That would be an over-
simplification. Clearly *in this case* the 'Ιουδαῖοι and ἀρχιερεῖς have the
same reference, and the identification is a fateful one. For the remainder of the Passion narrative they can no longer be properly
distinguished: the chief priests having been formally convicted of
plotting Jesus' death, now the Jewish people are seen to be
demanding it from the only authority with the power either to pass
the sentence or to carry it out. In none of the other gospel accounts
does the term 'Ιουδαῖοι occur except in the expression βασιλεὺς τῶν
'Ιουδαίων—a nugget of tradition[63] exploited by John with his
habitual irony—nowhere more tellingly employed than here. But
by replacing the synoptic ὄχλος with the more specific term οἱ
'Ιουδαῖοι, far from exonerating the general populace from complici-
ty in Jesus' death, John is inculpating them all the more.

---

[63] This is in fact the only point in the whole Gospel where John's use of 'Ιουδαῖοι
converges with that of the Synoptists.

But where does this leave the Pharisees? To begin with one must distinguish the passages discussed in the last section (where the Pharisees, as we saw, have survived in older stories reworked by the evangelist) from the deliberate conjunction of chief priests and Pharisees, which never occurs without some connection, direct or indirect, with the Passion. The evangelist may, it is true, have inherited a tradition of the Pharisees' bitter hatred of Jesus (according to Mark they begin plotting his death very early indeed: Mk. 3:6); but it does seem that in these texts he has introduced them, so to speak, on his own recognizance. (And no doubt it is on the same level of redaction that the puzzling 12:42 took its present shape.)[64] Martyn argues persuasively for the view that the chief priests, as actual contemporaries of the earthly Jesus, represent the *einmalig* level of the drama (i.e. the level at which the narrative refers to the events and people of Jesus' own day) the Pharisees, on the other hand, represent what he calls "the Gerousia of John's own city", since after the fall of Jerusalem they are the ones who picked up the reins of power in Jewish communities everywhere.[65]

Attractive as Martyn's theory is, it relates to the Pharisees, not to the Jews. If the evangelist sees the Pharisees, along with the chief priests, as engineering Jesus' downfall in the first place, we must not forget that they vanish from the scene altogether before the actual arrest and leave it to the Jews, along with the chief priests, to press for Jesus' execution. So it is not just the Pharisees that attract his ire and resentment: it is the Jewish people as a whole who are made the symbol of the human shadow.

The world

Any comprehensive reading of the role of the Ἰουδαῖοι in the Fourth Gospel must reckon not only with their frequent appearances but also with their disappearance—from the close of the Book of Signs until the beginning of the Passion narrative. The evangelist himself draws attention to this by the device of making Jesus refer back to an earlier statement that the Jews had found particularly enigmatic: "as I said to the Jews so now I say to you, 'Where I am going you cannot come' (13:33; cf. 7:36; 8:22). The significance of this remark changes slightly in the new context

---

[64] See *supra*, p. 62, n. 62.
[65] *History*, pp. 72 f.

because the perplexity of Jesus' new audience, though just as great as that of the Jews, is of a different order.

Given the setting of the Farewell Discourse, there is obviously no room for any direct confrontation with the Jews. Their physical absence at this point is not only unsurprising but necessary. The problem lies elsewhere, in the fact that when Jesus tells his disciples of the persecutions they will soon have to endure he warns them not against the Jews but against 'the world'. At one juncture he mentions the synagogue ban: ἀποσυναγώγους ποιήσουσιν ὑμᾶς (16:2). The shift from the singular to the plural is made earlier in the passage, at 15:20; so the plural cannot be said to be unexpected. 'They' of course are the Jews, but their role has already been usurped by ὁ κόσμος—the world; and though they are not far away (who else had the power to expel people from the synagogue?), they are not named.

In the Prologue, a general observation about the world's unreceptivity to the light (1:10) had been narrowed down to focus on a single state (τὰ ἴδια) and a single nation (οἱ ἴδιοι) soon to be specified as οἱ 'Ιουδαῖοι. In the body of the Gospel, where the sullen hostility of these same 'Ιουδαῖοι is a major theme, the movement of the Prologue is reversed, and after Jesus' retirement from the public scene the narrator's record of the unreceptivity of the Jews is followed by Jesus' own prophetic warning of the active hostility of the world. In the Farewell Discourse, where the word κόσμος occurs no fewer than 20 times (not counting ch. 17), there are no instances of the positive usage found elsewhere in the Gospel.[66]

Although neither in the Prologue nor in the Gospel proper is there any formal identification of 'Ιουδαῖοι and κόσμος[67] in both cases the reader is invited by the context to make the identification for himself. Here once again we must be careful to distinguish between sense and reference. One might argue that the world envisaged in the Farewell Discourse, like that of the Prologue, is really a very tiny one, a single nation; nevertheless it is experienced by the evangelist and his community as a *world*. The bleak

---

[66] Especially 3:16-19 and in the expression τὸ φῶς τοῦ κόσμου (8:12; 9:5; cf. 1:9; 12:46).

[67] Unless one counts 8:23, where the Jews (ὑμεῖς) are said, unlike Jesus, to be ἐκ τούτου τοῦ κόσμου. The additional οὗτος, which certainly affects the sense, is only found once in chs. 14-17 (16:11), but is frequent elsewhere: 8:23; 9:39; 11:9; 12:25, 31; 13:1; 18:36.

metaphysical statement of the Prologue, ὁ κόσμος αὐτὸν οὐκ ἔγνω (1:10) is echoed in a warning to the disciples: εἰ ὁ κόσμος ὑμᾶς μισεῖ, γινώσκετε ὅτι ἐμὲ πρῶτον ὑμῶν μεμίσηκεν (15:18). But these do not emerge out of the cosmic gloom of Gnosticism; rather they are the consequence of the intersection of tradition and experience. The sad failure of divine revelation (Wisdom/Logos) to enlighten the world in which it shone culminated in the rejection, by his own people, of that revelation incarnated in Jesus. The Christian community, hurt and bewildered by its own experience of rejection, could only make sense of it by interpreting it as a re-enactment of the career of its founder.[68] Yet Jesus does *not* say: "if *the Jews* hate you, remember that they hated me first". Why not?

On what we have called the *story* level this question poses no problems. We can simply say that the situations are different: the behaviour of Jesus, living as he did at a time when the inhabitants of Judea moved in constant fear of Roman reprisals and repression, naturally alarmed the religious authorities: "It is good that one man should die for the people". The dangers faced by his followers are no longer localized in this way—their profession of faith in Jesus (15:21—διὰ τὸ ὄνομά μου) will incur the enmity of the world at large. Of course such an answer is unsatisfactory: both Caiaphas' prophecy and Jesus' warning are intended to resound far beyond the confines of the rooms in which they were uttered. But if after scrutinizing the role of the Jews in the Gospel you conclude that the evangelist intends to portray them not just as the adversaries of Jesus but as a continuing threat to the wellbeing of the community, then you are left with the task of explaining why all direct reference to the Jews is dropped as soon as the situation of the community becomes the specific focus of interest. That writers on the role of the Jews in the Gospel mostly ignore this problem is I suppose to be explained by the fact that if the locus of one's enquiry is a word or an expression, one tends to leave out of consideration passages where the word or expression in question is not employed. Which, at least in this instance, is surely a matter of regret.

If in asking what in the world the world is doing here the questioner wants an answer on the level of *explanation*, the genesis of the ideas that dominate the Gospel, then the answer might be expressed

---

[68] See Wayne Meeks' deservedly famous article, "The Man from Heaven in Johannine sectarianism", *JBL* 91 (1972) 44-72.

in terms of the Gnostic myth of the endemic enmity of the world and its unnamed ruler. But on the level of *understanding*, that is of the meaning of the Gospel, any answer must include the distancing effect of a word ('world') which takes the author beyond the realm of immediate experience, a true dissociation of sensibility.

III. CONCLUSIONS

Compelled to choose between Lowe, anxious to prove that John's 'Ιουδαῖοι are properly confined to an area on the edge of the Mediterranean smaller than Wales, or von Wahlde, removing from the evangelist's purview all but a handful of highly-placed officials, and the vast, visionary exegesis of Bultmann, dissatisfied with anything less than an archetypal symbol of the sinfulness of mankind, one would, I think, have to opt for Bultmann, if only because he shows an incomparably greater understanding of the *meaning* of the Gospel. But is such a choice inescapable? Niels Dahl, one of the most penetrating and astute of recent writers on the Gospel, does not think so. Commenting on Bultmann's general thesis (which he accepts) that the Jews are the representatives of the world in its hostility to God, he adds: "it is, however, equally important that the *Jews* are those who represent the world".[69] Bultmann, for whom even the humanity of Jesus was no more than a contingent vehicle of divine revelation, would undoubtedly disagree with this proviso, which he would regard as a glorification of the happenstance, an illegitimate and dangerously mistaken exaltation of the importance of historical fact. We must acknowledge, I think, that we have to do here with interpretative options which proceed as much from the personal metaphysic of the individual exegete as from the book they are interpreting: the choice is between the historical, the theological and the historico-theological.

The issue is further complicated by the exciting suggestions of J. Louis Martyn, who adds an extra dimension to the historical approach with his theory of a two-level drama, a two-tier universe, and the consequent need of stereoptic vision. In an essay of as restricted a scope as this it would be foolish to do more than note the range of interpretative possibilities. It can be stated with some assurance though that to offer an interpretation of John or any

---

[69] N. A. Dahl in *Current Issues in New Testament Interpretation*, ed. W. Klassen and G. F. Snyder (New York/Evanson/London, 1962), p. 129.

aspect of his Gospel—from Jews to judgment, from Pharisees to fig-trees—without getting beyond the sheerly historical or referential is tantamount to hooding the eagle or seeling his eyes.

Before concluding it may be worth offering some final observations on the two distinctions which have guided the discussion.

Sense and reference

Perhaps no question in New Testament studies, certainly none of such importance, has been worse affected by the confusion between sense and reference than the one we have been considering. But however carefully it is drawn there must remain some area of possible disagreement. If the Fourth Gospel were a work of pure literature the sense of οἱ Ἰουδαῖοι, as I have argued, would be entirely determinable from within the work itself. Since this is not so, what we have seen to be the fundamental ambivalence of the word continues to present problems that cannot be properly elucidated without enquiring into the genesis of the Gospel. Bereft, apart from a few scattered instances, of the kind of contextual clues which make it so easy to establish the reference throughout the much more voluminous writings of Josephus, we require more *historical* evidence before we can be sure whether Lowe is correct in his conclusion that it was Judeans, not Jews in general, that the evangelist had in mind. And here the reference could affect the sense because of the delicate matter of what Frege calls "die verknüpfte Vorstellung". Galileans, Jews themselves, will have thought very differently about Judeans. (And would it *mean* the same thing to say, "the people of Samaria have no truck with the people of Judea" as to say, "Samaritans have no truck with Jews"?)

The two levels of understanding

Up to now I have distinguished between the *story* (avoiding the question-begging term 'history') and the meaning of the Gospel. This distinction is of course a modern version of the old distinction between letter and spirit, or the literal and the allegorical. In the topic we have been considering Bultmann's interpretation is surely the right one, but such confidence would in many cases be misplaced, partly because of the many unanswered questions regarding the genesis and growth of the text, partly because of the exceptional subtlety of the author and the delicacy of what one might call his interpenetrative technique.

The question why

Out of the answers to the first two questions (who were the 'Ιουδαῖοι and what function do they fill?) there emerges a third question (why?) which probes into the link between the who and the what: why does the writer assign *this* role to *these* people? This, unlike the other two, is a historical question. Why are the 'Ιουδαῖοι (Jews or Judeans as the case may be) selected along with the κόσμος to serve as the central symbol of negativity in a Gospel which, unlike the other three, is strongly marked by an ethical or soteriological if not a cosmological dualism? He could have chosen οἱ ἄρχοντες, with the possibilitiy of a conceptual link with ὁ ἄρχων τοῦ κόσμου: this would have retained the reference argued for by von Wahlde and provided a satisfactory sense as well. Alternatively, if he wanted to invite the kind of stereoptic reading Martyn attributes to him, he could have made more use than he does of the phrase ἀρχιερεῖς καὶ Φαρισαῖοι (which seems rather to reflect a different level of redaction). Or he could have further extended his use of ὄχλος (of which there are already 20 instances in the Gospel)—a general and unspecific term which would not have drawn undue attention to the Jewishness of Jesus' adversaries.

This difficulty, although for the most part passing unobserved,[70] is a real one: one reason why Lowe's thesis is so unsatisfactory as it stands is that it fails to explain *why* the evangelist should have evinced such hostility to the inhabitants of the tiny province of Judea. Indeed Lowe does not even raise the question or feel its force. Here I can only sketch in a provisional answer in successive stages.

(1) One might start by asking if there is anything in the tradition that might have furnished some platform, however narrow, for the edifice which came to be built. Indeed there was: the belief shared by all the evangelists that Jesus' message was rejected by his own people and the seed of his word sown on poor and unreceptive soil.

---

[70] Among those who *have* felt the need for an answer is Carl von Weizsäcker who, writing in 1864, attributed the bitterness of the Gospel to a sustained resentment on the part of the evangelist arising out of some soul-searing experience he had undergone at the hands of the Jews. *Untersuchung über die evangelische Geschichte*[2] (Tübingen/Leipzig, 1901), p. 187.

The inscription on the cross, which Pilate says is not to be erased, itself affords eloquent testimony to this rejection: "King of the Ἰουδαῖοι", king of those whose faith and confidence he failed to elicit. It would be hard to overvalue the significance of this one small fact: it is of the kind that resonates in the memory and generates myth. But if its presence in the tradition explains where the fourth evangelist derived the motif it does nothing to account for the use he made of it.

(2) In the second place it might seem as if the opposition between Galilee and Judea so persuasively argued by Meeks might give Lowe's thesis the stiffening it needs. For if an important episode in the history of the Johannine community had been somehow linked with the fortunes of a group of Galilean (and later, maybe, Samaritan) converts, then we might be able to give a plausible explanation of the deliberate blackening of the name of the Judean nation throughout the Gospel. Of course we should still be left with the task of explaining the allegorical significance subsequently invested in these same Judeans; but at least we could see why, given such an history, the Judeans would naturally have been picked for the role of Jesus' adversaries.

Unfortunately such an explanation overlooks the very restricted space occupied by the theme of Galilean acceptance versus Judean rejection. Only in two places (4:43 ff. and 7:47-52) is it at all prominent and in neither is the required thesis easy to sustain. In the first, in ch. 4, the passage from Judea to Galilee is, it is true, given unmistakable emphasis: it serves to bracket both the story of the woman at the well (4:3, 43, 45) and that of the nobleman's son (4:46, 54). But as it happens the key word Ἰουδαῖοι is missing. Its nearest occurrence is in the phrase "Salvation is from the Ἰουδαῖοι" (4:22; cf. 4:10). So the weight of contrast between those who rejected Jesus and those who welcomed him is borne by *Judea* and *Galilee* (and Galileans, who are said, oddly, to have 'seen' what Jesus did in Jerusalem: 4:45).

This might be dismissed as of no significance were it not for the fact that no Ἰουδαῖοι, at least by that name, figure in the second episode either. In this Jesus is championed unexpectedly by Nicodemus, who pops up out of nowhere to answer a mindless objection voiced not by the Judeans but by the *Pharisees*: Μή τις ἐκ τῶν ἀρχόντων ἐπίστευσεν εἰς αὐτὸν ἢ ἐκ τῶν Φαρισαίων; (7:48). The reader who recalls that Nicodemus was both ἐκ τῶν Φαρισαίων and an ἄρχων τῶν 'Ιουδαίων (3:1) can appreciate the ironic humour of his riposte, as he sides with the crowd of those "ignorant of the law" (7:4) and actually quotes the law in reply. This allusion to Nicodemus' authoritative position among the 'Ιουδαῖοι is at best flickering and indirect: not enough to offset the fact that it is not they but the Pharisees who occupy the centre of the stage.

This is not to deny the significance of the Galilean connection in this passage: both Nicodemus (explicitly) and the crowd (implicitly) are closely associated with this northern province from which neither Christ nor prophet could be expected, so that the story sardonically suggests the discomfiture of the sophisticated south by the unlettered north. But the 'Ιουδαῖοι as such—active enough earlier in the chapter—play no part whatever in this little episode.

So while the north/south opposition may well have fed into the community's traditions and given an extra impetus to the polarizing tendencies that permeate the Gospel as we have it, it is not a sufficiently strong theme to account for the role the 'Ιουδαῖοι are eventually asked to assume.

(3) One of the minor puzzles can be cleared up relatively simply. This is the evangelist's readiness to speak of Jesus (a Judean) and his disciples (Jews) as if they were of a different race and nation from the 'Ιουδαῖοι. Josephus uses a similar device when he records how a certain Justus urged the citizens of Tiberias "to take up arms and form an alliance with the Galileans, whose hatred of Sepphoris will make them willing recruits" (*Vita* 39; cf. 325). For Sepphoris, although one of the three largest towns of Galilee (*Vita* 123) and named by the Romans as its capital (*Vita* 38), had abandoned the Galilean cause (*B.J.* III 61: ἀποστῆναι Γαλιλαίων). Josephus, whose usage, like John's, is possibly affected by his personal interests here, might seem to imply that the people of Sepphoris are not really Galileans; but of course that cannot be his intention. Again like John, he expects his readers to supply the necessary qualifications for themselves.[71]

(4) This parallel from Josephus, though mildly illuminating, sheds no light at all on the real difficulty, which is that the fourth evangelist's antagonism towards the 'Ιουδαῖοι, grounded though it

---

[71] S. Freyne believes that by Josephus' day, "attitudes had hardened to the point that this very specialized use of the term 'Galileans' was justified without taking account of its purely geographical associations": *Galilee from Alexander the Great to Hadrian, 323 B.C.E. to 135 C.E.* (Notre Dame, 1980), p. 125.

may have been upon local rivalries, was predominantly religious and ideological. This is particularly true of the tense and acrimonious debates, especially in chs. 5, 8 and 10, that give the Gospel much of its distinctive character. Jesus goes so far as to call his adversaries children of the devil (8:44) and they, time and again, sought to kill him for his blasphemies. What still needs to be explained then is the extraordinary polemical thrust of the Gospel—noticed long ago by Bretschneider, who pointed out how closely it resembles in this respect the work of the 2nd century apologist Justin.[72]

(5) Once again it is Josephus, a contemporary of the evangelist, who offers some glimmer of light in this rather dark and impenetrable tunnel. Just occasionally in his substantial corpus are found glimpses of a usage of 'Ιουδαῖοι different from its habitual reference to those of Jewish race, whether in Judea or elsewhere. In one of his rare animadversions on the name itself, he tells us that it is derived from the tribe of Juda and dates ἐξ ἧς ἡμέρας ἀνέβησαν ἐκ Βαβυλῶνος (A.J. XI 173), suggesting that it properly belongs to the returning exiles (Jeremiah's basket of good figs) rather than to those who were left behind—a comment that supplements the earlier snippet of information that it was the same people (the returned exiles) who were responsible for the reconstruction of the temple (XI 84). Book XI concludes with the strange story of Alexander and the Samaritans, plus a postcript to the effect that Shechem provided a refuge for people accused of violating the dietary laws or the Sabbath regulations ''or any other such sin'' (XI 346), who fled from Jerusalem protesting their innocence.

Counterbalancing this picture of Shechem as a centre of religious dissidents inhabited, Josephus tells us, ὑπὸ τῶν ἀποστατῶν τοῦ 'Ιουδαίων ἔθνους (XI 340), is another picture, opposed and facing, of a Jerusalem reserved for the good and the pure. We are informed that soon after the re-dedication of the Temple, the priests and the Levites ''killed the passover lamb for all the returned exiles, for their fellow priests, and for themselves; it was eaten by the people of Israel who had returned from exile, and also by every one who had joined them and separated himself from the pollutions of the

---

[72] Carolus Theophilus (Karl Gottlieb) Bretschneider, *Probabilia de evangelii et epistolarum Joannis, apostoli, indole et origine* (Leipzig, 1820), pp. 118 f.

peoples of the land to worship the Lord, the God of Israel'' (Ezra 6:20-21).

Earlier, speaking of those who endeavoured to frustrate the efforts of the returned exiles to rebuild the temple as the עַם הָאָרֶץ (4:4), the Chronicler had made no distinction between these and "the adversaries of Judah and Benjamin" (4:2); and Josephus, who has Ezra as a source at this point, bluntly identifies the same group as the Samaritans (*A.J.* XI 19-30, 84-88).[73]

Whatever the precise relationship between the עַם הָאָרֶץ and the Samaritans, there seems to have been a real connection between the people of the north and those southerners who remained behind at the exile and subsequently earned the disapproval of the powerful group (*the* 'Ιουδαῖοι?) of which Ezra, the *bête noire* of the Samaritans, came to be a leading representative. And so it may be no coincidence that Jesus, besides being associated with the עַם הָאָרֶץ (Jn. 7:49), treated the 'Ιουδαῖοι as aliens and failed to rebut the charge that he himself was really a Samaritan (8:48).

(6) It is widely held nowadays that relations between the synagogue and the Johannine Christians were finally severed as a direct result of the activities of the Pharisees at Yavneh under the leadership of Gamaliel II.[74] But however attractive and plausible, this hypothesis does not explain all the features of the evangelist's use of οἱ 'Ιουδαῖοι. It seems that at the most important stage of its development the Johannine community must be located among the sects and parties of the Second Temple whose very existence the canonical documents of the period do so much to conceal. The Samaritans may not have been the only people of Jewish race reluc-

---

[73] R. J. Coggins, commenting on Ezra 4:4, declares that "there is no reason to link them [*sc.* the people of the land] with the Samaritans", *Samaritans and Jews* (Oxford, 1975), pp. 66 f.; and there are certainly difficulties (notably the use of the term in Hagg. 2:4 and Zech. 7:5) in the way of this. But Josephus, a contemporary of the fourth evangelist, does appear to do so; and Coggins himself, speaking of Second Isaiah, had already concluded of "the northerners and ... those who had remained in Judah during the exile" that "these two groups came to be identified with one another, and both would be dismissed as no part of the true people of God" (*Samaritans*, p. 37).

[74] The scholar most widely associated with this view is J. L. Martyn, who offers a particularly subtle and interesting version of it. But the theory of a nexus between the proceedings at Yavneh and the Fourth Gospel dates back at least as far as 1861, when M. von Aberle called the Gospel "der Absagebrief gegen das restaurirte Judenthum (*Theologische Quartalschrift* 42 (1861) 94).

tant to call themselves Ἰουδαῖοι when religious affiliations were in question.

Finally it is perhaps worth adding that while the *meaning* of the term Ἰουδαῖοι in the Gospel, its allegorical and symbolic function, is unaffected by such findings, they do raise the possibility that none of the previously suggested *identifications* has quite succeeded in hitting the mark.

WASHING IN THE POOL OF SILOAM—
A THEMATIC ANTICIPATION
OF THE JOHANNINE CROSS

by

BRUCE GRIGSBY
La Mirada, CA

Introduction

The Fourth Evangelist certainly intended his account of the blind man's healing to develop and enhance several ongoing literary motifs in his gospel. Above all else, this healing dramatically validates Christ's claim within the pericope itself to be the "light of the world". The "light versus dark" motif, begun in the prologue, is strikingly illustrated as the spiritual dimension of the man's restored sight is juxtaposed against the forboding darkness of the Pharisees' unbelief.

Yet alongside the more "obvious" symbolism of this healing pericope, one might argue that the Evangelist intended a more subtle, if not more complex, literary motif. To wit, it appears that a symbolic anticipation of the believer's salvific "bath" was intended by the Evangelist in the story. Christ's command to wash in the pool of Siloam, directed at the blind man, would thus become a universal command to all unbelievers to wash in the fountain of cleansing waters at Calvary.

To demonstrate this exegetical proposal, it will first be necessary to explore the various ways in which the Jews—influenced by Rabbinic speculation—regarded the symbolic role of Siloam's waters, both in their past history and their prophetic future. Thereupon it will be possible to explore the ways in which the Fourth Evangelist might have exploited such symbolism to serve his own literary ends. Specifically, it appears likely that the account of the blind man's washing, with the attendant symbolism attached to Siloam's waters, produces a *sensus plenior* that nicely accommodates the Evangelist's developing "living water" motif—a motif which culminates in the effluence of water from the crucified Christ.

Jewish Speculation about Siloam's Symbolic Role

The cultic dimension of Siloam's waters

The original audience which heard the instructions of Jesus to the blind man, as well as the Jewish segment of the Fourth Gospel's readership, would have regarded the pool of Siloam in a cultic sense. Its waters would have been revered as waters suitable for a ritual bath of purification, capable of affecting cleansing within the cultus. Within Judaism, the origin of such ritual deference towards Siloam's waters is obscure. However, Rabbinic speculation about the meaning of Isaiah 8:6 offers a clue. In the 16th *pisqa* of Pesiqta Rabbati,[1] the Rabbis puzzle over the location of the destination of Siloam's waters, given in the MT as "At" (אט). Disregarding the most natural contextual solution—i.e., "At" is not a *place* but, in combination with the prefixed ל, an *adverb*, "gently"—their geographical search is in vain. Thus, resorting to their oft-used hermeneutical device *gematria*, they solve the puzzle numerically. The term לאט "adds up" to forty,[2] which is precisely the number of *se'ahs* of water prescribed in Rabbinic thought for a ritual immersion bath.[3] Quite clearly then, the Rabbis reason, the inspired text is alluding to Hezekiah's intention that the pool of Siloam be used to promote sexual purity and restraint. Unfortunately, however, as Isaiah 8:7 points out, the Jews did not avail themselves of these purifying waters, receiving for their obstinance the flood waters of the Euphrates.

Significantly, Jesus' original audience and the earliest readership would have regarded Siloam's waters as not only cultic, but *living* as well. Their status as "living water", again a product of Rabbinic speculation, was especially prominent during the feast of Tabernacles, the backdrop for the John 9 episode. During each of the feast's seven water ceremonies, water from the pool of Siloam was ceremoniously transported in a golden flagon up the altar ramp in the temple.[4] This "water of expiation" (מֵי חַטָּאת) from Siloam, as spelled out in the highly embellished Rabbinic commentary on

---

[1] Pesiq. R. 16:6. For a discussion of Midrashic references to the cultic status of the pool of Siloam, see Str-B., 2: 531-32 and esp. the appended material, "Excurs über das Laubhüttenfest—die Wasserspende" (2: 799-805).

[2] ל(30) + א(1) + ט(9) = 40.

[3] For a Rabbinic discussion of what does and does not constitute a prescribed immersion bath, see m.Par. 5-11 and m.Mikw. 1-8.

[4] m.Sukk. 4: 9-10. See further Str-B., 2: 490-93.

Numbers 19:1-22,[5] is only effective in the cultus because it is drawn from a "living"—i.e., "flowing" (חיים/ζῶν)—source. It comes as no surprise, then, to encounter the Rabbinic description of the "waters of Shiloah" (מיא דשילוח) as a "fountain of living water" (באר מיין חיים) in the Targumic paraphrase of Song of Solomon 4:15.[6]

The prophetic dimension of Siloam's waters

In addition to regarding Siloam's waters in a cultic sense, the *auditores Christi* and the earliest *lectores Johannis* would have been aware of the Rabbinic discussion about the "sign of Siloam". This "sign" (σημεῖον), according to the pseudepigraphal *Lives of the Prophets*,[7] unfolded when Isaiah prayed for water while hovering close to death. God answered his prayer and miraculously sent him water from the fountain of Siloam. Subsequent reflection on this miracle established the Jewish axiom that a free-flowing fountain of Siloam signifies God's blessing—especially in the Messianic age—and a stagnant or dry fountain signifies God's wrath.[8]

Again, significant for discerning the Evangelist's intent in John 9, the Rabbis based their etymological understanding of the term, Siloam,[9] on this developing "sign of Siloam" theme. In the above

---

[5] m.Par. 3. In the second *mishnah* of this passage another water ceremony involving Siloam's water is described. Young children, after dipping out water from the pool of Siloam in earthen cups, transported it atop oxen to the temple where it was mixed in a pitcher with the ashes of the sacrificed red heifer, resulting in a cultic "potion".

[6] Tg. Hag. SSol 4:15 (Sperber edition cited). Of course the Rabbinic reference to a fountain of living water is reminiscent of the living water motif in Jn 4 and Rev 21. The pool of Siloam, kept continuously fresh by the influx of water from the aquaduct was quite naturally described as a fountain. Josephus (*Wars* v. 145) refers to the "Siloan fountain" (σιλωὰν πήγην) and to "that fountain of sweet and abundant water" (v. 140).

[7] Isaiah, v. 2. This work is undoubtedly a product of the first Christian century and free from Christian interpolation. So Franklin Young, "A Study of the Relationship of Isaiah to the Fourth Gospel" *ZNW* 46 (1955): 219, n. 18.

[8] According to Lam.R. XIX, Jeremiah said to Isaiah, "had you been worthy you would be dwelling in Jerusalem and drinking the waters of Siloam whose waters are pure and sweet." Josephus (*Wars* v. 410) blames the recent Jewish fall to the Romans on their iniquities. He notes that God is quite content to allow the waters of Siloam to flow copiously in Jerusalem for Titus, whereas in times past He would have dried up the fountain for Israel's enemies.

[9] The term Σιλωάμ in Jn 9:7 is found in Is 8:6 (LXX) as a transliteration of the Hebrew שִׁלֹחַ ([the waters of] Shiloah). The affixed "μ" might be seen as a later linguistic phenomenon of Palestinian Aramaic and Mishnaic Hebrew whereby

passage from *Lives of the Prophets* water was "sent" (ἀπεστάλη) to Isaiah from Siloam. On account of this, the writer concludes, the fountain is called Siloam "which is translated 'Sent'" (ὃ ἑρμηνεύεται ἀπεσταλμένος).[10]

There is a further etymological development within Rabbinic circles germane to the Evangelist's intent in the John 9 pericope. Probably due to the Messianic overtones surrounding the advent of God's final Sign of Siloam, the Messianic reign is associated with a substantival participle of the verb שָׁלַח/ἀποστέλλω.[11] The pertinent Rabbinic passage is Deuteronomy Rabbah, the seventh subsection of *parashah* six, which attempts to shed light on the eschatological import of Deuteronomy 22:7. The Jews are enjoined to "certainly send out" (שַׁלֵּחַ הְּשַׁלַּח) the mother bird if the mother's young are kept. This "sending out" activity is then extolled as characteristic behavior in the Messianic age by a dextrous, if not ingenious, cross-referencing with Isaiah 32:20. The Isaianic passage refers to a Messianic age populated by "those who will send out" (מְשַׁלְּחֵי/piel prtcp. in construct) the ox (= Messiah/Deut. 33:17) and the donkey (= carrier of Messiah/Zech. 9:9).

The Fourth Evangelist's Incorporation of Siloam's Symbolism into his Living Water Motif

With the preceding discussion of Siloam's Rabbinic background in mind, the *lectores Johannis* might well have regarded the inclusion of Siloam's waters into the John 9 story as a development of the Evangelist's "living water" motif. This motif, introduced in the interchange between Jesus and the Samaritan woman, places Christ in the role of the new Temple from which will flow living waters in

---

open-syllabled place names were often "closed" with either a " מ " or a " ן " (so E. Y. Kutscher, "The Language of the Genesis Apocryphon: A Preliminary Study" *Aspects of the Dead Sea Scrolls* [Jerusalem: Magnes Press, 1958], p. 23). At Qumran the Hebrew term appears in the form שילוח (3Q15:XI,7) and in the Mishnah as שילוח (m. Yad. 4:5) and שלוח (m. Par. 3:2). In Greek transliteration it frequently appears in Josephus as σιλωαμ or σιλωαν while in *Lives of the Prophets* σηλωμ is predominantly found. Whether this family of variant spellings is connected thematically or etymologically to the enigmatic and undoubtedly Messianic term "Shiloh" (שילה/σηλω[μ]) in Gen 49:10 will be considered below.

[10] Jn 9:7 similarly reads, ... ὃ ἑρμηνεύεται ἀπεσταλμένος. Technically שלח is not translated ἀπεσταλμένος (lit., "he who was sent"). The Greek would require a passive participle (שלוח). In addition, "that which is sent"—i.e., water—would require a neuter rather than masculine participle (ἀπεσταλμένον).

[11] Str-B. 2:530.

the new age. In the Evangelist's scheme, Christ proleptically refers to this outflow of eschatological waters in John 7:37-39. Here He dramatically extends a cryptic invitation to the religious pilgrims observing Tabernacles' climactic water ceremony:

> If any man thirsts, let him come to me;
> and let him drink, who believes in me.
> As the scripture said, 'from his belly
> shall flow rivers of living water'.[12]

Punctuating the verses in this fashion, Christ can be construed as the source of these eschatological rivers of living water, prophesied in Ezekiel 47:1-2 and Zechariah 14:8.[13] From his side[14] will flow rivers of living water—i.e., the Spirit—only after his glorification—i.e., his death. This prediction indeed transpires as the Johannine passion narrative reports the effluence of blood and water from the cross (19:34).

Focusing now on the miracle story of John 9, the role played by Siloam's waters accommodates this developing "living water" motif in three important ways.

---

[12] This so-called "Western" or "Christological" punctuation involves a full stop after ὁ πιστεύων εἰς ἐμέ in verse 38 and no punctuation after πινέτω in verse 37. Although this form of punctuation is rejected by the Textus Receptus (1873), Westcott and Hort (1881), Tischendorf (1869), von Soden (1913), Bover (1959), the UBS text (3rd ed., 1975) and Nestle-Aland (26th ed., 1979), it is accepted by several Johannine commentators of note (Bultmann, Boismard, Braun, Brown, Dodd, Forestell, Hoskyns, Jeremias, and MacGregor). In addition, it is the accepted reading of the *NEB*, the *Jerusalem Bible*, and is found in the margin of the *NIV*.

[13] Ezek. 47:1-2 appears to be the most likely OT spawning ground for this Johannine development of the "living water" theme in Jn 7:37-39. The religious pilgrims at the Feast of Tabernacles, who originally heard this dramatic invitation from Christ, would most naturally have interpreted his brief midrashic homily against a backdrop of Ezek. 47:1-12. For them, the daily water ceremony—such an integral part of this eight day Feast—symbolically anticipated the eschatological outpouring of living water as depicted in Ezekiel's vision. Their predisposition towards this specific passage is most clearly understood by considering the third chapter of tractate *Sukkah* ("Tabernacles") in the Tosefta. In this chapter (esp. *Halakoth* 3-9) the naming of the Water Gate, through which the daily libations of the water ceremony passed, is explained in terms of the prophetic role of the *south* gate in Ezek. 47:1-9. Significantly for Jn 7:38, the visionary river of Ezekiel is construed as a river of *living* water, in that the eighth *halakah* identifies this water with the eschatological river of living water described in Zech. 14:8.

[14] Christ is the new temple in Johannine thought (Jn 2:21; 4:21-23; cf. Rev. 21:22) and from him, as from the temple in Ezekiel's vision, the living water will flow.

1) *The waters of Siloam symbolically impart eternal life*

The blind man not only finds his physical vision restored but receives the gift of spiritual vision as well. Christ, the self-proclaimed light of the world, demonstrates his claim by bringing saving light to a life darkened by unbelief. In Johannine parlance, the man has passed from darkness to light, from judgment and death to absolution and life; and all of this was accomplished through obedience to Christ's command to wash in Siloam's waters.[15] The Sign of Siloam, a reference to God's outpouring of blessing on past generations of Jews is now being performed in the consummate, eschatological sense.

2) *The waters of Siloam cleanse from sin*

An important aspect of the "living water" theme in the Old Testament and subsequent Rabbinic material, as shown above, was the cleansing property of living water when mixed with the sacrificial ashes of the red heifer. Indeed, the living water of the new age, envisioned by both Ezekiel and Zechariah, is described by the latter as a "fountain for sin and impurity" opened up in the last days (Zech. 13:1).

For the Fourth Evangelist as well, his eschatology being "realized" in the gospel story, the living water offered by Jesus from the cross—this time mixed with his own sacrificial blood—will cleanse from sin. This cleansing water from the cross, where Christ is humiliated in death, is undoubtedly anticipated in the Johannine account where Christ assumes the "humiliating" task of washing the disciples' feet.[16] Here Peter is rendered "clean" (καθαρός), and

---

[15] Günther Reim finds little difference, thematically, between the blind man's *washing* and the Samaritan woman's *drinking*. Comparing the two passages, he is impressed with the literary similarities: "Erstaunliche Parallelen zu Arbeitsweise und Theologie des Evangelisten in Joh 9 gibt es in joh Material in Joh 4" ("Joh 9—Tradition und zeitgenössische messianische Diskussion", *Biblische Zeitschrift* 22 [1978]: 253, n. 30).

[16] Jn 13:1-20 appears to be far more than an exhortation to imitate Christ's humility in washing the disciples' feet despite the vigorous protestations of J. Michl ("Der Sinn der Fusswaschung" *Biblica* 40 [1959]: 697-708). Understanding the account as symbolic of Christ's passion is gathering a consensus of leading Johannine scholars. See esp. Theophil Müller (*Das Heilsgeschehen im Johannesevangelium* [Zürich: Gotthelf, 1961], pp. 68-69), M.-E. Boismard ("Le Lavement des Pieds" *RB* 71 [1964]: 8-10), James Dunn ("The Washing of the Disciple's Feet in John 13:1-20" *ZNW* 61 [1970]: 247-52), Herbert Klos (*Die Sakramente im Johannesevangelium* [Stuttgart: Verlag Katholisches Bibelwerk, 1970], pp. 89-91), and Raymond Brown (*The Gospel according to John*, 2:568).

thereby suitable to accept a "part" (μέρος) in Christ's kingdom, by "washing" (νίπτομαι) in the water offered by Christ. Peter's washing—anticipatory of the cross—is once and for all and his request for further washing in verse 10 is rebuked by Christ as redundant.[17] So too in the account of the Siloam miracle, the waters might be seen to prophetically anticipate the cleansing waters from Christ's side. The blind man, obeying Christ's command, is implicitly rendered "clean" and thereby suitable for eternal life, by "washing" (νίπτομαι) in waters made available by Christ—i.e., the pool of the one who is sent. His ultimate cleansing, depicted here only in (sacramental?)[18] symbol, must await his immersion in the fountain of living waters on Calvary.

3) The waters of Siloam are Messianic

Like the living waters throughout the Fourth Gospel, the waters of Siloam are dispensed by and through Christ.[19] Not only is the

---

[17] This interpretation is based on the acceptance of the short text in 13:10: "He who has bathed has no need to wash [further]" (ὁ λελουμένος οὐκ ἔχει χρείαν νίψασθαι). With this text, verse 10 becomes somewhat of a proverbial saying rather than a direct response to Peter's enthusiastic request of verse 9. Jesus is saying in effect, "Peter, there is no need to wash twice. My washing, such as you just underwent (vs. 8), is complete and removes all of your sins, since it represents the once for all cleansing of my death on the cross."

[18] It should come as no surprise to find the Siloam story interpreted as a baptismal miracle prefiguring the mystery of the sacrament. This exegesis is nearly as old as the text itself, going back at least to second century frescoes in the Roman Catacombs (see E. C. Hoskyns, *The Fourth Gospel* [London: Faber & Faber, 1940], pp. 355-56; 363-65). Dodd (*Historical Tradition in the Fourth Gospel* [Cambridge: At the University Press, 1963], p. 184) believes that baptismal imagery was "certainly intended", observing that the Evangelist has exploited baptismal symbolism by introducing the "washing" element to a healing pericope which originally (Markan version for Dodd) did not include this element.

[19] Could it be that the Jews themselves regarded the term Shiloaḥ as a Messianic title, prior to the first Christian century? Certainly they regarded a similar term, Shiloh (שילה) as a Messianic title. This is seen in Jewish commentary on Gen. 49:10 ("...the scepter shall not depart from Judah until Shiloh comes") in both Rabbinic and Qumran literature. See esp. R.Lam. 1:16 § 51 (Shiloh = Royal Messiah), Tg. Ps.-J. Gen 49:10 (Shiloh = King Messiah), Tg. Onq. Gen 49:10 (Shiloh = Messiah [משיחא/Sperber]), and QPatrBles 2:4 (Shiloh = Messiah of Righteousness). The plates of this Qumran fragment were published in 1956 by J. M. Allegro (*JBL* 75 [1956]: 174-76), and unfortunately contain only the Essenes' *translation* of the term Shiloh (משיח הצדק), the text portion being lost.

The LXX does not support a Messianic reading of Gen 49:10. "Until Shiloh comes" is rendered "until the things destined for him come" leading to the proposal (see *BDB* s.v. שׁילה) that שׁילה is a contraction of אֲשֶׁר לֹו—"until that *which is his* comes". In a mainline Rabbinic commentary on Gen 49:10 (Gen.R.

blind man directed to Siloam's healing waters by Christ, but the Evangelist informs his readership that the pool *belongs* to Christ. Through a dextrous twist of Siloam's popular etymology,[20] the pool of Siloam becomes for him and his readership the pool of "he who is sent" (ἀπεσταλμένος). And, of course, in Johannine parlance, "he who is sent" is a frequent Messianic construct applied to Christ.[21]

Owing to the Evangelist's free and, indeed, self-serving translation of שִׁלוֹחַ, the more astute among his readership might quite readily have regarded Christ's command to "wash in the pool of Siloam" as synonymous with "wash in *my* pool" or better, "wash in my fountain". Understood in this fashion, the command could then quite easily have been construed as a prophetic anticipation of the post-Easter mandate to wash in Calvary's cleansing fountain. This eschatological fountain, like Siloam, will gurgle forth from a rock as the crucified Christ of the Johannine passion narrative fulfills the Rabinically embellished role of the peripatetic rock in the Moses water miracle.[22] As Moses provided "rivers of living water"[23] by striking the rock, so Christ will provide his rivers of living water by being pierced.

---

xcvii.8), "until Shiloh comes" is rendered "Until a present will be brought" (יָבֹא שִׁילֹה) of the MT is explained as a transposition of (יוּבַל־שַׁי) to cross-reference with Isa 18:7: "In that time *shall a present be brought* (יוּבַל־שַׁי) to the Lord of hosts."

[20] So the phraseology of Dodd (*Historical Tradition*, p. 184). The translated Hebrew term is שִׁלֹחַ (Isa 8:6) which is a proper noun derived from the verb שָׁלַח. Of course, ἀπεσταλμένος is a substantival past participle which would more properly translate a participle of שָׁלַח in qal passive (שָׁלוּחַ) or pual (תְּשֻׁלַּח).

[21] 3:17; 4:34; 5:24, 30, 37; 6:29, 38, 39, 44, 57; 7:16, 18, 28, 33; 8:16, 18, 26, 29, 42; 9:4; 10:36; 11:42; etc.

[22] As shown above, Christ is the new temple in Johannine thought, and from him, as from the temple in Ezekiel's vision (47:1-12) the living water will flow. Actually though, Ezekiel's prophecy refers to the effluence of water from *underneath* the temple—i.e., the rock, Mt. Moriah. Thus it might be closer to the Evangelist's intent to regard the crucified Christ as the eschatological reenactment of the "struck" rock in the wilderness water miracle (Exod 17:1-7). As Moses struck the rock (which later followed the Israelites in their wanderings) to produce rivers of living water (t.Sukk. 3:11; Tg. Ket. Ps 78:16; cf. 1 Cor 10:4), so too was Christ pierced with the same result. Significantly, the Jews expected a reenactment of the Moses water miracle by the Messiah (Qoh.R. 1:9 § 1): "As the first redeemer caused the spring to arise (Moses at Horeb) so the last redeemer will cause water to rise up (Christ at Calvary)."

[23] So the phraseology of t.Sukk 3:11 and Tg. Ket. Ps 78:16. Cf. in this regard, M.-E. Boismard ("Les citations targumiques dans le quatrième évangile" *RB* 66 [1959]: 373-76).

Conclusion

A symbolic anticipation of the believer's salvific "bath" appears to have been intended by the Evangelist in the account of Jesus' encounter with the blind man and the subsequent restoration of his sight. When the earliest readership of the Fourth Gospel read that Jesus directed the blind man to wash in the pool of Siloam during the Feast of Tabernacles, those conversant with Rabbinic speculation about Siloam's waters would have connected these waters with the living waters prophetically offered by Christ in earlier contexts (4:10-14; 7:37-39) and dispensed by Him from the Johannine cross (19:34) and while risen.[24] The eschatological day when streams of healing, life-giving water would flow forth from the new Temple (Ezek. 47:1-12), or better, from the "struck" rock underneath the temple, had arrived typologically in the John 9 miracle. The Sign of Siloam, in its ultimate expression was upon them. And now, for all *lectores Johannis*, Christ's command to the blind man becomes the Evangelist's universal appeal: Wash away your sins in the fountain of living waters which flow from the new Temple on Calvary.

---

[24] That the Johannine account of the miraculous draught of fish (21:5-11) develops the Evangelist's ongoing "living water" motif has been recently discussed (B. Grigsby, "Gematria and John 21:11—Another look at Ezek 47:10," *ExT* 5 [1984] 177-78).

INDEX OF AUTHORS

INDEX OF BIBLICAL REFERENCES